"In the 1970s, the 2nd of June *l*
among the left. It was the guerril
denounced by the Red Army Faction as ..ppr.... p.
—*taz*

"This well-structured book allows us to revisit—and rethink—
the politics, practice, and consequences of the radical
left-wing opposition during the 1970s in West Germany."
—Geronimo, author of *Fire and Flames: A History
of the German Autonomist Movement*

"Ten bank robberies, a bombing, resisting arrest, illegal
possession of firearms. The defendants? Members of
the criminal organization '2nd of June Movement.'"
—*Der Spiegel*

"No urban guerrilla is no solution either."
—graffiti, Berlin

FROM HASH REBELS TO URBAN GUERRILLAS

A Documentary History of the
2nd of June Movement

Edited by Roman Danyluk and Gabriel Kuhn

From Hash Rebels to Urban Guerrillas: A Documentary History of the 2nd of June Movement
© 2024 Roman Danyluk and Gabriel Kuhn
This edition © 2024 PM Press

ISBN: 979-8-88744-061-3 (paperback)
ISBN: 979-8-88744-070-5 (ebook)
Library of Congress Control Number: 2024930555
Cover by John Yates / www.stealworks.com
Interior design by briandesign

10 9 8 7 6 5 4 3 2 1

PM Press
PO Box 23912
Oakland, CA 94623
www.pmpress.org

Kersplebedeb Publishing and Distribution
CP 63560
CCCP Van Horne
Montreal, Quebec
Canada H3W 3H8
www.kersplebedeb.com
www.leftwingbooks.net

Printed in the USA.

CONTENTS

DRENKMANN

BAUMANN

SAUBER

LORENZ

ANALYSIS

TRIALS

PRISON

DISSOLUTION (OR NOT)

EVALUATION

PREFACE

Gabriel Kuhn

This book does not have the most conventional of histories. Someone in North America who prefers to remain anonymous translated most of the documents collected in this volume more than a decade ago. With a collaborator, they intended to release a volume similar to the one you are holding in your hands. For various reasons, this never happened.

When, in 2019, German author-activist Roman Danyluk released an extensive history about the 2nd of June Movement titled *Blues der Städte. Die Bewegung 2. Juni—eine sozialrevolutionäre Geschichte* (Blues of the cities: The 2nd of June Movement—A social-revolutionary history), I reckoned that a summary of his book in English would make a useful companion to the translated 2nd of June Movement documents. So I checked in with the translator in North America and their collaborator. Since their volume still seemed a long way off, they generously allowed me to use the translations and conceive a 2nd of June Movement book together with Roman. They also provided material that proved very useful for the introduction and the notes included in this volume.

With access to unpublished 2nd of June Movement documents, I added a few translations of my own and gave the others an overhaul. The introduction is based on Roman's book.

The documents included here contain all of the texts released under the name of the 2nd of June Movement as well as texts by individual members that address the group's activities, trials, and prison terms. The documents range from interviews and articles to position papers and court statements. Some were written while the group was still active, some thereafter. Together, the texts not only provide a history of the group but also include important reflections on its successes and failures. Perhaps most importantly, the discussions these texts bring to life remain highly relevant for revolutionary politics in the "metropole" (First World/ Global North), the perennial question of armed struggle, and the relationship between the left and the working class. Readers will also be baffled by the fascinatingly accurate predictions of capitalism's development in the late twentieth and early twenty-first centuries (decline of the welfare state, neoliberalism, new factory regimes, new global rivalries). And all in a language that's accessible, bereft of academic jargon, and not even too loaded with the political lingo of the German far left at the time. As serious as the issues are, many texts are entertaining and outright funny.

Some published interviews and articles by former 2nd of June members were not included. This was to avoid redundancy, or because the texts included unsubstantiated claims. For the same reasons, a few (very few) of the included texts were shortened, with omissions indicated.

The documents included in this volume have been structured to create a narrative. They appear in chronological order with respect to the events they address, even if they were written or recorded at different times.

Some 2nd of June Movement members have written memoirs, but none of them sat well with core members of the group. Michael "Bommi" Baumann's *Wie alles anfing*—despite having been widely discredited from people within the movement upon its 1975 release—is the most famous of these accounts, especially outside of Germany due to an English translation titled *How It All Began* (1977). Till Meyer's *Staatsfeind* (State enemy, 1996) and Inge Viett's *Nie war ich furchtloser* (Never was I less afraid, 1997) also caused the irk of other 2nd of June members. Gabriele Rollnik included anecdotes from her time in the 2nd of June Movement in the interview book *Keine Angst vor niemand. Über die Siebziger, die Bewegung 2. Juni und die RAF* (Not fearing anybody: About the 1970s, the 2nd of June Movement, and the RAF, 2004). Like Viett, Rollnik joined the RAF in 1980 and declared the 2nd of June Movement dissolved—see the chapter "Dissolution (or Not)" in this book. Norbert "Knofo" Kröcher published a number of texts, including the autobiography *". . . warum mir die Linke"* (Why the left is . . .). However, former comrades advise people to read Kröcher's texts with caution, as he has allegedly always been prone to embellishment and fabulation.

Numerous documents from the milieu around the 2nd of June Movement were published in German in two volumes titled *Der Blues*, a reference to the name of the cultural and political underground scene of West Berlin that the group emerged from.

Several people apart from our unnamed friends in North America have helped to make this book a reality. A special thanks goes out to Klaus Viehmann, who has taken considerable time to provide material, check details, and help with annotations. The responsibility for any errors lies solely with the editors.

This book must not be read as a nostalgic tribute to militants of a distant past, but as a source of inspiration for revolutionary politics in a time that needs them as much as ever.

ACRONYMS AND ABBREVIATIONS

APO *Außerparlamentarische Opposition* (extraparliamentary opposition); shorthand for the broad-based, left-wing, extraparliamentary opposition in West Germany in the late 1960s and early 1970s.

CDU *Christlich Demokratische Union Deutschlands* (Christian Democratic Union of Germany); Germany's mainstream conservative party. The **CSU** (*Christlich-Soziale Union in Bayern*, Christian-Social Union in Bavaria) is its Bavarian sister party.

dpa *Deutsche Presse-Agentur* (German Press Agency).

DKP *Deutsche Kommunistische Partei* (German Communist Party); pro-Soviet communist party founded in 1968, claiming to be the successor of the original Communist Party of Germany (**KPD**), founded in 1919, banned by the Nazis and declared illegal by the West German postwar government in 1956.

FDP *Freie Demokratische Partei* (Free Democratic Party); Germany's mainstream liberal party, often a junior partner in government coalitions, both with the CDU and the SPD.

FRG *Bundesrepublik Deutschland* (Federal Republic of Germany); originally, the official name of West Germany; today, the official name of the reunited Germany.

GDR *Deutsche Demokratische Republik* (German Democratic Republic); the official name of real socialist East Germany from 1949 until its dissolution in 1990.

PFLP *Popular Front for the Liberation of Palestine*; founded in 1967 as a secular, nationalist, and socialist organization, the second-largest tendency within the **PLO** (*Palestinian Liberation Organization*) after Fatah. The **PFLP-EO** (*Popular Front for the Liberation of Palestine–External Operations*) was a PFLP offshoot, engaging in controversial actions such as skyjackings; it effectively dissolved in 1978 after the death of its leader, Wadie Haddad (1927–78).

RAF *Rote Armee Fraktion* (Red Army Faction); the best known of the German urban guerrilla groups of the 1970s; founded in 1970, it carried out actions until 1993 and officially dissolved in 1998.

RZ *Revolutionäre Zellen* (Revolutionary Cells); network founded in Germany in 1973, built around clandestine cells of aboveground activists engaging in militant action; mostly social-revolutionary, but with an internationalist/anti-imperialist wing in the 1970s. Together with its sister organization, the feminist **Rote Zora**, responsible for over a hundred militant actions. The RZ and the Rote Zora dissolved in the early 1990s.

SDS *Sozialistischer Deutscher Studentenbund* (Socialist German Students' Federation); socialist student organization of great importance for the APO.

SED *Sozialistische Einheitspartei Deutschlands* (Socialist Unity Party of Germany); founded in 1946, the SED—a merger of the East German branches of the SPD and KPD—was the ruling party in the GDR.

SPD *Sozialdemokratische Partei Deutschlands* (Social Democratic Party of Germany); Germany's mainstream social democratic party.

sponti *"spontaneists"*; influential antiauthoritarian tendency in Germany during the early 1970s.

Stasi *Ministerium für Staatssicherheit* (Ministry for State Security); the GDR secret police.

Conversions

1 centimeter = 0.4 inches

1 meter = 3.28 feet

1 kilometer = 0.62 miles

1 kilogram = 2.2 pounds

1 Deutschmark = 0.45 USD (rough average for the 1970s)

PROTAGONISTS

2nd of June Movement

The 2nd of June Movement had a couple of dozen underground members and many more aboveground helpers and collaborators. The following members are the ones you'll encounter most regularly in this book:

Ralf Reinders (born 1948) was a founding member; **Ronald Fritzsch** (1951–2022) joined soon thereafter. Both were arrested in 1975 and served fifteen years in prison, many in the same unit in Berlin-Moabit. **Klaus Viehmann** (born 1954) spent several years there with them, also serving a fifteen-year sentence. Viehmann was arrested in 1978.

Fritz Teufel (1943–2010) came to the 2nd of June Movement as a member of the Tupamaros Munich. He was arrested in 1975 and spent five years in prison. Contrary to his codefendants in the "Lorenz-Drenkmann trial" (see the relevant chapters in this book), he did not receive a fifteen-year sentence since he was able to produce an alibi for the actions he had been accused of—Teufel was working under a false name in a factory in Essen in the Ruhr Valley at the time. In the public eye, Teufel is closely associated with the term "fun guerrilla" (*Spaßguerilla*), apparently coined by himself. He combined political activism with humor, satire, and wordplay, characteristic for his writing (only partially conveyable in translation).

Gerald Klöpper (born 1953) was another defendant during the Lorenz-Drenkmann trial. Arrested in 1975, he had renounced the armed struggle before the trial began in 1980. Sentenced to eleven years in prison, he was prematurely released in 1982 and became active in green-alternative party politics.

Michael "Bommi" Baumann (1947–2016) and **Inge Viett** (1944–2022) were early 2nd of June Movement members. Baumann left the group before long and published a memoir in 1975, which was widely discredited by former comrades. He was arrested in a squat in Hackney in 1981 and extradited to Germany, where he spent five years in prison. Viett belonged to the 2nd of June faction that joined the Red Army Faction in 1980. She later found refuge in East Germany, together with other former Red Army Faction members. Altogether, she served seven years in prison.

Verena Becker (born 1952) was a 2nd of June member arrested in 1972 and freed as a result of the Peter Lorenz kidnapping in 1975 (see the relevant documents in this book). She later joined the Red Army Faction and spent roughly thirteen years in prison. Becker made numerous statements and collaborated with state security for years.

Ina Siepmann (1944–82) was another imprisoned 2nd of June member (arrested in 1973) who was freed as a result of the infamous kidnapping of CDU politician Peter Lorenz. After she had been flown to South Yemen with the other liberated prisoners, she joined a combat unit of the PFLP and died in Lebanon during an Israeli military operation in 1982.

Till Meyer (born 1944) joined the 2nd of June Movement in 1972 and was closer to the anti-imperialist politics of the Red Army Faction than most of the other 2nd of June members. His 1996 memoir *Staatsfeind* wasn't received well by former comrades. Meyer spent about twelve years in prison and served as a longtime informant for the Stasi.

Norbert "Knofo" Kröcher (1950–2016) was a cofounder of the 2nd of June Movement in 1972. Not long thereafter, he went into exile in Sweden, where he was involved in an ambitious plan to kidnap government official Anna-Greta Lejon (born 1939). Lejon was held responsible for the deportation of Red Army Faction member Siegfried Hausner (1952–75) only three days after he had been badly wounded during the ill-fated 1975 Red Army Faction occupation of the West German embassy in Stockholm. Hausner died a week after having been flown to Germany. Kröcher was arrested in Sweden in 1977 and deported to Germany, where he served an eight-year prison sentence. His wife **Gabriele Kröcher-Tiedemann** (1951–95) was another one of the 2nd of June Movement prisoners liberated during the Lorenz kidnapping.

Werner Philip Sauber (1947–75) came from a rich Swiss family (his brother Peter founded the Sauber Formula One team). He was trying to establish a factory guerrilla in the Ruhr Valley when he died in 1975 in a shootout with police in Cologne. His life is portrayed in the 2013 novel *Das Verschwinden des Philip S.* (The disappearance of Philip S.), authored by his former partner Ulrike Edschmid.

Karl Heinz Roth (born 1942), a physician, was also involved in the attempts to build a factory guerrilla. He was injured in the Cologne shootout and served two years in prison. He became a well-known labor historian and theorist.

The renowned novelist **Peter-Paul Zahl** (1944–2011) was a member of the Red Ruhr Army, one of the predecessors to the 2nd of June Movement. He was arrested in 1972 and served ten years in prison.

Thomas Weisbecker (1949–72) was switching from the 2nd of June to the Red Army Faction when he was shot dead by police trying to arrest him in Augsburg in March 1972. A squat in Berlin, the Tommy-Weisbecker-Haus, was named after him. It remains an important hub for the activist scene in the city to this day.

Georg von Rauch (1947–71) was an influential figure in the militant circles of West Berlin that led to the foundation of the 2nd of June Movement. He was shot dead by police in 1971. Like Weisbecker, he had a squat named after him, the Georg von Rauch House, which also remains an important gathering place for Berlin activists.

Andreas Thomas Vogel (born 1956) was an active 2nd of June member from 1974 until his arrest in 1976. He spent ten years in prison. He belonged to the anti-imperialist current within the 2nd of June Movement but, unlike others from that current, never joined the Red Army Faction.

Ulrich Schmücker (1951–74) was executed as a 2nd of June member turned police informant. The exact circumstances of his assassination remain unclear, but there are many indications that secret police had knowledge of it and decided not to intervene.

Red Army Faction

Throughout the book, readers will frequently encounter members of the Red Army Faction, the better-known Marxist-Leninist counterpart to the social-revolutionary 2nd of June Movement. **Andreas Baader** (1943–77) and prominent journalist **Ulrike Meinhof** (1934–76) were widely regarded as figureheads, together with **Jan-Carl Raspe** (1944–77) and Baader's partner, **Gudrun Ensslin** (1940–77). **Holger Meins** (1941–74), who died during a hunger strike in 1974, was another member well known to the public.

Lawyer **Horst Mahler** (born 1936) was an early RAF member and was arrested in 1970. In prison, he left the RAF and joined the KPD/AO, a small Maoist party. He refused to be part of the prisoner exchange during the Lorenz kidnapping. After serving ten years in prison, he briefly joined the FDP, before reemerging on the political scene as a spokesperson for the far right in the late 1990s. Since then, Mahler has repeatedly served prison sentences for Holocaust denial and hate speech.

Others

A highly influential figure within the radical left in West Germany and West Berlin during the time the urban guerrilla groups emerged was the SDS activist **Rudi Dutschke** (1940–79). In 1968, he survived an assassination attempt by a right-wing youth, but he succumbed to medical problems related to the attack a decade later.

Dieter Kunzelmann (1939–2018) was the most prominent member of Kommune 1, a commune in West Berlin that symbolized the late 1960s blend of cultural and political revolution.

Peter Urbach (1941–2011) was an effective infiltrator and agent provocateur within the radical left.

German statesmen who are named frequently in this volume are **Konrad Adenauer** (1876–1967), CDU member and West Germany's first chancellor, serving from 1949 to 1963; **Helmut Schmidt** (1918–2015), SPD member and chancellor from 1974 to 1982; **Hans-Dietrich Genscher** (1927–2016), FDP member, minister of the interior from 1969 to 1974, and vice chancellor in coalition governments with both the SPD and CDU from 1974 to 1992; longtime CDU chairman **Helmut Kohl** (1930–2017), who served as the country's chancellor from 1982 to 1998; and CSU stalwart **Franz Josef Strauß** (1915–88), CSU party chairman from 1961 until his death.

TIMELINE

The following timeline lists crucial events in the history of the 2nd of June Movement, as well as events referenced frequently in the book. It does not provide an exhaustive history of the German urban guerrilla overall; events related to the Red Army Faction, the Revolutionary Cells, and the Rote Zora are included only if they had direct relevance for the 2nd of June Movement.

——

1967
January 1: Kommune 1 founded in West Berlin, a prominent example of collective living in the spirit of the "Blues," the antiauthoritarian subculture of West Berlin.
June 2: Student Benno Ohnesorg is shot and killed by police officer Karl-Heinz Kurras during a demonstration against the Shah of Iran visiting West Berlin. (It was later revealed that Kurras was a longtime Stasi informant.)
September 6: The possibilities of an urban guerrilla in Germany is discussed by prominent SDS members at a conference in West Berlin.

1968
April: Georg von Rauch, Michael "Bommi" Baumann, and others form the Wieland Commune in West Berlin.
April 3: Andreas Baader, Gudrun Ensslin, Thorwald Proll, and Horst Söhnlein firebomb two Frankfurt department stores to protest the

escalation of the Vietnam War. The four are arrested the next day, put on trial, and sentenced to three years in prison.

April 11: Rudi Dutschke is shot and severely injured by a young man with right-wing sympathies. Many blame the antisocialist propaganda of the tabloid *Bild* for the deed. Since *Bild* is owned by the Springer publishing empire, Springer offices become the target of weeklong protests across Germany.

1969

February 27: While visiting West Berlin, US president Richard Nixon is met with massive demonstrations and an unsuccessful bombing attempt by Kommune 1 members against his motorcade.

June 13: While appealing their sentence for the Frankfurt department store firebombing, Andreas Baader and Gudrun Ensslin go underground.

Fall: The urban guerrilla groups Tupamaros West Berlin and Tupamaros Munich are formed. Members of the Tupamaros West Berlin train in a PLO camp in Jordan. The group is responsible for a series of firebomb attacks in Berlin.

November 9: The Tupamaros West Berlin plant a firebomb supplied by police infiltrator Peter Urbach at a Jewish community center in West Berlin; the incendiary device malfunctions.

1970

February 6: Bommi Baumann is arrested after a failed attack on a tabloid journalist and jailed for a year and a half.

April 4: Andreas Baader is arrested during a traffic stop in West Berlin.

May 14: An armed group breaks Andreas Baader out of the library of the Institute for Social Research, where he has obtained permission to work with journalist Ulrike Meinhof. An employee, Georg Linke, is shot and injured. The group, including Ulrike Meinhof, goes underground. The event is considered the beginning of the Red Army Faction.

May 22: The West Berlin radical magazine *Agit 883* publishes "Die Rote Armee aufbauen" (Building the Red Army), regarded as the RAF's founding document.

June 11: The so-called hand grenade law is passed, extending the police's arsenal.

July 19–20: Numerous Tupamaros West Berlin members are arrested.

September 29: Three simultaneous bank robberies are carried out in West Berlin by RAF and future 2nd of June members.

1971

May 1: RAF members meet with people from the Tupamaros West Berlin and the Blues scene to discuss a possible merger.

July 8: Thomas Weisbecker, Bommi Baumann, and Georg von Rauch go to trial for militant actions. Baumann and Weisbecker are released on bail; von Rauch is not. However, von Rauch leaves the courthouse pretending to be Weisbecker, whom he resembles. Once the confusion is cleared up, Weisbecker is released as well. All three go underground and are involved in forming the 2nd of June Movement.

December 4: During a manhunt in West Berlin, members of the Blues scene get involved in a shootout with the police. Georg von Rauch is shot and killed.

December 8: A vacant wing of the former Bethanien Hospital on Mariannenplatz in Berlin-Kreuzberg is occupied and named the Georg von Rauch House. It becomes an important center for the extraparliamentary left.

1972

January: Members of the Blues scene, the Tupamaros West Berlin, the "Central Council of the Roaming Hash Rebels," and the Red Ruhr Army found the 2nd of June Movement.

February 2: The 2nd of June Movement bombs the British Yacht Club and two British military trucks in West Berlin in response to the British army killings of protesters in Northern Ireland on "Bloody Sunday" in Derry, January 30. At the British Yacht Club, boatbuilder Erwin Beelitz finds the bomb and is killed when trying to disarm it.

February 28: Till Meyer is arrested in Bielefeld while trying to buy weapons from soldiers who have tipped the police.

March 2: Thomas Weisbecker is shot and killed by police in Augsburg.

May: The RAF responds to the sea blockade and carpet-bombing of Vietnam with a bombing campaign known as the May Offensive.

May 19: The RAF's 2nd of June Commando bombs the Springer Building in Hamburg; despite three warnings, the building is not cleared, and seventeen workers are injured.

May 24: The RAF's 15th of July Commando bombs the European head-quarters of the US Army in Heidelberg; three soldiers are killed.

May 7: Inge Viett and Ulrich Schmücker are arrested alongside other 2nd of June Movement members in a small town in Rhineland-Palatinate.

July 21: Verena Becker is arrested in the Kreuzberg neighborhood of West Berlin.

December 14: Peter-Paul Zahl seriously injures a police officer during a shootout in Düsseldorf. He is wounded himself.

1973

June 20: Inge Viett breaks out of the women's prison on Lehrter Straße in West Berlin.

July 7: Gabriele Kröcher-Tiedemann is arrested in Bochum, following a shootout with the police.

October 20: Ina Siepmann is arrested when entering a safe house in the Kreuzberg neighborhood of West Berlin.

November 11: Till Meyer escapes from the open Castrop-Rauxel institution.

1974

June 4: Ulrich Schmücker is executed in the Grunewald forest of West Berlin.

September 13: Prisoners from the RAF and the 2nd of June Movement go on hunger strike, demanding the end of isolation.

November 9: RAF member Holger Meins doesn't receive sufficient medical support and dies after two months on hunger strike.

November 10: In response to Holger Meins's death, 2nd of June members attempt to kidnap Günter von Drenkmann, president of the West Berlin district court; the attempt fails and von Drenkmann is shot and killed.

1975

February 27: The Berlin CDU chairman Peter Lorenz is kidnapped by the 2nd of June Movement; he is freed one week later after five political prisoners are released and flown to South Yemen.

April 24: The RAF's Holger Meins Commando occupies the German embassy in Stockholm, demanding the release of twenty-six RAF prisoners. As several deadlines pass, the commando kills two hostages. Late at night, an explosion rocks the building. RAF member Ulrich Wessel dies, and so does, ten days later, RAF member Siegfried Hausner, who is deported to Germany despite life-threatening injuries.

April 28: Ronald Fritzsch and Gerald Klöpper are arrested in a garage in the Tegel neighborhood of West Berlin.

May 9: Werner Sauber is shot and killed, alongside police officer Walter Pauli, during a shootout in Cologne; Karl Heinz Roth is shot and seriously injured.

June 6: In a shootout with police at the Yorckstraße subway station of West Berlin, Till Meyer is injured and subsequently arrested.

July 30–31: The 2nd of June Movement distributes "chocolate kisses" during bank robberies in West Berlin.

September 9: Ralf Reinders and Inge Viett are arrested alongside another 2nd of June Movement member in an apartment in the Steglitz neighborhood of West Berlin.

September 15: Gabriele Rollnik and Fritz Teufel are arrested in a hidden rear apartment in the Wedding neighborhood of West Berlin.

December 21: An OPEC conference in Vienna is stormed by a Palestinian-led commando including two West German militants, Hans-Joachim Klein, associated with the Revolutionary Cells, and Gabriele Kröcher-Tiedemann, from the 2nd of June Movement. An Austrian police officer, an Iraqi guard, and a Libyan government official are killed; Hans-Joachim Klein is seriously injured. The commando takes several hostages. They negotiate a free passage to Algeria, where they release the hostages, purportedly for a ransom of several million dollars.

December 24: 2nd of June Movement member Inge Viett is caught trying to break out of prison by sawing through the bars of her cell window.

1976

March 26: Andreas Vogel is arrested entering a safe house in the Schöneberg neighborhood of West Berlin.

June 27: A commando consisting of Palestinian militants and Revolutionary Cell members hijack an Air France airliner traveling from Tel Aviv to Paris. They divert the plane to Entebbe, Uganda, and demand the release of fifty-three political prisoners, including 2nd of June Movement members Ralf Reinders, Fritz Teufel, and Inge Viett. On July 4, an Israeli special operations unit storms the airport, killing the commando members as well as forty-five Ugandan soldiers. In Entebbe, the hijackers divided the passengers into two groups; whether the division was based on Israeli citizenship or Jewish identity is contested to this day.

July 7: Inge Viett and Gabriele Rollnik break out of the women's prison on Lehrter Straße in West Berlin alongside another 2nd of June member and a RAF member.

November (exact date unclear): Till Meyer attempts to escape from Tegel prison with the help of members of the 2nd of June Movement and the Revolutionary Cells; the effort fails when guards are alerted by sawing noises.

1977

March 31: Norbert "Knofo" Kröcher is arrested in Stockholm and extradited to West Germany.

May 21–22: The "torture weekend" occurs, during which 2nd of June Movement prisoners are severely abused by state security agents.

September 5: German industrialist and former SS officer Hanns Martin Schleyer is kidnapped by the RAF's Siegfried Hausner Commando. His chauffeur and three bodyguards are killed. The commando demands the release of eleven political prisoners. On October 13, a Palestinian commando hijacks a Lufthansa airliner traveling from Mallorca to Paris. The airliner eventually lands in Mogadishu, Somalia, where, on October 18, it is stormed by a German special police unit (GSG 9). Three of the four hijackers are killed; the passengers are freed. Shortly thereafter, RAF prisoners Andreas Baader, Gudrun Ensslin, and Jan-Carl Raspe are found dead in their cells in Stammheim prison. The authorities classify the deaths as suicides, a version refuted by many, including RAF prisoner Irmgard Möller, who survives the night badly injured in her Stammheim cell. On October 19, the Siegfried Hausner Commando executes Schleyer; his body is found in the trunk of a car parked in the border town of Mulhouse, France. The events become known as the "German Autumn."

November 9: 2nd of June Movement members and three Austrian supporters kidnap textile magnate Walter Palmers in Vienna. Palmers is released four days later in exchange for a ransom of several million US dollars. The three Austrian supporters are arrested within weeks.

December 20: Gabriele Kröcher-Tiedeman is arrested along the French-Swiss border, alongside another 2nd of June Movement member, following a shootout.

1978

January 27–29: The Tunix Congress is held in West Berlin; it brings together a cross-section of the radical left in West Germany to discuss how to proceed after the "German Autumn."

April 10: The so-called Lorenz-Drenkmann trial, addressing the Lorenz kidnapping as well as the assassination of Günter von Drenkmann, begins in West Berlin. The defendants are Ronald Fritzsch, Gerald Klöpper, Till Meyer, Ralf Reinders, Fritz Teufel, and Andreas Vogel.

May 27: Till Meyer is broken out of Moabit prison; the intended breakout of Andreas Vogel fails.

May 31: The Revolutionary Cells carry out two actions against the court-imposed lawyers in the Lorenz-Drenkmann trial. One of them is shot in the leg.

June 5: Klaus Viehmann is arrested in the Schöneberg neighborhood of West Berlin while getting into a car under police surveillance.

June 21: Till Meyer and Gabriele Rollnik are arrested in Bulgaria alongside two more 2nd of June Movement members. They are extradited to West Germany.

1980

January 19: Klaus Viehmann, Gabriele Rollnik, and two more 2nd of June members go on trial for the 1977 Palmers kidnapping in Vienna and the 1978 Till Meyer prison breakout.

June 2: 2nd of June Movement members hiding in France decide to dissolve the organization and join the RAF. They issue a statement, read in court by Gabriele Rollnik. In a text released soon thereafter, Ronnie Fritzsch, Ralf Reinders, and Klaus Viehmann strongly object to the statement. The 2nd of June Movement effectively splits into two camps, which marks the end of the group.

1981

February 10: Bommi Baumann is arrested in London and extradited to West Germany.

August 4: French police officer Francis Violleau is shot and seriously injured by Inge Viett during a chase.

1990

June: In the wake of the fall of the Berlin Wall, ten former RAF members who had received sanctuary in East Germany are arrested, among them Inge Viett.

INTRODUCTION: THE BLUES

Roman Danyluk

In the early 1970s, West Berlin is a front line separating the East from the West, a reality largely forgotten today. Just as the year 1972 begins, somewhere in the divided city, about a dozen activists from various militant groups have gathered to discuss a daring project that they hope can breathe fresh air into a flagging revolt. The antiauthoritarian rebellion started five years ago, and for the last two years, there have been numerous militant actions—and not just in Berlin. Across the planet, a young, euphoric generation shares a common spirit of revolt, with Berlin being one of its epicenters. Here, where real socialism and capitalism meet, an explosive storm of resistance has been brewing since the 1960s, made up of subcultural and countercultural initiatives, politicized students, rebellious young workers, women's groups, and lesbian and gay groups. In this boiling cauldron, the 2nd of June Movement emerges from half a dozen small militant groups as a new urban guerrilla. Its members are the children of the antiauthoritarian social revolt who understand their armed project as part of the social-revolutionary tradition.

Being the Subject of One's Own History

What does the era of West Berlin's urban guerrilla mean today? Can it provide any lessons for the twenty-first century and its struggles for liberation? In 2005, Karl Heinz Roth, an influential movement figure at the time, answered the question as follows:

What remains important about the 2nd of June Movement is this: it was the only armed group that had a solid relationship with the proletarian youth and subculture. If you focus on this particular aspect in the context of the revolt of the 1970s, you will find both the strengths and the weaknesses of this era. . . . Without a healthy degree of subversiveness and boldness any social resistance lacks perspective. Yet the people who resist need to know their limits if they don't want to end up in social isolation, turning into a bogus revolutionary elite.[1]

Since capitalism began to ravage both humanity and the planet, there have been two historical moments with world revolution on the agenda. The first was the period between 1905 and 1923, when the revolutionary left struggled for sharing the wealth, council democracy, and a noncapitalist economy—in short, for communism. The second period stretched, roughly speaking, from 1967 to 1977. You could see it everywhere: in the terms used at the time, in the First World, the Second World, and the Third World. Protest movements, anticolonial struggles, proletarian uprisings, and militant rebellions occurred both in the industrialized countries of the West, the real socialist countries of the East, and in the "Three Continents," or, as we say today, the Global South.

The armed left was a specific element of this era (as it is of any revolutionary era), and it is the subject of this book. The book's purpose is to uncover what remains useful of the experiences of the era's armed left. We will examine this from a standpoint of critical solidarity. The utopian demands of said era, freedom and equality the world over, remain as relevant as ever.

Mainstream historical accounts attempt to downplay liberation struggles, particularly armed initiatives. The dominant representations of the urban guerrilla cynically affirm the ruling conditions and are full of self-serving inaccuracies. They pay hardly any attention to the motivation behind the struggles. They draw on police reports and judicial records. But any such sources need to be approached with utter caution and skepticism. In the novel *Macht und Widerstand* (Power and resistance), Ilija Trojanow writes the following about a Bulgarian resistance group:

The charges, a monstrous frameup: five young men, unscrupulous, violent, ready to do anything, incited and supported by sinister foreign capitalist forces—a screeching hyperbolic account, thread-bare, dishonest. It wearies me. No word about the prosecutors' crimes, committed to disclose our alleged crimes. . . . Behind the demonization, no one sees what we have really done: creating a network of cells in resistance, carrying out a spectacular action. . . . No word about our hour-long debates, no word about the difficult path to the right deed. That's the nature of official records: they never include what's essential.[2]

When journalistic or academic treatments of the armed struggle refer to former protagonists as sources, we are usually confronted with renouncers, defectors, and crown witnesses. The attention paid to former militants who have returned to the bourgeois fold is considerable. All of the West German guerrilla groups had defectors who hoped to capitalize on their militant past as "guerrilla celebrities." They delivered sensational accounts and fairy tales that the media in the society of the spectacle longs for. Whenever interest in these storytellers known for their extensive media barrage (books, interviews, articles, talk show appearances, etc.) waned, they would, without fail, produce ever more fantastic "revelations"—for a fee, of course!

This contrived history-writing about the militant left must be resisted; the realization that ruling historiography is the historiography of rulers is hardly new, but the historiography of the militant German left serves as another example to confirm it.

Even within the left, vague assumptions and ideological prejudices characterize the portrayal of the armed left. But a left that portrays the militant struggles of the 1960s and '70s as nothing but mistaken and misguided is doing the ruling class a favor. What we need is an open debate about left history. Otherwise, the radical left will find itself floating aimlessly, no ground beneath its feet.

The 2nd of June Movement, which existed from 1972 to 1980, understood itself to be the "proletarian section of the armed left" in West Berlin and West Germany. I consider psychological or pathologizing attempts to explain the emergence of armed struggle in West Berlin and West Germany completely inappropriate. The rise of urban guerrilla groups in several industrialized countries at the time indicates that there existed a political, social, and economic base for them. The social developments of the time require special attention.

In Germany, Rhine capitalism laid the groundwork for the rebellion of the late 1960s.[3] It was broader and deeper than what many think today. It is difficult to find a label that does the complexity of the situation justice, but terms such as "antiauthoritarian social revolt" or "extraparliamentary opposition" *(außerparlamentarische Opposition,* APO) provide a reasonable conceptual framework. The rebellion consisted of at least six significant wings:

- the high school and university students;
- the New Left, both within and outside the institutions;
- second-wave feminists;
- lesbian and gay activists;
- the working class, particularly young workers, apprentices, and migrants;
- the subculture and the counterculture of hippies, communes, artists, Hash Rebels, the Blues, the Beat scene, etc.

There was, of course, much overlap between these wings, both ideologically and personally. Mobilization was so broad that it impacted all areas of life. Students struggled to democratize schools and universities. The APO targeted the Nazi legacy of the West German Federal Republic of Germany (FRG) as well as the emergency laws, the Springer press,[4] the Vietnam War, and more. The second-wave feminist movement struggled for equal wages, abortion rights, and a reform of marriage and divorce laws. Migrants rallied against poor pay, high-speed assembly lines, and the living conditions in the barracks they were housed in; they also demanded a summer vacation that was long enough to visit their home countries. Apprentices wanted to work under less authoritarian structures and with better pay—they were part of a broad working-class resistance demanding higher (fairer) wages and better working conditions. Declassed people (runaways, the homeless, prisoners, people in various institutions) were tired of marginalization and deprivation. Rebellious subcultures turned their backs on commercialization and materialism, and the lesbian and gay movement was picking up speed.

The breadth of the revolt of the 1960s needs to be understood in its social context. For the participants, the experiences were formative. People acted on their own, broke rules, aimed for self-transformation as well as social change, thought collectively, and championed solidarity. It is wrong to reduce the rebellion to a cultural revolution, glossing over its political, social, and economic dimensions. The revolutionaries of the time had a very political understanding of culture. Their anticommercial networks brought together artists and theorists, festivals and study circles. It was clear to them that the revolution required a strong cultural element. Emancipation meant breaking with bourgeois society.

The diversity and creativity expressed in political action at the time is hard to imagine for younger generations. There were demonstrations, rallies, provocations, sit-ins, teach-ins, smoke-ins, paint balloon attacks, free concerts, free festivals, rent strikes, squats, sabotage in the factories, street fights—lots of militancy. Communes were founded (urban and rural), as well as support networks for West German and American draft dodgers.

It is no surprise that, in such a climate, the possibilities of armed struggle were discussed. Eventually, different groups went from talk to action. They figured that armed resistance was a natural extension of the movement. None of the urban guerrilla groups, the 2nd of June Movement included, appeared out of thin air. They were part of a broad militant movement. But there was another element: in the early 1970s, it became clear that the early energy and optimism of the rebellion was slowly fading. The armed groups believed that the disintegration of the rebellion needed to be stopped by raising the resistance to new levels. They made mistakes and had their shortcomings, but their uncompromising rejection of reformism attracted quite a few on the left. There existed a particular aura around the armed groups.

The 2nd of June Movement

The 2nd of June Movement emerged out of various militant groups in West Berlin and West Germany. To outline the 2nd of June Movement's history, we need to look at three stages: the prehistory, the formation, and the practice. Thereafter, we will look at the beginning of the end of the 2nd of June Movement, and its final disbandment.

Prehistory

Shocking the bourgeois is, alas, easier than overthrowing him.
—Eric Hobsbawm, 1969

In July 1969, there was a meeting of militant leftists from West Berlin and West Germany with far-reaching consequences. The people gathered, coming from various groups, and evaluated the "Prison and

Justice Campaign" (*Knast- und Justizkampagne*). Within the antiauthoritarian currents of the APO, breaking the law and engaging in militant resistance—from street fighting to property destruction—had become accepted forms of resistance. "Direct action" would, as the saying goes, "deliver the goods." However, there was no shared position on targeting people.

The orthodox sections of the APO turned to party building; many different Marxist-Leninist and Maoist organizations were founded, with centralized leaderships and disciplined cadres. Armed struggle was not on their agenda. Many antiauthoritarian militants thought differently. They saw armed struggle as key to keeping the spirit of the rebellion alive. Some of them believed that a nationwide meeting on the outfall of the Prison and Justice Campaign would allow for relevant discussions. The meeting was held in Ebrach, a small town in Bavaria, under the name "Red Prison Week." On a meadow provided by a local farmer, two hundred militants assembled, hailing mainly from Munich, Frankfurt, and West Berlin.

Ebrach was chosen because the well-known activist Reinhard Wetter was imprisoned there. Wetter, a twenty-one-year-old philosophy student, had been sentenced for fare-dodging and attacks on the America House. He had also objected to the presence of plainclothes police officers at the University of Munich. Wetter was serving eight months with no possibility of parole. His sentencing had been the result of obvious collusion. In prison, Wetter helped other inmates with complaints and petitions.

Several actions accompanied the meeting. The Ebrach prison gate was demolished, the local cemetery (burying only representatives of the legal system) was vandalized, and a government office was occupied when local authorities tried to declare the meeting's campsite illegal.

During the meeting, two issues were central: one, establishing a nationwide infrastructure for the Prison and Justice Campaign to address the ever-increasing number of trials and prison sentences among leftists; two, procuring weapons and establishing contacts with Third World liberation movements. Among the participants were Andreas Baader, Gudrun Ensslin, Georg von Rauch, Fritz Teufel, and various other militants who over the subsequent years would play a role in the Red Army Faction and the 2nd of June Movement, respectively.

The goals of the Ebrach Red Prison Week proved too ambitious. The APO newspaper *Agit 883* published a sobering balance sheet of the gathering, calling it a chaotic failure, mainly due to poor preparation. Instead of decent food, there were mountains of hash. Nonetheless, the meeting had a lasting impact because of the informal discussions it enabled between the present militants. There were very concrete outcomes: the prisoner solidarity movement had been strengthened, and a seed for armed struggle had been sown.

The second half of 1969 proved crucial. An armed left was no longer just a lofty idea. The first steps to make it a reality were taken. Apart from Third World influences, inspiration was drawn from the Black Panthers and the Weather Underground as well as from Italian militants.

Of particular importance was Carlos Marighella's *Minimanual of the Urban Guerrilla*. Marighella was a Brazilian Communist Party member who founded an urban guerrilla group after the 1964 military coup in Brazil. He was shot dead in a military ambush on November 4, 1969, only a few months after the publication of his manual, which influenced urban guerrilla groups worldwide. A German translation was first published in the journal *Sozialistische Politik* (*SoPo*). But in order to become practically relevant, Marighella's ideas had to be applied to the conditions in the country.

West Berlin was probably home to the largest rebellious milieu in postwar Germany. The population of the city had decreased by about a million compared to the 1930s. The city was divided by a wall built on the orders of the GDR government in 1961. The wall made even more people leave the city, fearing that it would soon be administered by the Soviets. However, there was also an influx of many young people coming to the city from West Germany. From 1955 to 1965, the number of students increased by tens of thousands. Many young men moved to West Berlin to avoid military service. The city was filled with conscientious objectors, hippies, and people longing for a different kind of life. Many of them moved to working-class neighborhoods such as Kreuzberg and Neukölln, which were also the homes of many migrant workers, the so-called *Gastarbeiter* (literally "guest workers"). The result was the creation of subversive enclaves in West Berlin.

To describe the rebellion of the era as a "student rebellion" is as false as speaking of a "cultural revolution." The students were part of the rebellion, yes, and they shook up the traditional structure of German universities. Many democratic rights were won, and collective practices were established. But the rebellion was by no means limited to the academic milieu. The APO was much broader. Every conceivable aspect of life became a subject of political struggle. A prominent example was the connections made between socialist principles and psychotherapy, challenging social norms and fostering individual liberation.

Of course, the movement was not homogenous. Apart from political differences (e.g., libertarian/antiauthoritarian versus dogmatic/state socialist), the protagonists' social backgrounds and class allegiances mattered. The academic left and SDS members largely came from bourgeois families. They were primarily occupied with issues such as anticolonialism, the Vietnam War, and psychoanalysis. Young workers, on the other hand, rebelled first and foremost against the repressive conditions they experienced at home, at school, and at work. The Blues, Berlin's antibourgeois subculture of the late 1960s, was strongly rooted in the proletarian milieu. There were fewer theoretical debates in the Blues scene than among the students, and more immediate practice.

Militants from working-class families sensed a chasm within the left. While left-wing students and intellectuals could, at any time, decide to pursue a professional career, workers remained workers. In 1966, only 10 percent of students in West Germany and West Berlin came from working-class families.

The Blues created a rebellious energy in the city. Although overwhelmingly (sub)proletarian, it attracted a wide range of people. Among them were skilled Marxist and anarchist theorists and dropouts of all sorts: drug addicts, runaways, freaks, rockers, petty criminals, the voluntarily unemployed, and the occasional barefoot prophet. The Blues was a libidinous and hedonistic hodgepodge, with an explosive mixture of politics and counterculture that encompassed around a hundred collective houses and communes. The Blues was characterized by an aggressive nonconformity, a rejection of authorities of any kind, and a critique of industrial society. Members of the Blues struggled for liberated spaces and their own lifestyle. They valued self-expression, agitation, and provocation. The majority of the people involved always remained working-class.

Music was important. While most Germans hailed schmaltzy pop songs, the Blues rebels listened to R&B, soul, and psychedelic rock. So-called Krautrock was also popular. Bars like the Top Ten and Dicke Wirtin became important meeting places. Unlike in most major cities of West Germany, there was no curfew in Berlin. Many informal meetings were held on squares across the city. Underground printing presses published speeches by Malcolm X, articles by Frantz Fanon, and song lyrics by Bob Dylan.

The high spirits of the time were summed up a quarter of a century later, when 2nd of June Movement member Ralf Reinders said at a meeting to commemorate the twentieth anniversary of Ulrike Meinhof's death on May 3, 1996: "We would be sitting in a bar having drinks, and when people left, they would say, 'See you at the revolution!' That's how we felt."[5] You always know better in hindsight, but at the time, the West Berlin rebels could reasonably assume that there was considerable sympathy for their actions among the population, especially among the youth. Furthermore, their rebellion was part of a global uprising where the sky seemed the limit.

A significant part of the Blues consisted of "marginal groups" (*Randgruppen*). For many of the antiauthoritarians within the APO, these groups constituted an important revolutionary subject. The idea that the socially declassed—what Marx called the "lumpenproletariat"—had a particular revolutionary potential had already been developed theoretically by the German-American philosopher Herbert Marcuse. Marcuse reckoned that members of marginal groups, such as the homeless, prisoners, and patients in various asylums, were trapped in what sociologist Erving Goffman called "total institutions," experiencing the contradictions of capitalist society in concentrated form. In the West Germany of the 1960s, "beggars," "drifters," and "vagrants" could still be sentenced to several months in prison, based on laws dating back to the nineteenth century—and sometimes to the Nazis' penal code. Workhouses existed in West Germany until 1969. Poverty was treated as a crime rather than the expression of social ills.

In the late 1960s, a quarter of a million children in West Germany lived in reformatories, foster homes, and youth detention centers. Many were beaten, humiliated, and sexually abused. Most came from families living in extreme poverty. The institutions they were in demanded absolute obedience; the children were deprived of the most basic rights and freedoms. Many of the institutions were run by churches. "Discipline and order" was the rule of the day. Unsurprisingly, plenty of children escaped from these institutions as they grew older. In West Berlin alone, there were as many as two thousand young runaways living on the streets in the late 1960s.

Before joining the Red Army Faction, Ulrike Meinhof was an acclaimed left-wing journalist. She spent considerable time researching the conditions in the asylums, presenting her findings in magazine articles and radio programs. She demanded an end to gender segregation and any form of psychological and physical violence against the children. Positive reference points for Meinhof were the education system of Israeli kibbutzim and the theories of the Summerhill School founder A.S. Neill.

There was a concerted APO effort to draw attention to the conditions in the children and youth asylums through the *Heimkampagne* (asylum campaign) of the late 1960s. Inmates of the asylums were encouraged to rebel against the conditions they were living under, and living quarters for runaways were provided in political housing collectives.

By the early 1970s, much of the romanticism about this potentially new revolutionary subject had faded. It was hard to bridge the needs and ideas of the marginal groups and the high demands of the academic left. The orthodox Marxist-Leninist groups that emerged at the time shifted their focus elsewhere and relocated the revolutionary subject in the traditional working class. However, the subcultural proletarian milieu of the antiauthoritarian sections of the left remained open to the underclasses and continued to work with them. In its 1971 declaration "The Urban Guerrilla Concept," the Red Army Faction wrote: "Figure out where the asylums are and the large families and the subproletariat and the women workers, those who are only waiting to give a kick in the teeth to those who deserve it. They will take the lead."[6]

Of particular importance for integrating the asylum campaign into a broader political agenda was the December 1971 occupation of the former Bethanien Hospital in Berlin-Kreuzberg. The occupiers turned the building into a squat named the Georg von Rauch House, as the Tupamaros West Berlin member Georg von Rauch was killed in a shootout with police only days earlier. An entire floor of the building was occupied by runaways, while another was reserved for apprentices and young, unskilled workers. The relationship between the two groups wasn't always the best, but the Georg von Rauch House has played an important role for the counterculture and the political scene of West Berlin. The story of the squat is commemorated in the "Rauch Haus Song" by the band Ton Steine Scherben, a hugely influential musical mouthpiece of West Berlin's political subculture of the early 1970s.

Formation

No single incident provided the launching pad for the formation of the 2nd of June Movement, or the armed struggle in West Germany and West Berlin in general, but there are some historical moments of significance— the killing of Benno Ohnesorg by a police officer on June 2, 1967, being one of them.

Benno Ohnesorg was a twenty-six-year-old student, pacifist, and member of a Protestant church group who joined a demonstration against the Berlin visit by the Shah of Iran, Mohammad Reza Pahlavi. It was the first demonstration that Ohnesorg ever attended. He was among a crowd attacked by police outside the German Opera, awaiting the Shah's arrival. After the crowd was dispersed with the help of batons, water cannons, and tear gas, plainclothes police officer Karl-Heinz Kurras followed Ohnesorg into a courtyard and, according to numerous eyewitnesses, killed him with a shot in the back of the head. Despite forensic evidence backing up the witnesses' accounts, a widespread police cover-up ensured that Kurras was never convicted of any crime. The 2nd of June Movement would later reference the date of Ohnesorg's killing in its name.

Also of high significance was the assassination attempt on student leader Rudi Dutschke on April 11, 1968. The assassin was a young, far-right lone wolf claiming to have been inspired by the antistudent rhetoric of the *Bild Zeitung*, the flagship tabloid of the Springer press.

These two shootings, in the midst of the media's inflammatory rhetoric against the APO and an ever-increasing police repression and legal persecution, laid the groundwork for radical young leftists considering armed struggle as an option for West Germany and West Berlin.

The following groups must be named as predecessors of the 2nd of June Movement.

The Central Council of the Roaming Hash Rebels

Several political groups operated within the Blues scene in Berlin. The most iconic among them was the humorously named Central Council of the Roaming Hash Rebels (*Zentralrat der umherschweifenden Haschrebellen*), reminiscent of the US Yippies founded by Abbie Hoffman and Jerry Rubin, mixing anarchism and countercultural politics.

The Hash Rebels consisted mainly of working-class youth who had met in the subcultural drug scene. In April 1968, some of them founded the Wieland commune on West Berlin's Wielandstraße, where twenty people, including three children, lived. They all slept in one room. Petty crime was the main source of income. Stolen goods were sold in West German university towns, and hash was sold on the streets of Berlin, with American soldiers being among the most loyal customers. Both Michael "Bommi" Baumann and Georg von Rauch lived at the Wieland commune. Ralf Reinders lived in another Hash Rebels commune on Nimrodstraße.

The Hash Rebels associated an antibourgeois lifestyle with, as their name suggests, smoking copious amounts of hash. They considered themselves to be the "organic intellectuals" of the subproletariat, a class they thought would be most likely to adopt the urban guerrilla strategy in Germany—eventually, some of them would take that step themselves.

The Central Council of the Roaming Hash Rebels was formed in summer 1969 by members from the Wieland and Nimrod communes as well as from Kommune 1, the pioneering urban commune of West Berlin. The group meant to elevate the political consciousness within the Blues scene. Its name was an ironic play at the various Marxist-Leninist groups emerging from the APO at the time. Among the members were Bommi Baumann, Georg von Rauch, Ralf Reinders, Norbert Kröcher, Ronald Fritzsch, Ina Siepmann, Thomas Weisbecker, and Dieter Kunzelmann, the Kommune 1 poster boy.

The first Hash Rebels action was, fittingly, a smoke-in at West Berlin's Tiergarten park on July 5, 1969. The police kept their distance, but Georg von Rauch was arrested afterward, passed out in some bushes. The police had his stomach pumped, found out that von Rauch had consumed hash, and brought him to trial. He did a short stint in jail.

The Hash Rebels drew much inspiration from the Black Panthers, who defended local communities against police repression, helped addicts to detox, provided medical care for those in need, supported prisoners, and pushed dealers out of their neighborhoods. The Hash Rebels made an unrealistic, yet symbolically important demand: they wanted the West Berlin neighborhood of Kreuzberg, a stronghold of the Blues scene, to become an autonomous zone, closed off to the police. They produced numerous leaflets, which they distributed at concerts and festivals, and they had a weekly column in *Agit 883*. They called for people to leave the factories and universities and become professional revolutionaries.

Putting their money where their mouth was, the Hash Rebels acquired weapons and traveled to an anarchist commune in Austria for shooting training. Soon thereafter, they began firebombing banks and public offices. It didn't take long for the police to close in on them. The West Berlin neighborhoods where the Hash Rebels lived were flooded with hard drugs at the time, and the cops found it relatively easy to recruit informants. Some Hash Rebels were forced underground, among them Ralf Reinders.

But the militant actions in West Berlin didn't cease, not least because there were a few groups that were independent but closely associated with the Hash Rebels, such as the Black Cells, also rooted in the subproletariat and prone to stirring up trouble and confronting security forces. They also provided a support network for US military deserters. The far-left magazine *FIZZ* and the Black Aid group, an anarchist prisoner solidarity network, were closely tied to the Black Cells. They included a number of militants who would eventually go underground as 2nd of June Movement members, among them Inge Viett and Verena Becker.

The Central Council of the Roaming Hash Rebels ceased to operate when repression hit hard in 1970. But many protagonists became involved in a group that would leave an even stronger impact and that acted as a direct predecessor to the 2nd of June Movement: the Tupamaros West Berlin.

Tupamaros West Berlin

The Tupamaros West Berlin, named after the Uruguayan urban guerrilla movement founded a few years earlier,[7] emerged out of the abovementioned July 1969 Red Prison Week in Ebrach. They were arguably the most immediate predecessor to the 2nd of June Movement.

The Tupamaros West Berlin made early contact with the Red Brigades (*Brigate Rosse*) in Italy, facilitated by some Italian comrades who had attended the Red Prison Week. The Red Brigades kept a bit of a distance, as they found the Tupamaros from West Berlin too anarchist, but they got them in touch with Fatah militants who invited them to one of their training camps in Jordan. Ina Siepmann, who was part of the group that followed the invitation, decided to stay behind for some time, working with Palestinian paramedics. Most of the others left the Fatah camp eager to initiate the armed struggle in Germany.

The Tupamaros West Berlin were formed in collaboration with people from the Hash Rebels, with the intention to connect the political underground, the Blues subculture, and grassroots initiatives. In 1969, there was a firebombing campaign, targeting courthouses, prisons, and department stores. One action overshadowed any other. On November 9, 1969, on the sixty-first anniversary of the 1938 Kristallnacht, the Tupamaros West Berlin placed an incendiary device at the Jewish Community Center in West Berlin where 250 people attended a memorial event. The device failed to ignite and the action was meant to support the Palestinian liberation struggle, yet the antisemitic overtones were all too obvious, and the action tarnished the reputation of the Tupamaros West Berlin, also within the radical left. *Agit 883* announced that it would never again publish a Tupamaros West Berlin statement. The Palestine Committee in Frankfurt also denounced the action. As it turned out, the bomb had been placed by police infiltrator Peter Urbach.

In early 1970, the first arrests were made in connection with Tupamaros West Berlin actions, which, by then, amounted to about 120 attacks against the police, the legal system, and US interests. On February 6, 1970, Tupamaros West Berlin members, among them Bommi Baumann, Georg von Rauch, and Thomas Weisbecker, were arrested after a botched invasion of the home of tabloid journalist Horst Rieck.[8] Alarmed by neighbors, police units arrived before they were able to leave the property.

On July 19, 1970, Dieter Kunzelmann, who was wanted in connection with the attack on the Jewish Community Center, was arrested at Tempelhof airport. The following day, Siepmann and Weisbecker were arrested at a West Berlin safe house. The July 1971 trial of Bommi Baumann, Georg von Rauch, and Thomas Weisbecker ended with the infamous mix-up of von Rauch and Weisbecker. When Baumann and Weisbecker were released on bail but not von Rauch, von Rauch pretended to be Weisbecker and left the courthouse. When the authorities realized what had happened, they had to release Weisbecker as well, having been deeply embarrassed by the cocky militants. All three defendants went underground, determined to continue the armed struggle. Together with other Tupamaros West Berlin members on the loose, they organized safe houses, stole cars, and engaged in target practice in West Berlin's Tegel Forest.

By summer 1971, Tupamaros West Berlin militants and other Blues activists had sufficient material and strong enough infrastructure to escalate their strategy. Discussions about founding a committed urban guerrilla organization had become ever more serious. The militants agreed that such an organization would require a base in the proletariat and that it had to inspire the exploited and oppressed to revolt. The actions carried out should be such that anyone who wanted to should be able to replicate them. The organization itself should consist of autonomous cells, operating independently.

To further strengthen the material basis of their operations, soon-to-be 2nd of June members robbed a number of banks in fall 1971. However, tragedy struck on December 4. When a group of four militants wanted to move a stolen Ford Transit from the Schöneberg neighborhood to a more secure location, they didn't know that the van was under police observation. When the group arrived at the vehicle, they were confronted by plainclothes police, and in the shootout that followed Georg von Rauch was killed. The other three militants managed to escape.

Von Rauch had been one of the best-known militants of West Berlin, serving as a link between different sections of the radical left. His death led to numerous demonstrations and the occupation of the empty Bethanien Hospital, which was renamed the Georg von Rauch House.

The squatters received support from neighbors, who objected to the heavy-handed police response. The determination of the squatters, combined with the local support they received, forced the authorities to give in. The Georg von Rauch House remains an important gathering place for Berlin's left to this day.

With Georg von Rauch's death, the days of the Tupamaros West Berlin were over. The remaining militants, however, were determined to carry on in the 2nd of June Movement.

Tupamaros Munich

The Tupamaros Munich were, essentially, the Tupamaros West Berlin's sister organization. They, too, were an early example of the guerrilla strategy that would be embraced by the 2nd of June Movement later on.

Munich, the capital of Bavaria, is one of Germany's largest cities. In the 1960s, it had a strong counterculture and several left-wing and subcultural communes. Later members of both the RAF and the 2nd of June Movement got introduced to radical politics there.

One of the most important groups to arise in this context was, in 1969, the Aktion Südfront (Action South Front). It focused on the marginal groups in its politics and did much outreach in asylums and in workplaces with many apprentices. The group ran several collective houses in poor neighborhoods. They hoped that marginalized youth would become politically active, redefining the radical left's theoretical framework. After internal conflicts, one of the Aktion Südfront cells decided, in early 1970, to go underground and form the Tupamaros Munich.

On February 20, 1970, the Tupamaros Munich claimed its first action in a letter to the press: the group had placed several firebombs at the central courthouse in Munich. Three days later, two firebombs were thrown into the bedroom of a district court judge who had sentenced a twenty-seven-year-old university lecturer and draft dodger to seven months in prison. According to police records, there were about twenty suspected Tupamaros Munich members, several of whom would join the RAF or the 2nd of June Movement. One of them was Fritz Teufel, who was arrested on June 12, 1970, after a series of firebombings against courthouses and businesses involved in the war industry.

Despite Teufel's arrest being a harsh blow to the group, the Tupamaros Munich carried out firebombings until November 1971. A day after Teufel got sentenced to two years in prison, they firebombed the America House in Munich. Police stations, banks, and research institutions were also targets.

The end of the Tupamaros Munich came when key member Rolf Pohle was arrested in December 1971 while trying to purchase weapons for the group at a gun store in Ulm. The group had taken responsibility for twenty-four firebombings, in which no one got injured. Despite the end of the group, many of its members were just getting started.

Red Ruhr Army

The Red Ruhr Army is another group that deserves our attention in connection with the 2nd of June Movement. It was part predecessor and part parallel organization, with overlapping politics and personnel.

When Norbert Kröcher and Gabriele Tiedemann married in 1971, they used the marital loan of 3,000 Deutschmark they were entitled to as a young couple from West Berlin to buy two semiautomatic pistols and an assault rifle. They moved to North Rhine Westphalia, where they made contact with militants in Cologne and Düsseldorf. Together with Peter-Paul Zahl and a militant called Lothar Gend, they formed the core group of what became known as the Red Ruhr Army, a reference to a workers' movement of fifty thousand people that, in 1920, orchestrated the largest workers' uprising in German history. The modern-day Red Ruhr Army established contacts with various far-left groups in the Ruhr Valley and acquired safe houses, cars, weapons, and explosives.

A first setback occurred in December 1972, when Peter-Paul Zahl got injured and arrested during a shootout with police while trying to rent a car with false papers. He was sentenced to fifteen years in prison, as he had seriously injured a cop.

Norbert Kröcher was with Zahl at the time but managed to escape. He was questioned by comrades for not coming to Zahl's help and went into exile in Sweden, where he remained until his arrest and extradition to Germany in 1977.

With Gabriele Kröcher-Tiedemann arrested in July 1973, and Lothar Gend in March 1974, the Red Ruhr Army was devastated by arrests before it even got off the ground, but both its proletarian politics and several of its members found a home in the 2nd of June Movement.

Feminist Groups

The feminist movement of the time needs to be mentioned as another important influence on the 2nd of June Movement. Among various groups playing a role, the Brot und Rosen (Bread and Roses) collective was important insofar as it included future 2nd of June member Gabriele Rollnik. Bread and Roses focused on the situation of working-class women and established *Kinderläden*, feminist, left-wing kindergartens determined to strengthen children's autonomy. The collective also campaigned against section 218, the law limiting access to abortion. In 1972, the Bread and Roses collective published a women's handbook (*Frauenhandbuch*) addressing abortion rights, contraception, and the role of doctors, churches, and the pharmaceutical industry in controlling the female population, not least in the Third World. More than one hundred thousand copies of the handbook were distributed.

Another important feminist group was the Frauenbefreiungsfront (Women's Liberation Front), founded in 1970. It included a few future 2nd of June members, including Verena Becker and Ina Siepmann. Such as with others in the Blues scene, the women's income was, at least partly, based on petty crime. Many evenings were spent on postering and spray-painting feminist slogans in the Moabit neighborhood. They also carried out actions against misogynist gynecologists.

The Women's Liberation Front used *Agit 883* as a publishing outlet, criticizing other feminist groups as "bourgeois," but also, unlike some of the other radical feminist groups at the time, arguing for collaboration with male militants, seeing women's liberation tied to broader anticapitalist politics. Some of the Women's Liberation Front members were also active in a group called Die schwarze Braut (The Black Bride), carrying out actions against bridal stores and sex shops.

The personal overlap between all of these groups was strong, and it seems that the same women used different group names on different occasions. There was also a strong overlap with the abovementioned Black Aid prisoner support group.

The feminist groups of the era played an important role in the rise of the urban guerrilla in West Berlin and West Germany.

Founding and Practice of the 2nd of June Movement

Discussions about an urban guerrilla group based in West Berlin turned serious in late 1971. Several meetings were held at the Georg von Rauch House. Participants included members of the Hash Rebels, the Black Cells, the Women's Liberation Front, the Tupamaros West Berlin, the Tupamaros Munich, and the Red Ruhr Army, among them Ralf Reinders, Werner Sauber, Ina Siepmann, Norbert Kröcher, and Gabriele Kröcher-Tiedemann. They agreed that it was time for a more profound militant practice, and, as a result, the 2nd of June Movement was founded in January 1972. After the Red Army Faction, it was the second major urban guerrilla group in West Germany and West Berlin.

The name 2nd of June Movement was chosen because the death of Benno Ohnesorg was regarded as a turning point during the 1960s rebellion by students, artists, intellectuals, young workers, and Blues scenesters alike. Referencing the events of June 2, 1967, would also remind everyone of who had shot first. Equally important was the "movement" part of the name. The founders did not want to create a hierarchical structure but wanted to be the armed core of a broader revolutionary struggle.

Ideologically, there was no unity among members. While many drew upon anarchism, the group also included undogmatic Marxists and Maoists. What unified them was the conviction that there had to be freedom in the revolutionary process and that revolutionaries needed to ensure the revolution would lead to freedom. There was also agreement about focusing on local actions but tying them to global struggles.

The founders of the 2nd of June Movement reckoned that only members who were already sought by the police should go underground. Aboveground members were regarded as important. They helped avoid the logistical challenges of keeping a great number of people underground (everything from procuring false papers to safe houses) and were able to remain directly involved in aboveground discussions among the left. In a 2001 interview, former 2nd of June member Angelika Goder described her transition from aboveground to underground militant as follows:

> The 1975 Lorenz kidnapping was the action that really mobilized me. However, I had already had contact with the 2nd of June Movement before. That contact dated from 1973 or 1974, when I had done smaller tasks in support: observation, running errands, finding safe houses, establishing contacts, supplying false papers, and other logistical support. But the kidnapping of Peter Lorenz was crucial, because I saw that you could indeed resist the state and change things. At that point, I decided to go underground. . . . This was done after careful consideration, it was a gradual process. Before that, I was in contact with the same people, but I was still living aboveground, with a registered apartment, seeing my friends, and maintaining contact with legal groups.[9]

The early 2nd of June Movement members brought a basic supply of weapons with them. They had pistols, small-caliber rifles, and shotguns. Some of the weapons came from the RAF, others from contacts in Italy. But they had to build their arsenal. Apart from strengthening the group's structure and logistics, this was the biggest early challenge.

The group's infrastructure required apartments, garages, printshops, laboratories (for producing explosives), counterfeiting equipment, and a communication system. For safe houses, buildings with a rear courtyard and an exit into a back street were favored. They offered a safe passage for members and a steady flow of information. So-called dead mailboxes were placed in various buildings around the city. These were mailboxes with fake names placed next to the boxes of the building's real tenants. The boxes could be used to pass on notes and documents with little danger of being detected. They also allowed aboveground activists to maintain contact with the guerrilla without having to meet its members. As far as breaking into houses, stealing cars, and falsifying documents was concerned, there was plenty of shared experience within the group.

The intention of the 2nd of June Movement was to rejuvenate the radical left and fuel its revolutionary determination. It was a reaction to the "march through the institutions" that some former rebels from the 1960s had come to pursue. The SPD had profited strongly from this.

In 1969, they formed the West German government with the FDP as a junior partner, and in 1972, they scored a record outcome in the federal elections with 46 percent of the vote. SPD party membership increased by 40 percent between 1968 and 1976, reaching one million. The Jusos (short for Junge Sozialisten, or Young Socialists) also drew many new members.

The SPD pacified many radicals of the 1960s by relegalizing the DKP, by symbolic gestures such as the kneeling of chancellor Willy Brandt in front of the 1943 Warsaw Ghetto Uprising memorial in the Polish capital, and by an "Immunity Act" that eliminated many charges and sentences related to the protests of the 1960s. (This was not least in the self-interest of the party, as several thousands of its members, especially from the Jusos, were subjects of criminal proceedings.)

While the SPD government benefitted from giving itself a progressive aura, it intensified the repression of anyone unwilling to abide by its rules. For political radicals and outcasts of all sorts, surveillance, arrest, slander, persecution, prison, beatings, psychiatrization, and professional bans were part of everyday life. Infiltrators and agents provocateurs moved in their circles. The Springer press (and others) continued with their inflammatory rhetoric against the cultural and political underground.

There was also an increasing divide between academic leftists embracing scientific Marxism and working-class dropouts embracing sub- and countercultures. The 2nd of June Movement wanted to be a proletarian faction within the armed left. The group kept the language of their statements accessible and rejected both academic lingo and the messy sloganeering of the Marxist-Leninist "K-groups" (K for *Kommunismus*). They were convinced that in order to encourage revolutionary action you had to speak the language of the masses. This was also expressed in their actions, which often included humorous elements, something that led others from the far left to dismiss them as "populist" or a "fun guerrilla."

The 2nd of June Movement and the Red Army Faction

When the Red Army Faction was founded in 1970, it was the first urban guerrilla group in West Germany. Despite ideological differences, it served as an inspiration for the 2nd of June Movement, and it also supported the newfound group with material and information during its beginnings.

The RAF's story begins with an April 1968 firebombing of two department stores in Frankfurt, a response to the increasingly genocidal war led by the United States in Vietnam. Two of the four people convicted of the firebombing were Andreas Baader and Gudrun Ensslin, who would later become leading figures in the RAF. The immediate cause for the RAF's founding was the violent breakout of Baader from prison in May 1970. Renowned left-wing journalist Ulrike Meinhof played a central role in the breakout, as she had arranged for a meeting with Baader at a library where they, allegedly, were to work together on a book. During the breakout, library staff member George Linke was shot and severely injured. The RAF would prove to be the deadliest and most enduring of the armed groups in West Germany, carrying out numerous actions, some of them both spectacular and controversial, before officially folding in April 1998.

There was regular contact between the RAF and the groups who would go on to form the 2nd of June Movement. In 1970–71, members of the Blues scene, including Ralf Reinders, met with the RAF to discuss the possibility of common actions, but ideological differences as well as the arrest of numerous RAF members meant that nothing ever came of this.

Despite basic solidarity, the relationship between the RAF and the antiauthoritarian tendencies in Berlin was complicated. Antiauthoritarian publications such as *FIZZ* supported the actions of the RAF, but the overall support in the scene had its limits. When, in 1970, one of the 2nd of June Movement predecessors, the Tupamaros West Berlin, built a pirate radio transmitter with the capacity to interrupt TV audio signals, the RAF wasn't allowed to use it. The anarchist who had built the transmitter flatly refused to allow a "Marxist-Leninist organization" to put their hands on it.

The last important meeting between the RAF and the Tupamaros West Berlin happened in summer 1971. RAF members, including Andreas Baader and Gudrun Ensslin, traveled to West Berlin to recruit members of the West Berlin underground. They were particularly interested in Georg von Rauch because of his experience in militant politics. Georg von Rauch never joined the RAF, but the first RAF casualty, Petra Schelm, who was shot dead by a police officer in Hamburg in 1971, had indeed crossed over to the RAF from the Hash Rebels. Ralf Reinders was also in closer contact with the RAF for a while, but he then returned to the Berlin underground, dissatisfied with the RAF's hierarchical structure. Most members of the Berlin underground were anarchists who wanted to focus on actions in Berlin, while the RAF intended to operate in West Germany. The anarchists in Berlin also wanted to remain in close contact with aboveground comrades, which the RAF no longer could afford due to security concerns. The RAF demanded that all armed militants should break contact with

the legal left. This, effectively, blocked any way for RAF militants to return
to the aboveground.

Concerning tactics and strategies, there were also considerable
differences between the groups:

- The RAF believed that their actions spoke for themselves and
  would inspire the right people. This was based on the "*foco* theory"
  borrowed from Che Guevara, which called for a determined group
  of combatants (the *foco*) to directly attack the state. For the 2nd
  of June Movement, this approach created unclarity; they felt it
  was important to ensure that the population did understand
  their actions and not feel threatened by them, as this would only
  close the ranks of their opponents.
- The RAF argued that the militant left should attack "at the same
  level as the enemy." The 2nd of June Movement's armed strategy, however, sought to avoid deadly actions. The group always
  rejected a military rationale and encouraged low-level actions
  to be carried out in its name. The RAF considered such actions
  shallow and meaningless.
- The 2nd of June Movement was well connected with aboveground
  left-wing structures. These structures provided the group with
  maneuvering room, connections, and a social base. The RAF
  perceived this as a "mass tick" and "opportunism."

The 2nd of June Movement's Practice

The 2nd of June Movement did not believe that militant action could
wait until the revolution was imminent. The capitalist state had to be
attacked while the revolutionary movement was still taking shape. In a
1986 book chapter, former 2nd of June member Gerald Klöpper reflected
on the 2nd of June Movement's understanding of the interaction between
armed struggle and social movements: "Our strategy came down to how
useful our actions were for others, whether the actions concerned evictions, rent increases, layoffs, or factory closures. We hoped that others
would take our resistance as an example, adopt it, and begin to organize
themselves."[10]

An urban guerrilla is an armed political group, but for the 2nd of June
Movement weapons were, first and foremost, a means of self-defense and
a tool to facilitate actions such as bank robberies. They were very clear
about trying to avoid casualties.

In terms of internal organization, the 2nd of June Movement meant to operate in autonomous cells. Originally, there were two such cells in West Berlin. One consisted of militants with a couple of years of underground experience, including Ralf Reinders, Werner Sauber, and Ina Siepmann. Another consisted of relatively inexperienced militants, including Verena Becker and Inge Viett.

It was the latter who planted the bomb at the British Yacht Club in the Kladow neighborhood as the first action of the newly formed guerrilla. The group around Reinders bombed a British military vehicle in Berlin-Charlottenburg. Both actions were carried out in response to the January 30, 1972, killings of people protesting the British military presence in Derry, Northern Ireland, an event that has become known as "Bloody Sunday."

The bombing of the yacht club was ill-fated. Boatbuilder Erwin Beelitz found the bomb and set it off while trying to defuse it. He died from his injuries. This was not the action's only error. The militants who planted the bomb had also confused the yacht club with the actual target, the British officers' mess.

The bungled action led to heated discussions within the group. Bommi Baumann left because of it. Baumann had already been shaken by the death of Georg von Rauch, which he had witnessed up close. After he left the 2nd of June Movement, he went into exile in the UK.

The rocky road during the earliest phase of the 2nd of June Movement continued. When, not long after the yacht club disaster, members Harald Sommerfeld and Ulrich Schmücker were arrested, they made extensive statements. For Schmücker, this had disastrous consequences. After his release from prison in 1974, he was executed by a group calling itself the "Black June Commando." The group was based in West Germany and only loosely affiliated with comrades in Berlin, who largely rejected the action. The killing of Schmücker sent shockwaves through the radical left. Several investigations into the killing were carried out by German authorities, which concluded that the security services must have at least had knowledge about the assassination and decided not to intervene. Harald Sommerfeld served a short time in prison before becoming a priest.

Despite these setbacks, the new urban guerrilla group carried on. In March and April of 1972, successful bank robberies provided much-sought-after material support. The group's network of safe houses was steadily expanding. On March 3, the West Berlin police headquarters was bombed, one day after Thomas Weisbecker was killed by police in

Augsburg. On May 5, 1972, the 2nd of June Movement firebombed the law faculty at the Free University in Berlin in response to charges against police officers who had shot militants routinely being dropped. While the urban guerrilla turned up the heat, the security forces armed themselves with fully automatic handguns and grenades. Within a couple of years, the number of riot squad officers increased from 18,000 to 23,330, and that of state security staff from 1,016 to 1,409.

Considering the ever-increasing repression, the 2nd of June Movement's security protocol had to be adjusted. By 1973, meetings with aboveground supporters no longer took place in safe houses but in cafés and restaurants. Apartments and stolen cars were frequently changed. At times, the group kept watch on as many as twelve safe houses and thirty cars with fake license plates. Many of the cars were "doubles," meaning they had license plates indistinguishable from those on identical legal cars (same brand, model, and color). A provisional medical care facility was also established. Shooting practice took place in the Tegel Forest and Berlin-Grunewald. When taking an inventory of its arsenal in 1974, the 2nd of June Movement concluded that they had enough handguns but not enough larger weapons. On September 10, 1974, five members raided an arms store in Berlin-Spandau. Now the arsenal consisted of large-caliber revolvers and pistols, several rapid-fire and precision rifles, and shotguns and pump-action rifles. The group also possessed numerous sticks of dynamite, detonators, and fuses, as well as ammunition, tire spikes, license plates, burglary tools, wigs, and counterfeiting equipment.

The group's structure was as follows: the underground militants acted in small cells whose members generally lived together in a safe house. Each cell had its own circle of supporters. Representatives of all cells met regularly. Sometimes, aboveground members were invited to these meetings too, in order to report from the social movements and people's opinions on the guerrilla's direction and strategy. Personal contact to aboveground supporters was never entirely cut off. To varying degrees, 2nd of June Movement members kept in touch with members of the prisoner support organization Rote Hilfe (Red Aid), with kids in youth centers, and with factory groups. There were also contacts, even some common actions, with the Revolutionary Cells, another militant organization that emerged in 1973.

After two years of bank robberies, firebombings, shootouts with the police, and many arrests, the 2nd of June Movement carried out its most spectacular and successful action in February–March 1975. With many comrades behind bars, held in isolation, the 2nd of June Movement decided to liberate at least some of them. They figured that the kidnapping of a high-profile public figure would bring success. They set their sights on the West Berlin CDU chairman and mayoral candidate Peter Lorenz.

After observing Lorenz's movements for two months, the guerrilla chose Thursday, February 27, 1975, for the kidnapping. Lorenz routinely left his home at 8 a.m., accompanied only by his driver. Ironically, on the morning of the kidnapping, he left his home almost an hour late, which created a headache for the 2nd of June commando, as it was fairly exposed in the semirural area where Lorenz lived. Still, the plan held. Less than a mile from his home, Lorenz's car was blocked by a truck pulling out of a side street. A passenger car then rear-ended Lorenz's vehicle in what appeared to be an accident. When Lorenz's driver got out of the car, he was knocked out with an iron bar. The 2nd of June members from the truck got into Lorenz's car and drove off. Lorenz, a big and powerful man, struggled and kicked out the windshield. The commando eventually changed vehicles in an underground parking garage, with Lorenz being placed in the trunk. At a cemetery, there was another transfer of cars. This time Lorenz was placed in a large wooden box.

The commando's final destination was an unused retail space in West Berlin that the group had rented. They had turned part of the basement into a reasonably comfortable "people's prison." When they arrived, they ran into a slight snag. To get the box with Lorenz into the store, they had to walk by a group of elderly women chatting on the sidewalk. Fortunately, Lorenz proved a cooperative prisoner and made no fuss. Once he was situated in his makeshift cell, the kidnappers wrote their first communiqué. The main demands were "the immediate release of all demonstrators arrested and charged in the aftermath of the death of the revolutionary Holger Meins" and "the immediate release of: Verena Becker, Gabriele Kröcher-Tiedemann, Horst Mahler, Rolf Pohle, Ina Siepmann, Rolf Heißler."

The first demand related to the people arrested during clashes with the police in the aftermath of the November 9, 1974, hunger strike death of Holger Meins. The six named prisoners to be released were all connected to the 2nd of June Movement and the far left of West Berlin. Horst Mahler, a former RAF member who had now joined the small Maoist KPD/AO, declined to be released. He declared, "I am firmly convinced that the struggle of the revolutionary masses will open the prison doors for all political prisoners, and that the terrorist convictions against me will be swept away—which is why I reject being removed from this country in this way."

Authorities negotiated with the 2nd of June Movement for a week. As radio and TV announcements were a main part of the negotiations, it was easy for the German public to tune in. On March 4, the named prisoners whose release had been demanded (minus Mahler) boarded a Boeing 707 in the company of priest and former West Berlin mayor Heinrich Albertz. Albertz had been suggested as a mediator by the 2nd of June commando in order to ensure the prisoners' safety. He complied. With 120,000 Deutschmark in their pockets, the prisoners eventually landed in South Yemen. All of them would subsequently return to the underground, some as 2nd of June Movement members, others as members of the RAF. Ina Siepmann eventually joined a Palestinian women's brigade in Lebanon.

The same day that the prisoners landed in South Yemen, Lorenz was released. He was brought to a park at 11 p.m. with enough money to make a couple of phone calls. Before parting ways, Lorenz expressed regret that he had met his kidnappers under the given circumstances and suggested they come to one of his garden parties. Even later, Lorenz always claimed that the kidnappers were intelligent people who had treated him well. He did not cooperate with the police in their investigations. When subpoenaed to appear at their trial, he reiterated that his kidnappers were decent and respectful.

With the liberation of the prisoners, the Lorenz kidnapping was arguably the most successful guerrilla action carried out in West Berlin and West Germany. The subsequent attempts to win the release of prisoners through kidnappings ended in disaster.

The Beginning of the End

Personnel and logistics of the 2nd of June Movement were now in good shape, but the organization faced the question of how to proceed after the Lorenz victory. There were a couple of factions within the group. The differences concerned political, practical, and geographical aspects. Politically, the main disagreement was the one between an "anti-imperialist" and a "social-revolutionary" approach. Members like Inge Viett, Gabriele Rollnik, and Till Meyer championed the anti-imperialist line, while West Berliners from the Blues scene, such as Ralf Reinders and Ronald Fritzsch, favored the social-revolutionary one. The fledgling "factory guerrilla" in the Ruhr Valley, with a prominent member in Fritz Teufel, who worked in a plastics factory in Essen under a false name, constituted a third faction. Most aboveground supporters sympathized with the social-revolutionary approach and cooperation with the Revolutionary Cells.

Concrete suggestions for actions included supporting strikers and occupying supermarkets in low-income neighborhoods to distribute free food. The latter was inspired by the Tupamaros of Uruguay, who had diverted food delivery trucks in Montevideo to working-class neighborhoods, where they encouraged the population to empty them. But the anti-imperialists saw these actions as overly populist. They also wanted to move beyond the confines of West Berlin.

For some time, the conflict between the factions was mitigated by the 2nd of June Movement's cell principle. Members reckoned that anti-imperialist, social-revolutionary, and factory cells could exist alongside each other. This, however, did not resolve the underlying issue of rather different concepts of revolutionary politics. The anti-imperialist faction considered most openly to break from the others. When they established contact with the PFLP-EO, tensions within the group grew. The social-revolutionaries and the factory-guerrilla-to-be rejected participation in international actions.

What held the group together were pressing practical demands—first and foremost, how to free more prisoners. Escape plans were developed for comrades imprisoned in the Lehrter Straße women's prison in Berlin-Moabit. Some of the prisoners had discovered an antechamber in the prison library with a small skylight that had no mesh. But in order to escape through the likely forgotten skylight, they needed three keys: one for their cells, one for the corridor, and another for the library. During a handicraft workshop for prisoners, they were able to make plaster casts of the keys, which Inge Viett used to create wooden makeshift models that were smuggled to the outside.

After preparations lasting six months, three 2nd of June Movement members (Inge Viett, Gabriele Rollnik, and Juliane Plambeck) and one RAF member (Monika Berberich) managed to escape, even if they had to improvise: when only the cell key worked, they had to get the others by overpowering some guards.

Media coverage of the escape juxtaposed "perverted and lesbian female terrorists" with "decent and honorable German citizens," combining antifeminist and anticommunist tropes. The manhunt was intense, with patrol cars on every corner and door-to-door searches in activist neighborhoods. The population of Berlin was advised to report toilets in neighboring apartments being flushed more often than usual, as this might indicate hideouts. Police vans drove through the city flashing full-body photos of the escapees pasted on wooden boards.

Despite all these efforts, the three 2nd of June members managed to escape Berlin with the help of comrades from the Revolutionary Cells. Eventually, they made it to Baghdad, where they met up with some of the prisoners liberated during the Lorenz kidnapping. Only RAF member Monika Berberich was captured in Berlin within weeks after the escape.

While the 2nd of June Movement was regrouping and attempting to address its internal divisions, the international wing of the Revolutionary Cells was about to undertake an action that would deeply trouble the German guerrilla and the far left in general.

On June 27, 1976, a four-person commando made up of two members of the PFLP-EO and two members of the Revolutionary Cells, Wilfried Böse and Brigitte Kuhlmann, hijacked an Air France passenger plane traveling from Tel Aviv to Paris. They diverted it to Entebbe, Uganda, where the commando demanded the release of fifty-three political prisoners held in various countries. The Germans they demanded to be freed included the 2nd of June Movement members Ralf Reinders, Fritz Teufel, and Inge Viett. With many governments involved, negotiations carried on for a long time. After one week, the commando agreed to release all non-Israeli passengers. On July 4, Israeli special forces raided the airport, killing forty-five Ugandan soldiers and all of the guerrillas. They freed over one hundred Israeli hostages and returned with them to Israel. For the Revolutionary Cells, and the German guerrillas in general, Entebbe was a fiasco, militarily as well as politically. To this day, it is cited as a prime example for the latent antisemitism within the German left.

As 1976 came to an end, the situation for the 2nd of June Movement was as follows: fourteen members were in prison, and ten aboveground sympathizers faced charges for "supporting a criminal organization." Seven of them had already spent months in prison in remand. The charges against them included renting safe houses for the 2nd of June Movement and providing its members with cars and forged documents. A handful of members had gone into exile, a couple had crossed over to the RAF, and Werner Sauber had been killed. By the end of the year, only seven active members remained on the outside. It was a difficult time for the 2nd of June Movement, and the developments of 1977 didn't make things easier.

It was the RAF that heated things up. In spring 1977, it launched an offensive meant to win the freedom of many of its imprisoned members. On April 7, 1977, a RAF commando killed Attorney General Siegfried Buback on the way to work, alongside his driver and a bodyguard. The attackers fired from a motorcycle after pulling up next to Buback's car. The RAF justified the action as retaliation for the deaths of imprisoned RAF members during Buback's tenure. The group's communiqué read in part: "Buback was directly responsible for the murders of Holger Meins, Siegfried Hausner, and Ulrike Meinhof. In his function as attorney general—as the central figure connecting and coordinating matters between the justice system and the West German news services, in close cooperation with the CIA and the NATO Security Committee—he stage-managed and directed their murders."[11]

On July 30, the RAF killed Jürgen Ponto, the CEO of the Dresdner Bank, during a bungled kidnapping attempt. Unbeknown to Ponto, Susanne Albrecht, the sister of his goddaughter, had joined the RAF and arrived at his door with two comrades in tow. They were let in immediately, but when Ponto understood that he was about to be kidnapped, he resisted and was shot dead. Two weeks later, the RAF issued a short statement signed by Albrecht. It read:

> In a situation where the BAW [the federal prosecutors] and state security are scrambling to massacre the prisoners, we haven't got a lot of time for long statements. Regarding Ponto and the bullets that hit him in Oberursel, all we can say is that it was a revelation to us how these people, who launch wars in the Third World and exterminate entire peoples, can stand dumbfounded when confronted with violence in their own homes. The "big money" state security smear campaign is bullshit, as is everything that has been said about the attack. Naturally, it is always the case that the new confronts the old, and here that means the struggle for a world without prisons confronting a world based on cash, in which everything is a prison.[12]

On September 5, the RAF successfully kidnapped Hanns Martin Schleyer, who, as president of both the Confederation of German

Employers' Associations and the Federation of German Industries, was the most powerful industrialist in Germany. Schleyer was also a former SS officer. The kidnapping, during which three security guards and Schleyer's driver were killed, introduced the series of events that became known as the "German Autumn," during which West Germany was brought to a near standstill.

Schleyer's abduction lasted for five weeks. The RAF commando demanded the release of ten comrades, among them the most prominent members, such as Andreas Baader and Gudrun Ensslin. The state responded by effectively establishing martial law, locking down the country, mounting roadblocks, and conducting innumerable police raids against left-wing groups and projects, all the while slow-walking negotiations in the hope of tracking down Schleyer's whereabouts.

On October 13, more than a month after the kidnapping, there was a development that no one had foreseen. To support the RAF's demands, a four-member PFLP-EO commando seized a Lufthansa passenger plane flying German tourists from Mallorca to Frankfurt. The hijackers reiterated the RAF's demand, adding two of their own: the release of two Palestinians being held in Turkey and a payment of 15 million US dollars. After stops in Cyprus, Bahrain, and Dubai, the hijackers killed pilot Jürgen Schumann in Aden, South Yemen, after they had deemed an excursion he was allowed to undertake in order to inspect the plane suspiciously long.

In the early morning hours of October 17, the airliner landed in Mogadishu. The West German government was stalling for time while it maneuvered a GSG 9 antiterrorist unit into place for an assault. The assault came at 2 a.m. the next day. Three of the hijackers were killed, one was seriously wounded, and the hostages were freed.

Six hours later, Andreas Baader and Gudrun Ensslin were found dead in their cells at the Stammheim prison. Jan-Carl Raspe and Irmgard Möller were seriously wounded. Raspe died shortly thereafter. Möller survived and claimed she had been attacked and stabbed. The authorities ruled the deaths as suicides despite numerous circumstances that made a state killing of the prisoners appear plausible. The exact circumstances remain unclear.

It is virtually impossible to exaggerate the disorienting impact the "German Autumn" had on all of the German guerrilla groups and the left in the country at large, particularly following so closely on the heels of the

Entebbe debacle. The RAF itself would later write: "We made errors in 77, and the offensive was turned into our most serious defeat."[13]

Within the 2nd of June Movement, the anti-imperialist tendency had been weakened by the events of 1977, yet the social-revolutionary tendency wasn't faring much better. At the beginning of 1978, it seemed clear that some sort of unification of the armed left was needed to gain strength for the future. The anti-imperialists within the 2nd of June Movement argued for a merger with the RAF, while the social-revolutionary current eyed collaboration with the Revolutionary Cells. The 2nd of June social-revolutionaries were highly critical of the skyjackings of Entebbe and Mogadishu. Some even questioned the state murder theory concerning the Stammheim prisoners, which was a no-go for the RAF. Finally, the social-revolutionaries were wary of the close relationship some German militants had developed with Palestinian organizations. There was little space for compromise between the two factions. To the contrary, they grew further and further apart. At times, prisoners from both sides would no longer communicate.

Acquiring money remained an issue for everybody. But here, too, there were different approaches. Some 2nd of June members favored bank robberies, since, aside from providing financial means, they served as a good practice for armed actions and also had propagandistic value. Others thought more pragmatically and figured that a well-planned kidnapping could draw in much more money with relatively less effort.

The latter faction got its way. They chose Austria for a big action, hoping to avoid the attention of the extensive West Berlin and West German security apparatus. So, a group of 2nd of June members traveled to Vienna, the Austrian capital, and began to observe the routines of rich industrialists. They quickly homed in on Walter Palmers, head of Austria's largest textile manufacturing business. The reason was that Palmers was driving by himself every day from his home to his office. The 2nd of June members recruited three left-wing students from Austria—Reinhard Pitsch, Othmar Keplinger, and Thomas Gratt—as helpers.

Palmers was kidnapped outside his home on November 9, 1977. The 2nd of June Movement did not claim the action, as it was exclusively done for raising money. Thomas Gratt conducted the negotiations, and, after four days, the Palmers family paid a ransom of 30 million Austrian shillings (at the time, roughly 8 million USD) for Palmers's safe release. They did not involve the police. Palmers was released unharmed.

Two weeks later, Thomas Gratt and Othmar Keplinger were arrested at the Swiss-Italian border, carrying 2 million schillings of the ransom money, two guns, and the typewriter on which the ransom note had been written. Reinhard Pitsch was arrested on November 28 in Vienna. The three received prison sentences of four years (Keplinger), five and a half years (Pitsch), and fifteen years (Gratt).

Due to the arrests, the political nature of the kidnapping was revealed, something the 2nd of June Movement had hoped to avoid. But now they had money, and their own members who had been involved were still at large. But not for long.

The End of the 2nd of June Movement

During the crisis within the armed left following the "German Autumn," meetings between the 2nd of June Movement and the RAF had become more common again. They often happened in the new de facto headquarters of the 2nd of June Movement, a safe house in the Clichy neighborhood of Paris. The RAF presented a boiled-down version of their established criticisms of the 2nd of June Movement at these discussions: the 2nd of June Movement creating a "step-by-step consciousness" rather than a "frontline consciousness." The RAF suggested that the 2nd of June Movement was only clinging to its origins for nostalgic reasons. In their eyes, the attachment to a social-revolutionary subculture, the lofty proletarian aspirations, and the opportunistic babble about being close to the masses needed to be overcome in a process of ruthless self-criticism. The structure of the 2nd of June Movement was deemed "familial," rather than "revolutionary."

The 2nd of June Movement members who were present during the discussions were bothered by the RAF members' bravado. In her autobiography, Inge Viett recalls that she felt the new generation of RAF members lacked independence and substituted toughness for a lack of political direction.[14] However, she, as well as other 2nd of June members, retained general sympathies for the RAF's anti-imperialist line.

The discussions came to a halt when five women from the guerrilla—four from the 2nd of June Movement and one from the RAF—were arrested in Paris in May 1980 after the police received a tip from an Arab informant. The police also seized explosives, weapons, chemicals, technical manuals, counterfeiting equipment, and records of other safe houses in the Clichy area. Only Inge Viett and Juliane Plambeck were still at large. With contacts to other 2nd of June members cut off, and RAF members close by, they decided to switch groups. Their new RAF comrades insisted that they'd pen a 2nd of June Movement dissolution paper that blamed the 2nd of June Movement for the divisions within the armed left. The result was the infamous 2nd of June Movement "dissolution statement," released on June 2, 1980. It was published in the *taz* newspaper, which had emerged out of West Berlin's alternative scene in 1978. (Today, it is closely tied to the Green Party.) There was no mention that at least 1 million Deutschmark of the 2nd of June Movement assets (buried in a depot in Italy) and the group's remaining weapons were turned over to the RAF.

Reactions among the 2nd of June Movement members in prison were mixed. Some supported the decision. Gabrielle Rollnik, who at the time was on trial in Berlin together with Angelika Goder, Gudrun Stürmer, and Klaus Viehmann, read the statement in court, also in the name of Goder and Stürmer. Viehmann was vehemently opposed. Together with Ralf Reinders and Roland Fritzsch, he wrote a fierce rebuttal within days. This text also contains an outline for a future militant strategy, which was strikingly close to that of the Revolutionary Cells, the Rote Zora, and militant autonomist groups.[15] The strategy was trying to carve out an alternative both to the RAF's anti-imperialist line, the reformism of the sponti-turned-Green Party members, and the navel-gazing and hippieish alternative movement.

The "dissolution statement" and the response by Fritzsch, Reinders, and Viehmann sparked an open struggle over the heritage of the 2nd of June Movement as a proletarian urban guerrilla. With the prisoners divided, debates were equally contentious among aboveground supporters. Within the broader autonomist scene, people rejected the merger with the RAF. Local government offices in Berlin-Kreuzberg were bombed in the name of the 2nd of June Movement, suggesting that the organization wasn't dead and that it still had roots in West Berlin's social movements. The 2nd of June Movement was also credited for its historical links to the Blues scene of the late 1960s, which had significantly changed life in the city. The RAF, on the other hand, was deemed "authoritarian" and "elitist" by the autonomists.

The Revolutionary Cells clearly sided with the social-revolutionaries of the 2nd of June Movement. In an editorial of their newspaper *Revolutionärer Zorn* (Revolutionary rage), they wrote in January 1981:

> We agree with the 2nd of June Movement that we want a "popular guerrilla"! A guerrilla whose actions are understood by the people

and who enjoys their sympathy. A guerrilla whose actions can garner broad support in the long run, without being opportunist. A guerrilla whose actions are rooted in concrete social conflicts, and linked to the political struggles they entail. With regard to these actions, we must be able to answer questions such as "Do they take us further?" and "Do they deepen the social and political contradictions?"

The Revolutionary Cells and their feminist sister organization, the Rote Zora, carried on until the early 1990s, before their actions fizzled out. In 1992, the Revolutionary Cells published a statement titled "Das Ende unserer Politik" (The end of our politics), in which they stated:

> Today, we draw the consequences from our realization that the form and structure of our struggle was an expression of a particular phase of the development of the social contradictions in West Germany after 1968. With the collapse of real socialism and the following dissolution of left-wing forces, German reunification, and the "New World Order" emerging with the Second Gulf War, things have fundamentally changed.[16]

The RAF's last action dates from 1993. By then, the RAF had become very isolated. When, in 1998, a dissolution paper was published, most were surprised that the group still had members. The paper brought the era of the German urban guerrilla to an end.

Surprisingly, more than fifty years after the emergence of the urban guerrilla in Germany, balanced evaluations of its political impact, successes, and failures are still rare. The history of the urban guerrilla remains contentious, and ideological convictions—or simple prejudices—cloud people's views. Yet a thorough, unbiased investigation into the theory and practice of these groups remains important for revolutionary politics today and in the future. I hope that this book can make a relevant contribution.

THE BEGINNINGS

FROM THE HASH REBELS TO THE 2ND OF JUNE MOVEMENT
(1992)

Ronald Fritzsch and Ralf Reinders

This interview was recorded on November 22, 1992, in connection with a Berlin exhibition about the urban guerrilla struggle in Germany. The interviewers are Klaus Herrmann, who had written a chapter on the 2nd of June Movement for the exhibition catalog, and Peter Hein, editor of the bibliography *Stadtguerilla—Bewaffneter Kampf in der BRD und West-Berlin* (Urban guerrilla—Armed struggle in the FRG and West Berlin), released by Edition ID-Archiv in 1990. The interview was first published under the title "Von den Haschrebellen zur Bewegung 2. Juni" in the 1995 Edition ID-Archiv book *Die Bewegung 2. Juni. Gespräche über Haschrebellen, Lorenzentführung, Knast* (The 2nd of June Movement: Conversations on Hash Rebels, the Lorenz kidnapping, and prison).

Youth Movement in the 1960s: Rolling Stones, Long Hair, Vietnam
Klaus Herrmann: To understand the emergence of the 2nd of June Movement from a personal perspective, it would be nice if you told us a little bit about your background.

Ronald Fritzsch: I was born in Hanover in 1951 and grew up there: primary school, secondary school, then I intended to attend a business high school, but at the time there were no grants for students from working-class families. My father had no money but a few connections, and so I got an internship at the Hanover City Council, training to become a public employee. After two years I could have applied for a supervisor position, but I quit after a year and a half, not least because I wanted to escape the military. At the time, I was a convinced pacifist and thought, "No thanks!" Hanover I wanted to leave anyway, the entire city is full of public servants. Berlin seemed more appealing, it was a crazy time. I only considered Berlin or Hamburg, but the military issue brought me to Berlin.[1] So I left the internship and moved there in late 1970. I pretty quickly joined the anarcho circles.

Herrmann: Did you have personal contacts in Berlin before moving there?

Fritzsch: No, but I had visited a few times. In Hanover, there was a subculture too, but it was small. Everybody knew everybody. It was fun, and you had the typical stoner culture. People were looking for something other than a regular, square life, but they didn't drown their sorrows in alcohol, there were other things to do. We got politicized by the inflammatory crap that the *Bild* newspaper published. They always went after the Kommune 1 and free sex, writing about how everybody had sex with everybody, that kind of stuff. The more they went after that scene, the more outraged we got, because they were going after what we were into.

Herrmann: I have seen your profession listed as truck driver . . .

Fritzsch: I did work as a truck driver in Berlin for different companies. From the fall of 1971 to the summer of 1974, I worked as a truck driver for the railway services. That was a great job, and pretty well paid at the time. I earned twice the money that friends made in the private sector.

Herrmann: Ralf, what about you?

Ralf Reinders: I was born in Berlin in 1948 and grew up in the Reinickendorf district. I went to a normal primary school and left after eighth grade. The school was where the Märkische Viertel neighborhood stands today. At the time, it was hailed as a model school. Originally, it was planned for children from East Germany, but the GDR government prohibited children from the East to attend schools in the West. That means that we moved into an entirely new school that had been built for different purposes.

After school, I began an apprenticeship at Rotaprint.[2] Finishing the apprenticeship was my first goal in life [*laughs*], and I saw it all the way through. At the time, the *Gammler* subculture was emerging in Berlin and many people stopped wage-laboring.[3] When I left school, I felt caught in a bind—I didn't know if I should start an apprenticeship or not. My friends all quit their jobs, one after another, and hung out at the Kaiser Wilhelm

Memorial Church, playing their guitars and getting into trouble with the cops.[4] People let their hair grow. In the beginning, it was difficult for me to move between two different realities: in the afternoon, you let your hair down, and at work you combed it back with plenty of grease, looking like Elvis. It's easy to forget this today: at the time, many people lost their jobs and apprenticeships because they had long hair.

Herrmann: Yes, you could be thrown out of bars because you had long hair, you didn't get a beer, and so on.

Reinders: You got no beer, you were beaten up. Sometimes, some fools hanging out at street corners were trying to force you into getting a haircut. You had problems constantly. There were also conflicts about music. All my friends liked the new stuff from England, the Beatles, the Stones, but there was a bit of a rivalry between the Beatles and the Stones fans.

In 1965, the Stones came to play in Berlin for the first time, at the Waldbühne. For many of us, this marked a small breakthrough. We wanted to listen to the music, but they were charging twenty Deutschmark, a shitload of money at the time. We didn't have that much and decided to attend for free. We gathered in the Tegel neighborhood, fans of the Stones, but also of the Beatles and the Kinks, about 200 to 250 of us. Quite a few would later join the 2nd of June Movement.

Right when we got off the commuter train at Waldbühne, we hit the first police barricade. It was weak, and we muscled our way through. But there was a second barricade near the venue with mounted police. That one was more difficult to get past, but we managed. In the end, more than 200 of us were at the show for free, and right at the front. Some of the people with tickets didn't even get in . . .

That evening, I saw, for the first time, entirely unpolitical people getting really angry and frustrated with the cops. Once the concert was over—which, by the way, was really bad, I would have thrown a fit had I paid for it—people rose from their seats and demanded an encore, but the promoters simply turned off the lights. Chaos ensued. There were cracking noises that got louder and louder—everyone started to tear apart the seats. Suddenly, the lights came back on, and the cops appeared onstage, firing at us with water cannons! That caused a fierce battle, and our crew was at the forefront. We knew each other well and felt strong together. There was a pronounced sense of belonging.

Eventually, we wanted to leave the venue. Things had not gotten completely out of hand yet. Even the damage in the stands wasn't that bad. But then the cops started to beat up a group of forty to fifty girls who had hidden near the stage. It caused us to reenter the venue, and then all hell broke loose. Now everything was torn apart. The battle lasted for four to five hours and extended to the streets around the Waldbühne. For the first time, I saw people completely losing it and swinging at the cops. That was new to me. It continued in the commuter trains. They belonged to the East Germans, so no one in the West cared if they were trashed.

The next day, we regathered in Tegel—not the entire 200, but many of us, all of whom we knew. Among the later 2nd of June members were Shorty, Knolle, and Bommi Baumann.[5]

Right around that time, the students started with their actions. I joined some of the Vietnam demonstrations they organized. One of the first demonstrations went through the Neukölln neighborhood. Many residents turned out against us. For each of us, there were at least two umbrellas to get attacked with. The frontier town vigilantes of Berlin were outraged by the red flags and the communists. At the time, the SEW still joined events like these.[6]

Fritzsch: In Hanover, there was nothing of that at the time. Only on the occasion of Benno Ohnesorg's funeral did we see a bigger demonstration. He had grown up in Hanover and was buried there.

The first red flags appeared during the *Roter Punkt* actions in 1968–69.[7] I remember how angry people in the city were, and also the police, when they saw the red flags. The SDS had basically dissolved, and the Rote Garde and all the ML groups were forming.[8]

I was still part of an SDS "school base group" at the time, but I was soon expelled for "obstruction," because I raised my hand every time I didn't know a word, and that was about every other word being used. I wanted someone to explain to me what they meant. Eventually, they asked me and a friend to leave. But I hadn't meant to be a pain, I just wanted to know what they were talking about. We had learned not to swallow everything and to dare speak up. I ran into problems with that at school too, I didn't need this bullshit in politics—especially not when people liked to use the term "antiauthoritarian" without seeming to understand what it meant.

The Opposition Comes Together: Rockers, Students, Young Proletarians

Reinders: In Berlin, things were a little different. In 1964–65, the student protests and the slowly emerging youth revolt were still quite separate.

Herrmann: I remember the time around 1965. We were a small group and read our first critical texts, then taking the commuter train from Wilmersdorf to Neukölln to meet with our proletarian friends. It wasn't always easy, they were quite different. They also had less qualms about physical violence, something I was impressed by. At the same time, we had some reflections to offer that seemed to impress them. I found it to be a fruitful exchange. There was a spirit of solidarity.

Reinders: I think that was crucial and that's what brought every-one together, the students and the young workers. The latter yelled and protested and smashed things up, but they didn't always know what it was all about.

This was also the first time after the war that the economy in West Germany was in a bit of trouble. It wasn't so obvious yet, but in particular the youth began to feel it. In addition to that, there was much pressure from above: there were cops everywhere. The students got a beating when they demonstrated, not least as they turned against the US, the alleged bulwark of democracy. That's when it dawned on everyone: here is the bulwark of democracy, gives you a beating, and kills people in the Third World. So we took to the streets, and just our looks were provocative.

We were very interested in the situation of the Black community in the US. In 1965, entire neighborhoods such as Watts were up in flames. That's when people realized what racism was, when they themselves got a beating. They understood, or sensed, that they got a beating because they looked different, no matter what they did, no matter whether they had a job or not. They got a beating because the cops didn't like them, because they hadn't joined the army. That's why I always get a fright when I see people with shaved heads. I have seen these shaved heads so often, there is a lot entailed in them—a lot of military tradition.

Herrmann: Did you wear parkas back then?

Reinders: Yes, at some point we were wearing parkas. They were extremely practical, but also quite ugly.

Fritzsch: They were practical: warm, and easy to write slogans on.

Peter Hein: It was important to draw antinuclear symbols on them!

Reinders: It was good that everyone looked similar, so we could recognize each other. You were able to figure out the person next to you and knew whether you could rely on them or not, at least to a certain degree. "Look, there is someone who is also against the cops!" Today, it's different. Today, you can't tell much about a person from the way they look. But at the time you knew that if they looked a certain way, then . . .

Herrmann: . . . you weren't alone.

Reinders: Yes. There really were only a few who looked like us but weren't with us, maybe even helping the cops. Essentially, it was like this: if you looked a little different, you were not up for playing by the rules.

The real politicization began with the killing of Benno Ohnesorg on June 2, 1967. After all the beatings, we felt that the cops were now shooting at us—all of us. You could defend yourself against the beatings, at least to a certain degree. But to be shot at, that was at another level. I know many people whose lives were profoundly changed by that day. They suddenly felt they had to be on the streets, had to take a stand. They didn't necessarily support the students—or anything, for that matter—but they were against the police shooting people.

Ohnesorg's killing prompted one of the first big demonstrations in Berlin, a silent march of thirty to forty thousand, many students among them. And we still had the Kommune 1. Hardly anyone had visited these folks, but everyone had heard of them and thought they were intriguing. In some way, everyone wanted to live like them, especially after the prudish 1950s, when sex was only allowed behind closed curtains.

Herrmann: Ralf, didn't you live in the Wieland commune?

Reinders: No, that's a rumor spread by the cops. We, including Bernie, lived in Berlin-Tegel in the Nimrod commune.[9] It was a big house for four families, privately owned. On the ground floor lived an old woman and an old man. On the other floors, the owner rented out the rooms individually at a pretty steep price. But for us it was a free space. We had one and a half floors to ourselves and formed a kind of commune. We didn't have the same political ambitions as the Kommune 1. We simply had a shared kitchen and a shared bathroom, but it was like a collective house.

The cops came around quite regularly to look for hash. We did smoke on occasion, all of that was just starting at the time. It was all very harmless. There were three cops from the narcotics department who we all knew. As soon as they turned into our street, someone came and told us. We made sure that they would only search rooms where there was nothing to be found, and that was it.

Herrmann: How do you explain the Wielandstraße rumor?

Reinders: The cops were pretty lost back then. They didn't know what to do with me and Bernie. In fact, they hardly knew what to do with anybody in the Reinickendorf neighborhood. They threw us all into the same category, Georg von Rauch and Bommi Baumann included. I don't even know if the rumor came from the cops or if it was first spread by the media. In any case, we never lived there. We only took a bath there from time to time. They had a great bathtub!

Fritzsch: That was important.

Reinders: A bathtub where many people could take a bath at the same time, tiled, gigantic! I had never seen anything like it, and I haven't seen anything like it since.

I was confronted with politics from when I was very young. During a holiday in East Germany, I joined the Young Pioneers.[10] On occasion, I attended events there, for example on International Children's Day.[11] Nonsense like that. We always ran into problems with the cops. It leaves traces when you are twelve or thirteen, hanging out with other kids, and then the cops come and kick you out of the woods in Tegel, the only reason being that Young Pioneers were running around with their scarves, when carrying symbols of GDR youth organizations was forbidden. Well, in West Berlin they weren't actually forbidden, but the cops still went berserk when they saw them. One day, they harassed us while we were looking for Easter eggs—that shapes your image of "democracy and the rule of law." Today, the authorities act a little smarter.

Herrmann: Since you grew up in the north of Berlin, I have to ask: Did you have any contact to the rockers from the Märkische Viertel?

Reinders: No, we had no direct contact, we only saw them around. The Kommune 1 folks were in contact with them. We are talking about rockers on mopeds who gathered in discos. They were a little wild and attacked elderly people. No one really wanted to have anything to do with them. At some point, they got into a feud with an older rocker group from Wedding. We knew all the folks from Wedding, and there was no beef between us. They were simply rockers, had motorcycles, and did no one any harm. In any case, the younger ones looked for a fight with them at some point, because they thought these older folks were harmless, but then the younger ones got a serious whipping. After that, they stuck to their own stomping grounds.

Herrmann: I remember that, in the early to mid-1970s, we sat in the Georg von Rauch House behind barricaded doors, defending ourselves against rockers.

Reinders: That must have been different ones. The rockers from the Märkische Viertel were on our side during the Battle of Tegeler Weg.[12]

Some wondered whether they might switch sides the day after. They had scared a lot of the students because they were pretty brutal. But that's the way you had to act in the Märkische Viertel. Any confrontation there was like that. They weren't afraid of the cops. The regular cops still wore shakos back then, no helmets, only a few special units did. There were no problems with the rockers, we got pretty close over time.

Herrmann: I assume this wasn't based so much on political discussions but on a similar attitude to life.

Reinders: Well, we were both harassed, that was similar. The rockers always had troubles with the cops. The cops would confiscate their bikes at roadblocks. Other people gave them grief too.

The "Central Council of the Roaming Hash Rebels": Smoke-In, Raids, Street Battles

Hein: A tangent on the Roaming Hash Rebels: what was that about? Wasn't that a little more than just taking drugs?

Reinders: Yes, it was more than that. At a certain point, the repression by the cops became massive. The feds had gotten reinforcements, and in Berlin they started using methods that were new to us. They tried to get people to sell undercover cops fifty kilograms of hash, so that they could bust them. We all did a bit of dealing back then, mainly selling to US soldiers. They paid the best prices.

Many of us had stopped working, but we needed cash. Groceries we shoplifted. We were waiting for the Bolle delivery trucks in the morning, followed them, and grabbed all of the puddings.[13] Puddings were popular. We were stoned all the time, and you get cravings for sweets.

We dealt small amounts of hash, nothing big. But people understood that this offered opportunities, that you could make serious money. We knew them. There were some Turks who were very naive. They wanted to make a few thousand Deutschmark with one big deal and fell for cops posing as big distributors. We were involved in an incident in the Waidmannslust neighborhood. The cops took a few hundred grams from one of our cars. It was basically the entire supply for our house, where everyone smoked and sold a little. We were broke! Someone said, "This calls for revenge! Tonight, we'll blow up a cop car!"

We talked to some folks we knew from the student scene, and they brought us explosives. But we never blew up any cop car, Bommi was too scared. We hid the explosives in the house and forgot about them. It wasn't anything we could have blown up a cop car with anyway, a simple mix of cement and herbicide. At best, we would have gotten a good flame out of it.

We heard more and more people say, "We won't put up any longer with all the raids on the bars where we hang out, we'll fight back!" This mainly concerned the Zodiak at the Hallesche Ufer, the Park in the Halensee neighborhood, the Sun on Joachim-Friedrich-Straße, and the Mr. Go on Yorckstraße. It was at the Mr. Go where the last and wildest battle of the Hash Rebels took place. The first battle was outside the Park—that was the first time people fought back. We just wanted to smoke in peace. People were allowed to get wasted on alcohol too. That's why we organized a smoke-in at Tiergarten in July 1969. That's where you found the first leaflets signed by the "Roaming Hash Rebels."

The name was coined by Kunzelmann, even if he might deny it today. With the "Central Council of the Roaming Hash Rebels," we mainly wanted to provoke the students. They had already started founding parties, and used many terribly pretentious names. We wanted to poke fun at them. I recall a "Central Council of Roaming Absinthe Brothers" responding to our leaflet.

During the smoke-in at Tiergarten, I was in Sweden. When I returned, I heard that they had arrested Georg von Rauch. There had been 350 to 400 people at the smoke-in. They puffed on their joints, the cops watched and didn't do anything. But after everyone had left, Georg was still lying in the bushes half-conscious. He had eaten some pretty strong hash cookies. The cops took him to Moabit, had his stomach pumped, and detected 0.012 grams of hash. They charged him and he was sentenced to three or four months in prison.

Those were the beginnings of the Hash Rebels. Later, we got to know the people involved better. We met them a few times and discussed what we could do when the cops appeared for raids. We no longer wanted to put up with that shit. We began to appoint guards, for example at the Pan, next to the Jewish Community Center. It worked.

There was always a young girl there, shooting up. Whenever the cops came, she warned us. People carrying drugs had time to make a getaway. There was never a false alarm. We were wondering who she was but never pursued the matter, until she told us that her dad was well-informed and always gave her clues. One day, she was out of money, and Tommy Weisbecker and I drove her to Charlottenburg. We walked her to where she said she lived, and when the door opened, her father and a much younger fellow appeared.

Tommy looked at me and said, "I know the older guy." Then he turned to the girl and asked, "Is your dad gay?"

"No," was her answer. "That's his bodyguard."

"Bodyguard? What's your name?"

"Geus. Don't you know?"

So we were dealing with the daughter of Judge Geus, who apparently got informed whenever there was a raid because the cops knew his daughter was an addict.[14] He would then call her and tell her to make a move. And she would inform everyone else.

One night, we arrived at the Park and found it completely surrounded by cops. People were led outside with their hands over their heads. This was new to us. We unscrewed the gas cap on one of the patrol cars, pushed some paper inside, and tried to set it on fire. It didn't work, but it led to a whole column of cops fearing for their cars. They burst out of their hiding places to get a hold of us. This, in turn, encouraged others to start a riot. I think it was the first time for many to really resist.

Right around that time, the musical *Hair* was coming to Berlin. The performers were pretty cool. Almost all came from Berlin, but there were also a few Yanks and West Germans who sang and danced and jumped around. We knew many of them because they smoked with us and bought our stuff. They lived in a big apartment at Nollendorfplatz, a known hangout for artists. They asked us whether we wanted to do something for the premiere. Everyone with a name in Berlin was invited, including Tilla Darieux, an eighty-year-old actress. We said, "Okay, if you allow us backstage, we climb onstage with a joint and tell the audience that there are real people who smoke, that this isn't just theater, and that the cops are always after us."

Alas, one of the performers tipped off the theater, and they hired security. Together with the old folks from the Kommune 1, who always had a reasonable stash of pyrotechnics, we built a few firecrackers and a smoke bomb. We were simply trying to figure out how best to make a nuisance of ourselves. There was the odd but familiar feeling of wanting to do something but not knowing exactly what to do.

So the night came, and everyone was there, all dressed up. Outside the theater were people used to getting whacked on the head by cops for having a few grams of hash on them. Meanwhile, the high society watched the musical and applauded. We wanted to give them a taste of reality. First, we threw the smoke bomb, but it got caught in the doorway. The security guards weren't able to kick it away in time, and smoke filled the theater. Tilla Darieux got smoke poisoning and had to be taken to hospital. When the cops came, one of them pulled his gun and fired into the air. He seemed overwhelmed by the situation, as many cops were at the time. That night, they didn't catch any of us. That was the first time that the Hash Rebels did something more militant and organized—as far as more organized goes, it was also the last time.

There was another incident at the Zodiak. The cause was the cops taking pictures from a patrol car. It was just a hundred feet away, and we couldn't tolerate that. Some of us went to the car and shook it a bit. It was fun, there was an automated camera on the car whose flash went berserk. The cops inside panicked, locked the doors, and called for backup. But before their colleagues arrived, we managed to topple over the car, leaving it lying sideways. When the reinforcements came, a big riot ensued, and some folks got arrested. The clashes themselves were still pretty harmless, though.

The last incident related to hash was at the Go. That was later, we were just about to go underground. We were driving underneath the Yorkbrücken when we saw that there was a raid at the Go. We got out of the car, approached the bar, and witnessed an uncommon scene: for the first time in many months, the cops were there without helmets. Next to them stood the Kreuzberg mayor, supervising everything. The mood was damp. People watched their friends getting arrested. We wanted to instigate some resistance but failed. No one wanted to take the first step. Suddenly, a billboard on the other side of the road went up in flames. Right away, everyone tried to get their friends out of the police vans. Rocks were flying, and the cops fled in panic. The Kreuzberg mayor was beaten up badly. We knew that the cops would return the next day. They couldn't accept a defeat like that.

So we returned the next day as well. There were about 1,500 people outside the Go waiting. The days before, there had been riots in Amsterdam. People were inspired by that. At first, the cops didn't show up, they didn't do us that favor. We were ready, had the Molotov cocktails strategically placed, but the cops didn't come. Georg had an idea: "This will be easy. We smash the windows of the pharmacy and call the cops, reporting a breaking and entering." And that's what we did.

The first cops came around the corner very cautiously. At the time, they still had Volkswagen Beetles. There was one Beetle and a van. In an instant, everyone was out on the streets, and the cops were attacked with twenty Molotov cocktails. One caught fire, his colleague had to extinguish the flames. But we had them where we wanted them. After a while, there were blue lights flashing everywhere. I had never experienced a riot like that before.

The cops had a tactic which implied sacrificing colleagues. A unit consisting of a Beetle and two vans drove around and tried to chase people into side streets. The Beetle would arrive first and get covered in rocks. When the vans came, there were no rocks left to throw, and they could chase people. But the Beetle always got smashed.

That night at the Go, the cops also fired shots. One of them jumped out of the van and fired a machine gun into the air. Not a word about that in the newspapers. But the cops paid a price that night. Innumerable Molotov cocktails were thrown, mixed in one-liter Coke bottles, which were brand-new. We had taken the gas with a hose from trucks parked at gas stations. We had no money.

The First Go Underground: Life Underground, Smaller Actions, Arrests

Herrmann: When did all that happen?

Reinders: It must have been the summer of 1970. The following day—so, the third in a row—there was another riot at the Go, but we never made it there, because we had been under observation all day, with cops on our heels constantly. Maybe they thought that if they could keep us away, nothing would happen. But they were wrong. Even without us, it was another wild night. That was the Hash Rebels' last battle. In November 1970, we went underground.

Herrmann: Some people say that you going underground happened rather randomly. That someone like Peter Urbach forced explosives on you, so you'd get busted? Is that true?

Reinders: At the time of the Hash Rebels, we had contact with Urbach, but we had been warned by an old railroad worker that Urbach was a state security informant, which was why he had lost his job at the railways. Urbach also approached Bommi for a hash deal, claiming that he could get ten kilograms very cheaply. After that, everyone close to us stayed away from him. That he later appeared on the scene again was due to competition with the RAF. The RAF believed we were highly interested in Urbach's weapons and only said he was an informant to keep the RAF away. In particular, Mahler didn't take the warnings seriously. In my opinion, it was him who decided to maintain contact with Urbach. That was fatal.

But back to us: Bernie and I still had these homemade bombs we had intended to use for a cop car hidden in our house, pretty useless cement-herbicide blends, which we had all forgotten about. We heard of the attempted firebombing of the Jewish Community Center and thought it was crazy. But Bernie's brother knew about the bombs and suspected that it might have been us. He called the cops, who had promised a reward of 50,000 Deutschmark for anyone who would help them solve the case. So the cops came and found the bombs, each about the size of a tennis ball. It did indeed seem that a similar blend had been used at the Jewish Community Center. But I don't think it was exactly the same. Ours was cement and herbicide, the other was powdered sugar and herbicide. The cops were looking for us nonetheless. Bernie's brother knew that we were hanging out with Bommi, so now they were looking for Bommi, Bernie, and Bär [Bear], which was my nickname. At the time, the cops didn't know my real name. Then they found a photograph of Bernie and I, which a photographer friend of ours had taken. The picture was published in all the newspapers. But we didn't have anything to do with the firebomb at the Jewish Community Center. It remains unclear who was behind it. It's one of the things I still can't get my head around. Mahler once said that Urbach had put the bomb there, but I don't believe that. It was an excuse by Mahler to save face.

It might have been like this: Some of those who had trained with the Palestinians in Jordan were deeply impacted by the Israeli crimes they had witnessed. And the left here was still pro-Israel, we were brought up that way. Maybe that's why they carried out this idiotic action. It might have been that way, but I don't know.

In any case, due to the photograph that had been released, our identities were known to the police, and they were looking for us. Amazingly, everyone who knew me, people I had gone to school with, told the cops that they had no idea who I was. Nobody at the time wanted to give the cops anything. Bernie's brother? There are always the odd ones out . . .

All of that happened in October–November 1969. In February 1970, they caught us. We had gone underground and hid out with people we knew from the Park and other bars. In February 1970, we got arrested and were held in Moabit in remand. The arrest went down very calmly, in ways you can't even imagine today. Two cops came to the apartment and asked if we were the ones they were looking for. We said no. When they asked for identification, we said we had none. "Okay, then follow us," they said, and brought us down to the station. They were very friendly. We could have given them fake names, but somehow they figured out who we were and locked us in a cell. Then we got introduced to the prison in Moabit. Each cell there had a loudspeaker that was turned on three times a day: two hours in the morning, one at noon, and in the evening from eight to ten, as far as I recall.

Herrmann: That's when they played RIAS?[15]

Reinders: No, worse than that. The rabbi. What was his name?

Fritzsch: Estrongo Nachama.[16]

Reinders: Yes, every Friday. It was the time of the first criminal law reform. They were closing the old jails. During yard time, you were allowed to walk with a companion—before that, you always had to walk alone and were not allowed to talk to anybody. The guards ran the prisons in a way you can't believe. The language they used . . . I was thinking, "This can't be true." The first three, four days, I was just flabbergasted.

Fritzsch: During the day, you were not allowed to lie in bed. They had folding beds that were tied to the wall. If they saw you taking them down, they put a lock on them.

Reinders: When they entered your cell, you were supposed to get up from your stool, face the wall, and say your name and number.

Herrmann: What number?

Fritzsch: The prisoner registration number.

Reinders: The first political prisoners were already inside, like Georg von Rauch. Since they resisted, the cops were complaining: "The long-hairs mess with our regime!"

Three days before I was arrested, there was an incident. The prisoners used to exchange newspapers among one another. The guards circled around them like vultures, seizing every newspaper they could get their hands on, beaming with joy. RAF prisoner Ali Jansen had observed that a few times. So one day he shat into a copy of the *Stern*, rolled it up, and took it to the yard, making sure one of the guards would see him. Sure enough, a guard grabbed the paper and tore it apart . . . Ali went to the hole for it, but the guards never forgot.

The weekends in prison are dead. On Saturday, there is some activity in the morning, but the lawyers can only stay until noon, and then there's essentially nothing: no radio, nothing. There were always some prisoners who lost it on Saturdays, and on Sundays it only got worse. Some trashed their cells. Suicide attempts were common. The guards were wasted and provoked people. They wouldn't tune in the radio properly, which drove everyone nuts. Prisoners banged against the doors, and then the guards came and beat them up. That was the routine. The food, you can't imagine. I went hungry rather than eat it. I was shocked by what they served us. The prison experience was the final piece in the puzzle for me to become a militant.

Where to Get Weapons?
Discussions with the RAF, the Baader Liberation, Penny Markets, and Pirate Radios

Reinders: Bernie and I got out after six weeks. At the time, suspended sentences were still quite common. When my mother went to the state prosecutor asking for a visit, he said she'd have to speak to someone else; he was no longer able to deal with all of this. He was under a lot of pressure from above—people had to be put in prison for political reasons, whether they had done something or not. The president of the district court passed this pressure down to the prosecutors. One of them finally said he was no longer willing to put innocent people in jail, and so he quit.

Our case was given to—what was his name, the drunk?—Krause! Yes, Krause wanted to be the tough guy and refused to let us out. They knew we had nothing to do with the attack on the Jewish Community Center, but they thought we might know who was behind it.

Bernie and I had agreed to sit down with the interrogators without saying anything. We went there to get coffee and for a change of scenery. There were six cops, and they did their routine: two were very aggressive, one just sat there mimicking me, and then there was "the intellectual" who wanted to discuss social issues with us. He had probably read a book and smoked a pipe to make himself appear more interesting. He was entertaining. Another cop acted all indifferent and would say things like, "Just leave them alone" to the other cops, or, "Don't you want anything to eat?" to us.

We found the interrogations laughable. But there was nothing to laugh about in prison. I was more miserable during that time than during the fifteen years I did later on. I hadn't been prepared for any of it, I knew nothing about prison life. So much brutality, every day.

When we got out after six weeks, we reunited with everyone. I got to know Ulrike Meinhof and others, and the first discussions between us and the emerging RAF happened. They were planning to get Baader out and wanted to recruit some of us. That was in April 1970, an intense time. We talked to Kunzelmann and concluded that we needed to do other things.

May 1 seemed like the perfect day. May 1 was a huge thing. In Neukölln, there was a march with fifty thousand people. This was the "Revolutionary May 1" demonstration, not controlled by the unions. We planned three attacks: one against the Yanks, one against a bank (the Bank für Gemeinwirtschaft, BfG, owned by the unions), and one against the district court.

The attack on the Harnack House didn't really work.[17] Only one of the Molotov cocktails hit the target. The others burst at the walls. We didn't have enough throwing practice to get them into the first floor. The firebomb attack on the BfG branch near Schillertheater went well. And then there was the one on the district court. That was the most successful. We placed buckets and canisters full of gas there, with an immersion heater connected to a socket. We had little experience and had hardly left the building when everything exploded. Gasoline is a hellish thing. The immersion heater went through the plastic buckets and canisters like it was nothing, the gasoline leaked out, and then it all went boom. The blast blew two people from the balcony. One courtroom was totally destroyed.

In May, there was the Allied Troops Parade in Berlin. We went to observe the final rehearsal. At the time, there were so-called communication cops, a "discussion commando" called Group 47 or something like that. They approached us right away, having finally found victims to talk to. But behind us was another unit, trying to pull us away and hitting us. The communication cops were outraged since we hadn't done anything. They almost got into physical confrontations with their colleagues! There was quite a bit of pushing and shoving.

Of course, they didn't know that we had insulted a British army officer earlier. Georg had called him a "pig." In his proud British ways, he acted as if he hadn't noticed but then told the next best cops to ID us. That's why they harassed us.

There was also a plainclothes cop who took pictures, and when we tried to get the film, the situation escalated. The cops lost control, and when I wrestled with another plainclothes officer, some of his colleagues thought a passerby had attacked me. A fist in a gray glove flew past my head, knocking the plainclothes cop halfway down the street. They had already arrested Shorty and Hella, and eventually they got hold of me too.[18] But as they were bringing me to the van, Georg said, "You don't need to take him, you know who he is." The cops looked puzzled, wondering whether they should indeed know me—and then they let me go, which saved me six months in prison. Shorty and Hella were sentenced to six months on probation. Later, I was investigated for aggravated robbery because I had tried to take the cop's camera—incidentally, the bodyguard of Klaus Schütz, as we learned.[19] That cop was a mean bastard. While wrestling with him, he told me, "If you can take twenty bullets, the film is yours."

Back to what you said about random reasons for joining the urban guerrilla and becoming a militant: you have to know people. But whether you get to know them or not depends on you, on what you want to do, and on how you move in the scene. Sure, sometimes things happen randomly.

Fritzsch: In the end, though, it remains a conscious decision.

Reinders: You don't get into it from nowhere.

Fritzsch: You're also quickly out of the inner circle if you don't do anything. It's not all that random.

Herrmann: How did you go from spontaneous action to urban guerrilla?

Reinders: We've had plenty of discussions about wanting to do more. But there were problems: We discussed armed struggle, but we had no arms. Worse, nobody knew anything about arms. Those of us who had come from West Germany, like Ronnie, had come as pacifists, they were draft dodgers. And we who came from West Berlin, we had no clue about arms anyway.

We heard about places in Berlin where you could get guns. We knew many criminals from our time in Tegel. Some of the kids we hung out with during our teenage years had taken that path. But it was a scene you could not rely on. Betrayal was a big thing. We were also told that we could get weapons in Austria, Switzerland, Italy, or Belgium. But we had about 800 Deutschmark to get us through the month—all of us—so there wasn't exactly much left to purchase a weapon. In the evenings, we broke into supermarkets and cleared the shelves, and during the day we took our bags there to shoplift.

Meanwhile, the RAF was working on building an armed organization, with much commitment, a tight structure, and a Marxist-Leninist base. We were too far-out for them.

The RAF's goal was to get Andreas Baader out. We discussed this with them but didn't know if it was a good idea. Baader was only serving two or three years. On the one hand, we wanted to get him out. We had just come out of prison ourselves and knew what it meant to be there, knew that no one should be locked up. But on the other hand, it seemed a little too ambitious for us, and we didn't want to take that step. The RAF had approached Georg directly. They knew him, he had done many actions, and for them he was the most trustworthy and reliable among us. They really wanted him to be part of this. But he said that if our group didn't think we were ready, he wouldn't join. He only wanted to work with us.

Step by step, the RAF acquired weapons: pistols, small-caliber rifles, and so forth. And then, one morning, as we were lying in the bathtub, we heard the news: "Baader is free!" We knew right away that things would be heating up. And we were right. An insane state security apparatus was turned loose.

Meanwhile, we had intensified contacts with some of the criminals we knew. But we still didn't have any money. Where can you get money? In a bank. We needed to move from idea to action. We knew how to loot stores and how to break into buildings; we were comfortable with picking locks and stealing things we could sell. But everything else still seemed too big for us, even if we had got better at stealing cars. In the beginning, we had known nothing about that either. The students close to us certainly didn't know anything about it, they came from fine families. Me, personally, I just never had an interest in cars, and I knew no one who could steal a car. But then the RAF presented two "experts," we got a bit of advice, they shared knowledge with us.

We knew a super anarchist who was very well versed in technology, but he didn't want to have anything to do with the RAF. His take was, "Anarchists have to remain independent, and you are much closer to anarchism." He had built radio transmitters together with Rudi Dutschke and had his own television transmitter. We worked with him, made recordings, drove around, and disrupted public TV programs—unfortunately, we could only do that using audio. Furthermore, the reach was very limited, only a few hundred meters, or until we hit a solid wall. We could disrupt programs further away but couldn't use the frequency to air anything ourselves. We tested places where we got the most out of the means we had. The hill near Gesundbrunnen proved useful. From there, we could reach quite a lot of people. We always knew that the transmissions were working when the cops came. We made progress.

But then we ran into trouble with the RAF. They wanted the transmitter. But the super anarchist said, "No way! No Marxist-Leninists will ever get their hands on my transmitter, not in a million years!"

He also had connections in Italy, in Genoa. That was before the Red Brigades appeared on the scene. Through the Italians we got some pistols and small-caliber rifles. We also tested sawed-off shotguns and built pipe bombs.

"In January 1972, We United as the 2nd of June Movement": Building Counterpower, the "Ugly Face of Terror," and Three Banks in One Day

Hein: Wasn't there an infamous trip to Milan in the early days of the 2nd of June Movement?

Reinders: That was earlier, but I don't know much about it. Some of those who went to Jordan went to Milan first. But Fritz Teufel, for example, he went back to Munich and founded the Tupamaros Munich.

Hermann: In 1972, the 2nd of June Movement presented a program . . .

Fritzsch: There is a history behind that. Someone wrote the paper to summarize the positions in our circles at the time. We only read it after our arrests; it was in our files. Before that, none of us knew about it. [*Everyone laughs.*] Even today, nobody knows who the authors were. But the paper did indeed summarize the positions in our circles at the time.

Reinders: Essentially, someone had turned the minutes from meetings into a program.

Fritzsch: But it was never discussed as a program, and no one knew about it.

Herrmann: "Officially," though, this counts as the 2nd of June Movement's program.

Hein: I have also listed it as the official 2nd of June program in my bibliography.

Reinders: The judges used it as evidence against us. They read it in the courtroom. We thought it was so funny we peed ourselves. At some point, Geus realized that something was off. He asked us who the authors were. We said we would love to know! We asked around internally, but no one had a clue.

Herrmann: What was the difference between the 2nd of June Movement and a loose network of folks carrying out actions?

Reinders: Before we "officially" called ourselves the 2nd of June Movement, we had come together three or four times—about twelve people from three different groups that agreed on most things. That didn't happen often within the left. There was a strong anarchist faction, but also a smaller Stalinist faction. In January 1972, we decided to work together as the 2nd of June Movement. The 2nd of June was a date that everyone could relate to, the students as well as the young proles. Other left-wing groups started to drift apart. Presenting ourselves as the 2nd of June Movement, everyone knew what we stood for. Something else was even more important with regard to the name: the date would always remind people that it was the state who shot first.

Fritzsch: I would say the political debates at the time were still pretty open and broad. I didn't even know everyone in the group, but we all shared the same reference points. With regard to the wider circle of supporters, there were many people who hadn't been part of the original meetings at all.

Reinders: That's true. Everyone, no matter where they came from, discussed the 2nd of June Movement's politics in their respective groups. That created a broad base. Even when I was underground, I always knew where to go for a good political discussion. I did not know the circle around Knofo, however. The so-called Zahl-Knofo-Kröcher gang had their base in Neukölln. Zahl had his printshop there.

Fritzsch: In 1971, we founded the Yippies together with Knofo. The magazine *FIZZ* was printed at Zahl's printshop; it was a split from *Agit 883*. The conflict with *Agit 883* came after the militants there had disappeared overnight, they had gone underground, and now the reformists dominated. Soon, the radical folks were all gone.

Reinders: Dirk Schneider was among them.[20]

Fritzsch: And they helped bring out *FIZZ*. They did that for half a year, before Knofo and Zahl went underground.

Herrmann: Ronnie, how did you come to the 2nd of June Movement? Through Knofo and Zahl?

Fritzsch: No, they had already gone underground. I was with the Anarchistischer Arbeiterbund [Anarchist Workers' Association] for some time, but that didn't last long. I had always thought that anarchists were undogmatic, but there I experienced the opposite. They were everything but undogmatic. They threw someone out because he had attended a *Kapital* study circle and liked to reference Marx. It was absurd.

Hein: How did the 2nd of June Movement logo come about? Hadn't the Tricontinental used something similar?[21]

Reinders: We first used the logo during the Lorenz kidnapping. Someone thought we needed a symbol and copied that of the Tricontinental. It was supposed to stand for internationalism.

Herrmann: You've already responded to some of the questions I wanted to ask. But I would like to know what your goals were, even if you didn't write the 2nd of June program yourselves.

Fritzsch: As we've said, the program summarized our positions well.

Herrmann: In an interview you did in prison, you said that none of you was naive enough to think that the revolution would come within five years.[22] But what was the goal of the struggle then?

Fritzsch: We wanted to build counterpower, to strengthen the resistance. It's like this: when there are people who resist, who strike back if necessary, then the other side becomes more careful. That's how we reasoned. To believe that we could topple the state with two dozen people would have been ridiculous. That's not how it works. We envisioned an organization in the form of cells. We never got to that step. After the Lorenz kidnapping, we meant to divide the group into pairs who should build cells, each recruiting three to four new people. We also wanted to enter the factories with some of these cells. We really wanted to get into the factories.

Reinders: We had made contacts in some factories early on, for example in August 1970 at Linhof.[23] For the first time in decades, they laid off many people. We wanted to do an action against the layoffs together with the RAF. We wanted to break in, take the office furniture and equipment with us, write slogans on the walls, and destroy the managers' armchairs. We also wanted to burn the boss's car and throw a bomb in his garage. The problem, however, was that we could not convince the RAF to come along, even if they always talked about workers' power. We thought that the RAF could do the factory because they were better equipped and more knowledgeable about technical things. We could have done the car and the garage. In the end, the RAF didn't do anything, while we proceeded to torch the car.

Off we went with three people. One stayed in the getaway vehicle, and two went to the garage, which was open. They poured five liters of gasoline on the floor and left a pipe bomb with a short time fuse in the corner. When they left the garage, they wondered whether the bomb would really go off. To ensure it did, one of them lit a lighter and threw it back into the garage. This caused the "ugly face of terror," as it became known in the papers. Both of our comrades were blown all the way to the fence of the property. One was wearing clothes made of synthetics; they melted down to a third of their original size—no, let me correct that, to a tenth. The other one had really bad burns on his face because the sunglasses he was wearing had melted. As we drove away, he held his face out the window to cool the pain. We stopped at the first water fountain we saw.

Once again, we had to recognize that gasoline was a hellish thing. In Munich, there was once an attack on a judge where the cops searched for a dead body afterward. They were convinced that the person who had caused the blast could no longer be alive. Comrades had poured five liters of gasoline into the basement of a judge's house, using a lighter to ignite it. There wasn't even enough time to pull the hand back before the entire basement blew up. Luckily, the fellow got away unharmed because he stood behind a wall. After those experiences, we became very careful handling gasoline.

Fritzsch: Back to the "ugly face of terror": when the comrade in Berlin was arrested, his face was scarred and his hair was gone. The *Bayernkurier* published a photo and an article with the headline "The Ugly Face of Terror."[24]

Reinders: Mind you, they hadn't arrested him for that particular action. The cops still didn't know what had happened at the garage.

Sometime later, the RAF wanted to do three banks in one day. We should do a fourth. They said they had enough equipment, including weapons, to pull it off. We discussed with them and expressed concerns. For us, this came too early, because four banks would mean a lot of heat. The cops would mobilize their entire apparatus to come looking for us. But in the end we said, "Fuck it, we're in." We had talked about doing banks long enough, and it seemed like it was time to get started. Furthermore, with the RAF doing three other banks, there was a sense of protection.

In the end, only three banks got robbed that day. This was in September 1970. We had eyed a fourth one, but there were roadworks out front, which caused concerns. At one of the other banks, there was a sudden change of plans. When the comrades assigned to it saw a woman with a pram inside, they dropped the smoke bomb from the itinerary. While the banks were being robbed, comrades drove around disrupting the police radio. The command center was still able to reach the patrol cars, but the patrol cars weren't able to reach the command center.

The first robbery was at the corner of Hauptstraße and Rheinstraße. The alarm went off, and all cops went there. Then, there was a second alarm at Altonaer Straße. The cops turned around, because they thought the first alarm had been false. The third alarm came from the Steglitz neighborhood, precisely, from the corner of Breitenbachplatz and Südwestkorso. Everything went really well.

Herrmann: Were you ever charged for any of this?

Reinders: No, to the contrary!

Fritzsch: Everything that had happened before 1974, they wrote off as petty stuff.

Reinders: This is also interesting with regard to the persecution of the RAF and the lies of the cops. Some years later, a *Stern* journalist raised the issue with us. She said that the cops assumed that we had done one of the banks but never went after us since they wanted to pin it on the RAF. Unlike the RAF, we were still aboveground at the time. During our trial, the crown witness Hochstein appeared.[25] In response to him, I mentioned that we had done the bank on Altonaer Straße. I wanted to show how crooked the persecution's crown witnesses were. The next day, the newspapers wrote that I had confessed to a bank robbery, not saying a word about the lies of crown witness Ruhland, who had been prepared by the cops to help them convict people.[26]

The Bank Robberies: Closed Safes, Escape Routes, Chocolate Kisses

Herrmann: What was the purpose of the bank robberies?

Reinders: We needed money for weapons and for building our infrastructure. The robberies were also a good opportunity to observe people with a weapon in their hand. Smaller militant actions had served the same purpose. It was important to see how people reacted during an action that was more stressful than throwing a firebomb in the middle of the night. We wanted to know whether anyone got on a power trip carrying a weapon, or whether anyone got scared and freaked. That was important to know. And, yes, we needed the money. We never had enough money, especially after the first of us had gone underground and needed financial support. The families of those in prison also needed support. It was crucial how people behaved during an action, whether they remained cool or whether they lost it.

Herrmann: What was your plan if a bank clerk acted up and refused to hand over the money, or if a customer resisted?

Reinders: The plan was very simple: they'd be knocked over the head. In the worst case—and only in the worst case—they'd be shot in the leg.

Fritzsch: Our assumption was that there'd be no need to shoot. We wanted to avoid that at all costs.

Reinders: Our guns were almost always cocked. We only carried them in case we'd have a run-in with the cops. We absolutely didn't want to use them inside the bank, other than in the case of an emergency—say, some giant acting up, and then he'd get a load in his legs. But we realized quickly that because of our strength in numbers with clearly divided roles, no one dared to attack us.

There was one case, in Lichterfelde, where the cashier wouldn't hand over the money, and so we fired a warning shot. Didn't impress him, though. So we threatened to shoot a secretary, hoping he'd step out the valve. Didn't happen. At that point, we were all wondering: What next? We were just about to bail when we saw the keys to the valve just hanging there. The robbery was saved. Otherwise, we would have just let it go.

Herrmann: How does it feel to rob a bank? Weren't you afraid?

Fritzsch: Well, we had trained. The advantage of a bank is that a bank is static, so you can plan a robbery well. You can go through all sorts of possible scenarios: "What are we going to do if . . . ?" Most of what's going to happen is very predictable, and so we went through it, step by step. What are you going to do if someone freaks out, or if some grandpa attacks you with a cane? Something like that can always happen, there are enough nutcases out there.

Reinders: We always put someone big and strong in the middle of the room or at the door, in order to watch the customers and prevent them from leaving. But we soon realized that the customers hardly ever were a problem. They just froze in fear. They were in a state of shock, you could not talk to them, they didn't move. You could simply let them stand where they were.

Fritzsch: There are some psychological tricks. Say you're outside the valve and there is only this small opening that you can't get through. So someone has to get in from behind. And the cashier sits there staring at your weapon, being scared shitless, not moving. Sometimes, it is enough to yell, "Get out!" If that isn't enough, you can release the safety catch of your gun, and they'll usually be out in a second.

These were the kinds of details we discussed beforehand: the more resolute you are, the less likely it is that anything goes wrong. You need to be determined. It sounds brutal, and I guess it is. But it minimizes the risk of anything going haywire, because no one even has the time to have stupid ideas.

Reinders: None of the customers ever complained. To the contrary. During our trials, everyone spoke very highly of us, how friendly and kind we had been. Indeed, there were never any major incidents during our robberies.

Herrmann: What were the criteria for choosing a bank, for example the one on Grüner Weg?

Reinders: At the time, we had five, six people who practically knew every bank in Berlin. In my case, I almost went overboard: I navigated Berlin with banks as reference points, not streets. We really knew almost all of them, all the Sparkassen, Berliner Bank, and Bank für Handel und Industrie (BHI) branches. Commerzbank branches we didn't do, because their valves were completely closed.

Fritzsch: The most important criterion was where we suspected the most money.

Reinders: When I started, there were still seven or eight banks in Berlin without closed valves. They only had iron bars. After we had done the three banks in one day, all of that changed. However, the Sparkasse, Berliner Bank, and some of the BHI branches still kept a hole in the valve through which you could threaten the cashier. At the Commerzbank, the valve was completely closed, you couldn't do anything. But then something happened that worked in our favor: some criminal robbed a bank, and the cashier refused to come out of the valve. So the fellow got the boss and shot him in the leg. After that, everyone came out of their valves. The days of defiance were over.

Criminals cleared the path for us more than once. One time, we got hold of a manual that told bank employees what to do in the case of a robbery. The manual made it very clear that the bank was more concerned about having to pay a lifelong pension to an injured customer than to lose some cash that got replaced by the insurance company.

Fritzsch: Another important criterion were the escape routes. How do you get away? On Wilmersdorfer Straße, for example, you can't do a bank robbery. Especially not today! If you make it out of the bank, you'll be caught in traffic.

Reinders: We always made sure that the escape routes included a stretch where a vehicle couldn't follow us—just in case some random driver got stupid ideas. There, too, we wanted to avoid having to shoot. So the escape routes would include a change of vehicles on foot, where we'd run through an alley or some place a vehicle couldn't pass through. That was a safety measure. None of us wanted to shoot at someone chasing us.

It happened only once that someone did. We flashed our gun, he pulled over, and that was it. Another time, there was an alarm in a bank that we had set off ourselves. That bank was a mess. There was money everywhere, and the cashier needed to make a big round to collect everything. We opened the drawers, and one of us must have triggered an alarm button. You could hear the alarm outside, and when we got into our car, a street cleaner who saw his chance of becoming a hero rushed toward us from the other side of the street. In this case, even our weapons didn't deter him, he decided to jump on the car nonetheless. He paid for it with a hard landing on the concrete when our driver sped off. He later told the cops that he had wanted to stop the car, but that we ran over him and fired at him. Even the cops doubted that account. There was no evidence of any shooting.

Herrmann: Where did the famous "chocolate kisses" come from?[27]

Reinders: The bank on Grüner Weg in Neukölln appealed to us. We had already done it once, two years earlier. We had made 230,000 Deutschmark. There was a lot of money there, which is why the bank had stayed on our radar. Two years after the first robbery, nothing much had changed inside. The idea with the "chocolate kisses" came because of Stockholm.[28]

After the Lorenz kidnapping, we had enjoyed quite a bit of sympathy. But after Stockholm, things were different. There was a lot of propaganda suggesting that we'd also be targeting ordinary folks now, and people felt threatened. You could always hear that the flower lady at the corner would be kidnapped next, that she'd soon be sitting in a box like Lorenz. We wanted to make it clear that that was nonsense. The customers in a bank didn't need to be afraid of us.

The customers never ate the chocolate kisses. Maybe it was best that way. They were terrible, really old ones. We had grabbed them quickly at Woolworth's.

We needed money quite desperately at the time, since we had suffered a few losses. Ronnie had been arrested, and much of our infrastructure was gone. We actually wanted to do two banks that day, but it didn't happen for logistical reasons. One comrade had to cancel on short notice, and we had problems with the car. We needed to get a new one, which is why we did the bank in the Schmargendorf neighborhood the day after.

Herrmann: How did the people react to the chocolate kisses?

Reinders: At Grüner Weg, they were distributed by a woman. We had to calm down a child there, a twelve-year-old who was bawling her eyes out. We talked with her until she was quiet. In Schmargendorf, the people were frozen with terror. That's the problem: first and foremost, people are scared during robberies.

The RAF criticized us heavily for distributing the chocolate kisses. From that day on, they called us the "populist faction." In their eyes, we no longer cared for anything but populist action and no longer took the struggle seriously.

Herrmann: Where did the idea for the leaflet with the "Economic Stimulus Plan" come from?

Reinders: Well, we figured it wasn't enough to just distribute chocolate kisses. After all the arrests, we also wanted to make it clear that we still existed. The mood within the left was like a roller coaster, up and down, back and forth. Because of the arrests, many thought that what we did wasn't worth it, since everyone was going to get arrested anyway. So we wanted to take a stand. To speak of an "economic stimulus plan" was ironic, of course.[29]

Herrmann: What did you mean by the phrase "Hopefully, everything will work out okay," which was included in the leaflet?

Reinders: Well, exactly that. There's a thing you must not forget: the bank clerks don't want the cops to arrive early. The customers don't know what the bank clerks know, namely, that the cops are the biggest threat to them. Because when they arrive, there is no escape from the building.

Herrmann: How do you know that the bank clerks thought that? Did you talk to them?

Reinders: No, but you know that, you can feel it. They want you out of the bank. They do pretty much everything for you to get the money and leave.

Fritzsch: There are also cops who are afraid of arriving early. One of us always stayed home to listen to the police radio during the robberies. This was important for our evaluation of the action. Once, he listened to a cop driving past a bank that was robbed, just as he received the alarm. But all he said was, "I need instructions. Where is the bank? Instructions, please!"

Reinders: The cop was right there. All he would have needed to do was drive around the corner. But he didn't want to. As we were escaping, changing from one vehicle to another, many patrol cars went to the bank with their lights flashing. But that cop was still parked around the corner waiting for instructions. Some cops simply don't want to get involved.

Fritzsch: They are the clever ones!

Reinders: A big thing was the Munich story, where a fellow called Rammelmayr took an employee hostage during a bank robbery, and then she got shot dead. They said it was Rammelmayr, but in reality it was the cops. After that, any bank employee thought, "I hope the cops won't show up!" That's what I meant when I said earlier that the criminals sometimes cleared the path for us. They did things that we would have never done, but they caused more fear among the employees. Plus, we showed up with five people. The employees had no idea of what was going on. Usually, they were robbed by one person, maybe two. With a team of five, one can go behind the valve, one can secure the window, and so on.

The Left Aboveground and Underground: Social Rooting, Discussion, Funding

Herrmann: Your wording is interesting: you distinguish yourselves from "criminals," the media calls you "terrorists." How did you see yourselves?

Fritzsch: "Terrorists?" Come on. The terrorists are on the other side. Terror is indiscriminate violence, and we never used indiscriminate violence.

Reinders: We never did crime to benefit ourselves. That's the difference to criminals. They do a bank because they want to have a good life. We did a bank to continue the political struggle. What people today often forget with respect to the bank robberies is that they were also used to fund many legal projects. The Chile campaign after Pinochet's coup was almost exclusively funded by us. We were the only ones who could get money quickly, and we paid for the newspapers, the leaflets, the factory groups. Not all of them, but the biggest ones. There are plenty of such examples. The people who took the money to print their newspapers often became some of our fiercest enemies later on, spreading terrible rumors about us.

Herrmann: What was your contact with the legal left like? Did you even have time to discuss with them, considering that maintaining your infrastructure was pretty much a full-time job?

Reinders: We had aboveground members, and we discussed with them.

Fritzsch: The 2nd of June and the RAF differed in that respect. The RAF expected from its members to burn all bridges and render a return to the aboveground impossible. They expected you to go underground with false papers. We reasoned thus: as long as the cops weren't looking for you, you ought to stay aboveground. That made things easier for everyone. Every underground member needed people to provide them with documents, needed safe houses, all of that was extra work. Had we only had underground members, we wouldn't have managed.

Reinders: It was important for us to maintain contact with legal groups.

Fritzsch: I was still aboveground shortly before I was arrested. We were all active in legal groups.

Reinders: Sometimes, the people underground met with people who weren't 2nd of June members. We discussed with them; these were people we knew. They could also join as guests in one of our meetings. We didn't always have much to contribute to what they were concerned with, but the meetings helped us to get a sense of the overall mood within the left. Later, in prison, we concluded that we hadn't had enough such meetings. They should have happened more often.

Fritzsch: We participated in quite a few discussions. At least with people who were active. Think about the leaflet distribution after the Lorenz kidnapping. We had planned to distribute fifty thousand, and, in the end, it was thirty thousand. Our calculations were as follows: in half an hour, a person can throw the leaflet into 200 to 250 mailboxes. After half an hour, you must assume that the first leaflet will be found and that someone will call the cops. So you have half an hour for the entire action. And that's how we did it. On one and the same night, thirty thousand leaflets were distributed all over Berlin between 7:30 and 8:00 p.m. You can figure out yourself how many people were needed for that. That's what shocked the cops the most.

Reinders: It impressed them in a way. Not least because they were so present in the city during the time; there were cops at every corner.

With the Weapon in Hand: Revolutionary Violence, Power, Liberation

Herrmann: One more question about the group's structure. To carry a gun means that you have to be ready to use it, at least under certain circumstances. Is there no danger that the readiness to engage in violence impacts group dynamics and personal relationships? What was your experience?

Reinders: We discussed that quite often. We had a few people who had made important experiences early on. The case of Gerd Müller, a RAF member, is a good example. Gerd Müller, who would later act as a crown witness, shot and killed a cop in Hamburg. After that, there was a discussion in Hamburg between RAF members and Rolf Pohle, Ina Siepmann, and me. We were appalled, because Müller seemed to be excited about what had happened, even enthusiastic. Okay, there was a shootout, the cop was dead, and we weren't exactly crying over that; the cop had also fired shots and could have killed one of us. But there was still no reason to feel happy about having killed someone, even less for being proud of it. The discussion got so heated that we left. Among ourselves, we always had plenty of discussions about the use of weapons.

Fritzsch: You could see that the weapons changed some people. Some acted in a special way with a gun in their hand. For them, the weapon made a difference.

Herrmann: Did they get a rush of power?

Fritzsch: I guess so. We had two people whose behavior gave cause for much concern. One of them got arrested with me. That he got arrested was a coincidence, the cops weren't looking for him. We meant to get him aboveground again. Had the cops come one day later, they would not have found him.

Hein: Were there cases when you said, "That person, they should not have a gun"?

Fritzsch: Well, in the case of the person I mentioned, yes. That's why he was to go aboveground again. He said that, in that case, he wanted to be active in a factory.

Reinders: As we said, we always discussed the use of weapons. People were not expelled from the group if they said that they wouldn't pull the trigger. Of course, there's something unsettling about that too—if you're out there with someone you can't rely on, things can get very dangerous.

Fritzsch: There were many arguments, especially about the use of firearms. What do you do in certain situations, for example when you're confronted by cops on the street? It was always paramount for us to avoid bystanders being hit. If someone had said, "I don't care about that, all I care about is to get away," they wouldn't have stayed with us for very long.

It's no coincidence that we never had shootouts, apart from the situation with Georg, but that was different. You gotta think about how to approach this beforehand. Do you say, "If a cop comes my way, he's had bad luck," or do you say that there have to be other ways to handle the situation?

Reinders: We didn't just discuss bystanders being hit, also ordinary cops. We also wanted to avoid confrontations with them. They also want to go home at night. We wanted a scenario where the number of cops who would drive past a bank that was being robbed would increase, knowing that if they drove past, nothing would happen. As soon as a cop gets killed, other cops feel threatened. And once they feel threatened, they'll be much more motivated to go hunt for people.

Herrmann: But isn't it sometimes unavoidable to say, "Now, it's either the cop or me . . ."?

Reinders: Sure, there can be situations like that. But getting pulled over with a bad taillight is not one of them. There, you don't think, "Bad luck, cop!" We had our fake IDs, they were well done, and we could use them under such circumstances.

Herrmann: Have you ever met the state security agent Grünhagen?[30]

Fritzsch: Oddly enough, he never came to see us. I think he visited everyone else who got arrested. But the two of us and Fritz Teufel, no.

Reinders: The first time Grünhagen appeared on the scene was after the three of us had been arrested in 1970. During the raid of a collective house, the cops took Ina Siepmann with them. After they had interrogated her, Grünhagen chatted with her privately and told her that he wasn't a cop. We thought he was a psychologist, because the cops had just started to use psychologists. Then he reappeared during the Schmücker saga.

Hermann: You got arrested in 1975. At that time, did they suggest collaboration with state security? Did you get any offers?

Reinders: For six months, I didn't see a single cop. Then they came five or six times in short succession. That was just before Andreas Vogel got arrested in February 1976.

Herrmann: What about Grünhagen's colleague Möllenbrock?[31] Didn't he always turn up in connection with Grünhagen?

Reinders: I didn't see much of Möllenbrock.

Fritzsch: In my case, the cops tried to get me to talk in the beginning. After a few weeks, they stopped. They returned once, after Ralf and the others had gotten arrested. The media hadn't even reported the arrests yet, when they appeared gleefully, Przytarski, Möllenbrock, and two cops.[32] "Do you know them?" they asked, and put photographs of the arrested in front of me. "This is your last chance, one of them will talk!" I just burst out laughing.

Möllenbrock was a particular jerk. He returned one week later. My father was old at the time, and so Möllenbrock said, "Your father is seriously ill, he will die. If you want to see him once more, you better start talking. You don't have to say much, but you gotta say something, otherwise you won't see him again." I almost went for his throat. It was a lie, all of it. How low can you go? What a pig.

Actually, now I remember: already before that, Möllenbrock had offered to establish contact with "an authority not dealing with criminal persecution," in case I'd talk without officially appearing as a crown witness.

2ND OF JUNE MOVEMENT PROGRAM

(1972)

Anonymous

—

This paper was first made public in 1978, when it was presented as a piece of evidence by the prosecution during the Lorenz-Drenkmann trial. The authors remain unknown, but 2nd of June members have expressed repeatedly that it summarized the group's key principles—see also the previous interview with Ronald Fritzsch and Ralf Reinders.

—

The 2nd of June Movement sees itself as the basis for an organization consisting of different autonomous urban guerrilla groups.

1. The 2nd of June Movement is committed to a protracted revolutionary practice. Only in this way can it claim to be revolutionary. It understands itself to be antiauthoritarian, but it must never lack strategic planning, theoretical and practical principles, and the discipline required in any guerrilla movement.

2. The 2nd of June Movement sees itself as a part of the vanguard only as it is "among the first to pick up the weapon." It is not a part of the vanguard only because it says it is. Weapons and engaging in "revolutionary actions" alone are not sufficient justifications. The 2nd of June Movement must engage in action, develop a convincing revolutionary practice, and reach the masses through continuous and understandable actions. It must prove that only action builds the vanguard, and that any vanguard becomes superfluous once the masses become active, once the actions become mass actions.

3. In the age of advanced imperialism, it has become clear that the main task is not the construction of a party, but the initiation of revolutionary action, the building of an organization for armed revolutionary counterviolence by the people against the organized violence by the state.

4. The first task of the 2nd of June Movement is to systematically carry out actions, even if, in the beginning, its capacities are limited.

5. Decisive for the work of the organization are the groups' capabilities and initiatives. No commando, no coordinating council, no central committee, no plenary assembly has the right or the authority to thwart an initiative by any group directed at triggering revolutionary action. We assume that each group, based on rich theoretical foundations, will only carry out actions prone to serve the people.

6. The 2nd of June Movement's military line is neither independent of its political line nor subordinate to it. We consider both lines inextricably intertwined. They are two sides of the same revolutionary coin. The 2nd of June Movement's line unites political and military aspects. It is revolutionary. Aboveground comrades work at the grass roots, in neighborhoods, in factories, in base groups, in schools and universities, with the aim to help unite the urban mass front.

7. The comrades who are active in the 2nd of June Movement consider their work on the mass front, in logistics, and in the armed tactical units as full-time work. With the increasingly fascist traits of the industrialized nations of the West, the Prometheus plan,[1] the state of emergency, the hand grenade law, ever stricter immigration laws as a consequence of the militarization of the class struggle by capital, and the increasingly imperialist endeavors of the metropole's capital specifically, the task of the 2nd of June Movement is to contribute to the solution of the fundamental contradiction in the capitalist countries by providing examples of revolutionary methods of intervention. This includes *direct* support for mass struggles, propagating means of resistance by national and international masses of wageworkers, and spreading knowledge about possible new means of struggle. The success of the 2nd of June Movement's revolutionary practice is dependent on the ongoing, direct, and personal involvement of the members of the commandos.

8. The 2nd of June Movement is not the armed wing of a party or organization. The armed tactical units of the 2nd of June Movement are the independent politico-military commandos of the organization. It belongs to the work of the 2nd of June Movement members who have not yet been forced underground to propagate and initiate the formation of revolutionary militias in the organizations they work in. We do not distinguish between "legal" and "illegal." The only actions that can be successful are actions that the powerful define as "illegal." Any successful legal grassroots action will be declared illegal. Those who don't accept this cannot be called revolutionaries.

9. The 2nd of June Movement does not embrace the "romantic mythology" of "underground work." Its cadres are realistic about their work and the risks they are taking. They know that by constituting a vanguard in the building of a people's army alongside other guerrilla groups such as the RAF, they will be declared leading enemies of the state. That the number of revolutionary deaths will increase as the class struggle intensifies is clear. The terror currently unleashed against the urban guerrilla's cadres and propagandists only prepares us for the class struggles to come. The war against the state and capital will be a long one. Not least the history of the German workers' movement teaches us that we must learn how to wage war. But waging war can only be learned in practice. Practice means for us: the building of militant aboveground groups, of militias, of the urban guerrilla, and, finally, of the people's army.

10. The struggle against capital and the state is not a struggle against abstractions. It is a struggle against the 1.3 percent of the population who control more than 74 percent of the productive assets as well as against their uniformed and civilian stooges. Our goal is not a "dictatorship of the proletariat," but the destruction of the rule of pigs over people, the destruction of capital, parties, the state. Our goal is council democracy. The regime of the pigs will not be overthrown by formulas but by revolutionary struggle. This struggle can't be waged and won nationally; it is an international struggle. The 2nd of June Movement collaborates with all of the world's socialist guerrilla groups. In fact, this program is inspired by that of our Brazilian friends in the MLP.[2] The 2nd of June Movement is part of a worldwide socialist offensive. It struggles shoulder to shoulder with the IRA, the

Weathermen, the Gauche prolétarienne,[3] the Red Brigades, and all
other guerrilla organizations.

Build the revolutionary guerrilla!
   Oppose the organized violence by the state with organized revolu-
tionary violence!
   Victory to the people's war!
   All power to the people!

A NEST EGG FOR THE REVOLUTION: THE BANKS OF THE 2ND OF JUNE MOVEMENT

(2000)

Klaus Viehmann

Originally published as "Notgroschen der Revolution" in the book *Vabanque: Bankraub, Theorie, Praxis, Geschichte* (Vabanque: Bank robbery, theory, practice, history), edited by Klaus Schönberger (Berlin/Hamburg: Assoziation A, 2000).

> Assets in the national economic cycle have to be protected from unlawful appropriation, since extremist and radical groups often finance their improper activities by means of burglaries and holdups.
> —Klaus Bockslaff, Sicherheitsplanung für Geldinstitute, 1996

The "national economic cycle" leaves many running on a hamster wheel, while a few don't know what to do with all the money they earn. It's an asocial system, unsurprisingly drawing the ire of the poor and provoking resistance by "extremist and radical groups."

Politics cost money. Militant politics cost more money. Okay, the rock that you throw doesn't cost anything, and you'll hardly have to worry about gas prices and bottle refunds when throwing a Molotov cocktail either. But tools to forge documents already are more expensive, safe houses and cars even more so. That's why the urban guerrilla groups emerging in the early 1970s had to ponder the same questions as the entire left: Who is going to pay for all this? Who has those funds?

Important in finding a solution was that, unlike in everyday capitalism, no one was supposed to die in the course of it. Methods of desperate—or simply mindless and ruthless—thieves and robbers who ransack two-bedroom apartments or beat a corner-shop owner half to death for a few coins were out of the question. These folks are not chasing the crown jewels, they go after glass beads. They don't question the system, they try to make themselves richer, a sad mirror image of the greed that drives the system.

There is an old advertisement: "Money problems? Ask your bank!" A suggestion we took to heart. Robbing cash-in-transit trucks implied too big a risk of shootouts, and even robbing individual cash deliverers could have led to physical fights about the green. "Nonviolent" means of acquisition, such as forged checks, were no option either, since they didn't generate enough cash. So bank robberies were the last resort to fight the chronic lack of funds of left-wing activities, and, twenty to twenty-five years ago, they were, without doubt, the most common armed action.

There was no stairway of political activities, where robbing a bank was the next step up from smashing a bank window. Bank robberies were simply done for the money, even if the political messages implied were a nice bonus: redistributing wealth from the top to the bottom, acquiring money subversively and without wage labor and exploitation, and demonstrating the lucrative possibilities of militancy.

The public condemnation of "terrorists" often contrasted with the secret admiration for their courage and their perceived perfection. And since they had to cover their faces, they could be turned into anything by the media, allowing people to project onto them whatever they wanted. In that sense, there was no difference between the "terrorists" and regular bank robbers. But political bank robberies drew bigger public interest, even when the robberies themselves didn't differ from regular ones. There were other differences that mattered: political bank robbers never used the money they "withdrew" themselves, neither for purchases in the temples of consumerism nor for luxurious vacations. These anonymous robbers were no unemployed folks in debt, or desperate providers of families. They were convinced leftists who didn't need extra money to get by privately. The difference to other leftists in West Germany was that other leftists didn't give robbing banks much thought—which was one reason for the dearth of money in the cash registers of their projects.

In urban guerrilla groups, there were dynamic handymen, ideologically steadfast students, nervous stoics, and, last but not least, both men and women. Ninety percent of the women bank robbers in West German history (there weren't many) must have been women from the urban guerrilla.

Each form of action requires a special kind of courage as well as a special kind of cool. Not all comrades were able to do a bank. That's how we put it: "do a bank." Or, rather, we mostly just spoke of "banks," because what we wanted to do with them was clear anyway. We never spoke of "robbing a bank." Some, who had proven courage during other actions, found their knees knocking and their hands trembling when it came to banks. Conversely, there were stellar bank robbers who got very anxious over a comparably innocent midnight car theft because they were night-blind and imagined a cop behind every corner. People who, during an expropriation action, frantically point their gun at a window shut by a draft should probably give up their militant career and focus on unarmed projects—a decision certainly supported by all comrades who aren't bulletproof . . . (Let's not get into a different kind here, the notoriously macho and self-promoting figures who are a risk for all armed actions.)

When it said "professionally planned" after one of our banks in the newspapers (with the inevitable police spokesperson admitting in the evening news that the manhunt "had as of yet been unsuccessful"), there was a lot of truth in it. Especially in the beginning, our bank robberies were very well prepared—the first bank is always the hardest. The "professionalism" was the result of experience and routine.

In the early days of the urban guerrilla experience, it took weeks to find the right bank, to collect intelligence about the interior, the valve, the doors, and to get (steal) the right getaway cars. It took even longer to get the guns. After the second or third bank, all could be taken care of within a week, with one or two people looking for a suitable site, checking the hours of the garbage trucks on the getaway route (to get stuck behind a garbage truck on a narrow street trying to make your getaway is nothing you'd want to experience more than once), and stealing two cars (alternatively renting them with false papers). One or two more comrades were briefed a day before the action, and the next morning your team showed up, got the money, and ran.

There was a rule that when it came to banks, you would always have two experienced comrades and never more than two rookies. You needed a sense of trust for comrades that went beyond the standard security felt in collectives. The roles during the action were divided in a way that the rookies couldn't do much damage.

They had relatively simple tasks appointed to them. A typical role for a rookie was to be the getaway driver, which also meant to wait in a car in front of the bank, listen to the police radio, and blow the horn when, after two to three minutes, they could hear the announcement, "Alarm at bank X on street Y—all available units respond!" Then, the people inside the bank knew it was time to split.

Rookies were also positioned by the door to prevent customers from leaving. It's annoying when customers get outside and yell, "Robbery! Robbery!" which inevitably draws a crowd of curious onlookers, through which you have to make your getaway while wearing masks, heavy clothing, bags full of money, and shotguns.

The person at the door also had to usher in customers that were arriving. We couldn't afford open doors and passersby staring at terrified people with their mouths open. Such images shall be confined to television series, where they are popular. The two experienced comrades could use the rookies' help, because they were busy with collecting the money and moving clerks out of the way who blocked the path to the money boxes. It was rarely possible to just grab the cash and stuff it into a bag. One would think that in a German bank with German clerks everything was in order. Wrong by a long shot. Only some cash lay orderly in the money boxes or on the counting board. The rest could be found in various drawers, in the cookie jar, or at the bottom of the wastebasket—no wonder that we had to go through everything, with much useless crap landing on the floor. Amid all the stress, it could happen that someone stepped on an alarm button covered by a pile of papers, which not only caused hideous noise (at the time, alarms were still ringing really loudly) but also terrified excuses from various employees: "That wasn't me!"

At times, the sum that we later counted on the kitchen table was lower than the one named in the papers. It seemed that a clerk or two might have compensated for the fright they got by stashing away some of the dough themselves.

Coins we left behind, except for the obligatory roll for pinball and cigarette machines. Value and weight were highly disproportionate, even for well-trained fellows like us. However, we were happy to take small gold bars (sadly, there were never any big ones), gold coins, and blank checks. There were also bundles of fake money, with a real bill at the top and at the bottom and sheets of blank paper in between them. If you allowed a clerk to fill your bag, you ended up with half a dozen of them, so it was always better to do the job yourself. New bills with serial numbers were not burned, like in bad crime flicks, but wettened in a bag, thoroughly crumbled, dried, brushed, folded, and exchanged for clean bills through modest purchases in department stores. If, days later, one of those bills did indeed draw attention in a bank, it was almost impossible to trace its origins. At least at the time, fingerprints were no longer discernable.

If registered notes showed up during an arrest or in a safe house left in haste, they could only be associated with comrades who were already looking at fifteen years in prison anyway, because of actions more serious in the eyes of the law. A bank robbery wasn't going to add anything to their sentence, so they didn't need to bother.

Customers and Others

Doing a bank becomes a relatively safe affair when there is strength in numbers. Three people in a regular bank have very little uncovered ground behind them. A customer is only tempted to play the hero if they are up against a single robber. Flashing your guns and being friendly but clear go a long way. The employees never gave us any trouble. After the Munich disaster of 1971, they had orders to hand over the money as quickly as possible to avoid a hostage situation.[1] Many had been trained for such moments and didn't give the impression of being scared. Some stare at you, as they've been told to provide the cops with a "good description" of the perpetrators, and most will press the alarm button only when you're on the way out (which means the cops never make it in time and there won't be a shootout). Only a few were foolish enough to give chase.

Some bank clerks used the opportunity to go on extended sick leave after an allegedly shocking experience, but for some the experience must have been shocking indeed—like for the old man who yelled, "Don't shoot!" when no one even pointed a gun at him, or the boy who froze and raised his hands without being told to do so. Such images you carry with you, and they make you ponder how to make a bank robbery as agreeable as possible.

Witness statements from customers and employees were often bizarre. Someone described a Kalashnikov repeatedly as a "cane" ("the male perpetrator also had one"), and someone else identified a sawed-off shotgun as a "club." Luckily, no one ever tried to reach for the "canes" and "clubs" in their confusion. It is frustrating to be identified by disoriented or manipulated witnesses when you weren't even in the bank, but it is somewhat amusing when an admittedly short but adult comrade is described as a "child" by no less than two customers. Indeed, the first personal descriptions that went out over the police radio that day spoke of "a couple with a kid" as perpetrators. At least the witnesses expressed bewilderment at the child holding a gun.

Once, a radio reporter had exceptional luck, as he was a customer in one of the banks we did. He took plenty of notes, and before the cops arrived on the scene, he was already on his way to a live show in the studio. The host of the show burst with both envy and compassion when our roving reporter described his experience of coming eye to eye with the "terrorists." One comrade remembered the fellow clearly because of his odd behavior, but she didn't suspect him to be a journalist, rather a patient from the psychiatric ward where one of the getaway cars was waiting.

We always brought loaded guns when doing a bank. For one, people from the underground always carried them anyway, and they were also for safety in case the cops showed up early. Luckily, that never happened during 2nd of June actions. Once, a uniformed policeman entered the bank accidentally, but we had a man at the door who stood him up against the wall. Unfortunately, the comrade overlooked the concealed gun. Luckily, the cop didn't shoot at the getaway car, apparently because he didn't want to endanger bystanders. In truth, he probably had forgotten to load or cock the weapon.

Not to encounter the police during a bank, inside or outside, was wise and good fortune. We did our part by being quick; the cops sometimes helped with deliberate procrastination and pretended confusion. At first, they raced for any bank where a robbery was reported, expecting to catch an unfortunate fellow out of work and "armed" with a starter pistol. "Southwest," "Zeppelin," or whatever the unit's name was all tried to collect credit. But once more information reached them—for example, based on the account of some bank employee hiding in a back room— their determination waned. "To all units! Bank robbery at X street. Be alert for your own safety! Two female suspects and one male suspect, armed with machine guns!" (The comrade in the getaway car usually didn't get a mention.) Once this came over the radio, even the most thickheaded of patrolmen understood that they'd be up against "terrorists" with weapons equal to theirs. Suddenly, they took mysterious turns half a mile from the scene and asked for "new instructions," while people at the command center were puzzled that a well-signposted bank on a prominent street couldn't be found.

The Money

Even if we lived frugal lives, the urban guerrilla costs money. In the mid-1970s, a group of about ten people living underground needed roughly 20,000 Deutschmark per month just for running costs. Before actions, or to replace materials and safe houses lost during manhunts, they needed more. Impoverished leftists can hardly afford that. Much money went to real estate agents, travel agencies, landlords, and rental car companies. If you are urgently looking for a safe house, you take almost anything at any price, grinding your teeth as you pay extra for a worm-eaten cabinet. And once the house is no longer safe, it's hard to claim the deposit. Airplane and train tickets cost money too, and the rental cars that were so reliable and inconspicuous weren't cheap either. Money also went to printing presses, copy machines, and various tools. Weapons and ammunition were costly too, but they constituted only a small part of the overall expenses.

Part of the money we made went to left-wing projects, youth and social centers, prisoner support groups, newspapers, book publishers, neighborhood initiatives, and the Chile solidarity movement. So all of that was involuntarily sponsored by banks and credit unions during the 1970s. Some of the people didn't know why hundreds of Deutschmark suddenly filled their donation cans, and it was better that way, for the protection of both them and the people donating. Some people had a sense of where the money came from, and some people knew for sure, even if they later preferred to say that they always opposed illegal actions. The money they got out of them, they didn't reject.

What Remains?

Bank robberies are no longer a common way for the left to acquire money. They have been replaced by wage labor, inheritances, and scholarships from both private foundations and state institutions. That's legal and less dangerous for everyone involved but also more conformist—or, the other way around, less rebellious. Considering how common the expropriation of banks was in the radical left once upon a time, it is really surprising how much this has fallen out of fashion today. To finance left-wing politics and projects by means of expropriation leaves a mark, in the same way that wooing rich heirs or foundation staff, or filling out application forms, leaves a mark. In other words: a left using stolen money is different from a left using granted money. With the money being stolen, there is a different degree of independence, and a different relationship to state institutions, rich people, and established organizations.

Bank robberies can't redistribute social wealth overall, or secure income for the "impoverished masses," but they undermine the obligation to work and subvert the rules of capital for acquiring money—rules that entail at least as much robbery as that of any bank. A few people got long prison sentences for doing banks ("predatory extortion" in legal terms). A rough estimate suggests that 2nd of June members alone served more than one hundred years in prison for this "crime."

The question of whether the banks were worth it is a question of whether left-wing politics is worth it. Left-wing politics is not about profits but about winning. Without the banks, the urban guerrilla groups and other projects funded by the money would have been less effective. Their political success, of course, depended first and foremost on the historical situation and the balance of power. To have a sufficient nest egg was only one aspect, one less worry.

The Chocolate Kisses Banks

Hardly any expropriation action became as popular as the two banks where chocolate kisses were distributed. On July 30, 1975, at the usual hour, 9:30 a.m., five 2nd of June members did a bank in Berlin-Neukölln. While the money boxes were emptied, a comrade offered chocolate kisses to the customers and employees. No one helped themselves, maybe because of fear, maybe because of confusion—in any case, the chocolate kisses remained on the counter, while the money (about 100,000 Deutschmark) disappeared. The Berlin police launched a major manhunt, and, upon a tip, hundreds of heavily armed cops searched an entire apartment complex. At 4 a.m., they retreated empty-handed.

Six hours later, they were called back into action, since two men and three women of the 2nd of June Movement did another bank, in the same manner as the day before. The second set of chocolate kisses ended up in the police laboratory, where they were examined for narcotics—in vain.

Unlike the chocolate kisses, the leaflet distributed in the banks did not become part of left-wing folklore. It was short and referred to an economic stimulus program by the ruling SDP-FDP coalition.

The 2nd of June Movement's Economic Stimulus Program: With everyone saying that the ruble's gotta roll for the chimneys to smoke, we
want to contribute within our modest means—after all, we're all
sitting in the same shitty boat! Hopefully, everything will work out
okay. So: Hand over the cash! Revolutionary chocolate kisses from
the 2nd of June Movement urban guerrilla!

In the following weeks, inspired lefties distributed chocolate kisses
in banks on two occasions—this time, without any intention of emptying
the money boxes. In Munich, this led to a police operation and four-digit
fines; in Essen, the police contented itself with checking IDs. In a lefty
Berlin bar, chocolate kisses were offered for free on the 2nd of June for
years.

For many, the chocolate kiss banks became the symbol of a "fun guerrilla." This reveals plenty of ignorance, but maybe it was inevitable. In fact,
the chocolate kisses were chosen quite randomly. Sour drops could have
been distributed just as well. It was all just to keep the customers calm.
That the leaflet drew less attention than the sweets was quite surprising
for the 2nd of June militants.

There's something else that speaks against the idea of a "fun guerrilla": weapons certainly weren't brought for fun, and in the case of the
second chocolate kisses bank, the cops almost got there in time. There
was also a passenger car that gave chase, and the female driver could
only be stopped by having a gun pointed at her—no fun at all. Last but
not least, almost all participants were behind bars by the end of 1975.

It is no fun either when, more than twenty years later, you find Stasi
files with "firsthand" accounts of the robberies, recorded shortly after they
had occurred. These accounts include detailed information about the
participants, their respective roles, the people who handled the money,
the people who stored the money, the people who knew what the money
was going to be used for. We can only speculate what the Stasi did with
this information, but it could have had serious consequences if the files
had made it to the West before the deeds were prescribed, regardless of
how much truth they contained.

You weren't part of the guerrilla for fun, whether you distributed
chocolate kisses or not.

SCHMÜCKER

2ND OF JUNE MOVEMENT LEAFLET

(1974)

2nd of June Movement

This leaflet was distributed by the 2nd of June Movement after the execution of 2nd of June Movement member and police informant Ulrich Schmücker. The group responds to an "open letter" by the editors of the left-wing periodical *Langer Marsch* (Long March), who condemned Schmücker's execution. Who killed Schmücker remains unclear, as does to what the degree the state security apparatus was involved or knew about it. A "Kommando 'Schwarzer Juni'" (Black June Commando), which took responsibility for the killing in a paper titled "Kommuniqué über den Verrat" (Communiqué on treason), did not belong to the Berlin circle of the 2nd of June Movement.

We've read the letter by some old vanguardists about the execution of the agent Schmücker, and we can only call it whiny, moralistic, pacifistic, and divisive! And let us add this as well: the letter is characteristic of the bourgeoisie, and in this case the left bourgeoisie, which speaks of "the people" and "the grass roots" struggling for political survival while the revolutionary developments of the time pass by it. What are they doing about Putte, Fuchsbau, Belziger Straße, Weisbecker House, Kreisel, Zehlendorfer Tunnel, squatting, transit fare hikes, Ford (!!!), Lippstadt, etc., etc.?[1]

    The cautionary tone of the letter is so misplaced and arrogant that it bloody well reminds us of the words of our masters, superiors, and educators ("Your special knowledge is useful for us—our experiences are important and necessary for you"). Unlike you, we haven't experienced the class contradictions as privileged people. We would also like to ask whether you have encountered "the people" at your meetings, on your committees, on your panels, at your rock festivals, etc.? Or have you encountered them at the university, or perhaps next to your writing desk? If that is the case, you haven't learned much; otherwise, you would know that every class-conscious proletarian says that a traitor, an infiltrator, an agent must be sentenced.

The entire letter is psychological twaddle, has nothing to do with class struggle, and signifies the political degeneration of the 1968 left lobby. This is the only explanation for turning the liquidation of a tool used by the class enemy into a subjective, moral "problem"—as if it was the revolutionary movement that produced the traitor, infiltrator, and agent and not the class enemy who possesses a thousandfold of the means and resources we do.

It appears to us as if a couple of hesitant, disoriented, and frustrated left intellectuals want to make their criteria into a yardstick for the revolution. It's an old song from a never-ending story: the progressive bourgeoisie tells the dumb proletarians how to make revolution. You say that the people see the enemy in an entirely different light than the way we portray them. But you overlook, first, that we come from the people and, second, that we don't portray the enemy, we fight the enemy, step by step, inch by inch, every day.

You have no relationship to the underground struggle and you know nothing about it; your approach is purely personal and, hence, entirely apolitical.

Solidarity is not charity. People have tried to make you understand that over and over again. You only ever campaign when there is a "victim," that means when militants are in prison, murdered, hunted. But when they struggle and are on the offensive, you stab them in the back! Don't ever think of writing us another letter, because you don't represent the revolutionary forces we want to engage with.

DRENKMANN

THOSE WHO SOW VIOLENCE ...
(1974)

2nd of June Movement

First leaflet distributed by the 2nd of June Movement concerning the November 10, 1974, killing of Günter von Drenkmann, president of the Berlin district court.

—

When Petra Schelm was murdered, we said, "Retribution for Petra." When Georg von Rauch was murdered, we said, "Retribution for Georg." We said the same in response to all the other murders: Tommy Weisbecker, Ian McLeod, Günther Jendrian, Günter Routhier, Richard Epple,[1] and all of the "deceased" in German prisons. They were all shot and beaten to death under the collective responsibility of the legal system, the state prosecutors, state security, and the police. We were never in a position to respond to these legally protected crimes. Our words, we have to admit, had no power.

Prisoners are abused and tortured in every prison in West Germany—more here, less there. Only the crassest examples of "abuse" are exposed: Mannheim, Klingelpütz, Hamburg Glocke, the Tegel isolation units.[2] Some die in prison without anyone knowing why.

Yesterday, the revolutionary Holger Meins fell victim to judicial murder. He was on hunger strike with forty-two other prisoners. They are struggling for the abolition of isolation torture and the special conditions under which political prisoners are held. Holger Meins starved to death after fifty-eight days because he did not receive sufficient nutrition. Holger Meins struggled for the people, even if not everyone has understood that yet.

When the prisoners' hunger strike began, we said, "If the extermination strategy claims another revolutionary life, those responsible will have to pay."

Günter von Drenkmann was Berlin's highest judge. He belonged to the core of those responsible. He didn't want to listen to our demands that the prisoners' requests be met. He made it clear that he was willing to see more revolutionaries die in German prisons. Those who sow violence will reap violence.

We are once again demanding the abolition of inhumane prison conditions in West Germany and West Berlin!

REGARDING THE ASSASSINATION OF BERLIN'S HIGHEST JUDGE: TERROR OR RESISTANCE?!

(1974)

2nd of June Movement

Second leaflet distributed by the 2nd of June Movement concerning the November 10, 1974, killing of Günter von Drenkmann, president of the Berlin district court.

———

Who is "appalled" by the death of Günter von Drenkmann and why? The outcry over Drenkmann's death is the outcry of the powerful over the death of one of their own! It's not national security or the security of the people they see threatened (what interest do these folks have in "ordinary people" other than them providing votes in elections), only their own security. In this case, someone was held responsible for his actions who never had to care about responsibility before, because, as a "bearer of the law," he was untouchable. If he is now sold to us (among other things) as an antifascist only because he wasn't acting as a judge during the Nazi regime but as a legal adviser in Berlin's Chamber of Industry and Commerce, we must ask the question: Was that chamber antifascist?!?

Governments in Germany have changed, but the Drenkmanns always remained. Günter von Drenkmann's father was the president of the Supreme Court under Kaiser Wilhelm II, then came Weimar, then the Nazis. Günter von Drenkmann became a judge in 1937, and under our so-called free and democratic constitutional order, he became the highest judge of Berlin. It seems that the youngest of the Drenkmanns will carry on with this tradition; he is already a state court judge.

It is hardly a coincidence that everyone in the Drenkmann family has studied law, while the children of working-class parents become—workers! Our "democracy" (the "rule of the people") makes it appear as if the worker is both dumber and ("naturally") more criminal than the better off. Among university students, only 6 percent come from the working class, while the working class makes up 80 percent of the prison population! That's the "justice" of this system, that's the "order" that Drenkmann and his peers wanted to preserve at all costs!

Suddenly, we hear that "democracy is in danger"; not because the people don't effectively rule and are instead screwed over by folks ruling in the interest of the rich and power-hungry—no, because a very certain kind of people are afraid that their high positions and the protection through allegedly "universal" laws no longer guarantee that they can do whatever they want.

The actions of the armed left have never been directed against the people. The actions have always been directed against those who exploit, deceive, cheat, and betray the people. It is the powerful who, at the moment they sense danger to themselves, invent a danger to "the people"—the people who, under different circumstances, they wouldn't even share a meal with, the people who they expect to be one thing only, and that is to be submissive.

Suddenly, Judge Drenkmann was apparently a citizen like any other. As if the shots that hit him could have hit a toolmaker, a greengrocer, or a shop assistant at KaDeWe.[1] Come on, we do not struggle against our sisters and brothers! We struggle against those who tyrannize us and kill us on the installment plan, with inhumane living conditions, work speed-ups, an educational system that only educates *their* children, and prisons in which people die while those who don't are irretrievably destroyed.

Why would the working class care about the president of the district court, who, according to *Bild*, liked to wear pink shirts, and, according to *Tagesspiegel*,[2] was a "cosmopolitan man"? While normally everything is done to prevent solidarity among the people—through isolation at the workplace, at home, or in prison—we now hear calls for "solidarity" from the benches of the government and all political parties (oh, wait, there are no longer any parties, there are only Germans!). They demand "solidarity" in the fight against those who have shown, and continue to show, that resistance is necessary and possible. This is where their fear comes from! They are not worried about the people being threatened by "terrorists" (they know very well that armed actions only target themselves), but by a population that begins to resist the terror from above, that demands their rights and is willing to fight for them.

The killing of Berlin's highest judge was not an action directed against the people. The people have nothing to fear from the "terrorists"! The action against Berlin's highest judge shows that we are defending ourselves, that we will no longer quietly accept the murder of a comrade, and that we will make those responsible pay. In Berlin's legal system, the district court has long made a name for itself by delivering particularly reactionary rulings, decrees, and directives. That the president himself never sat on the podium is only logical. Is there any boss who gets his hands dirty? Regardless, he is still pulling the strings.

The deaths that the police, state security, and the justice system have on their conscience are innumerable: Richard Epple, Petra Schelm, Günther Jendrian, Georg von Rauch, Tommy Weisbecker, Günter Routhier, Ian McLeod, Benno Ohnesorg, and now Holger Meins[3] are only a few of the many who have been beaten and shot to death. All of the charges against their killers have been dropped. We neither can nor will continue to watch these state-protected crimes without taking action!

Deny these hypocrites "solidarity." Let them be by themselves on Thursday![4]

BAUMANN

FRIENDS, THROW AWAY THE GUN
(1974)

Michael "Bommi" Baumann

Interview published in the weekly news magazine *Der Spiegel* on February 11, 1974. Baumann was in exile in the UK at the time.

——

Do you have a gun in your pocket?
I haven't carried a gun for a year and a half. Not carrying one makes me feel better, freer. A gun can become your worst enemy.

In a poem you wrote, you express it thus: "I've laid down the gun, friends, because I have realized that not hate ought to be one's driving force but love." Sounds a bit hokey for an anarchist.
Maybe it does, but I no longer see myself as an anarchist.

You're demanding from your friends to "throw away the gun." Have you come to realize that violence only repels people?
For many years, I told people to pick up the gun. They need to know that this is over. I owe them that.

You've been living underground for four years now. You've planted bombs. Was that political action or some trip? How far-out were you?
I suppose we had dropped out of society in some sense. The boredom, the monotony—it disgusted us. Take a drive along the Siemensstadt factories one misty morning, and all you see is ugliness and emptiness keeping

a soulless machine running, day in, day out.[1] Your parents are addicted to TV and your colleagues to alcohol. When I worked as an apprentice in construction, I couldn't put words to it, but that's how I felt. It gave rise to an undefined disgust for everything that surrounded me.

In the beginning, the 2nd of June Movement, to which you belonged, wanted to do things differently, "more politically" than the Baader-Meinhof Group, instead of just robbing one bank after the other. What were you trying to achieve?
We wanted to gradually intensify the class struggle, for example during transit fare hikes and wage disputes—prepare a people's war by creating a revolutionary sentiment among the population.

Why?
It's propaganda by the deed, an old anarchist thing. You fuel conflict and look for militant solutions. We wanted a different society, a society in which you can be constructive and happy. After twenty years of Adenauer and no experiments, the revolutionary strategists came along and said, "It's not just us: it's the Persians, the Vietnamese, we have the shootings of Dutschke and Ohnesorg, it's the same enemy everywhere, we have to fight that enemy, wake up!"

And then you robbed banks. According to police investigations, you were involved in three robberies.
One, in Hermsdorf. Otherwise, I was just an accessory.

Were you afraid?
Afraid? I was up for an adventure. Dangerous experiences can be thrilling. The fear was never overwhelming.

Was that people's war for you?
We didn't think in those categories. It was fun. We laughed a lot about our disguises. I looked like a clown out of a comic book.

During the time you were active, there were two deaths: the boat-builder Beelitz, who was killed by a bomb you were involved in building, and Georg von Rauch, who was shot dead by West Berlin police on Eisenacher Straße, in your presence.

Those were endpoints. Those were deaths that changed my mind. With Beelitz, it was horror. With Georg von Rauch, it was, one more time, hatred. When you see someone like that fall next to you, you see him fall for a very long time.

Did you see him fall before that?
You knew there was a possibility, yes.

Who shot first on Eisenacher Straße?
It was Georg, but it was a close call.

When did you shoot?
When you hear a bang, you shoot, that's logical.

And now? "Bommi the Bomber," is that over?
I've returned to where I started. I still feel like part of a movement looking for happiness outside of this society, looking for other ways to live, moving in a big stream. "Look here, the prodigal son has returned"—that's never happening.

You don't intend to turn yourself in to the police?
Not at all. Why would I? I've already been to prison for eighteen months. I don't need to have that experience again. Prison doesn't solve my problems. When you take a step back and quietly reflect on things, you see the world differently. When you're no longer adrift, the ferryman is waiting for you and takes you to the other side of the river.

The Garden of Eden in the underground? Where are you heading?
There are concrete alternatives. I can't tell you mine, or it would no longer be one.

BOMMI BAUMANN: HOW IT ALL ENDS

(1976)

Members of the 2nd of June Movement

Originally circulated under the title "Bommi Baumann: Wie alles aufhört" in response to the 1975 release of Bommi Baumann's autobiographical account *Wie alles anfing* (English edition: *How It All Began*, Pulp Press, 1977).

Bommi is the talk of the town. Bommi is in magazines, Bommi is in books.

It's happening. The PR departments of various "left-wing" publishers, newspapers, and associations have put their heads together and come up with a campaign that is now approaching its peak. After food, sex, hash, and other fads, we now have Bommi! A genuine crusade against the violence from below.

Admen, psychologists, cops, newspaper editors, Stasi agents, anchormen, everyone's in it: Bommi in *Der Spiegel*, Bommi in *Berliner Zeitung*, Bommi in *Frankfurter Rundschau*, Bommi in films, Bommi on TV. An unprecedented campaign, a holy crusade for love, peace, and harmony— something not seen since Billy Graham. No option available in the Christian occident is overlooked, everything is marketed. The Jesus freaks weren't half as good. "But why? What has happened?" wonder the readers, listeners, and viewers. Is there a new messiah? No, it's not that bad.

In this case, a Paul turned into a Saul and then into a Paul again. Not, however, as once upon a time, on the outskirts of Damascus, but in Berlin.

Berlin, as you know, is a frontier town. Nowadays, that's enough for market value. And if you're able to deliver firsthand reports about the enemies of the state, the *Spiegel*'s bestseller list is awaiting you. A bit of Simmel, a bit of Semler, a touch of gossip, a few white lies, voilà![1]

Now, to avoid all desecrations and excommunications, we, the authors of this text, have decided to get more concrete.

Concrete Questions—and Answers

What are Bommi's goals? What are his motives for becoming a hench-man of the state? Has he been bought? With what? Is this campaign a preparation for overthrowing Schmidt? Bommi for president? Are secret machinations of dangerous terrorists behind it?

These are all questions we've had to grapple with. We have reflected, researched, deliberated, racked our brains, sat around long enough to get hemorrhoids—all for the purpose of finding answers. And we did indeed manage to shed some light on the story! This makes up for all the sacri-fices. Our astounding discovery in the neon light: *desire!*

Desire is behind everything. The desire to understand one's fear and to overcome it. The desire to be loved. The desire not to do anything. The desire to be free. Yes, especially the desire to be free! Be free, be high, here and now, in the Christian, capitalist occident. Everyone is an island, everyone can be free, here and now. Love here and now, love without fear, the world is beautiful. Love your comrades! Throw away the gun, and the cops will leave you in peace! Everything will work out fine. Beautiful, happy world! Don't do anything stupid, and you won't have anything stupid done to you.

There is no emancipation without revolution. Revolution without emancipation is counterrevolution.

Bommi also has the desire to make some money. Stories about our struggle, no matter how distorted, have market value. Lots of people like Bommi—in particular, people who know neither him nor us. They believe that he tells it the way it is. But because he doesn't, because we aren't like that, because *he* was like that, none of what he writes or says teaches you anything about what we do, how we live, and what we want. Bommi has played police and thief. He knows that, which is why he says that what we did was apolitical, that our struggle was nothing more than banks, cash, trips, and terror. Since he saw the gun as a substitute for his dick, it was the center of his life, he was a revolver man. Is he now a good citizen because he says that we're just a few people underground who play urban guerrilla? That we have no love, that we are cold, rational?

Believe him if you want. If you're not sure, ask and form your own opinion. Those who don't believe him know better.

SAUBER

BACKS AGAINST THE WALL?

(1975)

Werner Sauber and Comrades

Position paper written by Werner Sauber in collaboration with other militants under the title "Mit dem Rücken zur Wand?" against the backdrop of widespread wildcat strikes in West Germany in 1973, mainly led by migrant workers. Circulated internally.

——

The Crisis

Workers have retreated following the struggles of recent years. The bosses' attack, which, at first, was primarily directed against migrant and young, unskilled German workers, is now targeting the entire working class.

Any general summary of the crisis has a neutralizing effect and is too far removed from its brutal reality. We only have an inkling of what is awaiting us. When you lose your job, you lose security and confidence. You interpret being laid off as a personal failure—failing your wife, your children, society. The feeling of powerlessness breeds despair.

The summer of 1973 was a short summer of fresh air, of courage, and of hope for more humanity in the factories. For the bosses, it was a summer of panic, insecurity, and fear. That's why their response to the demands for slower assembly lines, less working hours, no wage grades, longer breaks, and longer vacation came swiftly and violently. First came the batons, then targeted sackings, and finally mass layoffs as a sweeping attack against a rebellion based on outrage over work speed-ups, deteriorating health, and alienating labor. With Helmut Schmidt taking office in May 1974, the excesses of the bosses became the norm.

German skilled workers don't experience the same pressure as their Turkish, Greek, Yugoslav, and Spanish colleagues, both men and women. The pressure the workers feel has many reasons: mass layoffs, raids, deportations, reduced child allowance, termination of apprenticeships, pressure in vocational schools, evictions of youth centers. Strongly affected are also those who are supposed to mediate between the exploited and the state: social workers have to deal with fewer rights, shorter contracts, transfers, and sackings, and there are professional bans for teachers and other public servants. Leftist groups working with minorities among the working class can also feel the heat. The "Winter Journey" (a nationwide wave of raids following the von Drenkmann assassination in 1974) was the largest police assault in West German history. The police raided one hundred homes and collectives. It was much more than just a demonstration of power. The raids meant to spread fear at the heart of the social resistance movements: in the factories, the immigrant ghettos, the youth centers, the prisons.

Since Helmut Schmidt took office in May 1974, the crisis has been used as an instrument to regain control over the working masses and to target rebellious minorities. Many among the latter are now put in detention awaiting deportation—or extermination.

The Situation in the Factories

Asked about these developments, most workers sigh and say, "Layoffs everywhere you look; you can do nothing about them but keep your head down and try to make ends meet, that's all there is to it." The wave of layoffs is indeed overwhelming. Today, more than one million people in West Germany are unemployed. Most affected are women, foreigners, and young, unskilled workers.

The first major wave of layoffs happened a year and a half ago after the strikes in the automobile and automobile supply industries. This was followed by temporary work contracts. Currently, there is a new major wave of layoffs. The prelude consisted of "voluntary layoffs with compensation." Compensation means in this case that you get a severance package based on your last monthly income, which you have to use up before you can apply for unemployment benefits. One wonders how many millions of Deutschmark the bosses are ready to pay to prevent factory occupations and to pacify working-class uprisings?

As a long-term strategy, layoffs are an excellent means of disciplining workers. Those who protest are the first to go. Then follow those who have no place in the new organization of labor. They become the main targets of the bosses' attacks. Judging from the most recent strikes, the assembly line no longer is the most effective tool for exploitation. The bosses admit openly that traditional mechanisms of dividing the workforce no longer have the same effect. They respond in two ways.

The first is to use a seemingly more transparent organization of labor to create a new identification with the labor's product in the workers' consciousness, thereby rendering them more exploitable. Assembly line workers are also increasingly organized in "homogenous groups." This is meant to facilitate workers disciplining themselves (there are group bonuses). Some automobile companies test workers for specific tasks, providing the illusion of treating them as skilled laborers.

The second response by the bosses is technological. It is characterized by the introduction of the new Bosch modular flexible assembly system, which combines the classic assembly line with intermediate, partially automated, individual workspaces, or even robots. This is meant to achieve two things: first, to isolate workers along the assembly line, and second, to make them fear being replaced by automated production. Exploitation is intensified everywhere by measuring manual tasks in miniscule temporary units.

It is clear that the first response, the apparent humanization of labor, provides a cover for the second, the enslavement of workers as industrial androids. The requirement to produce surplus value doesn't lead to the abolition of mass work but rather to its reconstruction. It may be that much mind-numbing assembly line piecework will disappear, but only to chain supervisors and workers, both responsible for several semiautomated machines, more strongly to the production line than ever before.

It appears as if we have reached a final stage of capitalist rule. We see major changes in the design and development departments. Even there, computers turn labor into a monotonous routine. It's only a matter of time before the intellectual workers affected will recognize their situation and begin to rebel.

But there is no sense of it yet, neither in the design and development departments nor in production. One reason is that, since the shock of 1973, the bosses have become less shortsighted and thoughtless. They changed their investment strategies according to a careful analysis of national economic development. Not all assembly line capital has been abolished. The surplus value created by assembly line exploitation is too significant for that. Should the assembly lines in West Germany cease to run smoothly, the bosses will either restructure them or relocate them to the European periphery and, in particular, to the most stable economic regions outside of Europe. Right now, for example, Ford workers are unsettled by rumors that Ford Europe is planning to relocate important parts of its production to Spain. That's not an isolated case. Most corporations make such decisions as soon as the workers' resistance in West Germany becomes too costly.

The Situation in the Urban Centers

The increasing pressure in the factories has an immediate impact on working-class neighborhoods. The social consequences depend on which corporations control the region. The greater the number of foreign workers laid off, the greater the intensity with which the political authorities act against them, particularly in the areas where they are most concentrated. Illegal immigrants are controlled, hunted—on their way to work, on public transport, or randomly on the street—and deported. Restricted immigration shall allow the state to regain control over the immigrant ghettos. Family reunification, a question of survival for immigrants as it prevents them from vegetating as industrial slaves in barracks, is made difficult by cutbacks in child allowances and restrictions on residency permits.

But not only immigrants are threatened. The bosses have made it clear to young German workers that they, too, can be sacked at any time given the ongoing restructuring of production. In certain industries, 15 percent of those laid off are young German workers without a high school diploma. Government measures for job training (better education, more apprenticeships and stipends) are flatly rejected by the capitalists. Instead, they demand increased funding for the police apparatus in order to stifle any sign of resistance by the masses of unemployed youth. Alleged breeding grounds of resistance, such as youth centers, are constantly harassed. The police is also expanding its gang units.

Women workers, already at the bottom of the pile, are heavily affected by the restructuring of labor. In many factories, low-wage categories are reintroduced. (In some, they never disappeared, despite the struggles of recent years.) Progressive abortion laws are revoked by the legal mafia. The women's rebellion is being crushed, and everything is done to prevent an uprising by women workers. The overexploited sections of the working class are under siege, with the situation of the working class worsening overall.

The Schmidt Government: Swinging the Cudgel for a New Imperialist Superpower

Against the background of a spy scandal, West German capital succeeded in changing government policy in May 1974.[1] The Schmidt-Genscher government is the most right-wing government possible in West Germany today.[2] Given the ongoing transformations in production, the managers of the major growth industries require a regime that combines significant changes in economic policy with strong measures of repression against all forms of resistance. A CDU/CSU government could never do that.

In its first year, the Schmidt-Genscher government was able to avoid large-scale clashes with the working class. Only social democrats can pull this off while real wages are falling and the unemployment rate is rising faster than in any other country. The Schmidt-Genscher government was able to sell it all by suggesting that "otherwise, it might get a whole lot worse."

The Schmidt-Genscher government dropped all ambitions for stronger government control of investments. The massive reduction in social policy has drastically expanded capitalism's room to maneuver. There is no more talk about improving health care, education, environmental laws, life overall. The change of policy coincides with inflation threatening the boom in commodity and capital export. It was justified as a "stability policy," with the consequence of one and a half million people being unemployed.

Today, the Schmidt-Genscher government channels billions of tax dollars squeezed from the working class to capitalists. It makes no attempt to hide this. In the most recent economic program (December 12, 1974), the government announced that it will cover 7.5 percent of new investments, and, until mid-1975, 60 percent of the wages of new employees at readjusted workplaces. Thanks to Schmidt and Genscher, the working class will pay for this. This is the plan: first, there are mass layoffs; then there is temporary employment at workplaces where all forms of resistance are suppressed; and, if all goes well, people will be rehired and expected to be grateful for it.

But that's not all. While the Brandt government still maintained relationships with non-European liberation movements, keeping a low profile in Western Europe, the Schmidt government aligns with growth capital. West German employers are still the most powerful in Europe, able to control their employees better than anyone else. The development of the European Economic Community is dependent on West German capital.[3] One result is a billion-dollar loan to Italy being tied to keeping the Italian Communist Party out of government and to downplay the involvement of the German Federal Intelligence Service in the Milan bombing.[4]

Where export capital and loans don't suffice, violence will do the job. The Brandt government was still hesitant to allow the transport of US military equipment during the latest war in the Middle East. During the next war in the Middle East, however, German army bases will serve as a hub in the supply chain for the US, which will be trying to take control of the region's oil refineries. With Schmidt, the axis Washington-Bonn has become a reality. For the US, Bonn has become the main ally in the extraction of Third World raw materials. By all means and for all purposes, West Germany acts today as an imperialist superpower. With Schmidt it has become clear that in Germany, too, the ruling classes would rather risk World War III than an international breakthrough of the working class.

What Are the Current Conditions for Resistance? Where Do We Begin?

Where do we still find pockets of counterpower? Are new ones emerging? While the workers are put on the defensive, the left has fragmented into a thousand pieces. There are no more common evaluations of the class enemy. In light of petty factional quibbling, fear of armed actions, and discouraging experiences, many have retreated. The situation is depressing—as it almost always is when the class enemy has seized the initiative.

Things seem to be going better for the reformists. They've been postponing workers' power to someday in a distant future, allowing them to wax endlessly about the oh-so-complicated conditions of developing anticapitalist consciousness. This has made them ever more accepting of capitalist progress during the course of the last century. But, as the 1973 summer strikes have shown, this no longer convinces large segments of the working class. The IG Metall union declared the Ford strike the most serious crisis it had experienced.[5] During fall 1973, there was much soul-searching to understand how shortcomings in the union had contributed to the summer's intense workers' resistance. Such a series of wildcat strikes is not to be repeated!

The reformist press, including that of the DKP, speculated about the reasons of the strike wave, the general tone being: "The workers' morale is on the decline, they have no desire to work, they skip work on Mondays; they don't care about shop stewards, factory councils, or the unions; all they want to do is to gorge themselves, get drunk, and get laid." The strikes, so went the conclusion, sabotaged production and progress.

The fear that the Ford strike struck among the unions and the reformists was answered with collective bargaining agreements serving the interests of the employers, means to "humanize" the production process, and a "reduction of the workload and dependence on low-skilled labor." The unions renounced violent actions against exploitation and demanded a "politicized discipline" of the workers that would enable "anticapitalist structural reforms." As the capitalists tried to win time, a temporary alliance with the reformists came in handy. In fall 1973, they offered IG Metall in Baden-Württemberg the following concessions: a limit to takt times, paid breaks of thirty minutes, contract rates at 125 percent of the factory wage average, net wages for up to seventy-two weeks after work-related injuries, and guaranteed wages for senior workers. These weren't peanuts, and the reformists rejoiced! Only a few months later, however, all employers in the steel industry seemed to have forgotten the agreements. Now, we're back at a stage where the reformists try to save even the shittiest of jobs during mass layoffs. They turn their coat depending on the level of capitalist development.

The only common denominator of the antireformists seems to be the rejection of the reformist line, and this happens more rhetorically than practically. A few years ago, the undogmatic groups around the newspaper *Wir wollen alles* (We want it all)[6] began to focus on the "multinational" worker in mass production. In 1973, they felt that their analysis was proven right. Unfortunately, they seemed satisfied by that. They made no effort to get involved in the proletarian resistance and to push its militancy further. The K-groups were only in very limited ways radicalized by the strike wave of 1973.[7] Only in rare cases did they revise their party doctrines, which are based on old—and lost—workers' struggles.

The antireformist left was splintered, weak, and only able to provide limited agitation during the workers' struggles of 1973. It could not take on any major initiative, even though the undogmatic groups, neighborhood initiatives, Red and Black Aid organizations, and migrant groups—for example, the Spanish Center in Essen—made a bigger effort than the

K-groups to connect with the migrants, workers, and proletarian youth. The problem wasn't so much a lack of contact between the social resistance movements and the antireformist tendencies, but rather the inability to create autonomous approaches to organizing that could have served as a basis for proletarian counterpower, enabling open and subversive resistance. To overcome this inability seems crucial for our attempts to develop the possibilities of real counterpower, which means armed workers' power!

There are two movements—the Red Army Faction and the 2nd of June Movement—that have so far attempted to turn this into political praxis.

The Red Army Faction

The offensive power of the RAF's anti-imperialist terrorism has been held in check by state repression over the, roughly speaking, last two years. We recognize that the comrades of the RAF, as partisans of the first hour, left the division between the personal and the political behind and took up the armed struggle in the here and now without risk coverage.

The RAF's revolutionary practice and its experience are worth more than the gazillion sheets of paper that various leftists have used to denounce it. The bombs in Frankfurt and Heidelberg were the right response at the right time.[8] In our confrontation with the class enemy, these comrades are our sisters and brothers, and their extermination is our extermination. Therefore, any criticism of the RAF can only be a criticism of solidarity, and it has to be expressed in practice, by realizing the armed mass line here and now. We summarize our criticism as follows.

The RAF disregards the struggles of the most exploited: women, foreigners, and young German unskilled workers. Any practical attempt to involve militant proletarians in the armed struggle has been rejected by the RAF. Instead, the RAF comrades act as a revolutionary "secret service," looking only at the liberation movements of the Three Continents.

It would have been more in line with their anti-imperialist concept to join a Third World liberation movement and fight with them against the metropole. The RAF is neither a fish in the sea nor a bird in the sky. It only collaborates with oppressed marginalized groups or the left to gain new allies for anti-imperialist terrorism, not to strengthen the class struggles of the oppressed in the metropole itself. Until 1972, this approach was understandable. But in the summer of 1973, they should have engaged with a workers' resistance that was strong enough for anyone to notice.

The anticapitalist struggle must arise from the daily resistance of workers trying to survive under the capitalist state of siege. Effective resistance is tied to daily experience. Resistance against the imperialist superstructure only, with no roots in the factories and neighborhoods, can easily be eradicated by the capitalist state with general police tactics.

The RAF is building a red army that, in the beginning, is standing on its own. It hopes that the bombs it plants will affect the consciousness of the masses, as if the development of mass resistance was primarily based on awareness of how bad living conditions are. Such a logic reduces revolutionary violence to a question of enlightenment. If revolutionary violence doesn't come from experiences of struggle and oppression within the class, it cannot become a means of counterpower. Among the left, people are sympathetic to militant activists on the run, but they have no idea what to do with the conflict between the state's terror and the RAF's anti-imperialist struggle.

Even in prison, RAF comrades stick to their elitist line. They act as if solitary confinement under particularly harsh conditions was designed specifically for them. But the justice system uses it against rebellious proletarian prisoners as well. It is the duty of the torture committees[9] and the RAF lawyers to support the many unknown resistance fighters just as much as they support their own comrades. For the undogmatic Red and Black Aid organizations, this has always been clear. The campaign and the mobilization of class violence against imprisonment as a form of extermination are absolutely vital. Those responsible need to be held accountable, whether they sit at a desk in an office or lock the cells in high-security wings. For centuries, the rebellion against prison conditions on both the inside and the outside has been the first sign of imminent revolution.

An Alternative: The 2nd of June Movement of Berlin

During the student movement, another militant and eventually armed group emerged besides the RAF in a much less spectacular manner: the 2nd of June Movement. Contrary to the actions of the RAF, the actions of this group, based in West Berlin, are carried out by proletarian comrades. The support for them doesn't come from left-wing celebrities and the left bourgeoisie, but from their own social circles. The group emerged from the Hash Rebels and the proletarian subculture, at first mainly supporting and strengthening the Justice Campaign with militant actions. In the underground newspaper *Agit 883*, it argued for organized mass militancy, with actions carried out by commandos.

When US troops marched into Cambodia in 1970, twenty comrades attacked the America House in West Berlin with firebombs, rocks, and clubs despite the building being protected by riot police. A few days later, the last remaining windows of this institution serving as an imperialist cultural center were smashed during a mass demonstration. Two of the police horses driven into the crowd were stabbed to death. The militants defended themselves against armed police with rocks, steel ball bearings, and welded iron plates.

Soon, most members of the group were driven underground. For more than three years, they attempted to become the armed wing of the undogmatic left in Berlin. They had two main goals: 1) within the context of anti-imperialist mass campaigns, they wanted to move from symbolic actions against institutions of power (particularly US institutions) to actions causing as much actual damage as possible; and 2) they wanted to carry out actions in collaboration with undogmatic factory and neighborhood groups in the proletarian neighborhoods of Berlin. These actions occurred in connection to evictions, layoffs, rent increases, and factory closures and were intended to motivate others to carry out similar ones. They were supposed to help transform the anger of the people into militant and eventually armed resistance.

Even if the 2nd of June Movement received generous support from many comrades, it was, ironically, their contacts in the neighborhoods and factories that stood in the way of offensive armed actions. These contacts didn't pass on necessary information, overslept, or suddenly left town. This undermined operations.

The few leaflets and communiqués released by the 2nd of June Movement didn't receive much attention and were largely ignored even by the left press. However, the members of the group weren't particularly keen on media attention anyway, as long as they hadn't bridged the gap between ambition and reality. This makes it easy to understand why, early on, it was primarily bank robberies that defined the image of the group. Even if they lived frugally, the comrades needed money for their operations and to support projects of the undogmatic radical left.

Georg von Rauch was killed, many comrades were arrested, others gave up, and a few tried to buy their release from prison through betrayal. Despite these serious setbacks (the group's infrastructure was repeatedly wiped out because of informants), the security forces have not yet been able to eradicate the group as a whole or to drive it from the city.

One example: In fall 1973, the police was on the heels of Ina Siepmann, a comrade on the run, after a tip from H. Brockmann.[10] In an unparalleled effort, the police hunted for a safe house in Kreuzberg. They tried to gather information from people by distributing twenty-five thousand leaflets and blasting messages from sound trucks. An anarchist neighborhood group responded with flyers and graffiti that called for solidarity with the 2nd of June comrades and explained the goals of the armed struggle. Two days later, the *Tagesspiegel* wrote that four tips had come in. The cops never found the safe house.

We need to keep in mind that the 2nd of June Movement was born during a phase of anti-imperialist mass struggles. First, it tried to turn this historical moment into a political perspective. However, it learned that a guerrilla trying to enlighten people can't connect to the people. The guerrilla can only do so by relating to the people's immediate, daily experiences and conflicts. Only this can be the basis for armed counterpower.

The 2nd of June Movement has learned that revolutionary force does not consist of a left "scene," but rather of the mass worker, the apprentice, the imprisoned prole, the rebellious woman in the factory and the neighborhood. But the group has not yet been able to make this strategy clear to everyone, since it hesitates to embellish modest beginnings for propagandistic reasons.

The 2nd of June Movement carries out revolutionary actions when they seem necessary, for example against representatives of the reactionary legal system and against traitors, informants, and the police. An example was the spontaneous attack against the highest representative of West Berlin's courts, von Drenkmann, after the murder of Holger Meins. It encouraged many comrades who felt desperate and powerless to keep fighting. The police held the city under siege for several weeks; they shut down roads and had patrol cars at all major intersections. Despite this, they have not yet been able to find the ones responsible for the action. And despite much drumming up, the West Berlin government could summon no more than fifteen thousand people for a march in von Drenkmann's name. The march was dominated by the state apparatus and the upper class. Meanwhile, the 2nd of June Movement distributed ten thousand leaflets in working-class neighborhoods. Any revolutionary group intending to launch an armed struggle will have to evaluate their experiences.

Realizing the Armed Mass Line

These sketches of the RAF and the 2nd of June Movement show that, within the undogmatic left, there is a choice between anti-imperialist terrorism and the armed mass line. The 2nd of June Movement is still active. It has drawn its conclusions from the demise of the extraparliamentary left and takes guidance from the daily resistance in the factories and working-class neighborhoods. It confirms that the rebellions against work speed-ups, declining wages, rent increases, evictions, and prisons have a mass perspective. If Orwell's *1984* is not to become tomorrow's capitalist reality, the net of surveillance and discipline that determines our lives must be torn apart. The current retreat of the left will only stop when an armed proletarian movement will make the social liberation of the exploited masses possible, regardless of the economic doctrines of the employers and the state.

There is a history of the armed mass line in the German working class. In 1920, the Red Ruhr Army, the partisan movement in central Germany, and armed farmers in Mecklenburg brought large areas under their control. The 1921 uprising in central Germany, as well as the 1923 uprising in Hamburg by an urban guerrilla group, are not simply "heroic battle stories." They are the living memory of old workers.[11] KPD fringe groups shot dead two police counterinsurgency experts during the Weimar period.

In 1943–44, not even public executions could prevent the armed resistance by forced laborers from different countries and young German proletarians. The violent rebellion spread widely. In Berlin, there were illegal groups of the KPD; in Hamburg, there was the Swing Youth (Swing-Jugend); in Cologne, there were the Edelweiss Pirates (Edelweißpiraten). They all chased Nazis out of bombed areas and working-class neighborhoods, and sometimes, when they could get their hands on a machine gun, they killed them. They liberated city blocks and were engaged in bitter battles with SS and Gestapo units.

The resistance continued after the war. This, too, is part of Germany's proletarian legacy. An underground group that survived in Hamburg sank numerous war ships in the city's harbors in the mid-1950s. There is a historical tradition behind the activities of today's armed groups engaged in struggles for revolutionary workers' power and the destruction of the capitalist system.

We are facing two options: either the armed mass line will become resilient enough to survive and continue its attacks, or West Germany will once again become a center of repression, this time enforcing the social massacre against the international workers' movement and the Third World liberation movements together with the USA.

REGARDING THE DEATH OF OUR COMRADE WERNER SAUBER
(1975)

2nd of June Movement

2nd of June Movement leaflet on Werner Sauber being killed during a shootout with police in Cologne.

—

We are calling on you to show practical solidarity with the internationalist and antifascist militant Werner Sauber, who was shot dead by police in Cologne. During many years, comrade Werner Sauber showed great determination in helping to organize the militant and armed struggle, both legally and illegally. We, and the entire revolutionary movement in Europe, have lost a strong militant. His death touches us deeply!!

We know that the police are not our main enemy. Our main enemies are capitalism, the state, and the greed for profit that destroys our lives. But we also know that it is the task of the police to capture us, dead or alive!

Capitalism looks differently in Europe, North America, or the Third World. Sometimes, it is openly fascist and totalitarian; sometimes, it appears "democratic." But the inherent destruction of humankind and the environment is the same everywhere. And everywhere, the governments have decided to exterminate the forces that fight and threaten them. The police are supposed to carry out this extermination. A confrontation with the police is therefore always a question of life or death for the guerrilla. We avoid confrontations with the police because it is not our goal to kill them. Everyone knows that they are hunting us, and that it is not us who are hunting them. But when we are attacked, strike back! Our comrades in Cologne fought bravely, and we are proud of it.

The death of our comrade Werner Sauber is painful. But we also know that the Viet Cong fought for thirty years and lost hundreds of thousands of sisters and brothers. We know that each liberation movement pays for its progress with blood and pain.

We call on all our comrades not to cower in fear. Learn from the Viet Cong! Learn from the heroic Palestinian people! Learn from Werner!

Liberation struggles don't appear out of thin air. They always start with a handful of determined militants. We call on all lawyers to defend each militant with equal zeal regardless of their group affiliation. We call on all doctors to act in solidarity with comrades engaged in armed struggle, providing them with medical care if necessary.

Organize and support the armed struggle! But don't carry out actions in blind rage. Carefully assess your strength, and never underestimate the enemy—particularly not when he carries a social democratic face! Stockholm has shown us what doesn't work!!!!!!![1]

Don't evoke fascism and its tendencies in words and in writing, but become an active part of the resistance against it. To fear fascism contributes to its victory!

LORENZ

THE LORENZ KIDNAPPING
(1995)

Ronald Fritzsch and Ralf Reinders

Interview published in the 1995 Edition ID-Archiv book *Die Bewegung 2. Juni. Gespräche über Haschrebellen, Lorenzentführung, Knast*, based on a series of interviews in the socialist daily *junge Welt*. There are no indications of whether the answer to a question comes from Fritzsch or Reinders.

———

A week after the kidnapping, *Der Spiegel* wrote: "Last Thursday was supposed to be a short day for Lorenz; for the first time in weeks, he was going to come home early. At 8:52 a.m., the leading candidate for the CDU said goodbye to his wife Marianne in Zehlendorf: 'The swans have arrived; it's spring. See you this evening!' Then he rolled away into what would become a very long day, through Grunewald and its single-family homes, his driver Werner Sowa behind the wheel in a black Mercedes, Lorenz's official car. Lorenz would next be seen twenty-four hours later, without his glasses, on a fresh eight-by-ten-centimeter Polaroid photo holding a cardboard sign bearing the word 'prisoner.' Those who had taken the photograph and sent it to dpa had kidnapped him at 8:55 a.m. that Thursday morning (February 27, 1975) about 1,500 meters from his home, after the Mercedes had been blocked by a four-ton truck and rammed by a Fiat, his driver Sowa knocked unconscious with a broomstick." Was that how it happened?

Almost. Except for the broomstick. That was camouflage. It was actually an iron bar wrapped in insulation tape. *Der Spiegel* couldn't know about all the problems we had run into. On one side of Quermatenweg, there's a forest, and on the other side is nothing but villas. The person who knocked down the driver had to stand on the side where the forest was, sweeping. Because Peter Lorenz was an hour late, the person had to sweep for an hour. Luckily, nobody took notice.

How long did you hold Lorenz prisoner?
Five days.

What were your demands?
One demand was that all people arrested at the Holger Meins demo were to be released.[1] We also wanted six prisoners to be flown out of the country: Gabi Kröcher-Tiedemann, Rolf Heißler, Rolf Pohle, Ina Siepmann, Verena Becker, and Horst Mahler.

The action seemed well-prepared. When did you start working on it?
At first, we had planned to do a kidnapping only for a ransom, because we were pretty skint. The bank robberies that we had done had brought in some money, but that was only ever enough for a couple of months. We also used the money to finance legal things like magazines and radio transmitters. So we thought we'd solve the financial problem by grabbing some rich fellow. We figured it could be a training run for a kidnapping to liberate prisoners later on.

We gathered intelligence about some of Berlin's richest people. We found someone we thought we could grab. We nicknamed him "sergeant," in reference to the Beatles album *Sgt. Pepper's Lonely Hearts Club Band*, because his actual name was Pepper. He was the co-owner of the Europa-Center.[2] Based on the information we had, he was worth around 6 million Deutschmark, so that's what he should have been able to cough up. He had his fingers in construction all over the city.

For an action like that, we needed a large basement or two apartments on top of each other. We wanted the person we kidnapped to be held in decent conditions. We didn't want any of those mafia stories, where people are locked into tiny boxes and physically damaged for life. Eventually, we found a store at Schenkendorfstraße 7. When we looked at it, we all agreed on something for the first time during the entire planning phase: this was the place we needed, despite a CDU office being located

right across the street and a police station on Friesenstraße, just around
the corner.

We started to make preparations to kidnap Pepper. We didn't want
the cops to suspect political militants but a gang of regular criminals.
The authorities shouldn't know that we were capable of such actions. We
acquired cars in a different manner than usual. We got them in front of
a post office. At the time, drivers in Berlin would still leave their vehicles
with the motor running. We chose a post office with garages close by.
The drivers had to walk about thirty meters to the postboxes. When a
driver with a suitable vehicle came, they got out of the car, left the motor
running, and it was ours. That's how we got cars for the action without
leaving any traces.

For the handover of the money, the car was to be converted into a
taxi, with a back seat that could be folded down, opening into the trunk.
The plan was for one of us to drive the taxi, pick up the person who would
hand over the money, and then have one of us in the trunk replace the
suitcase with the money with an identical suitcase that was empty. That
way, cops following us would only see two people in a taxi, not knowing
that a handover of money was taking place.

We started working on the basement at the Schenkendorfstraße
store. We stole everything we needed from construction sites. We wanted
to do the kidnapping in early to mid-December 1974, but developments
in the hunger strike of the political prisoners prevented that. The hunger
strike began on September 13, 1974, and lasted until February 5, 1974. The
demand was that the political prisoners be moved into general population and be treated in the same way as anyone else.

Initially, we didn't think the hunger strike would interfere with our
plans. We thought it would last three to four weeks, just like the first two
had done. But that was a huge underestimation. There were plenty of
support actions by legal groups. We took part in many legal—and not
so legal—actions, which meant that there wasn't much time to prepare
for bigger things. Most importantly, with the death of Holger Meins on
November 9, 1974, and the assassination of the district court president
Drenkmann the next day, there was little maneuvering room for the
kidnapping of Pepper. (The Drenkmann action was a direct response by
the 2nd of June Movement to Holger's death.)

We had planned the Pepper action for the Christmas season to capitalize on Christmas spirit. The manhunt after the Drenkmann killing

made it clear that if we later wanted to kidnap Lorenz, we needed more preparation. There was no time to pull off both actions. But the timeline for Lorenz was already set because of the election for the Berlin senate on March 2, 1975. So, eventually, we let the Pepper kidnapping go, even though this created some serious financial problems.

What was the objective of the Lorenz kidnapping?
To get prisoners out, and to boost our spirits. They weren't high at the time. The hunger strike resulting in Holger's death was a hard blow. There was a strong response, but psychologically many of us were badly affected. We also wanted to show that it was possible to confront the seemingly all-powerful state. Later, in prison, we had long discussions about whether the Lorenz kidnapping had been a mistake, because it seemed that it had prompted an almost exclusive focus on liberating prisoners, meaning that everything now was about the prisoners, while not much was happening politically.

We wanted the action to be a success. We wouldn't have done it had we not believed that there was a realistic chance for an exchange of prisoners. When the RAF's Commando Holger Meins occupied the German embassy in April 1975, it demanded the release of twenty-six prisoners—we assumed that the state would never let that many people go. We figured that six or seven people would be the maximum. Afterward, we were criticized for a preemptive compromise; some people didn't like that we hadn't tried the impossible.

There were long discussions about who to put on the list. We wanted to have someone included from each faction. We had thought of Ulrike Meinhof. Apart from her, there were Andreas Baader, Jan-Carl Raspe, and Gudrun Ensslin in Stammheim. We figured that they would never let all four of them go. But then the Stammheim prisoners said that they wanted to decide on who to put on the list.

You asked those in Stammheim?
We had to be very vague, of course, but they understood. Their response was: We have heard about a dozen planned liberation actions but none from the Berlin underground. Two or three weeks later, they discussed the issue again and asked us to explain in a letter to them what our plans were. We thought they had gone nuts. Several women at the Lehrter Straße prison—mostly RAF prisoners, but also Ina Siepmann—said: "All or none!"

Eventually, we decided to cut communication with the RAF prisoners, and we included none of them on the list. We made this decision knowing that the RAF was planning a liberation action of its own anyway. They wanted Revolutionary Cells and 2nd of June members to be part of it. Revolutionary Cells member Wilfried Böse was in Berlin at the time, trying to recruit people. We didn't know that this was about Stockholm. It all happened shortly before the Lorenz kidnapping.

The RAF plans for Stockholm were basically ready, and they wanted two or three of us to join. We declined. First, because we didn't like how the RAF had gone about it, and second, because of the method. They spoke about one action on the ground and one in the air. That translated into an occupation of the embassy and the hijacking of a plane. We said that we categorically rejected that.

Why?
Hijackings were primarily carried out by Palestinian groups. We had discussed this, and we figured they were doing it to draw attention to their specific cause. We didn't think it was our place to judge them, but for us, we rejected taking uninvolved third parties hostage. We figured that was counterrevolutionary. We refused to attack the people we were trying to mobilize for political action. And if you occupy an embassy, the enemy knows where you are and you can easily get trapped.

Back to the Lorenz action . . .
In the beginning, we had thought to only liberate prisoners who were serving time in Berlin. We didn't know who would make the final decision among the politicians. Later, we learned that there were two factions in the "Crisis Committee" in Bonn: the Strauß/Kohl faction was willing to do the exchange, while the Schmidt/Wehner faction followed a hard line: "We won't do it!"[3] Then the mayor of Berlin, Klaus Schütz, said that he'd offer a local solution if the federal government rejected an exchange, because he wanted to maintain "trading relations" with us. That caused the Crisis Committee to give in.

What were the different factions that the prisoners came from?
Before we called ourselves the 2nd of June Movement, we had carried out actions under different names. The two of us, for example, were previously in a group that called itself Tupamaros West Berlin. In Munich, there was

the Tupamaros Munich, and in the Ruhr Valley, there was the Red Ruhr Army. Rolf Heißler came out of the Tupamaros Munich and gravitated toward the RAF. But the main reason why he got on the list was that he was experiencing the worst solitary confinement of any prisoner in West Germany—the Bavarians held him in complete isolation. He was serving eight years for bank robbery. Rolf Pohle was also from the Tupamaros Munich; he was serving six years for buying weapons and minor things like faking a university degree. Horst Mahler was a founding member of the RAF who was serving twelve years for membership in a terrorist organization and bank robbery. By then, he had come close to one of the K-groups, the KPD/AO. Gabi Kröcher-Tiedemann was a former member of the Red Ruhr Army who was serving eight years for shooting at cops. Verena Becker and Ina Siepmann were from our group; Ina was doing thirteen years for bank robbery, Verena seven years for a bombing.

As we said, we had carefully considered how many prisoners we wanted to put on the list. We thought the most we could get out were five or six—and we couldn't get out six people serving life sentences, that would have been difficult too.

Didn't you ask other people from the 2nd of June Movement if they wanted to get out as well?
We asked Peter-Paul Zahl. He had been sentenced to four years in prison and said he didn't want to be included because it wasn't worth it. Then the prosecutors appealed his sentence, and he got fifteen years. That was really bad luck.

We also talked to Sigurd Debus.[4] But there was only one of us who knew him, and that person had nothing good to say about him. He called Debus a "Stalinist" who would do his thing without consideration for others. He also said that Debus would pose a risk for us in the Middle East after a possible release. In hindsight, it was a mistake to exclusively rely on one person's opinion.

Did the prisoners who were flown out indicate that they were okay with that?
We hadn't been able to reach all of them.

Who decided on the final list?
The list was discussed by everyone involved in the action. The final

decision was made when Lorenz was in the basement and we were typing out the demands.

How many people were involved in the action?
Six to fifteen.

Tell us about the planning.
That we'd take Lorenz was pretty clear from the outset. The polls indicated that Lorenz would win the election as the CDU front-runner. We figured that the ruling SPD would not let the projected winner of the election be put to the sword. We had also briefly discussed Lummer.[5]

That would have been tempting.
But he's among the people you can't really let go again. Besides, we wanted to succeed. Lorenz was too liberal for many in the CDU. Lummer, on the other hand, had paid his NPD buddies to paint Juso slogans on CDU posters.[6]

Lummer was lucky not to be a front-runner. It would have been embarrassing for him had we stuffed him into a shoebox—he's pretty tiny. However, he would have been much easier for us to carry than Lorenz.

When did things really get moving?
It all became pretty concrete during Christmas 1974. Everyone involved in the action gathered for a Christmas meeting. First, we fried a fish and put a goose in the oven. Then we sat down and, once more, read a collection of Tupamaros texts, especially a story about a kidnapping.[7] It was a hilarious story: The anesthetics didn't work on the guy they had kidnapped because he was an alcoholic. They had given him shots, but the guy just kept on blabbering, he simply got high. Once we were confronted with Lorenz, we understood what they had been writing about . . .

The next day, we used toy cars to stage the plan with the core group. We sketched all stages of the action and started dividing up tasks. Later, the group almost split. The reason were two people who fucked around a lot and were very quirky. One never did what he was supposed to do, and the other flashed his gun around at a youth center.

How was this resolved?
Well, the two of them had to engage in what was called "self-criticism." But we also had an objective problem: we only had eight weeks left. There

was no shortage of people we could have asked to replace the two, but they knew everything about the plan and had taken on tasks.

In January, we cleared out all our safe houses, because we figured that the search would be very intense. We hid a lot of stuff and buried all the weapons we didn't need at the time. It was quite difficult to recollect them—trees grow! When we were in prison, someone tried to locate some of the weapons. Well, explain to someone how to find things in the woods. One time, we tried to find a depot that our Swiss friend Säuberli [Werner Sauber] had set up. We dug and dug and were close to giving up. But we told ourselves, "That man is Swiss, we'll keep on digging!" And indeed, right when we thought we'd hit groundwater, we found the weapons. Säuberli did everything very properly.

After Christmas, we checked out Lorenz's routes. It was hard not to be detected in the area where he lived. He followed the same routine every day. His driver arrived and waited briefly by the door. Then Lorenz came out and got in the passenger seat. Everything unfolded like clockwork, every day. Only on the day of the kidnapping, he was an hour late . . .

We never came close to Lorenz, always just observed him from a distance. We had estimated that he was about six feet tall and weighed about 180 pounds. We needed those measurements to get him into the box. But on the day of the kidnapping, we realized we had a problem. He was gigantic and really heavy! We weren't even able to close the box, although he was very cooperative—nothing to complain about there, he was a good prisoner.

As we were scheming the kidnapping, there were numerous technical problems to solve: How to stop the car? How to get the driver out? How to keep Lorenz quiet? There was also the medical challenge of using an anesthetic. None of us knew anything about it. After much medical study and advice from, eh, "experts," we settled on haloperidol, because we were told that it wouldn't affect Lorenz's natural reflexes, and we didn't want him to choke on his tongue.

To stop his car, we used a truck that we had rented with phony papers. Then came the psychological challenge: How do we get the driver out of the car? The plan was: A truck would pull out of a side street and force Lorenz's car to stop. Then a woman driver would rear-end it. She would be wearing a pretty blonde wig and act all scared. The way guys are, we were sure that the driver would get out to comfort her. And he did, it worked perfectly—you should have seen him get out, estimate the damage, and be all cocky, like, "Well, honey, what have you done now?" Next thing he knew, he got whacked over the head.

But we almost blew it. The car rear-ending Lorenz's car had a radio and was meant to let the people in the truck know when Lorenz was coming. But when the people in the truck saw a black Mercedes approaching, they pulled out despite not having received a radio instruction, assuming that the radio was damaged. Yet that Mercedes was the official car of the president of the district court Schertz, who would later become West Berlin's chief of police. Schertz testified that he had noticed a truck first pull out and then back up, and that it seemed suspicious. We had come close to grabbing the wrong guy!

After Lorenz's driver had been knocked out cold, four of us jumped into Lorenz's car—two in the back, one grabbed the steering wheel, and one sat down on Lorenz's lap. In that configuration, we drove to an underground garage. As a cover, a second car followed. To change cars, we had chosen a perfectly suited garage on Kantstraße. But the person waiting there had been waiting a whole hour, not knowing what was going on, because he had no radio.

How did Lorenz react?
At first, he cried for help and struggled, kicking out the front window. His legs were bloody long. It all happened very quickly. Then he got punched in the nose and was told that he should think of Drenkmann and be quiet. He muttered, "Okay, okay, it's all good." Then someone cut open his pants and gave him the anesthetic. Lorenz was sitting in the passenger seat, with someone sitting on top of him, and from behind somebody was wrapping something around his head, a towel. That made him look even bigger. He was also wearing handcuffs.

So you drove off with a guy with a towel around his head and someone else sitting on his lap, with three more people in the car, and no windshield?
Yes, at 100 miles per hour on Avus.[8] Later, a witness who passed us came forward. He had been driving 75 miles per hour himself but claimed that he'd be able to identify a person in the driver's seat who was wearing a red tie.

We stopped at an autobahn exit, near the Funkturm.[9] The sight of us didn't bother anyone. There were cars next to us, and pedestrians looked in, but no one showed any reaction. In the underground garage, everything was quiet. Only the second car had had a hard time keeping up. It was a brand-new stolen car, but the clutch was fucked up.

Was Lorenz dazed by then?
Not yet. In the underground garage, he was transferred to the trunk of the other car. We had chosen a route where we avoided all throughways to Kreuzberg. We assumed that the cops would shut down all the major intersections. That was some drive . . .

Der Spiegel wrote: "Minutes after the kidnapping, the police launched the largest manhunt in the history of West Berlin: five helicopters, two hundred patrol cars, ten thousand cops, a 100,000 Deutschmark reward, and another 50,000 Deutschmark promised from the right-wing Bund Freies Deutschland."[10] Did you notice any of it?
At the time, no. One of us tried everything to keep Lorenz calm, but he blabbered on endlessly, wanting to know what was going to happen to him and so on. He really got on our nerves. Later, the police searched for a luxury limousine with a large trunk to hold Lorenz. That was our experience after the bank robberies: the police mostly stopped large cars. But you have no idea how large the trunk of a Golf can be.

We drove to a cemetery on a small side street in the Hasenheide area of Kreuzberg, where we had a clear view of the Friesenstraße police station entrance. We had parked a Ford Transit at the cemetery, and that's where we put Lorenz in the box. That was at 9:30 a.m. Then we drove to the store on Schenkendorfstraße. Then came the hardest part, because we had to get him into the store. Three old women were standing on the street yacking, as old people tend to do. The box itself was heavy enough without Lorenz—and now we had to carry him too! Don't let anybody say that being a revolutionary isn't hard work! And not all of us could help carry, because some had to drive the second car to a garage in Neukölln. On top of it all, the box suddenly opened, because Lorenz was nervous—but at least he was no longer yapping. I guess the anesthetic had finally had some effect. At that point, one hour had passed since he had gotten the shot.

What did you do about the old ladies?
Nothing, we could have waited forever. We just walked past them.

Were there four of you carrying the box?

Yes. Once we were inside the store, Lorenz had to climb down a ladder. We had made an extra opening to get to the basement, which now consisted of two rooms separated by a wall we had put in. One room had a very low ceiling and was accessible through a hatch on the ground floor. The other room was underneath the kitchen, where we had created the extra opening. The opening was covered by a carpet. This was the room we had prepared for Lorenz.

You were armed during the kidnapping, weren't you? What would you have done if the driver had been armed and fired?

That's why he got whacked over the head: to be on the safe side. We also patted him down to make sure. One of us was there with a semiautomatic pistol. We wanted to avoid a shootout at all costs. Had there been a fatality, chances for a prisoner exchange would have been minimal.

But you did whack the driver over the head with an iron bar . . .

We discussed that quite a bit; it's something that needs to be discussed quite a bit.

Did you practice? It seems hard to hit someone over the head with an iron bar without killing him.

It was done by someone with experience. A boxer who knew how hard he could hit. He dished out the blow with precision.

Once we were in the store, everybody took a good look at Lorenz. He wanted to talk to the bosses—the commandant or whatever. We said that we had no bosses.

Did you disguise yourselves?

We wore overalls that covered us, boiler suits with long arms. We also had hoods, homemade from sheets, with slits in them. During the action itself, everyone was disguised, with beards and so forth.

But Lorenz was blind anyway. He had glasses as thick as Teufel's, something around seven diopters. We hadn't known that, since he usually wore much thinner glasses for press photos.

In Lorenz's room, we had made a cell out of wire mesh. There was a red curtain, which we discreetly closed when he had to go to the toilet.

Next to the cell was the ladder leading up to the kitchen. The other room in the basement was used by the guards.

Lorenz had a cot, a bucket, a table, a chair, and a gymnastic program pinned to the wall with suggestions for morning exercises. It was pretty much like a regular prison cell. He had a lamp, even two. He also got reading material, political literature, although we censored the daily newspapers we gave him. We cut out everything related to the kidnapping. We did that so he wouldn't get any hidden messages. Essentially, he only got a few opinion pieces to read, and the ads. The newspapers we gave him looked like cutouts. That was the only thing he later complained about; he didn't like that. Another reason for censoring everything related to the kidnapping was that it might have made him anxious following the search closely. From the very first moment, he told us that his biggest fear was that the cops would find us. The "boys," as he always called them, he only spoke of the "boys."

That was his biggest fear?
Yes, he wasn't particularly afraid of us killing him, more of them killing him. He thought that if they found us, they might just fire indiscriminately and kill everyone, him included.

When Lorenz was in the basement, did you tell him who you were?
Yes, when we took that well-known photo. He resisted a bit; he didn't want to hold the sign. It didn't help that we were all sick. One of us had caught the flu and given it to everyone else.

Lorenz always insisted that he had been treated well by us. In the evening, he was bored and wanted to watch TV. We didn't allow him to watch the news, but, together with the guards, he was allowed to watch— what was it called?—oh yes, *Ohnsorg Theater*.[11] During the trial, he said that this made him realize that we could laugh too.

Didn't you also sew a button on his clothes for him?
We repaired his pants.

Well, it was you who had damaged them.
He got new underwear. We also played chess with him.

Masked?

In court he was asked whether he won in chess, and he said, "Yes, once in a while," but added that he was under the impression that we had let him win.

What did you do after you took the photo with the sign?
We wrote the first communiqué. Two people were always upstairs and two downstairs, so we had to do a lot of running around, since everybody wanted to have a say.

And then you wrote the following:

> This morning, armed women and men from the 2nd of June Movement took Peter Lorenz, the Berlin CDU chairman and front-runner for the March 2 parliamentary election, prisoner. The kidnapping had to happen with arms, since Lorenz was prepared for the scenario: his driver and bodyguard was armed too. Peter Lorenz is now a prisoner of the 2nd of June Movement. As such, he is not being tortured or treated inhumanely, contrary to the more than sixty thousand prisoners in the penitentiaries of West Germany and West Berlin. As our prisoner, he will fare better than the prisoners in the state's prisons. But he will not be as comfortable as he is at his Zehlendorf villa. Peter Lorenz will be interrogated. He will have to talk about his connections to industry, to capital, and to fascist governments. Lorenz was kidnapped by us because, as a representative of the reactionaries and the bigwigs, he is responsible for the speed-ups and the rigid regime at the factories, for the formation of security units on the shop floor and anti-guerrilla units on the streets, for professional bans, for stern demonstration laws, for limiting the rights of defense attorneys, and for upholding the discriminatory section 218.[12] As a big figure in the CDU, he has acted as a propagandist for Zionism and Israel's aggressive, expansionist policies in Palestine. Through visits and donations to Israel, he has actively participated in the persecution and oppression of the Palestinian people. He has also got his hands dirty by supporting the military coup in Chile by Pinochet and his cohorts. His party funds the junta's repression through generous financial contributions—a repression that tries to annihilate any form of free thought, eradicating it brutally. Thousands of Chileans

are tortured in concentration camps, while the junta stays in power due to daily bloodbaths.

Our demands are:

1. The immediate release and annulment of convictions of all those arrested and charged in connection with demonstrations following the death of the revolutionary Holger Meins. This demand must be met within twenty-four hours.

2. The immediate release of: Verena Becker, Gabriele Kröcher-Tiedemann, Horst Mahler, Rolf Pohle, Ina Siepmann, and Rolf Heißler. Kröcher, Pohle, and Heißler are held in West Germany and have to be brought to West Berlin within forty-eight hours. In West Berlin, a fully fueled Boeing 707 with a four-man crew shall be waiting for them. The prisoners will then be accompanied by a public figure until they have reached their final destination. This public figure is the pastor and former Berlin mayor Heinrich Albertz. The six comrades shall also receive 20,000 Deutschmark each. These demands must be met within seventy-two hours.

3. This statement must be published in the following daily newspapers: *Berliner Zeitung, Tagesspiegel, Abend, Hamburger Morgenpost, Weserkurier, Hannoversche Allgemeine Zeitung, Westdeutsche Allgemeine Zeitung, Frankfurter Rundschau, Süddeutsche Zeitung, Kölner Stadtanzeiger, Neue Rhein/Ruhr Zeitung, tz, Frankfurter Allgemeine Zeitung.*

4. During the entire time that Lorenz is imprisoned, we demand a ceasefire on the part of the police. No weapons, no patrols, no checkpoints, no raids, no arrests, no wanted posters, no requests for information from the public.

Noncompliance with these demands or attempts to deceive us pose a serious threat to the prisoner's well-being. All of the demands are equally important.

We are not interested in secret negotiations. Government messages, the liberation of the prisoners, including the departure of their flight, must be broadcast on television and the radio. If all demands will be met, the well-being and the release of the prisoner Lorenz is guaranteed. Otherwise, the consequences for him will be the same as they were for district court president G. v. Drenkmann.

To the comrades in prison: We wish we could get more of you out, but, currently, we don't have the strength to do so.

To the population of Berlin: The state authorities will carry out a smear campaign against us in the coming days. They will try to involve you in the hunt for us. Don't support them, let the police, the fat cats, and the media be by themselves.

Freedom for all prisoners!

How did you deliver this and your other communiqués?
We used dead mailboxes. This is how it worked: we put up extra mailboxes in old houses where nobody noticed, and then only we would use them. So one of us went from Schenkendorfstraße to one of the mailboxes, and then someone else would pick up the communiqué and forward it.

The first communiqué went to dpa and some other places. All of the communiqués were sent or delivered to at least three addresses. In the beginning, to media outlets, then to other people named Peter Lorenz. We just found them in the phone book. We also sent the communiqués to priests. We figured that you could put something like that under any door-mat, and four out of five people would forward it. The first communiqué included two photographs of Lorenz with his glasses on—he insisted on that, and for those photographs he also sat down properly.

Was there a search?
Yes, but only by undercover cops. The police tried to buy time. They needed to confirm whether Lorenz was still alive. The first photograph we sent could have been of his dead body, you couldn't see.

What else happened on the Thursday of the kidnapping?
Nothing. By the evening, Lorenz was fairly lucid again, so we tried to interrogate him. We had prepared questions about his activities in the CDU and his connections to the Berlin construction mafia. We set up a tape recorder, but we weren't experienced interrogators, and we gave up after an hour. We didn't want to be abusive to get him to speak, and he refused to say anything. In the following days, he became more talk-ative, especially because we were no longer taping. He said something about the "suffering" of the Christian Democrats in Chile. With regard to Palestine, he said that the people of Israel must be allowed to live in peace. We agreed, but added that the Palestinians must not pay the price for it.

For the most part, the things Lorenz told us were pretty banal. He was down there in the basement, we had all taken a good look at him, and then we started to wonder: Who was going to kill him if our plan went south? We no longer saw him as a pig, just as a rather naive fellow.

What about the next day?

We still had his briefcase. It contained a check for 10,000 Deutschmark from—who was that guy?—yes, Klingbeil.[13] A campaign contribution to the CDU. Klingbeil was known as a firm SPD supporter, because the SPD had helped him get all of the construction contracts in Berlin. We also found documents about planned price hikes in public transport that hadn't been announced yet. There were also documents about expected layoffs at the DeTeWe telecommunications company. Finally, we found letters to Lorenz from the mother of a disabled child. He didn't want to comment on them.

We had to close one dead mailbox, because on Friday, Rainer Hochstein, who was in contact with several of our people, was arrested in Hamburg. Luckily, he only knew about that one mailbox. We had refused to involve him in any of our actions, which is why he later offered himself to the federal prosecutors as a crown witness. The fool ended up where he belonged.[14]

What was your plan in case the cops would find the hiding place?

We didn't really have one. I think we said that in such a case we would forget about our demands and simply try to get out of there. But it would have been an unpleasant situation.

Was the place in any way secured?

We felt very secure. We had a camera monitoring the entrance. The guards had a screen downstairs.

We wrote our second communiqué on Friday. It went to Marianne Lorenz, the CDU Berlin headquarters, the dpa, Bishop Scharf, and the Berlin senate. It added little to the first communiqué, and the only purpose was to let people know that we were serious. Lorenz's wife also received a personal note from her husband: "The police shall do everything it takes to get me out of here unharmed. With love, your Peter." The communiqué itself read as follows:

> We demand from the abovementioned people and organizations
> to try to ensure that our first communiqué, which was sent to the

dpa, United Press International, and the Berlin senate, shall be read aloud during all of the ARD news broadcasts. The photographs of Lorenz's imprisonment must be shown as well. If you are interested in the prisoner Peter Lorenz being freed unharmed, you must also try to ensure that the conditions listed in the first communiqué will be met immediately. If the demands are not fulfilled, the ultimatum expires on Saturday at 12 p.m.

We wanted Lorenz to give us the name of a person he trusted, and ironically it was Pepper. So we called him. We asked him whether there was anything he could do for Lorenz. He just hung up; he wanted nothing to do with it. "I'll remember that," Lorenz said.

How did the police and the Crisis Committee communicate with you?
Through the media. Sometimes, they announced that there would be a message in the ARD evening news. On Friday, March 1, the following police statement was broadcast over SFB and RIAS[15] at five minutes past midnight:

> The police are turning to Peter Lorenz's kidnappers. First: The people arrested in connection with the demonstration after the death of Holger Meins have already been freed for some time, with the exception of Ettore Canella and Günter Jagdmann. These two will be released from prison on March 1, 1975, at 10 a.m. Second: You must provide us with convincing evidence that Peter Lorenz is still alive. Third: We are making every effort not to threaten the health and well-being of Peter Lorenz. To avoid any misunderstandings, it is necessary to clarify certain things. For example: How do you foresee the handover of Peter Lorenz, and how can you guarantee that he will remain unharmed? What will happen if any of the people on your list refuse to be flown out of the country? Fourth: As proof that we are dealing with the right people, give us Peter Lorenz's personal ID number.

How did you know this was going to be aired at five minutes past midnight?
Do you think that we ever turned off the radio, even just for five minutes? Usually, the messages were announced far in advance and repeated several times. They also used the messages to help the search by broadcasting them late at night. On the fourth night, they deployed all their

satellite trucks, because they hoped that at 4 a.m. not many television sets would be turned on in Berlin. But the whole city was glued to the television. In fact, the only ones not watching TV that night were us; we were so exhausted that even our guards had fallen asleep.

On Saturday, at 10 a.m., they released the last two people arrested at the Holger Meins demo. The authorities won some time by that, but it didn't bother us. When Jagdmann, an obvious drunk, was released, all the reporters jumped on him, but he just said: "I have absolutely nothing to do with it, I don't know anything about it." Then Canella got out, they all rushed toward him, but he just took to his heels and made a run for it. Jagdmann had randomly ended up at the demo, he had said so himself. He said that there had been trouble at home that day, that he had drowned his sorrow in alcohol, happened to come across the demo, and threw a rock at a cop—that was it. The proceedings were closed, and neither Jagdmann nor Canella ever heard from the cops again.

After the media had published our first communiqué, and Jagdmann and Canella had been released, it was clear to us that we were in control. On Saturday morning, March 1, we issued our third communiqué. We dropped it off at different addresses, among others the Protestant parish office in Zehlendorf. It read:

> If any of the comrades on our list do not want to be released, they should inform us of this in the presence of their lawyer during the SFB evening news on March 1, 1975. Our ultimatum will not be extended. It expires on Monday, March 3, at 9 a.m. By then, the released comrades and Pastor Albertz must have departed. After Albertz's return, we will clarify the modalities of Peter Lorenz's release. His well-being is exclusively in the hands of the state. We have not forgotten Fürstenfeldbruck and Rammelmayr.[16] If the police are preparing for a similar operation, it means Peter Lorenz's certain death. This is our final communiqué until our demands will be fulfilled.

Was this your final communiqué?
Nope. That evening, at 8 p.m., Pastor Albertz made a statement on radio and TV:

> I speak to you as a man of the cloth, ready and obliged to protect human life. That is why I immediately agreed to cooperate in this

difficult situation. However, I can only do so if the risk and danger is not on my side alone. The proposal presented to me by the mayor is unsatisfactory with regard to the safe release of Peter Lorenz. To fulfill my mission, I must receive a different answer than the one I have received so far. I have made myself available under the condition that I feel certain about the safe release of Peter Lorenz when I meet with you or your friends. For your part, you can rest assured that I will not participate in any undertaking that ends the way things ended in Fürstenfeldbruck.

Immediately afterward there was a statement from the police:

You have heard Pastor Albertz's statement: inform us immediately about the modalities of Peter Lorenz's release. To ensure who we are communicating with, tell us the name of the place where the wooden carving in the hallway of the Lorenz's house was purchased.

Clearly, these were things that only Lorenz could know.
Shortly before midnight, Mahler declared on the ARD news that he declined to be released:

To kidnap the enemy of the people Peter Lorenz in order to free political prisoners is the result of a politics detached from the struggles of the working class. It will inevitably lead to a dead end. The strategy of individual terror is not the strategy of the proletariat.

That was broadcast on TV. In a written statement, Mahler added:

During the show trial against Becker, Meinhof, and me in September last year, I made a public criticism that was, at the same time, a self-criticism, clarifying that my place was on the side of the revolutionary working class. I am firmly convinced that the struggle of the revolutionary masses will open the prison doors for all political prisoners and that the terrorist convictions against me will be swept away—which is why I reject being removed from this country in this way. . . . Long live the KPD!

In 1980, Mahler was released on parole. The prison doors were not opened for him by the revolutionary masses but by him crawling through

"Baum's tunnel."[17] After his release, Mahler got his revenge on the working class by training managers responsible for their oppression.[18]

Gabriele Kröcher-Tiedemann also declared that she did not want to be exchanged for Lorenz. The next day, however, at 10 p.m., Rolf Pohle demanded a telephone conversation with her, which the cops agreed to. After that, Kröcher-Tiedemann decided to come along. Later, when we could read her files, we understood the reason for her change of heart. Her initial refusal was based on a promise that she would only serve half or two-thirds of her sentence. But when she demanded a confirmation in writing, she never received it.

Was the telephone call your idea?
No, it was Rolf's initiative.

How did you react when two people declined to be freed?
It was quite a shock for us. Two! "Have they all lost their minds now? They're going nuts!" Those were the kinds of things we said. But we figured if they wanted to stay behind, they should serve their sentences. In the case of Kröcher-Tiedemann, we figured that she was just confused.

Did Lorenz know about any of that?
No. Although he probably heard us stomping about.

Did you consider demanding the release of other prisoners instead of the ones who declined?
We did consider it, yes. But the problem was that by naming two new people, the other side would have argued that it was impossible to keep the agreed-upon schedule, and we didn't want to back out of that. Then the following message reached us at midnight on Saturday:

> The police are addressing the kidnappers of Peter Lorenz once again. They have received communiqué no. 3. No further numbered communiqués have been received.
>
> 1. The police are assuming that Peter Lorenz is still alive.
>
> 2. It seems likely that only two prisoners are willing to be flown to Berlin. As you have heard, it is only possible for them to reach their ultimate destination via an airport in West Germany.

Therefore, it seems appropriate to assemble all the prisoners there. We await your response.

3. You have heard Pastor Albertz's statement, which clarified that a plan for the safe release of Peter Lorenz is mandatory.

4. You can rest assured that the objective of previous and future negotiations is solely to ensure the survival and well-being of Peter Lorenz.

5. Your means of negotiation make it very difficult to meet your demands. Choose a faster way.

6. To prove that the police are still negotiating with the right people, tell us where Frau Lorenz's wristwatch was purchased.

What kind of discussions did this prompt among yourselves?
There was not a lot of discussion at that point. You must understand that we had hardly slept in days. The overall mood, however, was great, because the cops' first statement had made it pretty clear that things were unfolding according to plan. The police complied with the demands to publish our communiqué and to release the demonstrators. So, up to that point, everything had gone smoothly. But it was clear that they were trying to buy time. The cops assumed that we would name a lawyer for handling the negotiations. That's why they were talking about a "faster way to negotiate." They hoped that this would lead them to us.

What did Lorenz think about all this?
He knew about our demands, but he knew nothing about the state of negotiations. All he ever wanted to know was what Biedenkopf's position was. Biedenkopf was the CDU strongman at the time. He was the party's general secretary and Kohl's adversary. When we told Lorenz that Biedenkopf supported the exchange of prisoners, he seemed relieved and optimistic.[19] From that point on, he assumed that our plan would work.

Then we released a communiqué accepting the decisions by Kröcher-Tiedemann and Mahler. We placed it in a postbox on Kurfürstendamm, together with a tape. At around 3 a.m., we called the cops and told them that they could find it there. It read:

> We accept the decisions made by Kröcher and Mahler. The imprisoned revolutionaries Siepmann, Becker, Heißler, and Pohle must be brought to Frankfurt/Main immediately. Pastor Albertz must fly

there with the comrades from Berlin. In Frankfurt, the comrades must have the opportunity to talk among themselves without supervision. Furthermore, they must be shown all of our communiqués. All four comrades shall then have the opportunity to declare, at the beginning of the 12:45 p.m. ARD news on Sunday, March 2, 1975, whether they wish to be flown out of the country or not. Herr Albertz and the comrades who have agreed to be flown out must depart before 9 a.m. on Monday in a Boeing 707 with a four-man crew. The comrades must receive the money (120,000 Deutschmark total) that we have demanded. P. Lorenz himself will speak about the modalities of his liberation on the accompanying tape. For us to know that the state has received this fourth communiqué, the contents must be read out on SFB immediately after its reception. Wristwatch = Madrid.

We had demanded 20,000 Deutschmark for each released comrade. When it became clear that not everyone wanted to be flown out, we still insisted on a total of 120,000 Deutschmark. The cops insisted on 20,000 Deutschmark per person, to which Rolf Pohle responded that we had demanded in writing a total of 120,000. After that, he received another 20,000, but later he also received an additional three-and-a-half-year sentence in Bavaria for extortionate robbery, simply because he had insisted that our demands be fulfilled.

In Lorenz's message on the tape, he thanked Albertz in advance, and added:

You yourself, Pastor Albertz, want to make sure that no catastrophe like the one in Munich will happen and, therefore, you want to know how and where I will be freed. My captors do not feel that they can announce the modalities because it would put them at risk. They say that they wouldn't trust the police, no matter what they guarantee. But I have received my captors' word of honor that I will be released immediately and without harm once you, Pastor Albertz, have returned by plane to Germany. I trust them to keep their word. Please send my warmest regards to my wife!

The cops confirmed the reception of our communiqué and the tape.

And then what happened on Sunday?

The Berlin election was held. The mood was very strange. On the one hand, the authorities acted tough; they held the elections and would not let themselves be blackmailed by anarchists. On the other hand, nobody talked about anything but the kidnapping; it was the only topic in every bar in town. Well, it's not too common that the winner of an election has just been kidnapped. The CDU with Lorenz got the majority of the votes, even if it was only half the increase that had been predicted. We went downstairs to Lorenz and said, "Herr Lorenz, congratulations, it seems that you'll be the next mayor of Berlin!" He beamed with joy.

Was he allowed to see the election results?
Sure.

And he remained calm the entire time?
He was cooperative. He didn't even complain about the food. We don't know who cooked that day, but it was terrible—worse than in prison.

And then you were anxious all night, wondering what would happen the next day?
Yes, the tension was growing, because at 2 p.m. on Sunday, the cops informed us that the prisoners would be flown to Frankfurt that day:

> The police are addressing Peter Lorenz's kidnappers with regard to the following. March 2, 1975, 2 p.m.: The prisoners Becker and Siepmann will leave Berlin for Frankfurt/Main today. Pohle and Heißler will also be in Frankfurt. . . . The schedule that you demanded cannot be met. . . . It is essential that you name the final destination of your flight now, so that the necessary arrangements can be made.

In the early morning hours of March 3, we dropped a letter addressed to "The Senate!! Code word: Gerd!!" in a mailbox on Marburger Straße. Once again, we informed the police where to pick it up:

> Communiqué no. 5.
>   1. We will not specify a destination. The pilot will receive instructions in the air.
>   2. The ultimatum will be extended for one hour. We demand that the boarding of the five comrades and Heinrich Albertz will

be broadcast on the ARD news at 10 a.m. The prisoners' statement
from Monday, 4 a.m., must also be broadcast.

3. The Boeing 707 must be fully fueled and depart with a four-
man crew.

4. Heinrich Albertz is no hostage.

5. Peter Lorenz and we are waiting for the immediate departure
of the five comrades and Heinrich Albertz.

We later learned that the federal government and the state governments involved had already decided to meet our demands before
receiving the communiqué: "The governments involved have decided
to accept the kidnappers' demands, because it still seems—shortly before
the ultimatum expires—that this decision is the only way to save Peter
Lorenz's life." The prisoners received the requested 120,000 Deutschmark,
and Ina Siepmann made a short statement that was broadcast on TV,
declaring at Frankfurt airport that they were about to depart. At around
9 a.m., they all boarded the plane, which departed at 9:56 a.m. in the
direction of Salzburg. The footage from boarding the Boeing 707 and the
departure of the airplane were shown on TV all day long.

**But it seems that you didn't have any way of verifying that they had
boarded a real airplane and taken off, that this wasn't just staged,
and that there really was an airplane flying them out?**
Well, Albertz pretty much guaranteed for that. We had also made sure
that Albertz got a code word from the prisoners after they had landed.
They were supposed to write a short statement in which the code word
was embedded. Albertz was to read the statement on TV upon his return.
That's how we were to know that the comrades had landed safely. We
were always updated about the position of the plane, so we could check
that everything went as planned. Had the prisoners been brought to a
different destination, Albertz would not have received the code word, and
we would have known that our agreement had been broken. Lorenz would
not have been released. We had explicitly said that there must be no
stopovers.

**But doesn't that mean that you had to be certain that a kite with the
code word had made it into prison?**
That had been confirmed to us.

Did the cops investigate this afterward?

Not sure. In any case, they never found out who the code word was delivered to.

What was the code word?

"Such a day, as wonderful as today." The kite didn't just contain the code word, but also the route. The information was very detailed. First, head to Rome, then, shortly before Rome, tell the pilot to head to Tripoli, then to Addis Ababa, then finally to Aden. Because everything was broadcast on the radio, we always knew where the plane was and that everything was going according to plan. We didn't want the cops to know the final destination. We wanted to confuse them, we sent greetings to Libya as we entered their airspace, things like that. On the radio, they always said they didn't know where the plane was headed. That's why we had chosen a Boeing 707. We had calculated beforehand how far it could fly. Rolf Pohle instructed the pilot.[20]

Did the crew really consist of no more than four people?

They wanted to double the crew, but the freed prisoners rejected that. The cops sent a second crew in another airplane trailing them.

So there were two airplanes?

Actually, three. The third one was carrying the state secretary for the chancellor's office, the experienced secret diplomat Wischnewski, "Ben Wisch."[21] He had a suitcase with 6 million Deutschmark with him to buy the prisoners back from the South Yemen government in exchange for a development project.

But how did he know that South Yemen was the destination?

He didn't. He would have tried to use the six million in whatever country the prisoners would have landed. And there weren't too many options. Realistically, it came down to Libya, Algeria, Somalia, South Yemen, maybe Iraq. In any case, the West German government had already promised the Yemenis a cement plant years earlier, and now they would have given it to them, but the Yemenis declined. The West German government tried several times to get the prisoners back but never succeeded.

What appalled Albertz, as he later said in the trial, was that the West German government had arranged for the Ethiopian army to storm the plane and shoot everyone, including him, if it had landed in Addis Ababa. A high-ranking official in Bonn had revealed that to him. Naturally, Albertz was horrified. After his return, the media always asked him if he had felt threatened by the prisoners, but the only real danger he faced came from the state. He was already frustrated with the cops, because they had him wired during the entire time leading up to the flight, even though he had been assured that he could talk freely with the prisoners.

What happened in South Yemen?
The airplane had to circle for a long time because it didn't get a landing permit. The South Yemeni government played dumb until it received an official request from the West German government for the airplane to land and for the prisoners to be received. At around 7 p.m., the landing permit was granted, and the airplane finally touched ground.

Is it true that you had clarified all of that with the Yemenis already a year in advance?
Well, not a year—it was basically just a month in advance. A person there took on the political responsibility and made the relevant arrangements. We would not have been able to do that ourselves. Without a prior arrangement for a landing permit, we wouldn't have had a chance.

Was that person a Palestinian?
Yes, he had enough influence to get it done. We were certain of that, based on the experience we had with these people. Well, let's say we were 99 percent certain.

After several hours, the prisoners were allowed to leave the plane on March 4. Then everyone gathered around a table at the airport, representatives of the South Yemeni government, the prisoners, and Albertz. First, they drank tea, as it is customary there. Then they talked about permanent resident permits. Eventually, Albertz was ready to return to the plane. At the last moment, the prisoners remembered that he needed the code word, so they quickly wrote a statement that he was supposed to read upon his return.

Did the other two airplanes also get landing permits?
No, they had to land in North Yemen. The West German ambassador in Sanaa, North Yemen, headed south in a jeep, but he was refused entry

at the border. At 8:30 a.m., Albertz departed from South Yemen, now all alone. From what we recall, there was a stopover and crew change somewhere. But the plane was back in Frankfurt the same day. The prisoners' message had been sent in advance, but Albertz read it once more on the ARD evening news:

> On the morning of March 4, 1975, we, the five liberated prisoners, the crew, and Pastor Albertz, left the Lufthansa airliner. In the airport lobby, we met with the South Yemeni state secretary for foreign affairs. He confirmed his government's decision to receive us in the People's Republic of South Yemen, where we can move freely and remain as long as we wish. The government guarantees these conditions as long as we guarantee that this text will lead to the release of P. Lorenz. We thank the crew for their work, and we thank Pastor Albertz for his efforts. We send greetings to the comrades in Germany, both to those on the outside and to those still in prison. We will put our energy into ensuring that they, too, will soon have such a day as wonderful as today. We will win! Ina Siepmann, Rolf Heißler, Gabi Kröcher-Tiedemann, Verena Becker, Rolf Pohle.

Albertz read this aloud?
Yes, on Tuesday evening on TV.

Was Lorenz allowed to know?
He watched the plane take off and depart together with us. Once it was in the air, he was happy. Everything became more relaxed.

Did you have champagne?
No, only wine, but we had a toast with Lorenz. He knew that he would be going home. We decided together with him how we'd go about it. He said that the box was terribly uncomfortable. We said that, technically, we could take a back exit, but someone might see us. In the end, we covered his glasses—no, we covered his eyes and then put his glasses on—which was also uncomfortable for him, but at least he could walk himself. This is how we led him to the car. That was about 11 p.m. that same night, after Albertz had read the message with the code word on TV.

The city was empty. There were no cops on the streets. They had pulled back all their forces. We drove with Lorenz to the city park in Wilmersdorf— the same place where he was arrested as a soldier by the Russians in 1945, but we didn't know that. We gave him three coins for a phone booth (three in case one wouldn't work), and said goodbye with a handshake.

Before we parted, Lorenz expressed regret that we got to meet under unfortunate circumstances. He said that maybe we'd get a chance to reunite under different ones. He was still blindfolded then. We were sitting on a park bench, and he said that he always had reunited with people who had played a role in his life and that he hoped that, when things were different, he would reunite with us as well. He even invited us to one of his garden parties.

We told him that he should avoid the front door when returning home because there would be plenty of reporters—a piece of advice he heeded. He just wanted to get home, home to his wife. He didn't want to talk to anybody.

But didn't he appear in the media right away, doing a big thing? Let me see . . . yes, in the afternoon of March 5, he already held an international press conference, so he couldn't have slept much.
From the transcripts:

> *Lorenz*: It was certainly an act of violence . . . but, considering the overall circumstances, they treated me well. I always had a place to wash, I always had something to eat, and they didn't harass or bully me . . .
>
> *Question*: Herr Lorenz, did you feel that the kidnappers were afraid of police raids, or did they feel entirely secure?
>
> *Lorenz*: The kidnappers gave the impression that they had taken all the necessary precautions. And I have to say that when I think of their operation, everything seemed very well planned and executed—even if one considers that the police purposely took a step back for a while. But, of course, they were always concerned that the police would come up with something . . .
>
> *Question*: Herr Lorenz, did the anarchists say anything about the election campaign?
>
> *Lorenz*: They just said that the kidnapping might affect the election results in one way or another.
>
> *Question*: Herr Lorenz, two of your party colleagues have demanded the death penalty for terrorists. What is your position?
>
> *Lorenz*: I have always been and always will be opposed to the reinstatement of the death penalty.

Question: Herr Lorenz, can you describe how you were fed and what you ate?

Lorenz: Regular food, bread, coffee, tea. I ate the usual way, putting the food in my mouth.

Question: Herr Lorenz, did you feel like you were at a real people's prison?

Lorenz: No, I had the impression that it was prepared for this specific case.

Question: How were you addressed by the kidnappers? Were they rude? Did they seem intelligent?

Lorenz: I found them to be intelligent. I don't want to elaborate here, but I want to say that I was not being blackmailed and that the treatment I received was correct. Of course, one has to consider the circumstances and the fact that I had been coerced into this situation.

For weeks, the cops tried to interrogate Peter Lorenz, but he was not interested. Eventually, the police released a psychological report about the sympathy that hostages can feel with their kidnappers, because it was so obvious that Lorenz was not willing to cooperate. His secretary always said that Lorenz wasn't home when the cops wanted to talk to him. He got really pissed, because they were observing him all the time, even when he was out for a walk.

Here is an excerpt from the psychological report:

Sympathy is a result of external pressure, common goals, and increased personal interaction. All of these factors are present in this case (the common goal is to release the prisoner unharmed). There is clear evidence of this in statements made by Lorenz: they were watching TV together, the kidnappers sewed his pants, they provided various utensils, they treated him politely, Lorenz apparently played chess with them, they had common discussions. In these discussions, phrases such as "Kids, please tell me" or "Wait for five minutes, please" were used. These phrases might have been used literally, or Herr Lorenz remembers them that way. In either case, they indicate a "companionship." Such companionship is possible based on the "code of honor" of communist and anarchist perpetrators (Herr L. has used this term himself), since they only act against the "system," not against individual "capitalists." (Even if this doesn't apply to all groups, and even if it doesn't prevent murder, if murder is seen as appropriate on political grounds.)

The development of sympathy also serves to reduce fear, which in turn leads to a more generous assessment of the situation and yet more sympathy for the perpetrators and their goals. We do not assume that this has influenced the accuracy of Herr Lorenz's statements or led to consciously false statements in order to protect the perpetrators. There is the possibility of an unconscious identification with the perpetrators, but we consider it very unlikely. There is also the possibility of memory loss due to shock or repression, but this, too, we consider unlikely, since medication prevented deeper psychological impact, terror, panic, etc. when Herr L. was most vulnerable.

After Lorenz was released, the manhunt began. The cops raided more than eighty homes and a few youth centers. Even in the mainstream media, the searches didn't go down very well. There is a photo of cops viciously swinging their clubs in the Weisbecker House. Before that, they had restrained themselves during raids—now, they were out for revenge. Everybody knew that Lorenz had not been in the Weisbecker House. We assumed that the manhunt would be most intense during the first three days and that it would be more covert thereafter, and that proved true. We kept a very low profile. The basement we left behind as it was; we only covered the opening on the ground floor with a cupboard. We planned to return the basement to its original state later on.

We had access to apartments that we hadn't previously used. These were legal apartments rented by people we knew but who weren't very close to the scene. The first three days, none of us went out. The suspects that the cops made public were Inge Viett, Ralf Reinders, Fritz Teufel, Norbert "Knofo" Kröcher, Till Meyer, Andreas Vogel, Werner Sauber, and Angela Luther, a total of eight people, half of whom were the wrong ones.

They were hunting for Angela Luther because she was so tall. Lorenz's driver believed he had recognized her—the hit he took to his head must have been harder than we thought. Regardless, the cops in Berlin went after any tall woman. It helped us relax, because we knew that they wouldn't find us that way.

After Lorenz was freed, we sent a package to Albertz with all the stuff we had found in Lorenz's briefcase. Among it were the letters from a certain Frau Busch, who had a disabled daughter and who had turned to Lorenz multiple times for help. Here is an excerpt from one of her letters:

> Dear Herr Peter Lorenz! I have been a CDU member for twenty-five years. I have a daughter with Down syndrome, who was born on December 24, 1960. Since then, I've had many disheartening experiences with people. Only people with no inner values can be so cruel. But it hurt when even the senate and the church dropped us like a hot potato, leaving us feeling like second-class citizens . . .

The woman tried everything, and Lorenz had obviously collected her letters, but he had never helped her. That's why we asked Albertz to help Frau Busch. The cash that Lorenz had on him, around 700 Deutschmark, we sent to her together with a letter explaining the circumstances. (We sent mail to many people at the time.)

Did the woman keep the money?
No, but later she regretted that.

Did Albertz advocate for Frau Busch?
We don't know.

Did Albertz later advocate for you?
Yes, for the release of Gerald Klöpper and Gabriele Kröcher-Tiedemann.

And you released a statement?
"The Kidnapping as We See It." It was distributed about twenty days after Lorenz's release. Three days after his release, we all met, discussed, and cowrote the text. It starts as follows:[22]

> Who Are We?
> After all the drama, we want to turn to the population of Berlin once more, directly, and as comprehensively as possible.
> We are doing this mainly for three reasons:
> 1. We want to tell you, as far as that's possible, what kind of people we are.
> 2. By doing that, we want to debunk some of the fantastic lies presented by the press and the politicians.
> 3. We want to explain why we kidnapped CDU-Lorenz.

We aren't the kind of people who—following the motto "The worse things are, the better"—indiscriminately strike out whenever we see an opportunity "for us." We know that "we" cannot dismantle, topple, and destroy the state. We're not the petty bourgeoisie on acid. Every one of us knows what factory work is; some of us don't even have a high school degree, let alone have visited a university.

Our enemies babble in ways that are no longer tolerable: "We're all in the same boat," "When will they kidnap the greengrocer on the corner?," "Nobody's safe on the streets anymore!" Okay, so suddenly everyone's the same? Is it no longer true that some live in run-down, overpriced rental apartments in Kreuzberg or Wedding while others live in a villa in Zehlendorf? Is it no longer true that some are earning 1,000 Deutschmark a month while others are spending 1,000 Deutschmark a day? Has the equality stipulated by the law suddenly become a reality, even though still less than 10 percent of all university students come from working-class families? (No, the reason is not that they are more stupid!) Do we suddenly have equality, even though the rich with their money and their connections enjoy a good life and travel abroad if they need an abortion while the CDU lobbies against making abortions legal in West Germany? Is there equality when the CDU supports the bosses fucking with the little guy? Anyone who resists is a "criminal," a "terrorist." No, not the piggish police who destroy youth centers, not the bosses who lay off hundreds of workers, not the judges who spare the construction mafia while cops shoot folks stealing pennies from vending machines.[23]

We believe that appeals are useless when trying to change what's wrong with this country. An awful lot has already been written about it, and millions of people experience it firsthand. Only a few enjoy a good life; the majority get a lousy deal. What kind of life is it when you toil all day and return home so beat that all you can do is watch TV? Where does the child abuse come from, the fistfights, the suicides? Why do they not happen in the villas of Zehlendorf and Dahlmen, but in the low-income neighborhoods of Moabit, Wedding, and Kreuzberg? Is it really because the people living in Zehlendorf and Dahlem are "finer," "better," "more honorable" people?

It is no coincidence that most working-class women show their age, while Mrs. Kressmann-Zschach can go about her crooked business as a stylish and youthful entrepreneur.[24] Look at all the efforts that Frau Busch has made to draw attention to her plight! Her letters prove that the SPD and the CDU are one and the same. The common people can choose between the devil and the deep blue sea. That is the free democratic order that everyone hails in West Germany!

"Our income is too high to starve to death, but too low to fill our bellies considering the current food prices. Is this what you want?! That workers have no life apart from working, eating, drinking, and paying rent?"

Frau Busch poses this question to all political parties. It seems as if the politicians' answer is yes. The bigger the workers' worries, the less likely they'll have "stupid ideas." This serves the political parties well, because there is nothing that the powerful fear more than people who resist and fight for their rights. Whoever has money has power, and whoever has power will not give it up voluntarily. Only we can force the powerful to do so. There are attempts: wildcat strikes, community groups, the struggle against the construction of the nuclear reactor at Wyhl.[25] There are also forms of resistance that are more covert, like calling in sick. The occupants of a house in Tempelhof were particularly creative: they poured boiling water over the cops who came to harass them; the cops never found those responsible.

We see our struggle as part of the overall resistance. Urban guerrilla means imagination and willingness to act. Both exist among the people. We don't act randomly but evaluate our options. Only then will we move to action. We learn from practice. For that reason alone, the Lorenz kidnapping was a "perfect" action. We are neither superheroes nor sick geniuses, no matter what political parties, the media, and the police are trying to make people (and themselves) believe. It's all just an attempt to cover up their incompetence.

We have realized that we must close ranks and organize ourselves if we want to achieve something. You start alone, but you cannot do much alone. This, however, doesn't mean you have to give up, it only means you need to seek out others who think like you and want to change things. There are tens of thousands of such people. Then you start doing things together, you learn from your own mistakes, and you must not be discouraged when things appear hopeless—they often do, especially in the beginning. The state and the police are not all-powerful, even if the density of police in West Berlin is higher than anywhere else in the world.

We produced the text on a Rotaprint machine in the Steglitz neighborhood, a run of thirty thousand. We had announced fifty thousand, but we didn't have enough time for that.

We distributed the thirty thousand copies in just half an hour on March 26. We had made a detailed plan: We made bundles of 250 copies and assigned them to a street each. The streets we chose were spread out across the city. We handed the bundles to people who divided them into even smaller ones. Distribution was to happen between 7:30 and 8 p.m. At 8 p.m. most of the entrances to the apartment buildings were locked. We limited the time of distribution to half an hour to avoid unnecessary risks. Had someone found the text right away and called the cops, they would have been there within twenty minutes. All in all, we had almost 120 people helping.

They all knew about this beforehand, and no one reported it?
Correct. Only recently someone told me that they had to burn the few copies they had kept in a hurry during one of the many raids at the Rauch House.

Our distribution plan followed an old pattern, the so-called snowball system: you speak to five or six people you trust, then they speak to people they trust, and so on. Things worked in a similar manner with the Drenkmann leaflet.[26]

The pressure on people distributing the Drenkmann leaflet was higher, and the discussions around it more heated. Some people refused to help because they didn't agree with the action; others were afraid.

The distribution of the Lorenz leaflet perplexed the cops more than the kidnapping itself. They probably believed it was fifty thousand copies too. They knew, of course, that if so many copies appeared all over town within such a short time span, the copies must have been distributed by more than a handful of people.

How many pages did the leaflet have?
Ten.

What did you do while it was being distributed?

We helped too. In Wedding, for example, around Putte, because the cops had increased patrols in that area.[27] We put the copies in mailboxes, telephone booths, and subway stations. There were no security cameras in the subway stations at the time. As we left, the first patrol cars arrived.

Did the press make a fuss?

Yes, because of the way the copies had been distributed, and because of the contents relating to the mass layoffs at DeTeWe and Loewe-Opta as well as the planned transit fare hikes.[28] It also caused a fuss that Klingbeil had donated to the CDU. We thought the press would try to keep that off the radar, but they didn't. So the press did make a fuss, which meant that even more people wanted to read the leaflet. It was reprinted a few times. The transit fare hikes were delayed by half a year. With regard to the mass layoffs, the bosses denied them.

Politically, the leaflet was a big success because it energized people, not least because we pulled off the mass distribution while the cops were searching for us on the streets. Even some of the mainstream media made fun of that. So all of that went fine, and we even managed to clear out the basement. We tore everything down, stuffed it into blue garbage bags, and distributed the bags around town.

What was in them?

Mostly Styrofoam, some stone wool, some wire mesh. But it was harder to get rid of this shit than we thought. I remember us stuffing a bag in a waste container somewhere, when a woman shouted from a nearby house, "Hey, don't fill up our containers!"

We spread out the rest, some in waste containers, some on vacant lots. According to *Der Spiegel*, young men unloaded twenty-one blue plastic bags in a high-rise housing estate in the Marienfelde neighborhood: "ochre-yellow woodchip wallpaper, brown adhesive tape, wire mesh, and red curtain fabric." The media caught on to it, because the CDU politician Berthold Rubin lived in the area, who had kidnapped himself in the early 1970s.[29] It gave people the ammunition they needed. Some leftists who thought that the Lorenz kidnapping had been staged to help the CDU win the election figured they were proven right. Meanwhile, the right-wingers thought that we had dropped the stuff intentionally near Rubin's house to make him a suspect.

For the cops, it created a lot of work. They had to check every piece of tape and everything else for fingerprints. Then they had to weigh everything. They had spread out the contents of all the blue garbage bags they had found over five garages, hoping that they'd be able to assemble an enormously big puzzle.

After some weeks, they gave up. They proceeded to try calculating how big the room holding Lorenz must have been. Lorenz had told them that he had had so-and-so many meters to walk, and then they used their findings to calculate how thick the insulation must have been.

At the time, the cops still wore blue uniforms and were always driving around wasted. The *Berliner Zeitung* published a joke with a wasted cop lying on the street and two men standing over him saying: "Look, there's another one of them blue garbage bags!"

Meanwhile, the cops went through hundreds of basements, and they did indeed look at the right one, but they couldn't find any traces. After two weeks, they found the truck that we had used to dump the garbage bags. In fact, we could have simply left the Styrofoam in there.

All in all, the cops weren't very successful in their search. That's no surprise, though. If you're out there looking for things for weeks, you'll eventually turn blind. They got so many stupid tips. In fact, we should have called in and left some more!

What was the mood like among the population?

Hard for us to say. We have to rely on what we've been told. But, generally, positive, we believe. It was kinda like after a big sports event where everything turned out well.

A week after the kidnapping, we left for Beirut. We had enough money, because some of us had done a bank just ten days prior to Lorenz. We were traveling different routes to Beirut. Two of us traveled via Italy and Greece, the rest via Denmark, all at different times. We assumed, correctly, that there wouldn't be thorough controls along those routes.

To travel through West Germany with false papers was too risky. Some folks brought us to the Friedrichstraße subway station, we handed them our weapons, and then we crossed into East Berlin. The East Germans gave us a visa without problem, and we took the train to Saßnitz on the Baltic Sea coast. But we had miscalculated the times, so we all found ourselves on the same ferry to Copenhagen. Luckily, the Danes showed little interest at the border. The West German authorities probably hadn't expected us to travel that way. Then we flew out of Copenhagen in different directions.

Our eventual meeting place was the beach in Beirut. The Palestinians had advised us not to meet in any of the cafés along the beach, but on the beach itself. The cafés were popular meeting places for intelligence agents. As a saying went, anyone sitting there for more than an hour was either a journalist or a secret agent, or both.

Didn't you want to meet the liberated prisoners?

Of course! That's why we went to Beirut in the first place. First, we had some training sessions there, which had been prearranged. We wanted to take it slow with meeting the liberated prisoners, not because of the Western intelligence agencies but because of the Israelis. They had been the only ones predicting the destination of the prisoners correctly.

In the end, unfortunately, we never had a meeting. Our Palestinian contacts explained that it wasn't a good time to meet, because there were so many different people—journalists, intelligence agents, relatives, etc.—already on their way to South Yemen with the same intention. The Yemenis weren't happy about that; they wanted peace and quiet. Then, when a meeting seemed possible, our Palestinian contacts told us, very politely, that we'd have to leave Lebanon as quickly as possible because the civil war was flaming up and they could no longer guarantee our safety. We didn't know how everything would develop, so half of us returned to Germany and the other half went to Damascus, the Syrian capital, before eventually returning home as well.

What happened to the liberated prisoners?

They all continued with the struggle, but in different ways.

Rolf Heißler was arrested in Frankfurt-Sachsenhausen in 1979. He was shot in the head during his arrest. He only survived because he had noticed beforehand that something wasn't right and covered his face with a briefcase filled with newspapers. This deflected the bullet. Elisabeth von Dyck and Willi Peter Stoll had already fallen victim to the "death squad searches."[30] Rolf had become a RAF member by then, which, essentially, he already was before being freed. He is still in prison in Bavaria, serving a life sentence.[31]

Rolf Pohle was arrested in Athens on July 21, 1976. There was a lot of back-and-forth about his extradition to Germany. He had much support in

Greece, with mass demonstrations. His Greek attorney during the extradition process later became minister of justice. The judge who initially rejected the extradition became president. It was the same judge on whom the Costa-Gavras film *Z* was based. But the West German government applied ever bigger pressure, and eventually a Greek high court agreed to having Rolf deported. Contrary to the extradition agreement with the Greeks, German courts sentenced Rolf to an additional three and a half years. He was released in the early '80s and now lives in Athens.[32]

Ina Siepmann first returned to Germany but moved to Lebanon in late 1977. For her, struggling without any perspective for change in Germany as an extended arm of the liberation movements of the so-called Third World became increasingly schizophrenic, so she decided to directly participate in the struggle in Palestine. As far as we know, she joined a Palestinian women's brigade and was killed during the 1982 Israeli invasion. In the territories they took control over, the Israelis dug up all the graves and found the corpse of a blonde woman. They said they were 95 percent sure that it was Ina.

Verena Becker was arrested together with Günter Sonnenberg in the spring of 1977, during the peak of the RAF manhunt.[33] Both were shot and injured during the arrest and later sentenced to life in prison. Verena was pardoned and released in 1989. She now lives in Berlin.

Gabriele Kröcher-Tiedemann was arrested together with Christian Möller after a shootout in December 1976 along the Swiss border.[34] She served thirteen years in Swiss prisons for attempted murder. In her case, too, the extradition process dragged on. She still had a pending prison sentence in West Germany and was accused of having participated in the attack on the OPEC conference in Vienna in 1975.[35] Finally, in 1989, she was handed over to German authorities. During the OPEC trial, she explicitly distanced herself from the armed struggle and said that it had all been one big mistake. Thereupon she was freed. She now lives in Germany and is seriously ill.

So you haven't seen any of the people you liberated in the past twenty years?
Only Verena Becker here in Berlin.

THE KIDNAPPING AS WE SEE IT

(1975)

2nd of June Movement

Ten-page, stapled leaflet (laid out like a wall newspaper), of which thirty thousand copies were distributed in Berlin by 2nd of June supporters in a concerted ninety-minute action three weeks after the release of Peter Lorenz. Statistics on transport, water, and gas price hikes in Berlin, the letters by Frau Busch, and a "Peter Lorenz Song" have been omitted.

Who Are We?

After all the drama, we want to turn to the population of Berlin once more, directly, and as comprehensively as possible.

We are doing this mainly for three reasons:

1. We want to tell you, as far as that's possible, what kind of people we are.
2. By doing that, we want to debunk some of the fantastic lies presented by the press and the politicians.
3. We want to explain why we kidnapped CDU-Lorenz.

We aren't the kind of people who—following the motto "The worse things are, the better"—indiscriminately strike out whenever we see an opportunity "for us." We know that "we" cannot dismantle, topple, and destroy the state. We're not the petty bourgeoisie on acid. Every one of us knows what factory work is; some of us don't even have a high school degree, let alone have visited a university.

Our enemies babble in ways that are no longer tolerable: "We're all in the same boat," "When will they kidnap the greengrocer on the corner?," "Nobody's safe on the streets anymore!" Okay, so suddenly everyone's the same? Is it no longer true that some live in run-down, overpriced rental apartments in Kreuzberg or Wedding while others live in a villa in Zehlendorf? Is it no longer true that some are earning 1,000 Deutschmark a month while others are spending 1,000 Deutschmark a day? Has the equality stipulated by the law suddenly become a reality, even though still less than 10 percent of all university students come from working-class families? (No, the reason is not that they are more stupid!) Do we suddenly have equality, even though the rich with their money and their connections enjoy a good life and travel abroad if they need an abortion while the CDU lobbies against making abortions legal in West Germany? Is there equality when the CDU supports the bosses fucking with the little guy? Anyone who resists is a "criminal," a "terrorist." No, not the piggish police who destroy youth centers, not the bosses who lay off hundreds of workers, not the judges who spare the construction mafia while cops shoot folks stealing pennies from vending machines.[1]

We believe that appeals are useless when trying to change what's wrong with this country. An awful lot has already been written about it, and millions of people experience it firsthand. Only a few enjoy a good life; the majority get a lousy deal. What kind of life is it when you toil all day and return home so beat that all you can do is watch TV? Where does the child abuse come from, the fistfights, the suicides? Why do they not happen in the villas of Zehlendorf and Dahlmen, but in the low-income neighborhoods of Moabit, Wedding, and Kreuzberg? Is it really because the people living in Zehlendorf and Dahlem are "finer," "better," "more honorable" people?

It is no coincidence that most working-class women show their age, while Mrs. Kressmann-Zschach can go about her crooked business as a stylish and youthful entrepreneur.[2] Look at all the efforts that Frau Busch has made to draw attention to her plight! Her letters prove that the SPD and the CDU are one and the same. The common people can choose between the devil and the deep blue sea. That is the free democratic order that everyone hails in West Germany!

"Our income is too high to starve to death, but too low to fill our bellies considering the current food prices. Is this what you want?! That workers have no life apart from working, eating, drinking, and paying rent?"

Frau Busch poses this question to all political parties. It seems as if the politicians' answer is yes. The bigger the workers' worries, the less likely they'll have "stupid ideas." This serves the political parties well, because there is nothing that the powerful fear more than people who resist and fight for their rights. Whoever has money has power, and whoever has power will not give it up voluntarily. Only we can force the powerful to do so. There are attempts: wildcat strikes, community groups, the struggle against the construction of the nuclear reactor at Wyhl.[3] There are also forms of resistance that are more covert, like calling in sick. The occupants of a house in Tempelhof were particularly creative: they poured boiling water over the cops who came to harass them; the cops never found those responsible.

We see our struggle as part of the overall resistance. Urban guerrilla means imagination and willingness to act. Both exist among the people. We don't act randomly but evaluate our options. Only then will we move to action. We learn from practice. For that reason alone, the Lorenz kidnapping was a "perfect" action. We are neither superheroes nor sick geniuses, no matter what political parties, the media, and the police are trying to make people (and themselves) believe. It's all just an attempt to cover up their incompetence.

We have realized that we must close ranks and organize ourselves if we want to achieve something. You start alone, but you cannot do much alone. This, however, doesn't mean you have to give up, it only means you need to seek out others who think like you and want to change things. There are tens of thousands of such people. Then you start doing things together, you learn from your own mistakes, and you must not be discouraged when things appear hopeless—they often do, especially in the beginning. The state and the police are not all-powerful, even if the density of police in West Berlin is higher than anywhere else in the world.

Who Is Peter L.?

We found some remarkable documents among Peter Lorenz's papers. We also managed to get some information from the conversations we had with him.

Peter Lorenz is a man who could fit in anywhere—in the CDU, the SPD, the FDP. He has always been depicted as a man of the people; a "man of the people" who has 50,000 Deutschmark a year to spend on whatever he likes, and who wears fake glasses on campaign posters so that the thickness of his real ones doesn't show (he is very short-sighted). A man who, even though he talks a lot about security, denied in his conversations with us that he had demanded—and received!—a driver for personal security who was an armed special forces agent.

Lorenz said that he had no explanation for that. Nor did he have an explanation for the fact that his official car, registered to the license plate B-1–2, had received a private license plate, B-AC-744.

Peter Lorenz is a man who never responded to the mother of a child with Down syndrome (a twenty-five-year CDU member!) who had reached out to him for help. The reason: he had "no time" during the election campaign. That's why we took the 700 Deutschmark he had on him and sent them to the woman's family. In a similar spirit, we will send a 10,000 Deutschmark donation that the CDU received from the Klingbeil Group[4] (one of Berlin's biggest construction criminals) to an organization for the disabled.

2nd of June Letter to Frau Busch

Dear Frau Busch!

We are Herr Lorenz's kidnappers. Don't be frightened, we only want to inform you that we have found your letter among Herr Lorenz's papers. We were greatly angered by the indifference with which the political parties met your needs and difficulties. But for us that's nothing new. Otherwise, we wouldn't take to the means we are taking to.

We have asked Peter Lorenz about his behavior and why he disregarded your needs. He said that he didn't have time to attend to individual cases of this sort; big politics and the election campaign were more important and required all of his attention. We, however, think that politics can go to hell if there's no time to react to the problems of the people and to provide help in such an urgent case as yours. You probably know that tens of thousands of people are in a similar situation.

When we took Herr Lorenz prisoner, he had 700 Deutschmark of personal money on him. As you know, politicians are not among the poorest in this country. That's why they aren't very interested in the problems of those who hardly have enough to get by. So we decided to send the 700 Deutschmark to you. They won't solve your problems, but perhaps they are of some help.

We have told Herr Lorenz what we were going to do with the money, and he has certainly already visited you to save his face or to convince you to reject the offer. But it's all the same to us.

We'd like to add that it's brave of you to fight for your rights, and that you should not stop doing it, even if it sometimes seems pointless.

2nd of June Movement

Peter Lorenz's Monthly Earnings

Peter Lorenz's monthly earnings exceed 20,000 Deutschmark. He's unlikely to experience hardship. His handwritten accounts reveal that, in nine months, he has had an extra income of 194,057.60 Deutschmark.

How Does He Earn So Much Money?

Besides salaries for management and board positions, as a member of the house of representatives and its vice president, and as a legal adviser to RIAS,[5] he makes most of his money by buying up houses and properties for redevelopment firms such as Mosch. These companies demolish the old buildings and build new apartments that no one can afford. They also build the concrete blocks that dominate the Märkische Viertel or the Steglitzer Kreisel, where Lorenz was involved as a solicitor.

Now, one might say that this is his business and no reason for us to kidnap him! Okay, that's one way of looking at it. But let's do a few comparisons: How long must a worker do shifts to reach the living standard of Peter Lorenz? Indeed, a hopeless calculation . . .

At Capital's Service

To all those who believe that you have to vote for the CDU because the SPD has been a useless failure, we can only say that the CDU, the SPD, and the FDP are essentially all the same mess. They all govern against the people!

The People's Democratic Republic of South Yemen

Our comrades were flown to the People's Republic of South Yemen, where they received residency permits. The Yemeni people remember very well what it means to be persecuted when fighting against capitalism, colonialism, and exploitation.

In 1859, the British invaded Yemen and occupied Aden, the capital city. They needed the city and, in particular, the harbor to establish new military bases in order to exploit their biggest colony, India, without placing war or merchant ships at risk. That's why the British tried to occupy all countries along the seaway to India, including Yemen.

The economic system they established in Aden catered exclusively to the needs of the British military and British trade. Nothing was done to satisfy the needs of the local population. Domestic husbandry and agriculture were left to large landowners, sultans, sheiks, and feudal lords. These worked hand in hand with the colonialists and shared the wealth with them. Small farmers, the rural proletariat, and the workers on the British-owned oil fields lived in misery.

Their first uprisings were brutally suppressed by the British military and the sheiks' private armies. But after World War II, when the British had already been driven out of Egypt, Palestine, and East Africa, they could no longer prevent popular resistance in Yemen. To at least regain control over one part of the country, they divided it into two, and North Yemen became part of the United Arab States.[6]

However, the British failed to reestablish themselves in South Yemen. In Aden, the dockworkers went on strike, and work at the British-owned oil refineries came to a halt. The Yemenis came to realize that political protest alone wouldn't get the British out of the country. They initiated an armed liberation struggle that lasted for many years. In 1967, they chased the colonialists away and began to use the wealth of the sheiks and the sultans, the country's capitalists, for the needs of the people. Schools, hospitals, roads, and jobs were created. After a rule of 128 years, the English had left nothing but poverty, illiteracy, and disease. In a country of more than one million people, there were exactly twelve doctors.

The Yemeni people's revolution is only in its beginnings. There are still many obstacles to overcome, as in any new country, but the Yemenis don't let themselves be discouraged. They bravely defend themselves against sabotage and counterrevolutionary attacks, both from the inside and the outside. They know that there still is a long way to go before the revolution and peaceful coexistence with all peoples.

ANALYSIS

TUNIX

(January 1978)

Revolutionary Guerrilla Opposition from the 2nd of June Movement's Bankruptcy Estate

The Tunix Congress was held in West Berlin in January 1978 to discuss the state of the radical left after the "German Autumn." Thousands of radicals participated. The following position paper was written by 2nd of June Movement prisoners leading up to the event. The self-irony expressed in the choice of the collective pen name matches that of the name "Tunix" for the congress, a wordplay on "Tu Nichts!" or "Do nothing!"

The thousandfold fear will be guarded a thousandfold! The thousandfold disaster will be laughed at a thousandfold! The thousandfold fire will be sparked a thousandfold!

Regarding the Tunix Meeting

We appreciate that comrades have taken the initiative to spark a long-overdue debate. We would appreciate it even more if Tunix helped to finally put an end to the complete fragmentation of the left. No, not everyone has to paint the same star in the same color. It would suffice to collectively depart to "Tuwas," as in: *Do something!* We are not delusional. We don't think that we, from the "comfort" of our prison cells, know more about the difficulties experienced by the resistance movement in recent years than those who are confronted with them every day. But we hope that we can contribute with a few critical, and self-critical, remarks.

Overcome the Fragmentation!

If we don't want to dig a political mass grave for ourselves, we have to overcome our fragmentation, here and now! We need to see a horizon beyond the mini-groups. While leftists in this country drive one another insane, rightists begin to assemble. The unprecedented reactionary offensive of recent years has partly been enabled by the hopeless and meaningless infighting of hundreds of leftist groups and groupuscules. Not only have the concessions won by the youth and student rebellions been rolled back, but the state has been strengthened to a point where it controls life, all aspects of life, in a way even the Third Reich could only dream of. And all of this happened with no resistance! Yes, the methods have become more sophisticated, and we haven't seen the reckless attacks and excessive brutality of the Third Reich yet. But this must not deceive us. The only reason we haven't is the weakness of the left. The fragmented, downhearted left of today—often seeking refuge in dogmatism—is not capable of threatening the capitalist order. Its fragmentation into dozens of groups has made it very easy for those in power to isolate them, to paralyze the appeal—and the danger—of concentrated street rebellion. Leftist groups, in their isolation, are blindly following the "one way" they believe to be true. They are preoccupied with fighting the "deviants" closest to them. This has led the entire anticapitalist opposition into a dead end.

The Alternatives

Those who feel they have created "free spaces" for themselves enthusiastically fill them with "alternative" projects. Euphoric and deluded by apparent victory, they forget that it is impossible to shed social conditions. You have to change them! But instead of allowing their projects to benefit the expansion of the social struggle, they want to prove that they are superior to all others.

If you don't want to serve the interests of the rulers, you have to put your own interests first. But if you only focus on your own project, this "consciousness of justification" will lead to a series of compromises to save them, until they become a caricature of what they were conceived to be. What was conceived as an alternative to society becomes an alternative to struggle, and the consciousness of a resistance fighter degenerates into the consciousness of a social worker. In short, the compromises lead to a compromised consciousness. This is true for most alternative projects; the others have been disciplined or destroyed by other means.

The March Through the Institutions

Where are those who marched through the institutions?[1] They've assimilated, or they've disappeared. Their march has changed nothing but the marchers. The institutions still serve the reactionaries, as they have always done. That was predictable. Those who want to enter the corridors of power need to fulfill the demands of power more than anyone else. They need to fulfill the demands of the state apparatus and protect the order of the powerful more than anyone else. If you don't, you won't reach the corridors of power.

The comrades who marched through the institutions see the state as a tool that can serve anyone and anything, a neutral polity where class struggle can unfold and where everyone can occupy positions of power—a racetrack where everyone tries to cross the finish line first. They overlook that the bourgeois state is a tool with very specific functions. Its primary function is to protect and maintain the capitalist order. The bourgeois state was created for that purpose. If formerly powerless people gain power, the tool doesn't change. The only thing that is new is that some people have got new roles. For a fundamental transformation of society—for a humane society without domination—the state is of no use. It will always stand in our way.

The Dear Contradictions

Of course, these comments were very general. Not every comrade who has fought for alternative projects, or tried to carry the struggle into the institutions, has been corrupted. There are enough people who prove that this wasn't the case—but they are no longer in the institutions.

We aren't saying that teachers or social workers do anything wrong by trying to raise people's consciousness in schools or youth centers, or by teaching the youth to stand up for themselves. There is nothing wrong with providing explanations for the dire situation they find themselves in, and with propagating resistance as an alternative to assimilation and surrender. What we are saying is that the contradiction between institutional role and revolutionary action leads to reformism, as soon as "tactical" thinking takes over and you're no longer willing to make personal sacrifices. To be uncompromising means to go beyond legal limitations, to no longer play the role you're expected to play, to engage in sabotage. This becomes very clear in the prison environment. Whoever thinks you can do revolutionary work as a jailer makes, in the best case, a fool of themselves. Any kind of jailer will lock the door to your cell, that's what jailers do. To make a personal sacrifice would mean to unlock the door. All else only helps cover up the brutality of the prison system, is a tactical, reformist move to mitigate conflict. But revolutionary politics can't shy away from conflict, they need to dismantle the techniques of power. Only then can you march through the institutions in a revolutionary manner.

Abolish the State, Don't Reform It!
We must also engage critically with another position that has gained traction among the militant and armed groups, namely the fixation on the state as the only evil. According to this view, a new social order will emerge the moment the state has been cast aside. The comrades holding this view forget that the bourgeois state is not the cause of the social conditions we live in but their effect. And it is not the only effect. The voluntary submission of the masses (cited so frequently by the left) does not solely rely on the violence of the state apparatus.

The power of the disinformation spread by the media, the education system, and fascist mass literature; the manipulation of the people through organizations claiming to act in their interests, such as trade unions and the so-called mass parties; the ideological confusion and bogus cures to unhappiness and aggression; and, above all, the threats of unemployment, professional bans, and, in the case of foreign colleagues, deportation—none of this must be underestimated. Smashing the state does not equal social revolution because it doesn't smash the colonized consciousness of the masses. Any such attempt is doomed to fail. Smashing the state cannot be done by an isolated group; it requires a broad collective effort. And we can't grow in numbers if we ignore people's misery and insecurity. We can only intensify social conflict when we take them seriously.

We are not advocating mass opportunism. Even if only one person among ten says that, no, the sky is not a banana, that person is right. The sky is no banana. But it doesn't suffice to state that the consciousness of the masses "hasn't developed enough." We must ask ourselves how it *can be developed.* A slow and long process.

Our Isolation Among the People

We have to take responsibility for the isolation of the left. That is also true for the urban guerrilla. Apart from a few actions (way too few, unfortunately) such as those against Kaußen, MAN, BVG, and section 218,[2] the majority of our militant comrades have abandoned intervention in social struggles for a military conflict with the state apparatus. This means that we have accepted the ghetto assigned to us rather than breaking out of it. Certainly, the lack of public debate within the left has contributed to this. Out of fear that the state will use leftist criticism of the guerrilla in their psychological warfare against us, all criticism was waved aside as police propaganda. We were blinded by equating the left with Cohn-Bendit and collectives like Sozialistisches Büro and Langer Marsch,[3] which publicly denounced comrades, or—as it happened in Frankfurt—even doing police work by creating sympathizer files. There is no base for discussion with auxiliary cops like these.

Critique of the RAF

We consider some of the armed groups' embrace of a new anti-imperialist concept a form of resignation. These comrades reckon that the masses in West Germany (which is a part of the metropole) have been so corrupted that broad proletarian counterpower is impossible. In their eyes, this makes the formation of a social resistance movement futile. Since the peoples of the Third World are the most oppressed and exploited, they are the only ones who can give rise to a worldwide revolutionary struggle. Nothing can happen in West Germany, which serves only as a basis for military operations. The politics of the comrades who believe this reflect these views.

We don't share them. Of course, practical solidarity with the peoples of the Third World and their liberation struggles is an important part of our struggle. But the most effective form of solidarity is the development of revolutionary resistance in the metropole. We need a movement in the metropole that makes it impossible for the capitalist state to realize its imperialist ambitions. It is defeatist to see the current weakness of the revolutionary movement as unchangeable. Capitalism's crisis is deepening, which creates much potential for everyone, and we need to focus on that.

Schmidt says that if the terrorist base isn't destroyed today, the army of unemployed youth might navigate toward it tomorrow. Kohl says that the state will lose if terrorism can't be eradicated within the next five years. These are very clear statements.

The massive current investment in the state apparatus is not the result of the weak and economically as well as militarily highly ineffective guerrilla, even if some leftists claim such nonsense. We will not persuade anyone of the necessity of revolutionary politics when they feel that this politics is directed against them. We all decried the fascist bombs in the railway stations of Bremen, Hamburg, and Cologne.[4] We have always said—all of us—that the actions and the politics of the guerrilla must never target the people, only the rulers. Who is boarding cheap charter flights to Mallorca?[5]

The People and the Guerrilla

In January 1975, comrade Werner Sauber wrote the following in an analysis of the anti-imperialist line:

> The RAF disregards the struggles of the most exploited: women, foreigners, and young German unskilled workers. Any practical attempt to involve militant proletarians in the armed struggle has been rejected by the RAF. Instead, the RAF comrades act as a revolutionary "secret service," looking only at the liberation movements of the Three Continents.
>
> It would have been more in line with their anti-imperialist concept to join a Third World liberation movement and fight with them against the metropole. The RAF is neither a fish in the sea nor a bird in the sky. It only collaborates with oppressed marginalized groups or the left to gain new allies for anti-imperialist terrorism, not to strengthen the class struggles of the oppressed in the metropole itself. Until 1972, this approach was understandable. But in the summer of 1973, they should have engaged with a workers' resistance that was strong enough for anyone to notice.
>
> The anticapitalist struggle must arise from the daily resistance of workers trying to survive under the capitalist state of siege. Effective resistance is tied to daily experience. Resistance against the imperialist superstructure only, with no roots in the factories and neighborhoods, can easily be eradicated by the capitalist state with general police tactics.
>
> The RAF is building a red army that, in the beginning, is standing on its own. It hopes that the bombs it plants will affect

the consciousness of the masses, as if the development of mass resistance was primarily based on awareness of how bad living conditions are. Such a logic reduces revolutionary violence to a question of enlightenment. If revolutionary violence doesn't come from experiences of struggle and oppression within the class, it cannot become a means of counterpower. Among the left, people are sympathetic to militant activists on the run, but they have no idea what to do with the conflict between the state's terror and the RAF's anti-imperialist struggle.[6]

Overall, this remains valid. Of course, it is problematic today to speak of workers who "survive—not live—under the capitalist state of siege" in such a general manner. It accounts neither for the bourgeoisification of big sections of the working class (sections who have been able to climb up the social ladder) nor for the specific situation of women, migrants, the youth, and the unemployed.

Everyday Resistance

It is crucial to recognize that our struggle can and must develop from the people's everyday resistance. Neither the terrain of everyday resistance nor the agents can be defined by traditional concepts of class. This becomes particularly clear in the militant wing of the antinuclear movement, which brings together farmers, university professors, and all sorts of people in between.

To develop the struggle from everyday resistance can, for example, mean . . .

. . . to destroy a police precinct or city hall when a squat like the Feuerwache is cleared and demolished.[7]

. . . to torch Springer news racks and delivery trucks when our printers are arrested.[8]

. . . to organize shoplifting-ins in department stores when food prices go up (don't forget the cash registers!).

. . . to strip *Kontaktbeamte* down to their underwear and tie them to lampposts when they get too nosy (a beating works as well).[9]

. . . to renovate the offices of piggish gynecologists (you can also dump some slaughterhouse waste there).

There are more than enough ways, and there's no limit to the imagination. The best way to prove practical international solidarity is to burn down companies that deliver weapons to Iran or build nuclear power plants in South Africa.

Legality—Whose Legality?

Of course, the other side will, at this point, raise the questions of violence and of legality versus illegality. Legal is whatever poses no threat to the ruling order. Anyone who wants to abolish the capitalist order and act upon their own principles is criminalized.

If not everyone who works to change the system is thrown into the penitentiary, it doesn't mean that there are legal ways to knock the rulers off their pedestal; it simply means that it is sometimes easier for the state to control legal groups, or that their practice is irrelevant, or that criminalization might do the state more harm than good in a certain historical moment, or all of the above. Legality is nothing stable; it is negotiated by relations of power.

During the Third Reich, laws were passed for everything. Everything that happened, happened legally. It's no different today. If you always respect the legal framework, you will also respect a fascist legal framework. It is not up to us to determine what's "illegal" in this country.

The *Info BUG* Example

Let's look at the *Info BUG* example: a journal that publishes leftist discussions and opinion pieces is criminalized.[10] The editorial collective splits over the two alternatives that present themselves: one faction edits a "conspiratorial" paper, which continues to serve our needs but puts the editors at risk (even though, as the case of the printers has shown, the risk is not significantly higher than it was before).[11] The other faction "professionalizes" the journal, with the editors coming forward under their own names, making self-censorship a constant issue.

What's the difference? While the first faction has adapted to new conditions, the second faction has abandoned its original principles. It is ironic that it is primarily them who claim that they *stick* to their principles.

We don't say that all forms of legal struggle shall be foregone or neglected. What we say is that the ruling system must not define the boundaries of our struggle. Nothing but the ultimate goal of our struggle—that is, revolution—can define those boundaries. Our actions cannot be determined by what's legal or not, only by the tactics we choose in the context of revolutionary strategy.

On the Question of Violence

There is not much to say about violence. Any newspaper reveals where the violence in today's society comes from. We cannot stop anyone from turning the left cheek when they're hit on the right, but it should be crystal-clear to everyone today that they are not making a great contribution to the struggle. Everyone who cannot be co-opted by the state must understand that with a state armed to its teeth, we cannot meet our needs and interests without the support of armed revolutionary groups. We cannot avoid an armed confrontation with the state. This confrontation is a political necessity. It is not a fetish.

How Do We Advance?

> Without relating the movement to the final goal, the movement
> as an end in itself is nothing to me, the final goal is everything.
> —Rosa Luxemburg

We can't ignore one another. And why should we? If we want to advance, we will be forced to recognize that one form of resistance cannot be separated from another, that we must not juxtapose different forms of resistance. We must understand that we all benefit from a debate with many voices, that we are all dependent on one another. Only uncompromising struggle—on all levels—will lead us to a place where we come together as "one big family"—a place where, at least within the undogmatic groups, there'll be an end to defamation, narrow-mindedness, competition, and hostility.

One thing is clear: to get to the sand, we need to clear the tarmac covering our brains.[12]

For an offensive in all areas of life!

For the organization of total resistance, here and now!

For a revolutionary guerrilla!

INDIANS DON'T CRY, THEY STRUGGLE
(1979)

Fritz Teufel

Originally published under the title "Indianer weinen nicht—sie kämp-fen" in the 1979 IVA-Verlag book *Klaut sie! (Selbst)Kritische Beiträge zur Krise der Linken und der Guerrilla* (Steal this! (Self-)critical reflections on the crisis of the left and the guerrilla). The references to Native Americans will be considered offensive by many readers. The language used was very common in the German-speaking world, leftist circles included.

—

The Time Is Ripe in the Metropole—But for What?
Let me sort out my thoughts, based on a) the (limited as well as frus-trating) perspective of several years of state security imprisonment in Moabit, and b) more or less engaging discussions between, around, and about Horst Mahler and Peter-Paul Zahl (PPZ) as well as the notorious Ernst Derlage.[1]

1
On the surface, this is about Horst Mahler and PPZ, about the prison conditions that state security and social state security prisoners are held in, and about the meaning or meaninglessness of amnesty campaigns. But if you dig deeper, it is also about the odds of the revolutionary move-ment (if there still is one), and about the fate, and the changes, of the 1968 antiauthoritarian movement in the metropole; it is about the poli-tics of the urban guerrilla, a critical, and self-critical, assessment of its

merits and flaws; it is about mass movements, about the tasks, problems, and possibilities of revolutionary politics; it is about life, death, and survival; it is about current forms of oppressive, revolutionary, and counterrevolutionary violence; it is about the relationship between the anti-imperialist and anticapitalist currents in the human liberation struggle at the beginning of the ninth decade of this century; it is about a deeper understanding of the antinuclear and environmental movements and their relationship to democratic and revolutionary socialism; it is about social reform and revolution, just like it was in the beginning of the nineteenth century (see for example the discussions between Eduard Bernstein and Rosa Luxemburg[2]); it is about the future of humankind, the alternative between barbarism and socialism.

2

The former APO warrior §§§-Hotte[3]—who, for reasons not yet known, is attempting to enter the camp of the palefaces stinking of the cheapest reformist liquor—offers a farewell present to his former comrades in the form of some thoughts whose analytical ambition might get drowned in the outcry over alleged or real betrayal. "Indians don't cry," says Mahler. It means that revolutionaries—and state security prisoners see themselves as revolutionaries as long as they haven't been broken—must endure prison and persecution and all sorts of ordeals without complaint. In that sense, Mahler is only formulating a revolutionary truism. In the struggle for our common cause (world communism), we must not thrust our own personal fate into the foreground, overestimating its importance. It is selflessness and high moral integrity, paired with intelligence and commitment, that has made people like Rosa Luxemburg, Che Guevara, Ulrike Meinhof, Ayatollah Khomeini, and others into shining examples for their contemporaries.[4] Unfortunately, Mahler doesn't content himself with criticizing the guerrilla's incorrect approach and flawed politics; he calls for leniency with regard to the crimes of state security, thereby doing exactly what he warns against, namely, pushing young radicals into acts of desperation and putschist politics. This has without doubt other motivations than the shabby egoism of someone trying to save his own skin. Those who believe that the latter is driving Mahler let their emotions speak, they don't think. Mahler is panicking. He once set a theoretical milestone for a particular current of revolutionary politics, and is now trying to "repent."[5] And not just in terms of the law! If he could, he would throw the baby of the revolution out with the bathwater of an imprisoned guerrilla that has, for the most part, turned into a sect. All of this in the colorful German republic.

3: A Balance Sheet of Ten Years

More important than Mahler Studies seems the attempt to draw a preliminary balance sheet after ten years of armed struggle in West Germany. As one of the earliest advocates, representatives, and practitioners of what many, also on the left, see as the source of all evil in the current repressive republic, I can't criticize the armed struggle from the outside; I can only offer self-criticism that proceeds from an understanding that not all of it was wrong.

The RAF has fulfilled its historical mission. Their actions served as a beacon, coming from the consciousness that more violence from below against the violence of capitalism and the Yankees' imperialist war in Vietnam was necessary and possible. Such a consciousness is prevalent today among unemployed youth, students, apprentices, and dropouts in the fully automated idiot factory FRG Inc. But it is the duty of the thinking left to prevent that revolutionary rage and impotent fury from leading to swinging blows blindly and desperately. Only an honest, courageous, and broad discussion about the meaning and meaninglessness of revolutionary violence can get us further.

4: The Lorenz Kidnapping

The Lorenz kidnapping, as well as a series of unconventional loans from capitalist financial institutions, has proven that, in the ideal case, armed action is possible without bloodshed. It is no exaggeration to rate the Lorenz kidnapping as a watershed moment, an unprecedented highlight in the history of armed action in West Germany. The Lehrter Straße women's liberation of July 7, 1976, belongs in a similar category.[6] Of course, there were precedents. But the planning, precision, analysis, imagination, drive, and wit of the Lorenz kidnapping was praised even in the more intelligent sections of the bourgeois press. For reasons that will probably be revealed in the course of the Lorenz-Drenkmann trial, I can join the choir without fear of self-praise.[7] The new quality in comparison to earlier and later actions of the so-called guerrilla was as obvious to me as it must have been to any halfway politically interested television viewer.

Of course, the Lorenz kidnapping could have ended differently. Today, the wise compliance of the authorities in the Lorenz case has largely been forgotten (as much as the quality of the kidnapping), due to subsequent events from Stockholm to Mogadishu. But the Lorenz kidnapping, regardless of how well it was executed, also had a number of political consequences (predictable or not) that need to be analyzed, as they can neither be denied nor ignored.

The successful prisoner liberation gave false hope both to prisoners and to guerrillas fighting on the outside; at the same time, it narrowed the political horizon. (It also created new terrible forms of competition among prisoners and their friends. The discussion of who did or didn't end up on which list and why was consciously or unconsciously a parody of the moralistic-bourgeois-capitalist justice system. Strangely enough— or maybe not—formal as well as hypocritical criteria emerged.)

Turning the liberation of a small number of prisoners into the central problem of the revolutionary movement in a country of sixty million people might be subjectively understandable, but everyone who does so is doomed to fail politically—even (or especially!) with respect to the liberation of prisoners, which is what almost all activity now focuses on. This must be made clear to the comrades of the RAF as well as to the so-called new 2nd of June Movement (which, in theory and practice, is no more than a new branch of the old RAF, or, shall we say, the aging RAF). Parts of the Revolutionary Cells must hear it too.

The RAF itself once had politics that saw resistance in all areas of life, in factories as well as in neighborhoods, as the core of revolutionary socialism. Today, their theory and practice are limited to demanding freedom for the prisoners who are alive and revenge for the prisoners who are dead. As the practice of several actions—Stockholm, Entebbe, Buback, Ponto, Schleyer, Mogadishu—has shown, they achieve rather the opposite (apart, perhaps, from the revenge). The Meyer liberation and the arrest of four comrades in Bulgaria were ideologically embedded in the narrow guerrilla concept of the "free-the-guerrilla guerrilla."[8] One step forward, two steps back.

We must not forget the Revolutionary Cells and new autonomist expressions of militant resistance connected to grassroots movements. The actions carried out by these groups were downplayed by the system's propaganda machine, in the same way that the actions of the RAF (which, at the end of the day, were neither particularly numerous nor particularly spectacular, at least by international standards) were being blown out of proportion. Far too many people fell for this, including the armed heroes themselves, who allowed the media lackeys of the powerful to portray them as "Lumumbas of the metropole" and similar nonsense.[9] These are heroes who need a reality check.

Sensible people should neither demonize nor romanticize the guerrilla. The biggest problem is the unwillingness to engage in self-criticism by millions of former Nazis and Nazi sympathizers, who openly wished that lynch mobs would get to the APO leaders of 1968 and who later fueled the mass hysteria caused by a modest West German urban guerrilla movement. With the reactionary pigheads in control of mass media chiming in, a climate was created that inevitably led to equally hysterical reactions by the fledgling guerrilla itself.

5

A reminder for everyone wanting to avoid hysteria: we have to bake buns one at a time, but they have to be tasty! The struggle for the freedom of all takes time, and we need to be patient. The shortsighted prisoner liberation politics of scattered guerrillas who react to every failure by becoming more militaristic reminds us of the rulers' nuclear power policy: after us the deluge!

Naturally, I consider the interests of tortured prisoners more legitimate than those of corporations wanting to make profits, but the only measures for revolutionary politics are the needs of the masses and their desire for a life in freedom and happiness and for a world without exploitation, borders, and armed oppression.

6: A Critique of Mogadishu

My criticism of the airplane hijacking to Mogadishu is also a self-criticism. I cannot and will not deny the fact that I myself was to be freed in a similar hijacking to Entebbe. I was on the list of prisoners to be exchanged. I had not been asked to be on the list and maybe ended up there due to false assumptions about my role in revolutionary politics—but had I been asked (no one did ask me), I would not have objected to a journey from Moabit to Africa. In fact, I would have probably started knitting a bobble hat for Idi Amin right away.[10] Yes, the Idi Amin that was, with great zeal, painted as a criminal by our oh-so-critical press (of course, with no racism and neocolonial superiority involved), while no criminal traits were recognized in the Filbingers of our time, not even in the defendants of the Majdanek trial.[11] Well, nothing came of it, and I eventually sent the bobble hat to PPZ, who thought it was a potato sack.

It was not like the Entebbe hijacking made much sense to me ... but I had taken comfort (at the time) in the fact that its key objective was the liberation of Palestinian prisoners who were fighting for a just cause. (There is a note in my manuscript, written by one of the fellow prisoners whom I had given it to read: "And you are fighting for an unjust case, or what shall I make of that?" Fair enough. My only explanation is that, most probably, I wasn't thinking quite right at the time.) Israeli airplanes still bomb Palestinian refugee camps. Women, children, and the elderly, forced from their homelands and driven into a life of misery, are killed by the most advanced means of capitalist military technology. Hospitalized Palestinian napalm victims were among the most important reasons for the formation of the urban guerrilla in West Berlin and West Germany in 1970. Yet it is quite possible that desperate actions against the civilian Israeli population and against Israeli passenger planes—actions threatening the lives of innocent people, of children, women, and the elderly—might damage rather than benefit the Palestinian cause.

In the aftermath of the Entebbe hijacking, we considered public criticism. I was opposed. Hence, I'm not in a position to act surprised about comrades who still believe that public criticism of Mogadishu would mean a lack of solidarity or surrender to state security policies or whatever. It is not easy to criticize comrades who risked and lost their lives in an effort to free other comrades. The brutality and military precision of the Israeli commando in Entebbe and the GSG 9 in Mogadishu,[12] as well as the death of comrades involved, caused a process of psychological denial among us, making it impossible to reflect on the action's meaning, or lack thereof. Essentially, reflecting on it was taboo.

If we criticize Mogadishu now, our critique becomes hypocritical if we don't acknowledge how close the ideas and actions of the involved comrades were to ours. It is our brothers and sisters who made these mistakes. Their motives were right, but their actions weren't fully thought through. We don't want to judge comrades, but we want to bring those who still advocate such actions back to a sane(r) revolutionary practice.

7: Practical Internationalism
The internationalist sloganeering of a guerrilla driven to desperate actions by the state's antiterrorism propaganda as well as the prison

conditions of their (and our) comrades must not prevent us from reflecting on practical internationalism.

The strong internationalism of the early European workers' movement brought different peoples together. Its organizational expression was the Socialist International. It suffered its first major defeat when the peoples of Europe and the vast majority of the workers' parties cheered as they were propelled into World War I.

However, in the wake of this bloodbath caused by imperialist madness, and after unspeakable suffering and sacrifice by the peoples of Europe, we witnessed, in Russia, the first successful proletarian and internationalist revolution. It triumphed over the weakest link in the chain of the European bourgeoisie, the feudal czarist regime.

The struggle by the European workers' movement intensified after World War I. There were small victories (the revolution in Hungary, the Munich Council Republic[13]) and enormous defeats. The sections of the working-class movement betraying internationalism had diminished across the continent, but the traitors (in the Weimar Republic, the SPD) were still stronger than the forces of the international proletarian revolution, not least due to their collaboration with the bourgeoisie. Whether the communist October Revolution was simply deformed or completely liquidated by Stalinism (as many of its best fighters clearly were) is an interesting, indeed burning question. Being cautious, I will not try to answer it. What is clear, however, is not just that the impact of the October Revolution was long-lasting (like that of the Paris Commune of 1871), but that it indeed changed the world.

Fascism showed its ugly face in Italy, Bulgaria, Hungary, Germany, and Spain. At first, it connected the most reactionary sections of the bourgeoisie with the particularly unstable and dishonorable sections of the declassed petty bourgeoisie and the lumpenproletariat. But it could only attain power with the help of pro-capitalist, half-hearted socialists such as Ebert, Noske, and Scheidemann.[14] These men choked the revolutionary proletarian offensive in blood and pacified it with false promises of social reform. It allowed fascism to ascend to power as a preventative (precautionary) counterrevolution, eventually unleashing the inferno of World War II. Large sections of the peoples threatened by fascism resisted heroically and made many sacrifices. The European workers' movement suffered tremendously but was morally strengthened. Politically, it was both strengthened and weakened, considering the division of Europe into a Western capitalist half and an Eastern communist one.

Once we broaden our perspective and look at the laws of history as well as contemporary developments outside of Europe, there is no way around the anticolonial and anti-imperialist revolutions in China, Algeria, Cuba, Vietnam, Libya, Angola, Mozambique, and Iran, to name but a few. They all happened during or after World War II and provided beacons of hope for humanity. (Today, some of that shining hope has been replaced by gloomy disappointment, but that is the flip side of the coin. Hope stays on top.)

Eventually, a diverse rebellious movement emerged among young workers and apprentices, both in the US and Europe's capitalist core countries. The resistance in France and the US against the imperialist colonial wars in Algeria and Vietnam were important for the victory of the Algerian and the Vietnamese peoples. The Vietnam movement triggered a tremendous antiauthoritarian movement. In the US, it spread from Berkeley to the entire country; in Europe, from Strasbourg, Paris, Berlin, Milan, Rome, Frankfurt, and London to the entire continent (as the events in Warsaw and Prague proved, it did not stop at the boundary between the military blocs). We saw an active international exchange of ideas, the development of new forms of struggle and new lifestyles, and the self-organization of oppressed minorities and territories in all countries of the metropole, in an intensity never seen before. In spite of the rulers attempting to cause divisions and splits; in spite of increased repression and half-hearted reforms; in spite of sectarianism and waning solidarity (particularly pronounced in the multicolored Federal Republic of Germany, causing depression among many), the movement of 1968 grew stronger and sparked multiple mass movements. Today, the antinuclear movement challenges the power of mighty corporations and their political lackeys. Millions of people—out of a sense of sheer self-preservation—are disputing the rights of capitalists to decide on billion-dollar investments. Wyhl and Malville represent the internationalism of the antinuclear movement—Seveso, Contergan, and, most recently, the near maximum credible accident of Harrisburg represent the international dimension of the deadly threat posed by capitalism's industrial mode of production.[15] An increased struggle against armament and militarism, for a demilitarized Europe, and for the disarmament of the superpowers are features of the current socialist movement. Considering the enormous challenges, and the difficulties to find solutions, the delusional monopoly on internationalism that the armed German student jetsetters believe they own is a bad joke. Is the most advanced internationalist the one who has been to the most airports? Up, up, and away!

The multinational character of wage earners in the multicolored republic, not least in connection to persistent mass unemployment and increasingly harsher antilabor immigration policies, offers the internationalist German left a vast terrain for action. There is certainly more internationalist consciousness and willingness to struggle alongside the German left among the immigrant workers than vice versa. Educational task for the German left: learn the languages of the immigrant workers! Practical task for the German left: support the struggles of the immigrant workers! Learn from the struggles and the political culture of our neighboring peoples!

We want everything: abolition of prisons! But if we return to our starting point—the controversy about prison conditions and the "correct demands" for changing them—then prison abolition must, once and for all, be seen as an international task, and, therefore, the practical struggle for prison abolition must be carried out internationally. (In this regard, and not only in this regard, the struggles for communism and for prison abolition go hand in hand.)

Amnesty International is a half-hearted, bourgeois project. It chooses the bourgeois tactics of information campaigns and appealing to people's morality, mainly condemns torture, and demands only the liberation of "political" prisoners. It does not challenge the loopy practice of rewarding the socially deviant behavior of underprivileged minorities and the diverse forms of struggle against social injustice with prison sentences. Sure, Amnesty can save the lives of the people they campaign for. Yet the abolition of all institutions of isolation and repression, and of all inhumane constraints anywhere in the world, is not the task of Amnesty International but of the international progressive and revolutionary movement.

Abolishing the private ownership of the means of production (and of gummy bears) is only a first necessary step toward the revolutionary world commune. Thereafter, all social inequalities, privileges, and authoritarian and undemocratic structures will be replaced by (ever-changing) collective forms of life, by collective decision-making, and by collective learning. This requires relentless communist, democratic, and anti-authoritarian struggle.

(The second-to-last sentence in the paragraph above contains the word *collective* three times. The already-cited comrade who has read my manuscript underlined the sentence three times and wrote: "If you make too many jokes, no one will take you seriously." If I interpret the note correctly, it is not questioning people's ability to work collectively, it is questioning my ability to work collectively. Indeed, within an isolated small group in prison, I have great difficulties in working collectively in a way that would satisfy the high expectations of my fellow prisoners. Among other things, my wavering, idiosyncratic, and self-centered position during a past hunger strike probably didn't help. I have heard that people felt that the paper with which I tried to contribute to the hunger strike discussion was subjectivist and demagogical.[16] Our attempts to formulate collective opinions on the state of the world—"As we see it"—also caused plenty of irritation. I suppose mostly because of my somewhat distinct—and foolish—approach to writing. So much for the comments of those who read my manuscripts.)

Crime and prison will be meaningless in the new society. Their meaninglessness can already be felt now. The movement of community groups,[17] and other rebellious projects, must not rest before all people—that is, 100 percent—have organized in a spirit of democracy, socialism, solidarity, and bacchanalia. Crimes against the revolution, socialism, and democracy must be fought with increased education, communication, and capacity for criticism and self-criticism (in a spirit of solidarity) and with all-encompassing tenderness.

In the European country with the highest incarceration rate, there is one prisoner for every one thousand inhabitants. The task of the prison abolition movement is to ensure that one thousand inhabitants collectively take care of that one prisoner. It is first and foremost the consequences of class society, social injustice, and class struggle—as well as statistical randomness—that puts a person in prison.

We must also find meaningful tasks for jailers, court officials, prosecutors, criminal court judges, and others whose lives are even more tragic than those of prisoners.

Prisons will not be abolished by a general amnesty or an act of mercy. Amnesty, even for individuals or smaller groups, requires mass movements. Prison abolition will be the result of a general intensification of revolutionary struggle and a strong sense of social responsibility.

The prison abolition struggle in the multicolored republic cannot be isolated from the struggle for prison abolition in East Germany and other neighboring countries. It belongs to the propaganda of the rulers to paint repression in other countries in the darkest of colors. It is the task of the revolutionary movements to fight repression in their own countries with courage, energy, patience, and humor, while not ignoring the repression in others.

8: Criminals and Drug Addicts

Criminals and drug addicts of all countries must be integrated into the progressive and revolutionary movement through solidarity and education. When the hardened and misanthropic custodians who serve as cogs in the parasitical extermination machine that defines the unjust current order speak of "rehabilitation," socialists must establish better forms of communication, material help, and personal support for prisoners—all prisoners—through international as well as local Red, Black, and Green Aids, powerful proletarian counterparts to Amnesty International. Concretely, that means letters, newspapers, books, packages, visits, meetings, and actions, the integration of released or liberated prisoners in living and working collectives, and fighting units of all kinds. No progressive group, no collective house, no socialist group of sleepyheads must dodge this responsibility.

The consequences of isolation and despair among those whom the left denies solidarity could lead to a vicious circle of even more isolation, even less solidarity, and irrational putschist politics. Disappointments and defeats are recipes for illusion, error, weakness, failure, and compromise.

9: Indians Don't Cry

None of this means that Indians readily surrender. The dirty tricks of the palefaces are known. Indians don't stop fighting for collective freedom and collective happiness.

My red sisters and brothers! Our love and solidarity, our imagination, our courage, our patience, our determination, our cleverness, our tenderness, our humor, our capacity for criticism and self-criticism, and our hope are stronger than everything the palefaces can buy with money.

Howgh, I have spoken!

TRIALS

OUR CONTRIBUTION TO THE TEACH-IN ON JANUARY 27

(1977)

The Moabit Gang of Six

The defendants in the Lorenz-Drenkmann trial (the "Moabit Gang of Six") comment on a legal case against Waltraud "Wally" Siepert and Christine "Tina" Doemeland, who were accused of having organized apartments and vehicles for the 2nd of June Movement. The "teach-in" was a meeting of supporters of the defendants in preparation for the trial. Siepert was eventually sentenced to three years and eight months in prison; Doemeland received a lighter sentence. The document was circulated internally under the header "unser beitrag zum teach-in am 27.1.77."

We don't want to repeat everything that's already been said—or that will be said—on the legal aspects of the so-called supporter trial. So we'll keep it short.

We are printers, truck drivers, welders, etc. Except for one of us, we are all workers. Almost all of us have a criminal record of trespassing, breach of the public peace, property damage, civil disorder, theft, arson, and other so-called offenses. What we did was always directed against the rulers, the proprietors, the occupiers, the imperialists, and their lackeys, but never against the people. We all have experiences from prisons or reformatories, this is nothing new to us. We say that because the times are gone when those accused of urban guerrilla activities came from the student scene.

We are workers, which is why the prosecutors try to intimidate us, speculating that we workers will break in prison, making it easy for them to take us to court. They follow the motto "A fuck and a bottle of wine, that's the prole's sunshine!" We've been offered both, they've tried to buy us. It's good to have proof, but it's even better to have traitors on your side. Buback and the prosecutors have neither in this case, which is why they are in trouble. They've been forced to come up with a new spin. They needed to avoid a huge embarrassment.

The second trial against Wally and Tina started yesterday. Officially, they are on trial for supporting us. In legal terms, they supported a criminal organization. In reality, the trial is about much more.

The objective of the trial against Wally and Tina is to reach a sentence that can be used in the trial against the 2nd of June Movement members themselves. It shall boost the position of the federal prosecutors who have a hard time providing evidence. They want to silence us during our trial and make it impossible to defend ourselves. That is why, under all circumstances and at all costs, the 2nd of June Movement has to be declared a criminal organization *before* our trial starts.

We are not interested in categories such as "criminal." Any revolutionary action against capitalist exploitation is criminal for those in power, because it is dangerous for them. In the trial against Wally and Tina, we shall be prejudged without being able to defend ourselves, since we aren't in the dock. So Buback can have us sentenced in peace and quiet. Then, in the trial against us, all he has to do is read the sentence from the trial against Wally and Tina, and that will be it.

The "Bubacksecution" and the political state prosecution here in Berlin try to ensure that the question of whether armed struggle against capitalist exploitation and imperialism (and therefore the actions of the 2nd of June Movement) are justified will not be raised in the trial against us. In addition to the reasons already mentioned, there are two more of importance:

1. There will probably be big national and international interest in our trial. People will follow it attentively.
2. Buback—the vain lawn gnome—wants to preside over the trial against us himself. He wants to present himself as a righteous man who can handle a spectacular trial against the urban guerrilla with his stubby fingers. That's why he wants to depoliticize the trial and cover up (or settle prior to it) anything related to the history, struggle, and intentions of the 2nd of June Movement—or the "criminal" 2nd of June Movement, as this label will be very

important for him. The possibilities for us and our defense to have an influence on the proceedings will be very limited. The trial will be, in the truest sense of the term, a show trial.

According to Buback's state security intentions, there can't be any propaganda for the goals and the armed struggle of the 2nd of June Movement. The only thing that shall be determined in the trial against us is who has done what and where. Although even that no longer seems necessary . . .

The main trial against the 2nd of June Movement is no longer the trial about the Drenkmann assassination, the Lorenz kidnapping, the liberation of revolutionaries from prison, or other revolutionary actions directed against exploitation and oppression. *The main trial is the trial against Wally and Tina!*

The political prosecutors will try to ensure a sentence that defines the 2nd of June Movement as a criminal organization. They want to do what they so far have failed to do in all the trials against members and so-called sympathizers of the 2nd of June Movement due to lack of evidence and inadequate proceedings.

We must understand and remember this. We must prevent class justice from quietly and secretly determining all aspects of the trial against Wally and Tina.

That is one aspect of the trial against them. Another one, equally important, is that the trial against them will not only target us but *everyone!* They want to make an example of Wally and Tina—especially Wally, who has already been imprisoned for a year and a half. But it's not only about these two. It's also about all the other alleged sympathizers of the armed struggle who are held in prison for months. There's the comrade EB who's been imprisoned for almost a year now and is hardly ever mentioned. He, too, must expect a trial before ours as an alleged supporter of the 2nd of June Movement.[1]

Much time in remand and long prison sentences shall intimidate and deter those willing to support, or join, the armed struggle of the 2nd of June Movement and other urban guerrilla groups against exploitation and domination, against oppression and imperialism, for self-organization and social liberation.

We do not have high hopes for being able to stop the trial against Wally and Tina, but we have to try. The release of Peter and Christoph has shown that it is worth fighting.[2] We don't appeal to charity, or "solidarity with the victims," and we need not rage against the crime of class justice either. We have to prevent the trial because it will set a legal precedent. This form of presentencing is new. And we won't be the only ones affected. Soon, the trials against the revolutionary left and the urban guerrilla will be held with the defendants not even being allowed to attend. That's why we must try to prevent the first showcase of this state security plot.

Our demands are:

- An immediate end to the proceedings against Wally, Tina, and all other alleged sympathizers of the 2nd of June Movement!!!!!!!
- The immediate release of Wally and EB!!! (And of us too, of course.)
- Be creative! Take initiative! This teach-in can only be the beginning.
- Use all means of counterinformation at your disposal: leaflets, chants, posters, pirate radio.
- Send masses of coffins and cakes to the house of Judge Kubach! All it takes is a phone call.
- Come en masse to the courtroom and *occupy it*!
- Bring chocolate kisses! Yummy, creamy faces of judges and prosecutors!
- It's also a guerrilla tactic to shit in an envelope and send it to the judge. Everyone can do it. The more, the better!
- Publish emergency issues of your papers!

Oh, and you have a mind of your own too! Chocolate kisses aren't everything. Support the movement, join the fight!

The Moabit Gang of Six

MAY 9 DECLARATION IN COURT
(1978)

2nd of June Defendants

The defendants in the Lorenz-Drenkmann trial read this statement in court on May 9, 1978. May 9 commemorates the surrender of the Nazi forces to the Red Army in 1945.

The day of liberation from fascism thirty-three years ago was a day of hope for the people of Germany and Europe. After the excessive terror of the brown hordes, after more than six million victims in the concentration camps, after sixty million casualties in the war, almost everyone agreed: never again!

But it didn't take long before it became clear that little more had changed in West Germany than the mask behind which the wirepullers of terror operate. Yes, some minions were lined up and executed, but the gentlemen Krupp, Abs, and Siemens were soon able to invest their war profits and make more profits.[1] No Rehse was ever held responsible for his murders. No Schleyer, Filbinger, or Kiesinger ever had any disadvantage because of their Nazi past—quite the contrary![2] Since 1945, the profits have been disappearing into the same pockets as before, while the same people have been disappearing in the prisons: socialists and communists.

Three years ago, the antifascist Werner Sauber died in a shootout in Cologne. Two years ago, the antifascist Ulrike Meinhof was murdered in Stammheim. They and others in this country joined legions of antifascists killed in the war and the concentration camps. Our anger and sadness prevent us from retreating into a corner. We are continuing the struggle for the German and the international working class.

In order to express our respect for the courageous antifascist fighters, we call on everyone in this room to rise from their seats and observe a minute of silence in honor of those who gave their lives in the antifascist resistance.

THE 1977 TORTURE WEEKEND
(1979)

Ralf Reinders

A written court statement by Ralf Reinders presented on February 22, 1979, addressing the "torture weekend" of 1977, during which he and other 2nd of June prisoners were severely mistreated by state security agents.

———

I refuse to accept the district court judges Geus, Weiss, and Bauer due to a possible conflict of interest.

The reason: On February 19, 1979, these three judges have ordered that the defendants (including myself) should be physically and mentally examined by a so-called expert. The so-called expert's report shall include an evaluation of the possible success of treatment. Since the three judges in their proceedings cite section 246a of the Code of Criminal Procedure, it needs to be made clear that the vague term "success of treatment" implies the psychiatrization of political prisoners.

Since the three named judges have shown with numerous decisions that they aim to defame, offend, and destroy the health of the defendants, we must assume that they will use section 246a to full effect, meaning that enforced psychiatrization is a possibility.

In the trials against the armed resistance groups, it is common to portray the defendants as sick. With respect to Ulrike Meinhof, the dissection of her brain could only be prevented at the very last moment by an international protest campaign. In the case of other political prisoners, too, public intervention was needed to prevent psychiatrization. Since the named judges have remained vague about their intentions, they might want to introduce psychiatrization through the back door. Hence, the conclusion that there is a conflict of interest.

The judges rejected an earlier motion by me to be medically examined by an antifascist commission. At the time, they argued that there was no reason for such an examination. Suddenly, there seems to be one. This only makes my suspicions stronger that by rejecting my motion, the judges wanted to cover up torture and its consequences. This, of course, is no longer just a conflict of interest; it is the facilitation of a crime.

When I speak of torture, I can give several examples. It would include the enforced cutting of my beard and hair on May 21 and 22, 1977, for subsequent lineups. This caused a number of injuries. Several state security agents and the prosecutor Dörfler were responsible. My hands, which, at first, were tied in front of my stomach, were twisted all the way behind my back. My lower arms were on the back of a chair, with a state security agent sitting on them. Some of his colleagues punched me in the stomach and the kidneys. They also hit me in the kidneys with their knees. To enable a barber to give me a haircut based on a drawing presented to him, one agent suffocated me. Gagging followed. This has been documented by Amnesty International. I will only list the injuries that I received during those two days: on my lower arms, the skin had cracked twenty-three times (1.5 to 3 cm); on my arms and legs, I had several hematomas (about 10×4 cm); I had a cut of 1 cm behind my ear; I could not move my lower arms or hands; I felt nothing around my left kidney; and I had piercing pain in my right shoulder. To this day, I cannot move my right shoulder or my lower left arm without pain. Using my left wrist is even worse. With my left hand, I can no longer hold a bottle without fearing to drop it. I have several scars on both hands.

The judges don't allow me to see doctors of my own choice to document the injuries. They know that if torture was confirmed, their trial would be considered unlawful in a country with a democratic constitution. The judges have, of course, no interest in doctors documenting the consequences of torture. They have an interest in receiving an "expert's report" that justifies enforced psychiatrization and preventive custody.

The judges do not give us any possibility to participate in the trial—and we are eight months into it! Despite having been in remand for four years, we were not given the opportunity to prepare our defense. This recalls the fascist legal system. There is no comparable example in postwar Germany. The judges have not missed a single opportunity to ensure that our prison and living conditions are the worst possible. They are cutting off our air. There are reasons for this, and we have presented them often enough. The same is true for the court now talking about preventive custody.

The courts serve a political agenda. It acts as the long arm of state security. Both the courts and state security are not satisfied with imprisoning resistance fighters; they want to break and destroy them.

The courts and state security aim to demonstrate to the underprivileged and the youth (deceived and disappointed by the regime) that resistance is futile and that everyone who resists will be destroyed. Egon Bahr from the SPD has made this very clear in his article on the "German Jusos."[1] The isolation and destruction of the untamable minorities (Bahr means us) is a task that we can confidently leave to our democratic/socialist colleagues in the corridors of state security. Egon "Noske" Bahr speaks repeatedly of "destruction," "defiance," and "anarchist/terrorist brutes." He provides the theory that his accomplices in the government offices and courtrooms put into practice. The accomplices ensure that judges from their law departments are channeled into the trials, something that was only revealed because some of them were talking carelessly. If you need confirmation, look at the career of Judge Paetzelt.[2]

There are several reasons why there is so much talk about "preventive custody" in this trial. First, the legal system believes that we aren't capable of mobilizing a movement against preventive custody and that, once established, it will be common practice for political prisoners. And this will not only concern armed resistance fighters but anyone who dares to criticize the democratic Federal Republic of Germany. What we see is a state in crisis threatening, intimidating, and destroying its critics. We will see more of it, since the worsening economic and political conditions will breed more resistance. In Celle, the authorities reserved eighty prison cells for the clashes expected in Gorleben.[3]

The state can reserve prison cells, threaten, intimidate, and destroy as much as it wants, but this won't stop the resistance. The capitalist crisis is in full swing and will proletarianize ever bigger sections of society. The proletarianization is the consequence of the increase of capitalism's productive resources, that is, a consequence of rationalization. Rationalization means the increase of labor productivity by the use of more effective technological and organizational tools in production and administration. That, in turn, means that fewer people will produce more value under more intensive and painful working conditions. Meanwhile, numerous jobs are being lost. Rationalization degrades workers and leads to lower wages and unemployment. This, in turn, leads to less purchasing power. But if the productivity of labor increases while purchasing power decreases, the capitalist productive forces will clash with capitalist tariff barriers, and capitalism will enter a crisis.

If capitalism wants to master this crisis, it must continue to increase productivity at lower (wage) costs. This, however, creates a spiral leading to the collapse of the entire system. We would have already seen the system's collapse had not the state come to its rescue with subsidies, new tax regulations, tariffs, and so on. The state and capital are increasingly melting together, with the state being capital's "class organization," controlling the production process. But that's not all. In capital's interest, the state also controls the sphere of reproduction. Struggles in that sphere (about homes, playgrounds, kindergartens, a sustainable environment, etc.) instantly clash with the interests of capital and the state serving it. Even if people are not conscious of it, the state will know and deem their resistance dangerous, because any form of resistance, conscious or unconscious, is a direct anticapitalist attack.

The reason the armed resistance is so dangerous is the fear that politically motivated military actions can be adopted, and expanded, by the people. The use and threat of preventive custody shall not only deter those who are ready for armed resistance now but also those who might be in the future. The central role that preventive custody plays in this trial confirms this. The trial will address the only exchange of prisoners that ever worked in West Germany, the consequence of a politically motivated military action. Worse, the people understood what our action was about. It found approval among large parts of the population. This could not have been expected.

The leaders of West Germany and West Berlin suffered a unique defeat. This cannot be undone. Revenge is all they have. Their revengefulness shall serve as a brutal deterrent for others.

Judges who try to introduce enforced psychiatrization of political prisoners through the back door, who help to cover up torture, and who demand preventive custody on behalf of a regime looking both for revenge and deterrence reveal a conflict of interest and must step down.

THE UNRELENTING OF THE SPREE
(1978)

Interview conducted in 1978 in writing by Wolfram Bortfeldt, journalist of the weekly news magazine *Stern*, with Fritz Teufel, Ralf Reinders, Gerald Klöpper, and Ronald Fritzsch during the Lorenz-Drenkmann trial. The interview was never published in the *Stern*, but it was released as a pamphlet under the title *Die Unbeugsamen von der Spree*. The Spree is the biggest river crossing Berlin.

———

How did the 2nd of June Movement emerge? What personal and political experiences led to the decision to start an urban guerrilla and go underground?

On the 2nd of June 1878, Kaiser Wilhelm was lying in hospital with a royal bum full of lead, pondering why people were turning against him. He had been attacked heading for the zoo with the Shah of Persia, who was visiting Berlin. On the 2nd of June 1967, while another Shah of Persia was visiting Berlin, the student Benno Ohnesorg was shot dead by police officer Kurras in alleged (putative) self-defense. Apart from that, the origins of the 2nd of June Movement lie in a number of more or less pleasurable sex acts committed by more or less inhibited married German couples during the 1940s and 50s, leading to the protagonists, freaks, and free-sex maniacs of the 2nd of June Movement to be conceived.

In the criminal fantasies of state attorneys, the 2nd of June Movement is one of various associations committing terrorist crimes, with a membership list, bylaws, leaders, specialists, and sympathizers.

The establishment refuses to believe that this association contributes to the common good. In the revolutionary fantasies of other people, the 2nd of June Movement is a subversive force that arose and developed in the aftermath of the 2nd of June 1967. It has its stomping grounds in Berlin, which is one of numerous stomping grounds in Germany for autonomous movements trying to change society and replace the hell of capitalist exploitation and alienation with a socialist society of free people—no rulers, no coercion.

When it started out in the early 1970s, the 2nd of June Movement served as a political and ideological umbrella for militant actions against the occupying forces,[1] class justice, capitalists, cops, and the messy web of Berlin's dipshit politicians. The protagonists came from the radical-left scene. They struck and disappeared as it suited them, to the best of their knowledge and conscience.

What experiences moved, and still move, these people? The things we experience every day! The fetters of industrial capitalist life and the mode of production: the family, the school, the factory, the office, the university, the prison, the high-rise apartment building, the terrorist madness characteristic of life in capitalism. This led youth throughout the world to the barricades and to experiments with new forms of struggle and community. It led to the desire to live autonomously, not as puppets, cogs, robots, as manipulated, consuming idiots of a system pretending to be natural while it is entirely controlled by profit interest.

Underground? What does that mean? After every action that doesn't fit into our popular yet remarkably odd system, the cops fill out a lottery ticket. It could have been her, or maybe him, or maybe some other "violent terrorist" (police language) on wanted posters.

As soon as you discover a more or less reasonable likeness of yourself on the wall, you need to make a choice: either you choose life aboveground, the police state, the society of yesteryear, and you turn yourself in, allowing the police to milk you for information ("No, it wasn't me, but maybe it was my buddy?!"), doing a few years in prison nonetheless, just because; or you choose life underground, the society of tomorrow ("Kiss my ass!"). In that case, you'll be living on the run.

Wait, is this a choice forced on you by the cops? Can you only "choose freely" between two murderous ways to live? Don't we have to ask a very different question? Isn't it the very task of the movement to render the frameworks and the straitjackets of the police unusable? A computer only knows yes and no, 1 and 0. The revolutionary knows life and learns about it from all angles. The transitions between legality and illegality are fluid. People who aren't sought by the police can do all sorts of illegal things; people who are sought by the police can live for years without involvement in urban guerrilla actions. They can live abroad, in rural communes, or they can work with false papers in an office, in a factory, or wherever else.

What was permitted yesterday may be banned today; it all depends on the whim of the rulers. In the past few years alone, around five hundred assholes in Bonn have nearly suffocated a few dozen people in prison with a whole pile of shitty new laws.

Have you been influenced by theoretical writings?
If you're asking about the books that need to be banned to protect the state, it's all of them! Everything that feeds the imagination is dangerous. Books about American Indians, travel accounts, magazines—*The Manipulated Man* in the *Stern* is incredibly dangerous.[2] Various writings provide food for thought and explain complex relationships. But the motivation to engage in armed resistance comes from concrete, practical experience, the lack of rights at work, the terror of social norms, the contradiction between formal rights and the lack of power to implement them.

Horst Mahler has said that the decision to go underground is not an easy one. How does the underground change you?
We must not think that anything is easy. Illegality, legality, the factory, the prison, the CDU, the SPD—our "free choices" are always between ick and ugh. Nobody goes underground voluntarily, and if we're criminalized, we defend ourselves against labels such as "illegals" and "terrorists." To defend yourself and resist is possible and necessary in all areas of life and in any situation.

Illegality is nothing special. It can happen to anyone, like stepping in dog shit. This is proven by the persecution of antinuclear activists at Brokdorf and Grohnde, or by the raids against the Frankfurt women's groups.[3] We will neither glorify nor demonize illegality. In a police state, it's everyday business, and we need to remain levelheaded. Mahler once said that revolutionary politics are necessarily criminal, and he is the alleged author of a very popular pamphlet.[4] At the time, he lived in a forest of exclamation marks: "Understand! Act already! Do something!" Today, he lives in a forest of question marks and allows himself to be presented to an educated audience as an antiterrorist scarecrow. Mahler is probably genuine, but, like many others, he's gone from exuberant enthusiasm to exuberant bitterness. What is needed is a sober relationship to reality, also the reality of life underground. In the mixed coniferous forest of our progressive everyday life, we see exclamation marks and question marks and circle-As. A capacity to act, enthusiasm, to be "on it," and the ability to engage in self-criticism (which includes taking the criticism of others seriously, even if the cops make every effort to use any type of criticism to their advantage) must not exclude each other.

Doesn't life underground undermine contact to the masses, the ultimate goal?

Criminalization is a means by the police to isolate people they consider dangerous. Of course it is. But there's isolation in capitalism everywhere. The struggle against isolation and for solidarity is central to any revolutionary practice. It is not life underground that undermines contact to the masses, but the smelly vanguardist arrogance that may result from it. We are not preachers who promise salvation. The task of the guerrilla is to demonstrate and organize possibilities of resistance against a seemingly all-powerful state and its beneficiaries. When antinuclear activists prevent environmental destruction through sabotage or the occupation of construction sites; when women's groups organize abortion clinics or journeys to get abortions abroad; when students gain a day of freedom from the performance terror in the learning factory through an anonymous bomb threat—then all of that is guerrilla too. Guerrilla is no religion but the very form in which the masses struggle.

Were your actions rather spontaneous or well planned? How did you feel afterward?

The conditions of the struggle do, of course, demand a certain degree of planning. But spontaneity is an important part of it, since no action, in reality, will unfold as planned.

The RAF has strong hierarchical tendencies. What's the situation like in the 2nd of June Movement? How are decisions made? What is the relationship with the RAF like?

We don't know all that much about the RAF. Active RAF members always say that their organization is characterized by tenderness and a strong sense of belonging. In the case of the 2nd of June Movement, the women oppress the men, the proles oppress the students, and vice versa. Decisions are made by throwing dice or by brawling—sadly, whatever the outcome, the decisions are always wrong. Our relationship with the RAF is erotic and family-like.

Have there been people who decided to leave your group?
Yes!

After the Till Meyer breakout, the Revolutionary Cells published a statement. Was that not a 2nd of June action?
The Revolutionary Cells took responsibility for the actions against the court-imposed lawyers. As Till Meyer has stated during his trial, the liberation was carried out by the "Nabil Harb Commando."

There was something written about the "2nd of June Movement bankruptcy assets." Is the 2nd of June Movement about to dissolve?
The 2nd of June Movement is a political concept. It stands for the daily manifestation of the resistance that arose from the youth revolt of the 1960s. The 2nd of June Movement is embodied by anyone who has tried, and continues to try, to resist everyday capitalist terror and to open up alternatives. That includes squatting and taking control over your youth center; it includes prison and women's groups, self-managed day cares, alternative newspapers, organizers of rent strikes and abortion trips; and it includes the internationalist solidarity committees with the peoples of Vietnam, Iran, Palestine, Angola, West Sahara, and so on.

The armed commandos are an expression and a result of this movement—they came from it, were nurtured by it, and were dependent on it, even if some people today deny that. They intended to transform the latent revolutionary character of the movement into exemplary revolutionary actions in order to help overcome the feeling of powerlessness vis-à-vis, for example, the prison system and the police.

Neither the movement nor its armed groups have dissolved. But there has been a far-reaching process of transformation, and it is continuing. Today, there is no longer much talk about the "terror of consumption." Unemployment has become a big issue. It is no longer the fear for emergency laws that brings political opposition to the streets, it is the police and the state security apparatus staging a civil war in which laws count for nothing—look at Grohnde, Brokdorf, Stammheim, border control, surveillance, BEFA, big brother DISPOL, factory security (including keeping files on workers), and so on and so forth.[5] The social downward spiral that the majority of the population is caught in creates a different kind of dissatisfaction than the moral outrage of the students against imperialist bloodbaths far away.

If you will, we are witnessing a period in which the idealistic character of resistance is transforming into a material one. This also means a shift in the balance between armed and unarmed actions, and a restructuring of resistance, that is, of the forms of resistance and organization.

Karl-Heinz Dellwo has said that some actions puzzle and alienate sympathizers. Is Bommi Baumann right when he says that the guerrilla now follows a dynamic it no longer controls?
That's true. The skyjacking to Mogadishu was an action against the people. Some folks say that it is populist to seek the sympathy of the people, while it is revolutionary not to give a fuck about that. We are on the side of populism because we can never lose the sympathies of the masses given our dazzling looks.

Bommi Baumann follows a particular dynamic: whenever he needs money, he comes up with a new story, because the old ones no longer sell. One example is the stuff about "nuclear blackmail."[6] For us, this is where the fun ends. It was racist Yanks who dropped nuclear bombs on Japanese megacities. We've been fearing for a long time that nuclear profiteers and their political lackeys will blame us for the first bigger nuclear disaster, whether it will occur at a nuclear power plant or during warfare. That Bommi is joining in the choir shows where you can end up when you decide to become the rulers' propaganda whore.

Did the 2nd of June Movement, when it was founded, see West Germany as a fascist state? Has your analysis changed?
Nonsense! The West German state wasn't and isn't fascist. But the state bureaucracy, first and foremost the police and the justice system, have not changed since the Third Reich—in fact, they haven't changed since Kaiser Wilhelm. Even in the Weimar Republic they served the powerful, the reactionaries, capital. That's how things are in class society. The state bureaucracy is responsible for the terror of the state in times of crisis.

Individual judges, state prosecutors, and cops might, of course, feel completely unbiased. The repressive apparatus functions through (Prussian) drills and (class) reflexes. We would have to be blind not to see any difference between Freisler trials at the Nazis' "People's Court" (*Volksgerichtshof*), which led to off-with-his-head verdicts within ten minutes, and our trial, which will extend over months, even years, also leading to a predetermined sentence of course, but—at least apparently— within a constitutional framework. We are even allowed to do interviews. Very nice!

Fascism can't simply be juxtaposed to the normal bourgeois state, like black to white. The transitions are fluid. Both are forms of capitalist rule. West Germany is not a fascist state, but it has fascist tendencies, which have become considerably more pronounced in recent years. Of course, the methods today are much more refined and subtle. Let's take the prisons as an example: prisoners are still frequently beaten up and tossed into padded cells, where they may be injected with sedatives against their will. During the hunger strike in summer 1977, the concern for the welfare of RAF prisoners in Hamburg was so great that wooden wedges were used to smash their teeth in when they refused to be force-fed. Our wrists were tied with iron shackles by a state security SWAT team in May 1977 until they bled, our hair was pulled out in handfuls, and our kidneys received a bastion of kicks. Why? To break our resistance to mandatory haircuts and to punish us for grimacing during lineups. Amnesty International raised concerns. A renowned legal expert spoke of torture. The media remained silent.

There are also dead wings, where, for example, Astrid Proll and Ulrike Meinhof were completely isolated for months and years.[7] It was correct to speak of "white torture" in these cases. The contact ban renders prisoners defenseless and deprives them of their rights at the whim of the regime in Bonn. Filbinger can be considered a horrifying jurist.[8] Incidents in a prison in Baden-Württemberg, where he is minister-president, were never investigated and were covered up with tall tales and an impenetrable blanket of official statements. Yes, all of this pales in comparison to the torture techniques and the atrocities committed during the Nazi regime—but the Nazi regime is no meaningful standard.

The question about fascism keeps the majority of the left in West Germany from addressing the issue of armed resistance in a reasonable way. To them, it appears that armed struggle is only legitimate when it targets openly fascist expressions of capitalist rule. But German history has shown that by then it can be too late. Armed struggle does not need to be justified by frantic attempts to prove that we live in a fascist state. Some comrades have wasted way too much time and energy on that.

The actions of the 2nd of June Movement and the RAF have led to more funding for the police and to stricter laws. This also affects the legal left. Did you consider these consequences before you took action?

When you obey your master and allow others to exploit you, you need not fear reprisal. When you don't do that, there'll be attempts to violently coerce you. The stronger the resistance, the more pronounced the master's terror. If it was otherwise, there would be no masters and no subjects. To abandon the idea of self-determination only to avoid being subjected to the master's terror is no sustainable alternative.

Revolutionary actions are always a pretext for limiting civil rights granted by the bourgeoisie and for expanding the apparatus of oppression. But they are not the reason for this. The emergency laws and the "hand grenade law" were implemented before there was revolutionary action. Also the mobile task force commandos were established long before the first bigger guerrilla actions were carried out. The guerrilla cannot be blamed for the professional bans either.

That actions—or suspected actions—by minorities and small groups are used to justify repression is something we are all too familiar with from fascism. Let us turn this line of argument against the rulers themselves: the exploitation of the people as well as the terror of the police and the prison system have always caused increased resistance and bloody revolutions. Do the rulers consider these consequences? Apparently, they do.

During your trial, Ralf Reinders said, "It is and remains our goal to win over the majority of the population." How does that fit in with the skyjacking of a Lufthansa airliner carrying vacationers?

It doesn't!

Horst Mahler has said that the state uses the terrorists to gradually liquidate the civil liberties that were conceded to the people in 1949, following the collapse of fascism. Shouldn't we focus on defending these liberties right now?

The bosses say: "Blame the lazy if we pay lower wages!" The lawmakers say: "Blame the thickheaded people if we use thicker clubs!" The SS said: "Blame the partisans if we massacre the entire village!" But how can you use these arguments in a democracy in which, supposedly, the people rule? Are we stupid enough to exploit, oppress, and massacre ourselves? The logic of liberation is not the same as the logic of oppression. But okay, we will kiss our torturers' asses so that Horst Mahler gets a color TV.

Bommi Baumann has called Mogadishu "elitist madness." He has also said that the murder of Schleyer caused a political setback. Isn't political progress first and foremost coming from legal grassroots organization, the kind we see in the antinuclear groups or the community groups?[9]
The kidnapping and the death of the old Nazi and industrial leader Schleyer is in a different category than Mogadishu. But comparing a correct action with a false action does not only confuse people like Bommi Baumann. Only schematic thought and dogmatism on both sides allow maintaining the division between legal and illegal movements, between armed and unarmed citizens' groups. This thinking, these divisions, impede political progress. We struggle against that.

Was there any point, perhaps now in prison, where you felt that you got to a place where you were no longer doing what you had set out to do—where you felt that you needed to revisit your departure point?
Society is not fixed and stable. There are constant changes, processes, transformations, shifts in the balance of power. This means that your politics must always be reviewed and revisited. If that doesn't happen, your politics degenerate into dogmatism, become detached from reality, and end up being a blueprint for defeat. Or, as Marx says, "Proletarian revolutions . . . constantly criticize themselves, constantly interrupt themselves in their own course, return to the apparently accomplished, in order to begin anew; they deride with cruel thoroughness the half-measures, weaknesses, and paltriness of their first attempts, seem to throw down their opponents only so the latter may draw new strength from the earth and rise before them again more gigantic than ever, recoil constantly from the indefinite colossalness of their own goals—until a situation is created which makes all turning back impossible, and the conditions themselves call out: *hic Rhodus, hic salta!* Here is the rose, here dance!"[10]

On some days of the trial, the mood in the dock seems quite cheerful. What are you able to laugh about while facing life in prison?
"Life is serious enough, it becomes only bearable through laughing," as Gerald (Klöpper) likes to say. But seriously: this question can only be asked because sourpusses—or, let's say, sourpussness—has entered the colorful spectrum of left-wing sects. The perspective that capital offers us is ugly, whether it means life in prison or lifelong exploitation, imperialist war, and nuclear devastation. If you accepted any of these lots, there would indeed be nothing to laugh about. Yet the concept of the fun guerrilla is that life should be fun. It seems that people haven't understood the concept yet. It also means that the revolutionary struggle must be fun, because otherwise no one will join it. Those who resist can have fun too. It requires state violence to enforce dullness and prevent the Moabit puppet show from being drowned by laughter. Shall we remain serious when Peter Lorenz arrives to testify?

Andreas Vogel is currently without a lawyer of his choice. He refuses to cooperate with the court-imposed lawyer. Is he still able to mount a defense?
With a little goodwill, everything is possible: space flights without spaceships, legal defenses without lawyers. But it's much worse for the other side: they have to sit through the trial without morals, humanity, or reason.

What are your thoughts on the trial overall?
If we weren't prisoners, we wouldn't go. Sometimes it's exhausting, but it's still more entertaining than sitting in a prison cell. We also tried to use every opportunity to say things we wanted to say.

The trial has shown that courts are ill-equipped for defendants like us. When public interest waned—a natural process, we aren't the center of the universe—the federal prosecutors and the criminal division increasingly tried to steamroll us.

The special laws that can be used to limit the defense and to exclude the defendants from participating in the trial have been used to full capacity. Barely three months into the trial, the prosecutors had filed complaints with the court against all of our chosen lawyers for statements they had made during the proceedings. For the most part, our lawyers are young and inexperienced. Lawyers with experience in state security trials are either subject to the professional bans, like Henning

Spangenberg, or they were rejected with reference to section 146 of the Code of Criminal Procedure (ban on representing multiple clients). Lawyers from outside Berlin were not accepted either. Technically, they could have moved to Berlin, but that proved too costly.

We were excluded from the proceedings regularly, first for a day at a time, then indefinitely. The reason was our objections to the massive police contingent at the trial beating our friends and relatives in the audience whenever anyone made a sound. We also objected to the court-imposed lawyers acting against our will, for example by interrogating witnesses. Our attempts to speak during the trial were routinely ignored—even our lawyers of confidence weren't granted that right.

On certain days, it seemed as if the court had been promised bonuses if they concluded a particular task before a given deadline, for example when they were reading the indictment. An audio recording of the trial has been categorically denied. The presiding judge always makes sure that the minutes are to his liking. Any request by our lawyers to add anything is rejected. When a witness says, "I signed everything the authorities put in front of me," you will find nothing of it in the minutes. The presiding judge, on his part, seems pressured by members of the senate and the federal prosecutors. We and our lawyers certainly are under a lot of pressure from them! When we were banned from the trial indefinitely, we signed a statement declaring that we will behave much better in the future. The court deemed the statement insincere and insulting.

This is not just about a denial of democratic rights. Most frighteningly, state security measures are integrated into class justice. Normal prisoners (in prison jargon: cons) have never been able to invoke the rights they have on paper. To invoke these rights, you need money (such as successful financial fraudsters do), extraordinary public interest (as in the case of the *Spiegel* affair or the first student trials[11]), or a Nazi past, which guarantees a sympathetic application of the law by your peers. Judge Weiß, an associate judge of Friedrich Geus, acquitted for example Judge Rehse, once an associate judge at the Nazis' People's Court. And Judge Weiß is typical for the people working in Berlin's legal system. It is no different at other district courts, and not at the federal supreme court in Karlsruhe either. It has been suggested that the federal supreme court's German acronym BGH stands for "Brown Gangster Huddle" (*Brauner Gangsterhaufen*), but that is a joke. When we say that we expect a fair sentence in our trial, pretty much everyone gets the irony.

In a certain sense, the trial is already over for us, because our exclusion from it means that we can no longer defend or speak for ourselves. Even the limited options for a defense we had at the start no longer exist.

Have the prison conditions worsened since Till Meyer's escape, and if so, how?
Nothing has changed other than that partitions during visits are now mandatory. Before that (since a law reform passed on June 1), this only applied to lawyers visiting. The partitions are also mandatory for the defendants in the so-called supporter trials, and they were mandatory for the *Info BUG* printers as well.[12] In any case, rest assured that the prison conditions are shitty.

How have the partitions affected your preparation for the trial and the communication with the lawyers? How does it feel to sit behind a glass window?
It feels like you're sitting behind a store window looking out. Human contact? Forget it. It is difficult to go through the files with the lawyers because each sheet of paper has to be held up against the glass. Written documents that you could previously exchange during visits (the lawyers were always searched going in and out) now have to pass through the courts, which can take days, sometimes weeks. A focused preparation for specific stages of the trial is no longer possible.

How many visitors (relatives, friends) are you allowed to receive?
You are allowed a half-hour visit every fourteen days, with two security agents and a prison lawyer listening in. As we said, now there's always a partition. Since this has become mandatory, we have refused to accept visits. This is how it works in practice: we receive the visitors, so that they can see the partition, and then we call the visit off.

Which books and magazines are you allowed to read? Which ones are denied?
We still receive *Stern*, *Spiegel*, and bourgeois dailies. In the case of some West German prisoners, the publications are carefully censored. Newspapers and magazines that lean ever so slightly to the left cannot be

received. Even the social democratic *Neues Forum* from Vienna is deemed a security risk. Books have to go through the prison authorities, and they refuse to facilitate orders, so, right now, we don't get any books.

How often do you see each other as a group outside of the courtroom?
The six of us have one daily hour in the yard, and once a week two hours of table tennis and two common hours in order to exchange books, magazines, and documents, all of which is prohibited otherwise.

Do you have contact with other prisoners in remand?
Where shouting across the yard is possible, it is sanctioned with so-called institutional penalties (purchasing bans, denial of yard time, the hole) and transfers, both for us and the prisoners we communicate with. We can write letters, which will be censored, and which put the correspondents at risk. Repercussions for communicating with us are likely. There have been cases of prisoners being denied parole because they had corresponded with us. Otherwise, we have zero contact, we remain constantly isolated.

How often are your cells searched?
According to a court ruling, seven times in fourteen days, mostly in our absence. State security agents do their own searches on special occasions sanctioned by the judge—unofficially, they do searches every day. Our lawyers' files are read, photographed, copied, and stolen. Once, the federal prosecutors had a response to a motion ready that hadn't even been presented in court yet. Völz was embarrassed and his face was almost as red as his robe, but Judge Geus had no interest in mentioning any of it in the minutes.

To return to the searches: once a week, all of our possessions, including our food, are packed up and x-rayed by special staff in the so-called screening room. Our possessions end up on a table and are x-rayed from above without any radioprotection. Year in, year out. When our lawyers filed a complaint, the prison doctor said that there was no health risk whatsoever. Yet the staff working there received radioprotective clothing earlier this year, and on July 31, 1978, they shut the screening room down entirely. Could this be connected to the suspected colon cancer of prisoner Eberhard Dreher, who was subjected to the same routines as us?[13] Probably not. Now, our possessions are x-rayed in another room by a completely shielded device.

During the trial, the prison conditions have often been harshly criticized. What needs to change?

What do you mean, "What needs to change?" Prisons should be abolished because they keep class society intact. Obviously, prisons can only be abolished when there is general social transformation. We struggle for conditions that make survival possible, that secure our physical and psychological well-being. Not just ours, that of all prisoners. Concretely, this means integration into the general population and an end to special conditions. It also means that all prisoners must enjoy what now only a small, privileged minority in Moabit enjoys, namely, to be housed in groups.

We may add that the conditions in Moabit are worse than in all prisons of West Germany. If you're in general population, you get one hour a day of shared yard time. That's all the social contact you'll have for months or years. The rest of the time, twenty-three hours a day, you're alone in a cell. If you're housed in one of the groups, your cell will be opened seven and a half hours a day, and each evening you get two and a half hours of shared TV time.

The group unit has been presented by Baumann as a model for all prisoners serving more than a year.[14] In reality, only a fraction of those eligible end up there.

THE LORENZ TRIAL CLOSING STATEMENT MARATHON
(1980)

Ralf Reinders

This is the manuscript of Ralf Reinders's closing statement in the Lorenz-Drenkmann trial. It was never presented in court. Reinders refused to present it after Ronald Fritzsch was stopped by the presiding judge fifteen minutes into his closing statement. After consultation, the court sustained this decision with the following explanation: "The defendant Fritzsch has abused his right to a final statement. In spite of repeated warnings from the presiding judge, he read out severe insults from the trial minutes that the defendants had directed against participants in the proceedings. It served a purpose irrelevant to the proceedings, namely, to repeat the insults and to amuse parts of the audience. The defendant Fritzsch could have, and should have, changed his behavior following the warnings, had his intention been to use the quotes in a purposeful manner."

———

When the trial began, we had discussions about whether we should appear in the courtroom at all. There were good arguments against it. There was a clear risk that we would be degraded to extras who, through their presence, provided sustenance to a so-called democratic and constitutional theater.

The effort to reduce us to lifeless objects ran through this trial like the famous red thread. Expelling us was always the ultimate measure when we tried to defend ourselves. From the beginning, we weren't allowed to formulate and motivate motions the way we wanted to. There was an attempt to depoliticize the trial by focusing on criminal proceedings. That was the strategy of the court and the federal prosecutors. Why did the court and the federal prosecutors try to prove that we were common criminals who enriched themselves, living at the expense of others? Why these shenanigans when any child knows that revolutionary politics are necessarily illegal. You can't defeat the ruling system by abiding its laws. A regime that acknowledges a revolutionary struggle directed against it and doesn't treat it as criminal abandons itself. What regime could afford to acknowledge revolution as a necessity?

With regard to common criminals in a capitalist state, Brecht put it aptly: What's robbing a bank against founding a bank? The federal prosecutors Oh My, Ivory Tower, Know Nothing, and Speculator always say that we and our politics are entirely irrelevant, that we don't speak for anybody and not to anybody. If that was the case, this trial would have unfolded differently. In that case, the court and the federal prosecutors would have acted calmly and paternalistically and given us long sentences without denying our political motives. All of the mudslinging against our defense attorneys and ourselves would have been nothing but shadowboxing had it not been for a purpose. Since we knew what this purpose was, we decided to participate in the trial. We knew that they wanted to make us extras at our own trial, and that their objective was to make our goals, our politics, and our struggle appear as dead in the eyes of the public.

Our options are limited in any courtroom. The power lies with the state. Still, we were not prepared to abandon the field without a fight. Trials provide us with the opportunity to turn the courts into soapboxes for our struggle. Many people are interested in our trials, and we have to use them, as far as possible, for agitation and propaganda, conveying our politics to those we hope to win over.

Both sides—the court and the prosecution versus us—attempted from the outset to use the trial as a political stage. Our position was unquestionably the weaker: we were the visiting team, so to speak, and the outcome was a foregone conclusion. But we didn't lose on the terrain of the class struggle. In spite of the abuse and the mistreatment we experienced, of being thrown out of court, of being denied the right to speak, of being denied to file motions, and of having our lawyers appointed to us by the court, we scored a political victory by points.

Okay, we had our weak moments. Despite our extensive experience, we were sometimes staggered by the lies and the idiocy we were confronted with. But we were able to get our politics across. In the end, we will be convicted for the strength of our political convictions. Trials, and especially show trials like this one, are in bourgeois class society always a sword raised against those who wish to free themselves, who consciously or unconsciously struggle against a system that destroys both people and the natural world. With regard to the federal prosecutors' summation, which is legally and politically as meaningful as a losing ticket in a county fair raffle, we have nothing to say.

But for now, let's stay with the legal system. Taking a closer look and considering the last couple of years, even the healthiest person would fall ill. The eye of the law sits in the face of the ruling class, as Bloch once put it.[1] The justice system is never a neutral agency to protect the interests of all; it rather is a violent enforcer of the interests of bourgeois class society.

In 1945, with fascism lying in ruins, the Potsdam Agreement meant to make a resurgence of German imperialism impossible by eradicating all of the necessary conditions of an imperialist program.[2] This entailed breaking up monopolies and carrying out a rigorous denazification campaign—a denazification campaign that should have hit the German justice system hard. But the victorious Western capitalist powers needed a legal system, and, very soon, a specifically anticommunist legal system, with a clear idea of who the enemies were and with experience in how to prosecute them.

There was an anticapitalist sentiment among the German population following the fall of fascism. It dawned on the German people that the main responsibility for World War II didn't lie with Hitler but with German capital. Even the CDU paid lip service to this and demanded the expropriation of large industries and banks in the Ahlen Program.[3] In 1946, the population of Hesse voted in a referendum to abolish capitalism.[4] The referendum was declared illegal by an occupying general named Clay. The gentleman has gone down in history as the hero of the airlift, but no one has ever talked about how he undermined the will of the people.[5]

The anticapitalist sentiment of the population didn't suit the victorious Western powers, and it suited them even less that that Soviet Union had gained substantial prestige across the world due to its efforts, and the enormous losses it suffered, in fighting and defeating fascism. As a consequence of World War II and the liberation struggle in China, the balance of power between capitalism and socialism had shifted toward the latter.

The response of the Western powers was the division of Germany, so that the remainder, now known as the Federal Republic of Germany, could be turned into a capitalist bulwark against the Soviet Union. This entailed abandoning the denazification campaign in West Germany.

This was only a tiny historical sketch meant to clarify in whose interest it was, only six years after the closure of the concentration camps, to again imprison and persecute people in Germany because of their political beliefs. In order to set the persecution of communists into motion, a commission had to gather and hammer out a criminal law reform bill in 1951. It should come as no surprise that sixteen of the twenty-five jurists making up the commission had a Nazi past. Among them was a certain K.H. Scharpenseel, who until recently served at the federal supreme court and denied many of our grievances. Formerly, he served as a high-ranking Nazi legal administrator.

An even bigger fish was Herr Kanter, a West German supreme court judge in 1958–59. When Denmark was occupied by the Nazis during World War II, he handed out a number of death sentences. One of his successors in the West German supreme court, Judge Jagusch, had been a Nazi Party member. But let us go beyond the judges here. Let us also look at the federal prosecutor general Wolfgang Immerwahr Fränkel—as a Nazi federal prosecutor, he was involved in demanding close to fifty death sentences for political opponents. Is anyone surprised to discover that the definition of treason in the 1951 criminal law reform bill was almost identical to the one the Nazis had introduced in 1934?

These kinds of judges and prosecutors formed the basis on which the legal system of the Federal Republic of Germany was to be erected. Only a demagogue—a devoted pupil of Goebbels[6]—can deny that and speak of a democratic system. We can see through his fancy hairdo, ostensibly used as a disguise![7]

While people like Emil Bechtle, Fritz Rische, and Oskar Weyrich[8]—to name only a few among thousands—lost their health in prison after being sentenced by the same Nazi judges who had already sentenced them before 1945, the judges themselves remained comfortable in their positions, without any concern of having to pay for their crimes. These people, who once belonged to one of the biggest criminal organizations ever, came to convict antifascists under section 129 for forming or participating in criminal organizations. This is the historical link between us and those who freed themselves from the Buchenwald concentration

camp.[9] We are connected to those who sat in Hitler and Adenauer's penitentiaries, but not to the officers who tried to topple Hitler on July 20—they
weren't antifascists, they only held Hitler responsible for Germany's military defeat.[10]

Former war criminals did not just survive in the legal system, they
survived all throughout society. Globke, Oberländer, Kiesinger, Lübke,
Filbinger in politics; Abs, Schneidewind, Krupp, Thyssen, Schleyer in
industry; Heusinger in NATO.[11] The Bundeswehr inherited all of the
Reich's military officers.

These are only a few names, the ones best known. They are the
personified expression of what the restoration of capitalism looked like
in West Germany—a capitalism that from the outset was marked by a
new (old) aggressiveness, both externally against the socialist states and
internally against the left opposition.

Externally, Adenauer was quick to call for the so-called liberation of
the former eastern territories. In doing so, he fueled tensions. Internally,
there reigned legal terror, documented by six hundred thousand preliminary proceedings against political opponents between 1951 and 1964.
There were blacklists in factories and bans on strikes. Meanwhile, wages
were among the lowest in Europe. Even in the productive sector, the legal
system wasn't idle. On June 4, 1955, the federal supreme court ruled that
mass and general strikes as well as mass demonstrations could be judged
as violence equaling high treason. Yes, mass and general strikes as high
treason! There is a predecessor to this, namely, section 6 of the Nazis' Act
Targeting Treason Against the German People and Treasonous Activities,
passed on February 28, 1933.

Even today, political and wildcat strikes are banned and illegal in
West Germany. German capitalism has become competitive again due
to low wages and the repression against political opponents. Its old
economic base has been resurrected, and, since 1950, it has returned
as a competitor on the imperialist stage. Between 1950 and 1957, the
export turnover of German industrial products rose twice as fast as
domestic sales. West Germany conquered an ever-growing percentage
of the market in a struggle against both the US and Europe's old colonial
powers. It began to conduct business in Latin America only in 1950, but
just three years later it had displaced British capital from the number
two position in regional market shares. (The US remains number one.)
With the rise of German imperialism's economic power, in particular

its increased capital exports, the country's influence on international politics has grown remarkably. This dynamic of expansion was based on the increased exploitation of the population at home—a population for whom any socialist or radical democratic activity brought the risk of persecution and unemployment.

The role of postwar union leaders bought off by capital or put in place by the CIA—like Sickert[12]—was significant when it came to preventing class struggle. This country, with its imperialist ambitions, its role in the Cold War, its terror against dissidents at home, and its neocapitalism ensured by bought-off union leaders, portrays itself as the "freest state" that has ever existed on German soil.

We grew up during the postwar years. The biographical accounts of us presented by the court are everything but individual aberrations. Our biographies must be interpreted in a political context and not as personal histories. They reflect life in a country that, since its foundation, has used terror (in proud German tradition) to secure the power of the ruling class. That explains why the defendant Teufel asked a detective witness: "Aren't *you* the member of a well-paid and well-armed hierarchical terrorist organization?"

In this country, the interests of capital have always taken precedence over the interests of the people. The short historical overview of West Germany's political, economic, and social development that I have provided above shall make it clear to the young comrades fighting on the streets today how much their experiences have in common with ours. We grew up in a country where old Nazis got their jobs back. Today, they are enjoying pensions and retirement benefits, while the victims of the Nazi regime are turned away empty-handed. In school, we learned that the autobahn was built by Hitler, but we didn't hear anything about the atrocities committed in the concentration camps. We've been told that Hitler provided six million unemployed men and women with work, but nothing about the six million Germans—yes, the exact same number— who lost their lives during the war. Some of our teachers even gave a Nazi salute when reminiscing about their heroics during the war.

We are speaking about a country where Ernst Thälmann's killers wander the streets with no worry or concern,[13] while communists are still persecuted for having killed SS henchmen in the concentration camps. (This concerns the inmates in Buchenwald, in particular, who tried to liberate themselves.[14]) We grew up in a country that didn't allow children to vacation or join festivals and congresses in East Germany. On August 5, 1951, a teenager drowned trying to cross the border illegally, swimming across the Elbe from the West to the East. We grew up in a country where the offices of newspapers were searched and shut down, where editors were arrested, where poets were denounced and boycotted, where books were confiscated for identifying Nazis and other war criminals (for example, the *Brown Book* in October 1967[15]), where demonstrators were beaten and, at times, shot and killed, such as the twenty-one-year-old Philip Müller in Essen on May 11, 1962, when the police dispersed, with live ammunition, a youth caravan organized by the West German chapter of the FDJ.[16] We grew up in a country where, on August 2, 1954, Emil Bechtle was sentenced to three years in prison for helping to organize a petition against West German remilitarization. Almost ten million people had signed the petition even though the government had declared it illegal. In short, we lived through an economic miracle built on the backs of the working class, a system that prepared the population for the terror of consumption, causing debt and ensuring that not only fathers but also mothers had to go to work.

Drunkenness, illness, and violence defined life for many families. But what were people supposed to do? Not only did the system threaten to persecute and deny work to anyone who resisted, but it also carried out a war against the people's minds. Radio, television, and particularly the press hammered the people all day long: how good they had it; how important consumption was; how pointless resistance was; how everything that didn't correspond to the rotten norms of capitalism posed a threat to their monthly installments. The pogrom sentiment among the population was fueled to the point that "longhairs" couldn't get a job, were hunted down in the streets and often beaten. The war on the mind was to ensure that we would turn into pawns for the capitalist machine, and it was carried out not only by schools, universities, and bosses, but also by our parents.

Today, the war on the mind has changed. It has become more subtle and less transparent, but its purpose for the system remains the same. The youth shall become robots for capital. If you need the robot, you turn it on full throttle; if you don't, you put it in the corner. The staggering number of unemployed youth demonstrates this. But not everyone complies. After a long phase of disorientation, a section of today's youth has grasped that they need to act if they want to change things. They are like us, ready for rebellion. The things we see today across Europe, in

Zurich, Amsterdam, Bristol, Oslo, Paris, Frankfurt, and Bremen, are only precursors to a new revolt.

Our revolt had a strong political basis, the Easter March movement.[17] Even if the Easter Marches were boring strolls that didn't have much effect, they were an important part of our political training, a launching pad for the extraparliamentary opposition. APO—these three letters gave hope to an entire generation, even if revisionists today, both from the right and the left, distort the memory by claiming to know what APO was and wanted, while they clearly don't.

Our revolt was neither limited to the universities nor reduced to an anti-imperialist agenda. It was what the three letters stood for: *außerparlamentarische Opposition*, "extraparliamentary opposition." All sections of the young generation were represented. The general political expression of the revolt was the desire and the will to determine our own destiny, individually as well as collectively. It was an attempt to shape our lives freely and independently, and to no longer allow dumbshit authorities and capitalist interests to control us.

We rose up against oppression, and, in the course of the struggle, developed clearer ideas of what we wanted. It dawned on us that capitalism meant exploitation, destruction, and war, and that only socialism could solve the problems of our time. The capitalist state had to be eradicated—that was an important discovery. The way the capitalist state confronted us—with a police force able to get away with just about anything, with a legal system that in blind submission to the ruling order prosecuted and sentenced demonstrators, and with an ally that carried out a Nazi-style genocide in Vietnam—left only the option of opposing the violence of the oppressor with the violence of the oppressed.

What made us so euphoric was that we were not struggling alone. All over the world, people were fighting capitalism, imperialism, and archaic forms of domination. In Vietnam, a small and courageous people embarrassed a giant. The almost unimaginable sacrifices and the will to victory of the Vietnamese people gave us the courage to believe in the giant's defeat in our own country as well. In America, some cities were in flames, the nonwhite population fought back, and the opponents of the Vietnam War protested against it. In France, the door to the socialist revolution almost opened, but it was shut closed by the Communist Party. In China, there was the Cultural Revolution, our great hope, since it embodied the ideals we dreamed of: self-determination, collectivity, direct democracy, equality in education and work, no separation of intellectual and manual labor. The Cultural Revolution was the first attempt to move from socialism to communism.

Since then, we have learned a lot and needed to do so: in particular, that anti-imperialism, which had increasingly defined our political lives, was not the struggle that would change everything. The realization that our anti-imperialism lacked the material basis necessary to smash imperialism once and for all was a bitter one. Our anti-imperialism was idealistic, nothing more than moral support for Third World liberation movements.

Certainly, support for liberation movements struggling against imperialism—and particularly US imperialism—was important and remains important. But the anti-imperialist struggle in support of the Third World cannot be the main pillar of the struggle against the capitalist machine. The anti-imperialist struggle must not become the straw we reach for in order not to drown in our own incompetence, that is, our inability to carry out the struggle against the economic and political basis of imperialism here and now.

The Third World liberation struggle provided no revolutionary perspective for us since it couldn't help ending our own oppression. The longer we pondered what we actually wanted, and the longer we studied colonial revolutions, the more we realized that imperialism could not be defeated in the periphery. In his *Introduction to Marxist Economic Theory*, Ernest Mandel wrote the following:

> The balance, so far as the colonial revolution is concerned, paradoxical as this may seem, has not as yet resulted in a substantial loss to the capitalist world. On the contrary, one of the concomitant factors explaining the scale of economic expansion of the imperialist countries occurring in this phase, is the fact that, insofar as the colonial revolution remains in the framework of the capitalist world market (except where it gives birth to other so-called socialist states), it serves as a stimulus to the production and export of industrial equipment, the products of heavy industry in the imperialist countries.[18]

Since few of the newly independent countries joined the socialist camp or broke away from the world market, they remained within imperialism's realm. Even if, in the long run, the Third World revolutions will place limits on imperialism, some of these limits are ones that imperialism is asking for.

The exploitation of the new "sovereign" nation-states goes further than simply plundering raw materials. The UN has determined that the exploitation of Third World countries today is two hundred times higher than it was during the colonial period. Dependence has only taken on a new face. Since this face is the façade of sovereign statehood, and since the newly independent states sometimes vote against imperialist interests in the United Nations, the theory that the Third World anti-imperialist struggle will do away with imperialism has gained much traction.

The assertions that raw materials become more expensive after the revolution, that markets disappear, and that capitalists in the metropole are forced to squeeze out more of their own proletariat is only partially true and only shows the consequences of Third World revolutions for the primary imperialist contradiction: proletariat versus bourgeoisie.

However, we must beware not to draw the opposite conclusion either: we must not reject the anti-imperialist revolutions, or withhold solidarity, only because the majority of them cannot break from imperialism or because they might even contribute to its expansion. This cannot and must not be our stance. What we need to do is analyze and understand the significance of anti-imperialist revolutions. Every struggle against imperialist domination in the Third World must be supported, as imperialism always means exploitation, hunger, and poverty. Imperialism must be eliminated. Yet we must not allow our emotional perception to determine our analysis. Instead of simply observing the expressions of imperialism, we must reflect on its causes. It was an error in 1968 that we stuck to emotional perception, impressed by the rigor and intensity of the struggle in the Third World and touched by the misery that people experienced. This led to making the liberation from imperialism the center of our politics.

Emotional perception, imperialism, and notions of the principal evil and the principal contradiction led us to apply our images of the Third World to the industrial nations. To put it succinctly and bluntly, we failed to break away from emotional perception and only reached the first rung on the ladder to human knowledge. The next one, rational reflection, we only reached later.

If we interpret our anti-imperialist struggle exclusively as support for the liberation struggles in the Third World, acting as their long arm in the metropole, we will never threaten the core of imperialism. The Third World struggle against imperialism can under certain circumstances amplify imperialism's internal contradictions, but it cannot do away with them. We can only do away with imperialism by resolving its inner contradictions. We must not make the mistake of confusing imperialist reality—which includes Third World resistance against it—with its end. The imperialist powers survive due to the wealth generated by "their" proletariat. It is the exploitation of the proletariat in our part of the world, the ongoing domination of one class over another, that provides the imperialist countries with the economic and military power to exploit foreign countries and to blackmail them based on military might.

To smash imperialist power requires eradicating class rule in the metropole, which, in turn, requires deepening the class struggle in the metropole. Comments like "What do the Third World revolutions have to do with us?" or, conversely, "Nothing can be done here in West Germany, we're struggling for the interests of the Third World," do not only, each in their own way, express a lack of solidarity but are political nonsense. We have shown why resolving the contradictions in the heart of the beast must be a priority for us, and why the main battle will occur here where imperialism has its economic base and where it accumulates the wealth that makes it such a potent international player.

We are not denying the impact of the Third World liberation struggles on capitalism. We support the liberation struggles in the Third World. Solidarity must be more than a hollow phrase. All who struggle against capitalism and imperialism must support one another, be it through financial/material contributions or be it through demonstrations and actions. It is possible to criticize actions such as the occupation of the America House in Berlin because it was conducted the wrong way, or because the communiqués were shallow.[19] The form can always be criticized, but, objectively, the relevance of the action cannot be denied. It was correct, and important, because it demonstrated practical solidarity with the people of Iran at a time when the imperialist states vilified the revolutionary developments in the country. It also showed the Iranian people that there are still men and women in West Germany who refuse to accept the ruling-class story about the Islamic Revolution. In West Germany itself, such actions help to oppose misinformation and slander, essential elements in a strategy of dumbing down the population.

Militant solidarity with the liberation struggles in the Third World must be made an integral part of our politics and our own liberation struggles. Only through our own struggles *and* through the solidarity with other struggles will we be able to recognize all struggles' true significance and act effectively.

As the extraparliamentary opposition slowly dissolved in 1969–70, with our rebellious storm turning into a gentle breeze, we constantly discussed the question of "How do we carry on?" Increasingly, we turned against each other. Some believed that they needed to enter the factories and mobilize there; others favored the neighborhoods, the schools, the universities, or the women's movement; some formed parties; some attempted to win the subculture over to the resistance; and some formed an urban guerrilla modeled after the Tupamaros in Uruguay. All approaches aimed to shift the idealistic character of our rebellion to one of material resistance. All wanted to be where things were happening. However, instead of finding one another, people lost one another.

Each group believed in their own doctrine of salvation and prioritized the issue they themselves saw as most important. The urban guerrilla thought it was the only fundamental opposition and the most revolutionary current of them all. The factory workers claimed the factories were key, the neighborhood groups focused on the neighborhoods, the prison groups on the prisons, and on and on it went. Even today, we encounter such nonsense, luckily no longer as often. Instead of grasping that our resistance consists of various struggles that can only exist and survive when they are united, individual groups retreat into their own shells and deteriorate into sects. But when those who are meant to be the driving force of the resistance movement isolate themselves, the entire movement becomes isolated. Only today—ten years later—do people realize that the struggle is not about one issue or one particular sect. People are searching for new alliances. It is the duty of the '68 rebels to share their experiences and to help younger comrades avoid the same mistakes.

Lorenz

Since we now have decided to present a closing statement—not least to share some experiences with younger comrades—we should say something about kidnapping Lorenz. The action is still very popular within the left, which requires us to talk about the sociopolitical context in which it unfolded. It's an aspect that was neglected in the trial, by both sides. That's why we need to elaborate on it now.

Let us begin by paraphrasing Rosa Luxemburg:

> If a so-called "free" citizen is forced against their will to stay for some time in a small and filthy dungeon, everyone understands that it is an act of violence. But if it is sanctioned by a book called *Code of Criminal Procedure*, and the dungeon is called Moabit prison, then it is simply an act of upholding the law. If a human being is forced by another human being against their will to systematically kill people, it is an act of violence. But if it is sanctioned by what's called *military service* or police duty, it is an act of upholding the law. In short, what is presented to us as bourgeois lawfulness is nothing but the violence of the ruling class as an enforced norm.

Peter Lorenz had the privilege to learn firsthand about the counter-violence of the oppressed—a kind of violence that can only be understood by those who suffer under the violence of bourgeois class society. No shriveled bourgeois legal brain can deliver a judgment on it.

The legal violence of the state is meant to guarantee exploitation and oppression by the ruling class. It has only one agenda: to exterminate and destroy everything that gets in its way. The violence of the oppressed, on the other hand, is justified violence, directed against oppression and exploitation. Its goal is a classless society. It is necessary because capitalism will not disappear voluntarily.

Back to Peter Lorenz. His performance in the courtroom was marvelous. He was what they call a "good witness." Not in a legal sense (yikes!), but, from a political standpoint, his statements were good. He is still—although he doesn't even know it—the 2nd of June Movement's best propagandist.

After the statements about his time with the 2nd of June Movement, we must wonder if even one of the sixty thousand prisoners in the penitentiaries of West Germany would speak as positively about their experience as Lorenz. Is there even one prisoner in the penitentiaries of West Germany who can say, "I was not abused or beaten"?

Anyone who cares to look and search will realize that it is easier in West Germany to find a prisoner beaten to death than one who has never been abused. P. Lorenz has not said a bad thing about the 2nd of June Movement to this day, even though quite a few gentlemen would like him to. He doesn't, because his personal experience doesn't correspond to the propaganda shite of the federal prosecutors and a media sitting in the lap of state security.

Peter Lorenz was treated as a human being. He is a human being, even if he is an enemy. The experience must have been overwhelming for him. Federal prosecutor Völz asked P. Lorenz about the conditions of his imprisonment, and then immediately withdrew the question. We understood the demagogic point of this: raising a question without letting it be answered. Völz wanted everyone to believe that Herr Lorenz was subjected to inhumane conditions. Demagogy is like a stink bomb: it might blow up in your face. In this case, the stink bomb blew up in the pockets of the federal prosecutor's pants.

To let the smell linger a little longer, there's not even a point in comparing the conditions of our own imprisonment with those of Lorenz's. It suffices to look at the conditions of regular social inmates. Following their arrest, they are often held for days in a 1.5×3-meter cell at Gothaer Straße, with no radio, no newspaper, no company, and no yard time. If they want to use the toilet, they must ring a bell—and wait.

When they are transferred to Moabit—in cabins that are hardly bigger than the box and the closet we kept P. Lorenz in—they have yard time and loudspeakers for the prison program. But we have not heard of anyone receiving wine or beer, or even food, whenever they wish. In Moabit, dinner is served shortly after 3 p.m., and then the day is over. Should anyone dare to speak to other prisoners through the window after that, they risk a beating and other punishment. Some of the punishments were defined as torture by the UN in 1948. A game of chess or a bit of TV, for example, can be off the table for quite some time.

Imagine the outcry had the 2nd of June Movement treated their prisoner in the same way that prisoners are commonly treated in West Germany. In that case, the federal prosecutors would have used words like "torture" and "abuse." But that was impossible. Socialist revolutionaries fighting torture and inhumanity would betray themselves if they tortured or abused people, prisoners included.

"We didn't struggle against torture for years to then use it!" That was Fidel Castro's answer to an American reporter who accused the Cubans of torture. We think and act the same way, whether we were part of the Lorenz action or not.

The relationship between Peter Lorenz and his kidnappers was so warm and fuzzy that they even congratulated him on his electoral victory. These congratulations led to the accusation that the 2nd of June Movement wanted to ensure a CDU success by kidnapping Lorenz and that the group's members were happy about the CDU victory. Whoever spouts such a theory insinuates carelessly two things: one, that the 2nd of June Movement wants things to become as bad as possible, that it wants fascism; two, that there is a huge difference between the SPD and the CDU. But there is not that much of a difference. It would, of course, be too easy to say there's not much of a difference only because the SPD, like the CDU, protects the interests and rule of capital. Here, there can't be a difference, since this country is ruled by monopoly capital, and it is monopoly capital that determines politics, not some political party. Political parties must operate within this framework, in which they fight against other sections of monopoly capital. So there's no difference in the content of the parties, but rather in their form. While the CDU often hits out at anything that appears just a tad rebellious with a sledgehammer, the SPD understands nuances within the left and is, on the basis of decades of experience in deception and betrayal, able to mitigate growing unrest among the population.

Every time the extraparliamentary opposition rises and gains strength, the SPD offers reforms, which, on closer examination, aren't reforms (or aren't implemented). In 1968, at the height of the student and youth movement, the SPD was able to fake relevance by suggesting reforms, winning over a part of the rebels. Today, it is fair to ask, "What did the reforms bring us?" Democracy? The social democrats promised more, they promised that they would be daring. And what did we get? Professional bans! More power for factory and neighborhood councils? No, near perfect and total surveillance; youth unemployment; a police force that would do any police state proud. There are plenty such examples. The SPD hasn't kept a single one of their reform promises, and it couldn't have; not because the reforms would have brought the CDU into power, but because they contradicted the logic of capital. The system of repression was expanded knowing that there'd be resistance against the coming capitalist crisis.

Today, the SPD no longer promises reforms. Today, the professional banners of yesterday offer a milder form of the professional ban. They need to present themselves as the lesser evil compared to the CDU. They try to scare people with the prospect of Franz Josef Strauß becoming ever more powerful. They believe they can sell people a foul compromise.

Essentially, they say: the SPD might burn your fingers, but Strauß would chop them off. But with burned fingers you won't get very far either.

Since German history teaches us that capital determines politics, we'll need our fingers to resist. The political parties serve the logic of capital. Capital needs unemployment—the parties ensure that there is unemployment. Capital needs protection from foreign competition—the parties introduce tariff barriers. Capital needs markets in Eastern Europe—the parties become friendly with the East. Capital needs armament—the parties secure the funds. And when capital needs another war, the parties pave the way with public swearing-in ceremonies.

All political parties are part of this. A party moving within the realm of the capitalist system will naturally subject itself to the capitalist strategy and support it. In the process, the people will be deceived, lied to, and manipulated. It can't be any other way. Since CDU, SPD, and FDP are committed to the capitalist strategy, there is nothing much to choose between them. They all need to be fought equally. The capitalist strategy doesn't rely on randomness; it uses a wide range of tools to secure power, from bourgeois democracy with waves of repression to open fascism—it all depends on how favorable or unfavorable the conditions are.

Not to see the difference between democracy and fascism would entail not to find the right strategy and tactics against the dominant form of capitalist rule at the given time. Within bourgeois democracy, we see elements and tendencies of fascism, but they must not blind us; differences remain, and we must be careful not to simply equate bourgeois democracy with fascism, even if bourgeois democracy and fascism have the same goal, namely, to keep the capitalist system alive.

A form of rule that cannot be defined by established terms such as bourgeois democracy or fascism is "institutional fascism," which increasingly determines life in West Germany. It is a form of rule with a new quality, oscillating between the poles of bourgeois democracy and fascism, and entailing much of both. The fascism of old was a mass movement, able to both mobilize and reflect the masses, while institutional fascism is based on surveillance and control. It does not have the power to mobilize the masses, as the funerals of Drenkmann and Buback have made painfully clear. It draws its legitimacy from what the rulers like to call the "silent majority." There exists a silent majority; it would be foolish to deny that. But it is equally foolish to believe that the consciousness of this silent majority, and the legitimacy it provides for the regime, is unchangeable. Of course, the rulers always try to use the contradictions within the classes for their own benefit, and it is the contradictions within the classes that prevent a united resistance against the system, which, in turn, contributes to the passiveness of the silent majority.

How much the silent majority is needed to legitimize new laws is well demonstrated by the manipulation of the people. With the help of the media, they are turned into obedient voters. In order for the system not to lose control over them, they are isolated at work and at home; they no longer know how to resist and how to break out of this invisible stranglehold. If there is no mass base behind the system, only a silent majority, then the system loses all legitimacy as soon as people resist. A silent majority turning into a vocal majority is a danger to the capitalist system and its current form of rule, institutional fascism.

Institutional fascism is a technocracy. That is its biggest danger. A technocracy is harder to detect than classical fascism. Emotional perception tells you that something is wrong when security agents knock on your door, but when you're under surveillance by a computer system you might not even notice it. You hate the security agents, but you don't see the computers. Yet technocratic repression also has its disadvantages. Once people realize what's going on, they (the silent majority) will feel alienated from those who claim to represent them.

In West Germany, there clearly exists disillusionment with the state. There's a crisis of legitimacy. The bigger the technocratic repression, the bigger the nuclear state (this monster), the bigger the alienation of the people from the state. It is our task to deepen this alienation and to amplify people's dissatisfaction and disillusionment with the political system. In our political practice, we need to overcome isolation and bring together all forms of individual rebellion. When individual forms of rebellion turn into a solid bloc, when technocratic repression loses its grip, then it is easy to realize what classical and institutional fascism have in common: brutality. Yet, contrary to traditional fascism, which didn't accept any opposition, institutional fascism will offer free zones inherited from bourgeois democracy. It would be dangerous and politically careless to separate institutional fascism from bourgeois democracy or indeed see bourgeois democracy as pursuing a different end.

The nuclear state indicates more domination; bourgeois democracy indicates less domination. The dismantling of democracy across West Germany (and all of Europe) proves that democracy is a nuisance for the bourgeoisie in times of increased economic and social crisis. It puts hegemonic power and oppression at risk. By dismantling democracy, the bourgeoisie wants to nip any resistance in the bud.

When the rulers try to take away democratic rights, we must defend and, ideally, expand them. Cynics see an irresolvable contradiction here: on the one hand, we are fighting bourgeois democracy as a rule of capital; on the other hand, we are defending democratic rights. But this apparent contradiction can be explained.

We do not chain ourselves to bourgeois democracy when opposing the nuclear state. Why would we sit on the rotten branch of a tree? Our struggle is not about a little more or a little less freedom; that would be reformism. We support the struggle for democracy to build conscious-ness and set into a motion an emancipatory process, in which people shall create their own politics, self-management, and self-organization. This shall enable them to determine their own destiny.

The Wendländer in Gorleben have tried it, and the squatters are trying it.[20] Squatting is not simply a struggle against real estate specu-lation or failed redevelopment and housing policies. It demonstrates that democracy does not begin with the Promised Land. It can be practiced here and now, and people must learn how to practice it. And they do! Self-management and self-organization in today's resistance movements builds the foundation for tomorrow's socialist revolution.

In this difficult and protracted struggle, the people will mature and emancipate themselves. They will not only go beyond bourgeois rule, but they'll be able to repel any fascist—or, for that matter, Stalinist—charge for power. But it is madness to believe that capitalism can be abolished peacefully, solely by struggling for democratic rights, let alone by parlia-mentarian efforts. It is a pipe dream to believe that the journey from capitalism to socialism simply requires to take one step at a time.

For our comrades in Chile, this pipe dream turned into a nightmare.[21] No ruling class has ever passively accepted that its property was taken away, that its profits were limited, and that the exploitation of the masses was ended. The ruling classes defend their privileges to the bitter end with the utmost brutality. They have pillaged and exterminated entire peoples to protect their privileges. No means or method is beneath the ruling classes when it comes to defending their power. That's why the struggle for democracy doesn't replace the need for revolution. Without the abolition of capitalism, there can be no socialist democracy.

The capitalist strategy is not dependent on any particular political party or individual. The person Lorenz could be replaced by any other. Individuals only play a role insofar as politicians bear personal responsibility and are corrupted. Who is Peter Lorenz? Why was he kidnapped? What is his role in the system?

As the chairman of the CDU in Berlin and the vice president of the Berlin parliament, Lorenz's overall political significance was rather limited. At the time of his kidnapping, he was significant only because the CDU was the projected winner of the West Berlin elections. That's why the governing SPD could not afford to sacrifice him. Otherwise, the people of Berlin would have wondered whether the SPD had gleefully rid itself of a political opponent, espousing a hard line not to secure the authority of the state but to strengthen its own position.

This constellation caused a dilemma for the government, but that wasn't all of it. The CDU didn't want to sacrifice their man either, which made a common front of the political parties against a deal with the 2nd of June Movement practically impossible, as long as the 2nd of June Movement's demands weren't entirely unrealistic. And they weren't. To the contrary, one might think they were too modest.

But these weren't the only reasons why the prisoner exchange worked. And they weren't the only reasons for making P. Lorenz the first political prisoner not to be incarcerated by the state. (What an honor!) But what were the reasons then? Sure, P. Lorenz is photogenic, but that's not a good enough reason to imprison someone. There are others. As we heard in his testimony, he was, during his imprisonment, confronted by the 2nd of June Movement about a trip to occupied Palestine, where he had discussed economic and political support for the colonial entity called Israel with members of the Zionist government. In this very courtroom, P. Lorenz defended his decision—a violation of international law—by stating that the Jewish people must have the right to a place where they can live in peace. These are the usual arguments by a media loyal to the state. It's not that we're in disagreement with P. Lorenz and the CDU about the basics. We, too, believe that the Jewish people shall live in peace and prosperity in a place they can call home. But not at the cost of the Arab people of Palestine; not at the cost of bombed-out refugee camps; not at the cost of children blown up by toys stuffed with explosives; not at the cost of occupied territories in which people are forced to carry transit permits and have no rights.

The Palestinian people haven't done anything to the Jewish people. It was the German people who wanted to exterminate the Jewish people, and now the Palestinian people are paying the price for it. A guilty conscience toward the Jewish people must not be a reason to cover up and finance Israeli crimes. (If the guilty conscience is even real and not just a propaganda tool.) The true reasons for financing Israel were summarized by the KPD parliamentary club during a 1953 Bundestag session discussing the Luxembourg Convention:

> In the name of reparations, Israeli industrialists obtain everything they need from West Germany for the construction of basic industries. The facts prove that this agreement has nothing to do with reparations. . . . Persecuted individuals in Israel do not receive a single penny from the 3 billion Deutschmark, while the industrialists make great profits. But the industrialists are not the agreement's only beneficiaries. There are also the gentlemen from the American armament industry and from American high finance. . . . Nothing here is done out of humanitarianism and philanthropy. There are very concrete reasons for these policies. American imperialists are building a strong military base of strategic importance in the Middle East. . . . With support of the industrial imports from West Germany, the Americans want to turn the state of Israel, which is entirely under their control, into a well-armed operative base.[22]

That was said in 1953, and it is still valid today. Since Israel is respected and protected by our media as an imperialist watchdog, we hear nothing about the Israeli massacres against women and children in the refugee camps. They can be traced back to the carnage of 1948 in Deir Yassin and Katamon.[23]

The Deir Yassin and Katamon massacres are only two of innumerable ones that have targeted the Arab population. Their special significance stems from two facts: one, they set into motion the expulsion of the Arabs of Palestine; two, they were ordered by Israel's then prime minister, Menachem Begin.[24] You cannot ignore the massacres and the bombing of refugee camps when thinking of the people whom P. Lorenz met while visiting Israel.

Since the PLO—the only legitimate representative of the Palestinian people—has declared martial law in Palestine, anyone who morally or materially supports the Zionist entity is, at a minimum, guilty of supporting war crimes and crimes against humanity. Those who pass judgment on the actions of the Palestinians resisting the Israeli occupation should consult the statement released by Matzpen, an Israeli socialist organization, on March 22, 1968.[25] We need to stress, however, that when we speak of the Palestinian resistance, we do not include operations by Palestinians acting on behalf of some government's secret service. Here is an excerpt from the Matzpen statement:

> It is both the right and duty of every conquered and subjugated people to resist and to struggle for its freedom. The ways, means and methods necessary and appropriate for such struggle must be determined by the people itself and it would be hypocritical for strangers—especially if they belong to the oppressing nation—to preach to it, saying, "Thus shalt thou do, and thus shalt thou not do." While recognizing the unconditional right of the conquered to resist occupation, we can support only such organizations which, in addition to resisting occupation, also recognize the right of the Israeli people for self-determination. On such a basis the struggle of the Palestinian people can become combined in a joint struggle of Arabs and Jews in the region for a common future.[26]

The PLO program outlined by Arafat in his speech at the United Nations foresees a democratic Palestine in which Jews, Muslims, and Christians can live in peace and equality with one another.[27] It overlaps in some points with the programs of anti-imperialist and anti-Zionist Jews in Israel. By pointing out the moral and material support that P. Lorenz and the CDU had offered Israel, the 2nd of June Movement made people a little more aware about the Palestinian revolution.

Another thing that the 2nd of June Movement criticized P. Lorenz for was his support of Pinochet's torture regime in Chile. P. Lorenz rejected this criticism, claiming that Christian Democrats were persecuted in Chile too. Well, it's hard to lose the spirits you have summoned. Still, weeks after the killing of Allende, Chilean (and not only Chilean) Christian Democrats welcomed the coup and hoped that the military would help them regain power. Only now, when it seems that the military won't include the Christian Democrats in the government, have they started to resist and therefore turned into victims of persecution.

Based on everything that P. Lorenz told us, we believe him when he says that he personally rejects the regime in Chile. But he belongs to a party that doesn't. Bruno Heck of the CDU as well as the CSU chairman Franz Josef Strauß have visited Chile and have called the torture regime legitimate.[28] Heck visited the sports stadiums where prisoners had been held on a beautiful and sunny day, not giving a thought that people had been brutally murdered there. Strauß said the following during the visit: "Whoever says that Allende was murdered must say the same about the Stammheim prisoners!" We spare ourselves any comments.

Back to P. Lorenz: We do not recall him ever making a public statement against the regime in Chile. We do not recall him ever signing a petition. Both would have been impossible for him, since the imperialist-industrial circles that back the CDU would have immediately ensured the end of his political career.

With regard to another criticism of the 2nd of June Movement, P. Lorenz responded with the usual hypocritical charm of professional politicians. Why, he asked, should he carry any responsibility for upholding the discriminatory section 218?[29] P. Lorenz acted as if he, the regular citizen Lorenz, knew nothing, absolutely nothing, about any decision that P. Lorenz, the Berlin chairman of the CDU, has made. He acted as if the CDU did not have a party platform and had never passed any laws. This was a rather bold move. Was it not the CDU, supported by the church, that called all women murderers who had had an abortion and dared decide about their own life and body? There are no official statistics about how many women have risked their lives by having illegal abortions in a basement or back alley because of laws passed by the CDU that gave them no other choice, but the seemingly ignorant Herr Lorenz might be appalled if he ever cared to find out. Unfortunately, the way we got to know him, he won't bother.

Even today, the CDU still calls on doctors not to perform abortions, even though women have successfully struggled for a reform of section 218. Therefore, the CDU bears a responsibility for the poor treatment that women receive in certain clinics even when their abortions have been approved. Section 218 remains discriminatory because it still denies women the control over their own body.[30]

In a class society, women from the lower classes are particularly affected by discrimination of this kind. The wives of parliamentarians have other options, abroad or with the help of a family doctor. But section 218 has something in common with the political system in West Germany: one day, it will exit the scene.

These were just a few accusations levied against P. Lorenz and the CDU, and the same accusations could be levied against Schütz and the SPD or Oxfort and the FDP.[31] But our action targeted Peter Lorenz. To evaluate this action today without reading the leaflet "The Kidnapping as We See It" is impossible.[32] It is equally impossible to feel as positive about the action as we did four years ago, considering everything that has happened since. There has not been a sober analysis of the kidnapping yet. It has either been vilified as a "police act" or hailed as "truly proletarian."

It wasn't a police act for the reason alone that police acts are always directed against the people, never against the rulers. Whether the action was proletarian is up for debate. It was a populist action, at least in the sense of it being popular (the truest sense of the term *populist*). The action had all of the elements characteristic of people resisting: imagination, determination, cleverness, and wit. Given how smoothly the action unfolded and the political circumstances of the day (the Berlin elections), the rulers were forced to negotiate with the 2nd of June Movement. That meant that one of the political objectives of the 2nd of June Movement was achieved right away. The next political objective—the liberation of the prisoners—we probably need to say more about.

There are folks today who claim that liberating prisoners has been a part of the tactics and strategy of any guerrilla. In West Germany, this has partly become a reality. Luckily, that wasn't the case for the 2nd of June Movement when Lorenz was kidnapped. Had it been the case, it would have probably been better for everyone had the kidnappers packed their bags and left the country than the liberated prisoners. It is utter nonsense to reduce the political struggle to the liberation of prisoners, and everyone who believes in this nonsense should step away from the armed struggle for a while. The way the Lorenz action was conducted made it clear that the 2nd of June Movement did not entertain any such dangerous rubbish.

The worst things that can happen in political struggle are either to lose sight of one's objectives or to give up. Once either has happened, it won't be long before you're content with partial victories—or before partial victories become your objective. What once was a mere tactic takes on a dynamic of its own and is suddenly seen as a strategy in itself. This, inevitably, sets the stage for defeat. A guerrilla whose tactic and strategy circles around the liberation of prisoners is ludicrous. It essentially invites the enemy to kill the prisoners, as it can always be put under pressure via the prisoners. Murdering them could be the end of it. After all, what's

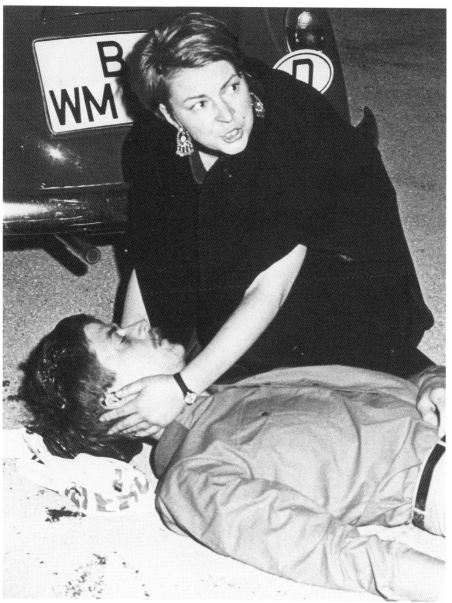

Benno Ohnesorg, shot dead by police on June 2, 1967. Photograph by Jürgen Henschel.

Participants of the "Red Prison Week" in Ebrach, Bavaria, July 1969.

Poster advertising a Hash Rebel teach-in, Berlin, November 1969.

Squatters in Kreuzberg, Berlin. Photograph by Tom Ordelman.

"An attack on the Georg von Rauch House is an attack on all of us. Let us fight back together!"

Logo of the Tupamaros
Munich.

Extrablatt

B·Z· Die Täter kamen mit Maschinenpistolen:

Kostenloser Sonderdruck · Donnerstag, 27. 2. 75

Die größte Zeitung Berlins

CDU-Chef

Lorenz

entführt

A special edition of the *Berliner Zeitung* announces the kidnapping of Peter Lorenz.

Schenkendorfstraße 7. The store where Peter Lorenz was held captive. Photograph by Jürgen Henschel.

Cover of the 2nd of June Movement leaflet "The Kidnapping as We See It," using a widely publicized photograph of Peter Lorenz during his captivity.

Der Spiegel cover after three 2nd of June Movement members and a RAF member escaped from the women's prison at Lehrter Straße, Berlin.

FREIHEIT FÜR DIE AGIT-DRUCKER!

Support for the *Agit 883/ Info BUG* printers arrested in November 1977.

die unbeugsamen von der spree

interview mit ronald fritsch   gerald klöpper   ralf reinders   fritz teufel

Cover of the pamphlet "The Unrelenting of the Spree."

Ronald Fritzsch and Ralf Reinders on trial, 1980.

DEMONSTRATION
gegen Hochsicherheitstrakte
und Isolationshaft !
WANN: 9.MAI Bi
WO: AlterMarkt Zeit: 10³⁰

Flyer for a
demonstration against
high-security and
isolation units.

a guerrilla gonna do when the entire basis for its tactics and strategy is gone? Prison is just one part of the system of domination, the final rung on the ladder of repression, the most brutal one, used against those still able to resist. Prison is supposed to scare the ones who haven't been scared enough yet by families, schools, universities, factories, and neighbors. The long arm of repression reaches everywhere; it oppresses and controls people with the help of teachers, bosses, cops, and, as of late, computers.

Prison is no engine of the capitalist machinery, nor is it the main fuse that brings the machinery to a halt when it overheats. Prison is one fuse among many. But each blown fuse impedes the smooth operation of the machinery and marks an accident. Yet to conclude that the system would fall apart if we managed to burn down all prisons is a misinterpretation of reality. Only when all systems of people oppressing people are destroyed, along with their mechanisms of domination, can the abolition of prisons be long-lasting. The struggle against prisons is only one aspect of the overall struggle, and the liberation of prisoners must be no more than one tactic of this struggle as well—a tactic aiming to overcome the sense of powerlessness by the people in light of the system's monopoly on violence.

To turn the liberation of prisoners into a strategy (the main strategy) means to ignore all other forms of oppression. It indicates that you don't understand the capitalist machinery. Ignorance and poor analysis are recipes for defeat. When conceiving a political action in West Germany, you must consider its impact on the entire resistance movement in the country. We can't leave the consequences of our actions to chance.

If we don't care about the consequences of our actions for the entire resistance movement, and rather think, "After us, the deluge," we must not be surprised when defeats wash us away. If we don't care about the consequences, repeating old mistakes again and again, our actions will isolate us, and we will no longer be part of a broader resistance movement. Our actions will follow their own logic, revolve around themselves, and be carried out for their own sake. It's the end of any guerrilla.

If our goal is to give armed resistance a solid basis, we must assess the strategic value of any action. The struggle for the prisoners is part of the overall struggle and has to consider the overall struggle. You cannot pick one part (in this case, prison) and declare it to be the whole. A group that does this, a group that, for example, confuses the Lorenz action with strategy, loses touch and pretends to have a significance it doesn't have. Any group that grossly overestimates its own importance becomes detached from politics on the ground, inevitably heading into a dead end.

If we hand those who confuse a part of the struggle with the whole a piece of cake and say, "Here is the entire cake," they would probably complain and be very aware of that modest piece not being the entire cake. In "The Kidnapping as We See It," we very clearly state that the 2nd of June Movement sees itself as a part of the overall resistance—as a *part*, because it knows full well that the guerrilla is but one means of the struggle, one among many.

Before the Lorenz action, the 2nd of June Movement considered whether its consequences for the left would be positive or negative. What, then, were the consequences of the action? It's a question the 2nd of June Movement needs to answer. The answer is that the action forced the government to recognize us as a negotiation partner, that it liberated seven prisoners,[33] that it helped overcome a sense of resignation within the left, and that it showed many comrades (and not just comrades) that the power of system has its holes. The 2nd of June Movement proved that it was possible to cause defeat for the West German regime. It tarnished the image of those who appeared so self-assured when presenting West Germany as a model country for safety and order, both in Germany and abroad. They can no longer do that; they can no longer be that arrogant.

Of course, the state has not been demoralized or significantly weakened. Unfortunately, things aren't that easy. But the state's monopoly of violence was undermined. This provided hope and gave courage to everyone in this country affected by professional bans, by the highly advanced apparatus of surveillance, by unemployment, prison, housing estates, and environmental pollution. For them, the defeat suffered by the system was satisfying and inspirational.

The Lorenz action was also satisfying for the liberation movements of the Third World, as they were able to witness the mighty West German government receiving a blow from the resistance movement within the country. It is not surprising that the Third World liberation movements are delighted about resistance at the heart of imperialism when we consider how unabashed and open West German imperialism has become again, for example using people in the Third World as medical guinea pigs. Schering has tested anti-baby pills on Indian women in South America, Rollei exploits the population of Singapore, who has no social security net to fall back on, and Siemens opens nuclear facilities in South Korea, where safety standards are much lower than at home.[34] Meanwhile, the West German government sends money and weapons to these countries' feudal and fascist regimes.

The Third World liberation movements know that, when push comes to shove, the main battle against imperialism will occur in the heart of the beast. That's where imperialism will be defeated. Whether the 2nd of June Movement received support from liberation movements or anti-imperialist states during the Lorenz action is a question that speculators on a state payroll can concern themselves with. Our task is to remind everyone that the prisoners were flown to a country of their choice, and that they were welcomed there. The People's Republic of Yemen has rejected a lot of money offered by the West German government to extradite them. Only those who know the poverty that British imperialism has left behind in Yemen can fully appreciate how the People's Republic has handled this. It must have confused many a capitalist politician's brain. Here they come with their moneybags from thousands of kilometers away, thinking that anything in the world can be bought with them—but they hit a brick wall and have to realize that their own pathetic corruptness is not mirrored by a socialist government. The Yemenis honored their promise: they received the liberated prisoners and granted them full freedom of movement.

But we also want to talk about the negative consequences of the Lorenz action. After Lorenz's release, the regime's fury targeted anyone eager to leave the constraints of the system behind, including youth ready to determine their own destiny. The brutality that the cops showed at the Weisbecker House and the Rauch House is a case in point.[35] The attempts to intimidate the legal left, and indeed everyone not fitting into the square box of a bourgeois existence, are further proof. We saw manhunts, raids, and threats. Some comrades were paralyzed by the wave of repression that followed Lorenz's release. Their joy about the liberated prisoners soon gave way to resignation. The state demonstrated its power and did everything to put the resistance in Berlin on the defensive. It didn't only go after the armed members of the 2nd of June Movement; it tried to silence everyone.

But the state's offensive wasn't very successful and received much critique from the population, as well as from people who had been opposed to the Lorenz action. With a poor reaction to the criticism from within its own ranks and the increased ridicule from the public, the state only widened the gap between the rulers and the people—that's exactly what the 2nd of June Movement had wanted. The state unveiled the brutality of legalized state violence at a time when everyone could compare it to the revolutionary violence of the oppressed. This was an error on the side of the state that set the stage for defeat. Had it managed to make people feel hopeless and powerless by its show of strength, it would have been successful. It would have detached the Lorenz action from any broader movement and turned it into a fluke. But this didn't happen. Right in the middle of the state's repercussions, the 2nd of June Movement explained to the left, and the population at large, the motivations behind the Lorenz kidnapping with the "The Kidnapping as We See It" leaflet. To explain an action is always important, but especially when the enemy is keen to vilify it, using all of its counterpropagandist means.

That it was possible to distribute a leaflet so widely proves how rooted the 2nd of June Movement was in Berlin. Otherwise, it would have been impossible to remain on the political offensive and inflict a defeat on the Berlin government. After all, it had unleashed its entire apparatus onto the streets to intimidate the people, in a city with the highest concentration of cops anywhere in the world, and yet the 2nd of June Movement managed to distribute the leaflet right in the middle of it. It was a show of strength and prevented the onset of resignation. People no longer saw the state as all-powerful; they realized that it could be powerless.

Helping to distribute the leaflet allowed more people to identify with the 2nd of June Movement. It made them a part of the action and gave them a sense of having contributed to its success. But the Lorenz action is no blueprint, and the success of copycat actions also is far from guaranteed. Blueprints are not only boring but also dangerous. Whoever follows blueprints forgets that the political circumstances of no two actions resemble one another. The enemy is always learning, and you never know how it will react.

But the enemy learning is only one thing. Another is more important, namely, that the political circumstances change after every action because of the action. The people involved must always ask themselves whether they assessed the political consequences of the action correctly and whether the consequences correspond to the aims of the action. If the answer is yes, then everything works in the activists' favor. Then, they retain what is most important under any action, namely, the initiative. If the answer is no, they lose the initiative. The action then enters a stage where the group or commando involved must ask itself whether it can take the initiative back. Otherwise, it must consider ending the action.

During the Lorenz kidnapping, the 2nd of June Movement never lost the initiative, not even for one second. Even when it looked as if the group was making concessions, obeying the orders of the police, the police was far from taking the initiative. To the contrary, the police was forced to make all communiqués of the 2nd of June Movement public, which confirmed that the group was in control. A guerrilla cannot afford to lose the initiative during an action; otherwise defeat is certain.

After the Lorenz action, the 2nd of June Movement could not have called the shots during an action in similar ways. Had it tried, defeat would have been certain. But the distribution of the leaflet showed that the initiative could be kept in other ways. It was almost as if the group was following a principle by von Clausewitz and Mao: when a guerrilla is backed up against the wall and the enemy's lines draw closer, it must not attempt to break through the encirclement by military means; rather, it must seek new political (political-military) ways to conquer the consciousness of the people.[36] The enemy will always attempt to back us up against a wall, to isolate, and to suffocate us, trying to push us into a direct military confrontation with the militarily superior state apparatus. The more spectacular the action, the more certain the state's attempt to turn it against ourselves. The state will try to force or lure us onto the battlefields, where it can dictate the form and content of the struggle, and where we can only perish. The state is superior not only militarily but also politically. It is a political error to accept this confrontation, and it will show in military defeat. When the enemy has encircled us, we must evade. When it tries to lure us onto the battlefield, we must take the political initiative in a way the state isn't prepared for. We need to find methods the state cannot prevent despite its military superiority.

You cannot evade an enemy when you are dogmatic. You need to remain flexible, you need to be able to react to changes within the enemy lines, and you need to be able to adapt your strategy. (Not your goals!) An example for this comes in the actions discussed in the courtroom under the name of the "chocolate kiss banks." It is widely assumed that the chocolate kisses were distributed for fun. That is false. The actions might have been fun, but more importantly, the 2nd of June Movement demonstrated how differently it treated the fat cats and ordinary people, both during actions and in general: the fat cats are kidnapped; the ordinary people get chocolate kisses.

A social-revolutionary group does not only win people over with their goals, but also with their conduct. For any goal, there are zillions of possible actions. When the state tries to convince the public that a revolutionary group's actions are as dangerous for the lady selling flowers on the corner as they are for future mayors of Berlin, it is important to demonstrate that this is not the case. By making revolutionary politics transparent, the state propaganda will become hollow. Actions by the 2nd of June Movement never posed any threat to innocent bystanders. It was—and is—important to make that clear.

If the oppressed classes feel threatened by our actions, they will turn against us and collaborate with the state. If, on the other hand, we gain their sympathy, they will rally around us, or at least remain neutral. An urban guerrilla has no liberated territories to fall back onto like a guerrilla operating in the countryside does. The population approving of their actions is key for their survival.

To build an effective urban guerrilla remains crucial. We do not want to talk about the past alone. We must also consider the present and the future. But we cannot outline a strategy. If anyone expected that from us, they will be disappointed. But how can we outline a strategy from prison? Our own experiences are not sufficient. We don't have the full picture of the struggles on the outside. We have no experience in some of the most important current confrontations. Without that, you cannot outline a strategy.

There are enough bourgeois propagandists, but also comrades, who talk about the imperialist countries as a unified bloc without noteworthy contradictions—countries under total control of the US. As proof, they name the obvious alliances: NATO, the Trilateral Commission, the IMF.[37] Alliances that supposedly facilitate the peaceful division of the Third World between the imperialist powers. But this division is much less peaceful than it may seem. The forms of conflict between the imperialist powers change and aren't always easy to detect. But if you analyze the statistics of the imperialists' commodity and capital exports, you'll notice that the steel, automobile, textile, currency, and armament wars stem from nation-states trying to expand their interests and spheres of influence as the administrators of capital against one another. And since this competition increases with shrinking markets, the tensions within the imperialist camp will increase too. True, the imperialist countries' common interests still dominate: to protect, and expand, the so-called Free West against the COMECON states.[38] The politics of the Cold War and the rivalry with the Soviet Union will weaken the Western camp economically, since Western countries will be forced to reserve significant parts of their national revenue for the ongoing arms race. While the US uses 5 percent of its gross national product for armament, the Soviet Union, being at a technological disadvantage, uses 17 percent.

The Americans know very well: as long as the Soviet Union has to keep up with the American level of armament, it cannot operate in the Third World as it would like to. But the "strategy of tension" fulfills yet another purpose: the European NATO allies are presented with the image of a dangerous, highly armed Soviet enemy. This highly armed foe of capital creates fear. In the context of the strategy of tension, it then appears logical for Western Europe to follow the US's lead. The old imperialist strategy of encircling the Soviet Union shall be maintained that way, now using nuclear weapons. The goal is to tie the hands of the Soviet Union. The US hopes to kill two birds with one stone: the second bird is the European Community, an increasingly stronger competitor for the US on increasingly smaller markets. West Germany replaced the US as the world's leading country in commodity exports in 1978. West Germany has also replaced the US as the world's leading country in capital exports. And this is just West Germany! When we consider the trend of an economic and political concentration of power within the European Community, it is easy to see that it has become a highly dangerous competitor for the US.

We are still at the beginning of the strategy of tension. It is not easy to analyze. Nor are the tactics used by the individual capitalist states. But one thing is becoming increasingly clear: the Americans want to weaken the rising imperialism of the European Community. There have been open discussions in the US about a war in Europe and such a war's economic benefit for the US. World War II has shown what destruction in Europe can mean for America.

"Learn everything, don't forget anything!" Karl Liebknecht has left us with this saying.[39] We must not forget that armament on full throttle, a capitalism in crisis, and the social tensions this creates make the onset of warfare less and less controllable. It won't matter whether the trigger is a dead heir apparent in Sarajevo, the pope in Rome, the Iraq-Iran conflict, or some other relatively banal occurrence. It will only be the spark hitting a powder keg filled to the brim, setting the earth on fire.

"Learn everything, don't forget anything!" To learn everything means to oppose everything that is open preparation for war: military conscription in the US, the US nuclear war strategy, jokes about the radioactive contamination of Iran, the development of the neutron bomb and NATO midrange missiles, the expansion and increased operational authorities of the West German navy. Not to forget anything means that warfare is also prepared psychologically and that public swearing-in ceremonies serve that purpose. Anyone who protests them keeps the tradition of the revolutionary workers' movement alive, reviving (knowingly or not) the political spirit of Karl Liebknecht and Rosa Luxemburg. "The Main Enemy Is in Your Own Country!" These words, too, are by Karl Liebknecht, and they remain true to this day.[40]

Capital regularly presents us with external enemies, be it the Soviet Union, be it the oil sheiks, be it the ayatollahs, be it Japanese industrialists, be it the people of Vietnam. This is not surprising. When a crisis deepens capitalism's internal contradictions, an external enemy is needed to distract from increased domestic exploitation and repression. If the distraction strategy works, the peoples of the world will start fighting each other. In that case, the only one who loses is the little guy. What we need in order to prevent the war between the races is the war between the classes.

Class war in the heart of the beast is the only possible way to eradicate war and imperialism once and for all. The capitalist state has recognized this too. That's why it turns all those into enemies who resist the madness of the arms race—the madness of an industry only interested in profit, while destroying humanity and the natural environment in the process; the madness of housing ghettos and high-rise buildings unfit for the human spirit; the madness of factories, schools, universities, everything that follows the capitalist clock. Capital has realized that resistance in all areas of life, the struggle for self-management and self-organization, is the beginning of a social revolt it needs to nip in the bud before it can take root and turn into a revolution.

For those of us who want to eradicate this madness, it is not enough to propagate resistance against run-down neighborhoods, nuclear power plants, or war. That won't suffice. The struggles must intensify, and they must unite with the goal of an economic and cultural revolution from below, from the people, on to a political revolution. It won't be enough to destroy political power and the capitalist state. We must attack the state's economic base. We must occupy and defend people's homes, then their neighborhoods. Undercover cops must be thrown out of them—indeed, all cops must be thrown out. We must occupy the factories and run them ourselves. Like the Polish working class, we must build and organize free unions. We must abolish nuclear power plants, midrange missiles, and all other crap.

We will do everything in order to bring together the sparks of resistance across society for a socialist revolution. Only when the resistance is united do we have the chance to liberate everyone. And only in unity and in revolutionary struggle do we have the chance to prevent the madness of a limited (or unlimited) nuclear war—or, for that matter, of any war. "War Against War" (*Krieg dem Krieg*) means direct attack against the conditions that bring about war, which means it is a war against capitalism. We, as the armed part of the resistance, must strive for the unity of resistance as well. Our struggle is a part of many struggles. Either we will become a part of these struggles or we will be rendered politically insignificant.

Should the enemy succeed in separating and isolating our struggles, we must analyze the errors that have made this possible. We must do this thoroughly and honestly in order to avoid the armed struggle becoming an end in itself. Armed resistance that defines and understands itself as part of the overall resistance, and that uses armed actions for the benefit of the overall resistance, won't run the danger of isolation. It will carry on the politics of resistance in everyday life by other means. And it will make clear that the politics of resistance does not only consist of armed actions. It will not declare the armed struggle the vanguard of the resistance. The vanguard will always be the politics. It is not the level of violence that determines the vanguard or the most advanced form of the struggle; what determines the vanguard or the most advanced form of the struggle is using the most effective means to achieve our goals. Our political goals are primary; the forms and the means are secondary. Politics command the gun, not vice versa.

We must never stubbornly stick to one form of struggle alone. This leads to dogmatism, to fetishism, and, in the end, to dead politics. The question of violence is for us not a question of principle but of necessity. We are confronted with violence; we didn't invent it. It is no coincidence that the proletarian sections of the left, which experience violence every day, turn much quicker to counterviolence than the bourgeois sections. Nonviolent and militant activists should not argue about the level of violence used in resistance; they should discuss how to most effectively expand the resistance together.

The nonviolent resistance in Gorleben has shown that there are moments when it is more effective to forgo active counterviolence. Meanwhile, the open counterviolence in Bremen has shown that there are moments when active counterviolence is more effective.[41] The active resisters from Bremen and the passive resisters from Gorleben should not criticize one another but engage in dialogue and stress the common aspects of their resistance. Both poles of the movement go through processes of learning, and they each need the experiences of the other, at least if they see themselves as one movement, which, we assume, they do. They need to exchange ideas with each other and define a common goal in order to develop appropriate tactics and a fitting strategy. Dialogue among ourselves will bring us forward; slimy dialogue with those in power will not.

We can only make steps forward independently if we take these steps ourselves. We can't buy them from the powerful by surrendering our radicalness. This is true on the individual as well as on the collective level.

We, the armed part of the movement, must in the future not bark louder than we can bite. We will do everything for militant and armed resistance to expand and take root in a way that makes long, resilient guerrilla war possible. But it must not be concentrated in the urban centers alone, as it makes people understand that, in the end, only a violent transformation can overthrow the system.

The minutes from the trial for the first 193 days (up until August 1, 1980) note the following:

365 witnesses
22 experts

Disturbances
Teufel: 52
Meyer: 27
Reinders: 59

Fritzsch: 55
Klöpper: 63
Vogel: 26

Warnings
Teufel: 20
Meyer: 13
Reinders: 44
Fritzsch: 39
Klöpper: 40
Vogel: 8

Melees in the left defendants' box: 2
Melees in the right defendants' box: 5

Courtroom
Demonstrations of approval and disapproval, commotion, applause, laughter: 614
Melees: 10
Clearances: 11
Unpermitted interaction with the defendants: 46
Orders of silence: 211
Threats of expulsion: 88

PIGS TO OUTER SPACE
(1981)

Klaus Viehmann

This is Klaus Viehmann's closing statement in the trial against himself and three 2nd of June codefendants, presented in February 1981. The first part of the statement was published under the title "Schweine ins Weltall" in the autonomist journal *Radikal*, no. 98, October 1981, and the second part in the subsequent *Radikal* issue, no. 99, November–December 1981.

Part I

I am neither a legal fortune teller nor do I intend to dwell on stories from the glorious (or, for that matter, not so glorious) old days. We shall look into the future and not cry over the past. We are awaiting a decade that will feel like a high-speed train compared to the relatively tame 1970s. And if we, the left, want to achieve anything during this decade, we need to finally analyze past experiences, at least if they are still relevant, and use them productively in the future. The main requirement for any productive analysis is discussion among the various factions of the left, and consciousness about the necessity of collaboration, which will become ever more important in West Germany.

The principal questions are always the same: What is our current situation? What do we want to achieve? Who is our enemy? How, and with whom, are we going to fight to reach our goals? These questions cannot be answered from a writing desk, especially not a writing desk in prison, where you are rather isolated from everyday life on the outside. The final answers need to be given on the street.

Whoever poses these questions seriously and intends to answer them has to be clear about one thing: those who fight for social revolution do it because they want the revolution to be victorious one day, not because they want to cry over the debris of defeat. We'll encounter many defeats along our way, that is inevitable, but we can—and must—learn from them in order not to repeat the same mistakes. We can't afford to. Those in power have been evaluating and improving counterinsurgency measures for centuries, while the left repeatedly must start all over again, especially in West Germany, where the workers' movement has been brutally smashed and forcibly assimilated over the past one hundred years. The APO of the late 1960s and the youth revolt, too, are at risk of passing on too few experiences and too little knowledge to today's movements; they can't rely on professional revisionists and old leftists with rather comfortable lives.

So if the new fires under the lounge chairs of the rulers shall be more than short-lived flares, we need to learn from the past and look into what is going to come in the future. We need to look beyond the boundaries of our immediate circles, whether they are defined by "special issues" (such as prison, factory work, or the environment) or by the rims of our muesli bowls. This also applies to the armed left. All factions need to see themselves as a part of the whole, that is, the entire left and its allies. The whole must not be understood as an assembly of parts. The old mistake of thinking in exclusions rather than inclusions, in black and white, without ever seeing two different sides complementing each other, has for a long time led to a political situation characterized by division rather than reasonable compromise.

The situation will be even tougher for the left in the coming years (for all of its currents, that is), due to a number of urgent problems ranging from the instability of global politics to the rebellion in the metropole. The repression that the different currents of the left will be confronted with will only vary in small degrees, since the rulers want to weaken the left as a whole. They don't want to allow a consciousness that understands the new situation and realizes that the rulers' power is on the decline. They want to prevent those who struggle to unite against them. This applies to the unemployed youth as much as to the pensioner forced out onto the street by development schemes, the people in Lower Saxony contaminated by nuclear waste, and the Turk next door. Without a connection between the radical left and the emerging declassed groups, there won't be a mass movement with any chance of success.

The radical left alone won't be enough. It faces the same problem as the guerrilla: either it will grow or it will become insignificant. But the declassed groups alone won't be enough either. They cannot be successful alone, because they need the experiences of resistance of recent years, the direct struggle against oppression, if they want to avoid terrible losses due to wrong tactics and strategies.

There is no doubt that the question of violence will play a role in the coming struggles. (On our part. For the other side, violence is a given, it needs not be discussed.) Relevant debates often remind me of conversations between people with hearing aids: in particular, nonviolent activists turn their position into an ideology, while accusing everyone who thinks differently of exactly that. That is, of course, nonsense.

It is clear for any revolutionary that they only use violence when necessary, that violence has to be directed against the enemy only, and that its use must allow us to improve our position in the struggle. We consider violence one means of many in the fight of the oppressed against the oppressors, and as such it is justified. How this differs from using violence simply for the sake of violence should have become evident, at the very latest, with the fascist attack on the Munich Oktoberfest.[1] This is a kind of violence directed against the people, and Munich was certainly not the last attack of that sort. West Germany is a country in which neofascists can amass arms with the state turning a blind eye, while any leftist with a slingshot stands for the "decline of the Christian West," at least if you believe the press and the legal system.

Some people—I don't know if they are true pacifists or just the nonviolent types who want to take away our guns to weaken and divide us—even object to fundraisers for weapons sent to the liberation movement in El Salvador, arguing that such donations would only fuel the cycle of violence.[2] This is rather cynical, because everyone who pays taxes here, or simply drinks a cup of coffee from El Salvador, supports the war of the junta against its own people. It is frustrating that public resistance against violence is stronger when there is an attempt to arm people who are murdered than when their murderers go out to slaughter them. Had there not been violence in social relationships all throughout history, left militants certainly wouldn't take to violence today.

We can use a more trivial example than the liberation war in El Salvador. Let's consider a street fight: Who turns the other cheek when the first blow has given them a concussion? It'd be a rather foolish thing to do. And who benefits if we refrain from militant resistance by principle? (A type of resistance referred to as "brutal violence" by people who are brutally violent in the name of the state.) Certainly not us. If, every once in a while, you see one of the state's minions taking to their heels, let's say during a protest, it provides encouragement and indicates what is possible when the tables are turned.

Those who embrace nonviolence as an ethical guideline for their lives will get a good beating or two over the coming years, considering the intensification of social conflict. The result is quite likely that they will stop taking to the streets. To always be at the receiving end of violence and never take a swing yourself is a recipe for fear and resignation, and bolsters the myth of the omnipotent state. We use violence to one day abolish violence, nothing more and nothing less.

It would be grotesque to allow the state that we fight and aim to defeat to dictate the means of our struggle. The state will only offer us means that doesn't threaten it. We ourselves need to determine the means of our struggle, morally and politically.

The question of violence has always determined the discussions of the left about the urban guerrilla—unfortunately, the urban guerrilla itself was rarely involved in these discussions. People haven't differentiated much between different forms of violence either. After all, violence can run the gamut from sabotage along assembly lines to bombings and kidnappings. Even among groups where there was principal agreement on having to accept violence as necessary under certain circumstances, the urban guerrilla could still be regarded as consisting of "killers" and "adventurists."

The loudest criticism has come from people who feel the armed struggle threatens the life choices they have made. Either directly, by fearing for a career or status they have achieved by adapting to the system, or indirectly, by joining the long line of know-it-alls who no longer seek salvation in the confrontation with the state but in the comfortable niches provided by the state. In the worst case, they justify having made

peace with domination by suggesting that the state and its representatives really don't want an increase in violence, or domestic armament,
but that "baby-eating terrorists" have left them with no choice. This is a
very odd line of argumentation. There were mobile task forces, emergency
laws, army exercises against striking workers, and high-tech manhunts
in West Germany and West Berlin long before there was any sight of an
urban guerrilla.

It is also wrong to claim that the armed struggle delivered the justification for the state's repression against the left. First, it would be rather
naive to think that the state won't defend itself when attacked, or when
the fat cats fear that their profits and their power are in danger. Second,
the powerful have always found a justification for their preposterous
acts. Once upon a time, the Jews were to blame; today, it is the asylum
seekers, the radical foreigners, and the militants spreading "chaos."[3] The
communists have always served as a default punching bag, especially in
this country, where the elite was politically socialized during the anti-
Bolshevist Nazi era.

In a climate where political positions are primarily defined by
distancing themselves from others, critique and self-critique of the
urban guerrilla becomes impossible. But such a critique would be of
great importance, especially now, in order to provide the coming social
movements with the extensive experiences that the urban guerrilla has
made over the last twelve years during its confrontation with the state. It
won't help us when, out of fear, we only address the errors of the urban
guerrilla (there have been errors, no doubt) without considering its intentions and the potentials of its methods. There is a lot of psychological
repression. Sober and rational analysis is difficult, as people would rather
talk about things that the urban guerrilla never has been involved with,
other than, perhaps, in the imagination of some individuals. Members
of the Revolutionary Cells have aptly called this the "myth of the armed
struggle."

Neither the image of the crazy adventurist blindly pulling the trigger
nor that of the heroic guerrilla fighter (the "new man") is anchored in
reality. Sure, if someone believes that this country is the freest on earth,
then anyone fighting it must appear crazy. And everyone who considers
the system unassailable and invincible must perceive those who fight
it nonetheless as heroes. In reality, we are always dealing with human
beings, with all their strengths and weaknesses. It is sad when they are

robbed of their humanity by one myth or another, especially when this renders resistance far-fetched and seemingly impossible—something that is not worth getting involved with.

With regard to the possibility of resistance, an ETA commando wrote the following in a report about the halfway ascension to heaven by Franco's deputy Carrero Blanco:

> In brief, it doesn't take a mining engineer to make a tunnel! Nor an expert in explosives to dynamite the tunnel. Nor does one have to be a specialist in optics to have a car well placed, signaling the exact spot to be dynamited. Nor is it impossible to have a man standing nearby, ready to give the go-ahead signal. All that myth must be eliminated. Nobody is a god—nor is a god needed. This was the work of normal men.[4]

What ETA says about a relatively complicated action can be applied to all resistance: everyone can learn. *Legal—illegal—scheißegal* ("Legal—illegal—who gives a shit?") is a slogan that has recently appeared on the walls of Berlin (if I can trust the photographs I receive from the outside). If this refers to the way by which we choose our actions, then fine, since we don't ask for the approval of the rulers. But if "illegal" means to have your face on wanted posters all across the city and be hunted by the cops, then it makes a bloody big difference.

Life underground requires a few changes in life, but it doesn't mean that you are constantly anxious and on the run. The cops only say that so that the enormous means they employ to catch you don't seem blown out of proportion. Most of the problems of living underground can be solved through practice. The real problems start when an organization and its members turn the necessity of secret logistics into a virtue; in other words, when life underground becomes an organizational principle and everything else appears less important and "not really revolutionary." Life underground as an organizational principle is very time-consuming. Legal comrades need to solve far less problems before they carry out actions, including illegal ones. If you live underground, you first need to take care of your everyday survival and safety.

The political danger of living underground lies in the possible alienation from the left, and from everyday life in general. This is what leads to actions that focus exclusively on the problems of the guerrilla and not on the mobilization of the people. This can only be avoided through

constant exchange between the comrades underground, the urban guerrilla, and legal activists. No one says that this is easy. Besides, since the
verdict in the *Agit 883* case, self-censorship among leftist publishers has
become rampant.[5] There is no blueprint for how to have an exchange
between the underground and the legal left, and if there was, it couldn't
be publicly advertised.

The cops know how crucial that exchange is. It is in their utmost
interest to prevent it. They probably understand better than many on the
left what would happen if the knowledge and the operational capacities
of the urban guerrilla merged with the mass struggles of the 1980s. A
former minister of police doesn't sit down at a table with a former enemy
of the state such as Mahler because he doesn't have anything better to
do.[6] There's a reason for this. We can assume that both know very well
that there's an enormous time bomb ticking that needs to be defused,
because otherwise it's going to blow off their asses. Their "dialogue" and
the tales about a "soft approach" serve to divide the left by integrating
parts of it, just as they did with broad sections of the APO. Everyone else,
everyone not satisfied with hollow promises and crumbs from the tables
of the rulers, will be criminalized. The carrot and the stick, divide and
conquer—it's an age-old strategy of oppression in a new, shiny package.

Among those who are targeted by new laws and police tactics are the
autonomist groups of the antinuclear movement, known for their mass
militancy. The events of Kalkar 1977, when, within a few hours, tens of
thousands of protesters were ID'd and searched before they had even laid
eyes on the nuclear power plant construction site, has made it bitterly
clear that mass militancy stands no chance against a well-prepared,
better-equipped opponent. With the means at your disposal (assuming
that the cops haven't taken them from you yet), you might be able to
withstand water cannons and tear gas, but it'd be sheer madness to take
on machine guns and hand grenades should the situation escalate. So far,
antinuclear protesters have only been met by hand grenades in France
(Vital Michalon died on July 13, 1977, in Malville), but under certain circumstances West German authorities won't shy away from similar means. If
you needed any proof, look at Albrecht's statements during the demonstration in Grohnde, where he came very close to giving a firing order.[7]

Criminalization creates two alternatives: either you become less
active and retreat from political life, or you prepare for life underground.
Whoever thinks I'm exaggerating runs the risk of naively waiting for the

day when the government gets serious about eliminating the entire left. To believe that they don't have plans for such an undertaking proves a lack of both historical understanding and imagination. To have no illegal and subversive structures means to be more controllable by the tools of surveillance and state-paid snoops.

A current example for the criminalization of militants are the imprisoned Kreuzberg squatters. As long as you're looking at relatively mild prison sentences, you can always say, "Okay, I'm willing to pay the price," even if, of course, it should never be the cops who decide whom to send to prison and whom not. If we left that exercise to them, we'd only find our comrades there, and never those who'd deserve it much more. What the Kreuzberg example demonstrates is that you must not only think about a possible life underground but also about a possible life in prison. Ideally, this would lead to a deep, collective reflection on the prison system as a whole—a reflection that would also include people with little risk of ending up there themselves, but with the will to fight the system of incarceration and total control.

The history of prisoners as well as activists on the outside fighting against this most obvious form of state power (poured into concrete) is not as rich in West Germany as it is, for example, in France and Spain, but, in recent years, awareness has been growing. Special forms of prison play an important role in the current discussions. The high-security unit in Moabit I know firsthand. High-security unit means . . .

. . . that everything you say and do happens in the midst of concrete walls, security cameras, microphones, neon lights, and bulletproof windows;

. . . isolation for years in small (tiny) groups with no diversion;

. . . physical and psychological damage;

. . . blueprints for newly built and planned prisons, for example the new women's prison in Plötzensee;

. . . an elaborate pyramid of punishments and rewards, the apex of technocratic prison reform;

. . . counterinsurgency, the attempt to eliminate all opposition and deviancy;

. . . approaches that might be more or less high-security, but always inhumane.

High-security units have sparked resistance. The hunger strikes prove this, fistfights with guards prove this, and the relatively broad public campaigns and actions against them prove this. The high-security units have punctured the liberal mask of the state; fascism has become more visible. There's a logic to it. The threat of fascism shall spread fear and deter. The rulers want everyone to know what happens when you dare confront the state. (As an aside, it is quite remarkable that the traditional prisons apparently no longer provide sufficient deterrence when it comes to today's resistance movements.) The high-security units are built for militants who are committed to resist all forms of exploitation and oppression, also in prison, where they are considered "dangerous" and "disruptive."

Therapy is offered to prisoners who leave their deviant ways behind and are willing to return to the everyday assembly line. Open prisons are offered to prisoners who shall be punished but not lost as cheap labor. Today, there are different forms of imprisonment next to the traditional detention units, where prisoners are pretty much left to themselves. The degree to which these old units will be replaced by new ones depends on the finances of the state and the level of social conflict. There exist parallels between the technological developments in the prison system and the automation in production—from work and detention units of yesteryear to total surveillance in the spirit of Orwell's 1984. This is the future according to those in charge of the prison system; it's a future that can only be prevented if we stop these desk murderers.

It is incredibly difficult to establish unity among inmates in a prison. After all, you have junkies, foreigners, safecrackers, men not paying child support, pimps, drug dealers, and people with various state-imposed labels. Among the left-wing prisoners, there are different ideas about the prison struggle and the demands it should entail. "Peace, happiness, and sunshine" is not what defines the interactions among prisoners, as little as it defines social relationships in general. The big prison (society) is reflected in the small one (the penitentiary). But all prisoners have a common goal: to get out, and to abolish the institutions of incarceration. If you keep that in mind, you have at least a common denominator. Just as it does on the outside, resistance in prison comes in eruptions that are impossible to predict. But with each one, there is growing awareness that your enemy is not the person standing next to you but the person facing you.

One discussion has been crucial in the context of the prison struggle and the prisoner solidarity movement in recent years: Shall prisoners from the guerrilla demand their own units, or shall they be integrated into the general population? It will probably be a contentious issue for some time to come. There is little collaboration between the people arguing for one line or the other. The only commonality during the last big hunger strike was that all prisoners rejected the conditions they are held in now.[8]

In the beginning, there were two hundred prisoners involved (in the entire country) with different concerns, reaching from very specific demands in regional prisons to the abolition of special units to the demands of the RAF prisoners to be housed together. The public remembered little more than the RAF prisoners' demands after Sigurd Debus was force-fed to death and the hunger strike was called off.[9] Even in left-wing papers, you could read that the prisoners had gone on hunger strike solely in solidarity with the demands of the RAF prisoners. Unfortunately, the public, the left included, falls victim to sensationalism (and cynicism) easily; there isn't much interest, as long as lives aren't in danger and people die. Only then will the issue be discussed in newspaper columns, usually poorly.

Now that the hunger strike is over, some people say they couldn't support it because they disagreed with the demands of the RAF prisoners. That is dishonest. The people who say that have never shown any solidarity with prisoners and their demands—at best, they have paid lip service to some of them. Their arguments only provide their guilty conscience with a soft pillow to lie on.

There are also folks who reject any discussion about right or wrong in the prison struggle altogether. Their approach is purely moralistic: if comrades die, they say, their demands must have been right. But we need a discussion about the prison struggle, especially now. We need to tackle the key issues—politically, not moralistically. I am hoping for extensive discussions. All I can do here is add my own two cents.

To me, the following arguments are the most important when it comes to not housing prisoners from the guerrilla in separate units: Separate units for prisoners from the guerrilla will mean (in some form) high-security units, and it is false to believe that these units can be changed from the inside. Any demand for units for up to fifteen prisoners (smaller groups are much more likely, and we will see them in the future) correspond to what the prison commanders of West Germany are already planning anyway, that is, a parcellation of prisons into smaller units. The main objective of this prison reform is to have small groups under expensive high-tech surveillance and permanent observation. Even youth prisons are planned that way. It is a reaction by those in power to the subculture that developed in the old prisons, where inmates still had contact with one another—a subculture the authorities found hard to control. In the long run, however, the most important argument against separate units for prisoners from the guerrilla is a political one: by isolating them, they lose all contact with the (both current and future) social-revolutionary, oppositional movements in and around the prisons.

The Red Brigades have drawn the consequences of the escalating situation in Italy by kidnapping Judge D'Urso.[10] Their strategy is to build unity between all prisoners ready to fight. The aim is to abolish high-security prisons and, in the long run, prisons altogether. They, correctly, believe that the prison system will be an increasingly important issue during the coming social confrontations. Prison has always been the tool the powerful revert to when they face rebellion and open resistance. Therefore, it is of strategic importance—and not just of moral importance, as some fans of charity believe—to smash the high-security units first, and then the prisons altogether.

The situation in West Germany and West Berlin is not the same as in Italy yet, but the development is comparable. The strategy of the Red Brigades can be a model for prison struggles here. As far as prisoners' support on the outside is concerned, it can't depend on whether you agree with the prisoners' demands or not. The prisoners never dictate the conditions in prison; it is the cops who put them there.

The demand for integration into the general population requires some clarification. It is not very clear. It considers political unity among prisoners mandatory for a common struggle for the equal treatment of all and against parcellation and isolation. The corresponding outside strategy is to mobilize the base—as far as possible, in coordination with the prisoners. But a strategy that excludes potential comrades is not sustainable. Integration into the general population is a misleading demand, because there is no "standard" life in prison, and there probably never was. Prison doesn't equal prison. There are numerous different units and, soon, there will be even more. Prisoners will be divided according to what they got sentenced for, according to their level of resistance inside prison, and, not least, according to gender. It is wrong to believe that we would achieve anything substantial by becoming part of "standard" prison life.

It might make it easier to bring together all prisoners in struggle, but it won't do much more.

Of course, unity among prisoners is necessary, especially in light of the constant attempts by the prison commanders to divide the inmates. Without the collective organization of a critical mass of inmates, it will be impossible to change conditions on the inside. We can see inmates starting to rebel. We have seen that a little push can be enough to start a revolt, and the revolt grows stronger every time. Collectivity—the unity of the prisoners—is our priority and must determine the forms of the struggle and its demands.

The struggle in prison is connected to the struggle outside. It is no coincidence that things heat up in prison when people on the outside prove that resistance is possible. Prisoner solidarity should be lifted to a new level. The left needs to see it as an integral part of their political practice. The demand for amnesty or slogans such as "One, two, three, set the people free!" do not suffice, as their practical consequences are limited. Left groups must also provide structures that allow released prisoners to continue the struggle outside against an enemy they have only seen a very specific side of behind bars.

Struggles on the inside and the outside also need to be connected to prevent the silence characteristic of prison cells from spreading to the streets. Otherwise, hope will die quickly. Hope is "every prisoner's sister," if you believe an old saying among cons. The critique of special units, and prisons altogether, must go hand in hand with a critique of the prison regime encroaching on our cities. Look at the difference between the old rental barracks of Kreuzberg and the new concrete blocks of the Märkische Viertel—it corresponds to the difference between the one-hundred-year-old holes of Moabit and the air of "urban development" that the high-security units carry. At intersections and public buildings in Berlin, you'll find the same security cameras that are used in the high-security units. In the old Moabit prison, inmates are still able to communicate fairly easily, sometimes by chance, even if they are kept in single cells. In the high-security units, the inmates are as isolated as tenants in high-rise buildings: no one even knows who lives next door.

Some comrades believe that only a special group of prisoners will benefit from campaigns against high-security units. That is not true. To begin with, the population of the high-security units has become quite diverse. The majority still comes from the urban guerrilla, but in Hamburg there are also former escapees, and in Celle and Stammheim they keep even neo-Nazis there. Second, all prisoners, no matter where they are held, know that they might end up in high security as soon as they resist. That's why campaigns against the high-security units are not only campaigns against tomorrow's prisons but also against new models of general bourgeois rule. They must be understood and conducted as such.

Another important aspect of the prison struggle is the urban guerrilla's relationship to prison and the prisoners. During the past eleven years, there have been many attempts to get people out of prison. Lorenz and the escape at Lehrter Straße are the prime examples of successful actions; Schleyer and Mogadishu are the prime examples of complete failure. The liberation of prisoners was always symbolic for liberation in general, and an escaped prisoner is always a thorn in the side of the powerful and their alleged omnipotence, always a blow against the control of the state over human beings. Any escape from prison is justified; there are no two ways about it. However, it is problematic when the struggle for liberation is reduced to the struggle for the liberation of prisoners and when this is sold to the people as the urban guerrilla's strategy. Prison is a terrain of struggle, but not the only one. This must become clear in our political practice.

By 1977 at the latest, it was clear that the liberation of prisoners as a political strategy had reached a dead end, that an exclusive focus on logistics and actions to get comrades out no longer corresponded to the necessity of revolutionary practice. During a phase in which the urban guerrilla needed to reconstitute after the "German Autumn," with new strategies in order to regain lost terrain and trust within the left, the liberation of Till [Meyer] in Moabit no longer had strategic significance. Politically, it would have been more meaningful had the prison struggle focused on campaigns and actions against the special units rather than another prisoner liberation. It would have also been less costly.

The following is equally true for the urban guerrilla, the prison struggle, and the left in general: we must break out of our relative isolation and reach a mass base. It was the lack of such a base that allowed every small defeat and error of the urban guerrilla to cause political paralysis.

Part II

All groups and movements of the past years that were unwilling or unable to grow failed or remained irrelevant. Some developed gigantic plans for half the world revolution without having even one foot on the ground. Others lost sight of their goals and ideals and became preoccupied with daily tasks, losing all strategic perspective. What many of the sects calling themselves communist had in common was that they tried to compensate for their weakness in numbers with vanguardist arrogance, for their lack of concrete tactics with abstract strategy, and for their poor connection to grassroots struggles with triumphant programs. The other side of the coin, the reformism and parliamentarism hoping for a peaceful and legal transformation of the state, forgot the military and illegal dimensions of revolutionary change; these comrades also forgot the experience that many had made in the APO, when they were chewed up and frustrated by the march through the institutions or shat out as convinced social democrats. One thing we must never forget is that institutions always prevail, unless they are confronted by a mass movement.

Both of these pitfalls, sectarianism and reformism, can only be avoided if we don't lose sight of ordinary life under capitalism and if we don't lose touch with what's happening on the ground. We must not allow the servants of the state to pacify us. Reality is radical, and we need to be radical. But reality is also buried under tons of debris in people's minds, which is not surprising after years of propaganda and, not least, twelve years of fascism and three decades of anticommunism. Weighed down by the press, Valium, toothpaste ads, and television news, people are denied information about the country they live in. State-ordered disinformation is a requirement for mass loyalty, (un)social peace, and capital's asocial market economy.

Left politics means fighting mass loyalty and destroying the false consciousness of the people around us all "sitting in the same boat," or, as the current version has it, "all in one oil tanker." The image of a galley, on which many are forced to row while a selected few give commands, is much closer to reality. When the ship no longer generates enough profits and careens off course, the ones working below deck pay the price.

Two things are careening off course today. First, economic stability, expressed by full employment, economic growth, and stable currency rates. Second, foreign relations, including international trade as well as strategic, political, and military relationships. Both are necessary for the mass loyalty capitalism relies on. Certain individuals are already dropping off. There's a new term for it, *Staatsverdrossenheit*, "being tired of the state." The rulers use it for people who haven't turned to open and organized rebellion yet; for those who have, they reserve terms such as "insurrectionism" and "terrorism."

The rulers also like to speak about "tightening the belt," asking us to "work harder and perform better!" The "fat years" are supposedly over, and we are obliged to "make sacrifices." Well, most people never saw much of the fat years, and considering the way the economy is going, they will continue to make sacrifices for quite some time—at least if the fat cats have it their way.

The world has one foot in a global economic crisis not seen since 1929. There are more than twenty million unemployed people in the industrialized countries. Inflation is way above 10 percent. The trade balance of most countries is negative, and people speculate with billions of dollars on the financial markets, causing fixed currency rates to tumble. Only billions of petrodollars serving as assets in the banks of the metropole prevent the capitalist economy from collapsing like a house of cards. But even the mighty United States of America can't let their money-printing machines run on with no end without eventually paying a price. Difficult times will arrive for the global superpower when an increasing number of countries will refuse to accept the US dollar as the world trade currency. Then, it will no longer be possible to pay for their oil by printing a few green pieces of paper.

Competition between corporations on the world market will also grow stronger, mediated by the nation-states that host their headquarters. Japan, the US, and the European Community have started to fight about the last pieces of the global cake. The ramifications for branches losing out in the respective regions will be huge. The corporations will raise prices and increase inflation, or they'll demand bailouts in order to "save jobs" (read: their profits), or they'll invest heavily in the rationalization of labor. Hard-working people will have to pay threefold for these developments: by a decline in real wages, by taxes, and by working even harder. Work-related accidents and illnesses are already on the rise, with the individual worker producing more than ever before. Wages have not been raised accordingly. The exploitation of the individual worker is growing, while work, rationalized for profit, is becoming increasingly mind-numbing. Human beings are turned into stooges of automation. That's the perspective the system has to offer. No future!

Skilled workers will disappear. They'll be replaced by a new class of casual and temporary laborers, hired and fired at the bosses' will.

Considering these prospects, quite a few prefer a life on the dole, but they will meet more obstacles to collect their money from the unemployment offices, and cutbacks will eventually force them to accept shit jobs just to get by.

During earlier crises, the state was able to stimulate the economy by digging into resources and taking loans, making new investments appear profitable with the help of subsidies and tax cuts. Public employment was used to lower the unemployment rate. But public employees need wages too, which has led to today's hiring freezes and the so-called cost control measures in health care. Unsurprisingly, the death rate in state hospitals is on the rise. An increasing number of people are dying prematurely due to insufficient care, since they're not allowed to become a burden on the state's balance sheet.

At a time when West Germany is asked to take on increasing responsibility in upholding imperialist rule, its main role is no longer to be the poster boy for economic reconstruction but the sponsor of fascist dictatorships that the US can no longer fund alone. The millions and billions that West Germany is paying to the Turkish military to uphold their torture regime, or to Egypt to comply with the Camp David Accords,[11] come almost exclusively from funds earlier used for domestic policies. The frantic armament by West Germany and other NATO member states also leads to funds previously used to secure "social peace" at home drying up. The people of all countries have to pay the price for the imperialist agenda, whether they are asked to "tighten the belt" for an alleged "common good" or whether they are asked to bleed to death as soldiers for capital.

The energy crisis, which is first and foremost a crisis of capitalist profit, shall, for example, be resolved by violence. The Iranian Revolution shall be smashed by the imperialist stooge Saddam Hussein and his Iraqi army. US soldiers are fighting worldwide for the interests of Exxon, Standard Oil, and US Steel, and for the exploitation of the "American Way of Life" by the grace of Coca-Cola. French imperialism has instigated one coup after another in Africa since it was defeated in Algeria. Together with other NATO member states it intervenes openly whenever a country seems to slip from its sphere of influence. Behind all the ado about Afghanistan, the demand for profit and cheap, accessible energy is all too obvious.

For historical reasons, West Germany has not yet deployed soldiers in open conflict, but West German capital has been a competitor in sharing the plunder of the Third World for decades. By delivering weapons to fascist dictatorships (or so-called friendly regimes), it helps to keep them in power. German-based transnational corporations operate today in almost all countries on the planet. AEG, BASF, Bayer, Siemens, Daimler-Benz, and Volkswagen have turned Latin America into their work yard. They make huge profits by collaborating tightly with the continent's military regimes. In the Volkswagen plant in São Paulo, a seven-hundred-men-strong paramilitary force ensures that exploitation proceeds as smoothly as possible. The Berlin-based Schering company uses Indigenous women in Ecuador and Colombia for the same kind of medical experiments that were conducted by the German pharma industry in the Nazi concentration camps. Mind you, even in Germany people are still experimented with, as long as they don't know about it and can't protest.

Deutsche Bank investors such as Bosch, Henkel, Hoechst, and BMW help keep the racist regime in South Africa in power. German companies use subsidiaries for profit, defying UN resolutions. Daimler-Benz is building plants for tank engines and has delivered Unimogs to the Boer police force, the kind they use, in slightly modified form, to suppress the uprisings in Soweto. In Guatemala, Heckler & Koch guns in the hands of the military ensure that there is peace (for the dead) and order (for the capitalists). Licenses for the production of tanks contribute to keep the military regime in Argentina in power. KWU nuclear plants allow the Brazilian dictatorship to pursue its nuclear dreams.[12] Using intermediaries, West German arms manufacturers deliver war material to Israel to be used for the suppression of the Arab left and the Palestinian liberation struggle. So-called anti-insurgency materials, such as water cannons and CN tear gas, even handcuffs and batons, are delivered by German companies (for example, the state-owned Diag) to torturers such as Paraguay's Stroessner. Once upon a time, the same companies also delivered to the Shah in Iran. Food companies from the European Community force Third World countries to grow luxury foodstuffs instead of urgently needed staples. Every day, tomatoes and eggplants are exported by plane from famine-ridden countries in the Sahel region to the cities of the metropole. It is pure cynicism when people speak of "natural catastrophes" during their fundraisers fighting world hunger. The real "natural catastrophe" is the enforced imperialist order of the world market and its corrupt regimes. In the Ivory Coast, entire regions are deforested, which causes desertification and poverty, because the rich of the world need teakwood for their cabinets and desks. No one in Western Europe will talk about this, unless we do.

Even though the riches of the Third World have been brought to the metropole for hundreds of years, it is too simple to call the workers of the industrial nations parasites of the Third World. After all, there is also a contradiction between the exploiters and the exploited in the metropole. Yes, it is in a different form, since the misery here is not comparable to the misery in the slums of the Third World, but social wealth is not in the hands of the people either. Instead, it fills the pockets of the corporations or is used for armament and the military protection of imperial rule. Left arguments that claim that all who live in the metropole are chauvinists and exploiters of the Third World run the risk of denying that there is a class society in the metropole too. There is no unity among the people in the metropole against the oppressed peoples, and where it appears to exist, the reason is racist, state-sponsored disinformation campaigns. It's a problem that needs to be resolved, but it is not proof that everyone here is profiting from the plunder of other countries.

Consciousness about the global connections between economic exploitation and political oppression has been growing again in the past year or two, after many years of silence on the streets. Internationalism means to support the struggles of the liberation movements through actions. These actions have to be carried out under the conditions of the social struggles here.

A current example for a legal solidarity campaign with a liberation struggle is "Weapons for El Salvador." Of course, it is right to collect as much money as possible for this cause and to transfer it from the metropole to the Third World. But it is hard to accept that only leftists, who usually don't have much money, shall donate, while the ones upholding the imperialist system—thereby being, directly or indirectly, responsible for the situation in El Salvador—can go about their business as they please. It is hard to accept that they sit comfortably in their villas and watch their money grow without ever being confronted with people sitting in refugee camps, starving, and not having a weapon in their hand to attack the oppressor. Money in the hands of the liberation movements makes much more sense than in the bank accounts of the capitalists. "Peace to the shacks! War on the palaces!" is a well-known slogan.[13] Putting it into practice means: money for the struggles for national liberation and self-determination, and war on the moneybags in Europe.

State prosecutors have declared that the kidnapping of the multimillionaire Palmers was an ordinary criminal act. However, they are still searching for the villas in Ticino that the "criminal" kidnappers supposedly bought for themselves with the 4.5 million Deutschmark they collected as a ransom. Yes, it is hard for a bourgeois mind to comprehend that money can be redistributed instead of being used for personal gain, and that this redistribution is part of a struggle for a more just division of wealth between the North and the South. But this struggle has only just started! No matter how much money the liberation movements get from the vaults of the banks in the metropole, they can attack only the limbs of the imperialist squid; its heart can be destroyed only at the center itself. As long as imperialist power has incredible wealth to fall back on, and as long as it possesses the technological and military means that are produced by the working class in the metropole, imperialism will continue to exist.

Overcoming class society in the metropole is key to destroying imperial exploitation. How to get hold of the key is a question of strategy. Some believe that the only way to victory lies in close collaboration with Third World liberation movements. Solidarity is necessary—but the attempt to go beyond that and create operational unity was doomed to fail. All groups that have attempted to let international politics dictate their practice have suffered defeat in their own country and lost political autonomy.

Revolutionary practice is always concrete. It has to consider the realities and conditions of the struggle where it takes place. Internationalism brings together many lines of resistance, but it is not possible to derive the right tactics and strategies from abstract unity. The ways to revolution are determined by historical and cultural factors, by the political and economic development in each country. Practice unfolds from the concrete to the abstract, from the national to the international. Revolutions can be supported from the outside, but they can never be directed from afar and never fit into the same framework. Any attempt in that direction would stand the historical process on its head.

One of Che Guevara's armed companions said that it was important to keep international relationships in mind but that you had to focus on concrete, national problems, as otherwise you wouldn't get anywhere. This means for us to fight locally in order to one day achieve the liberation of humanity worldwide. However, in this struggle for liberation, time is becoming of the essence. The old revolutionary strategists from Marx to Bakunin couldn't foresee what we know now, namely, that the earth might no longer be inhabitable when the exploiters disappear, since they're leaving us with a contaminated wasteland. There are enough arms today to destroy the earth multiple times. In West Germany alone, there are about seven thousand nuclear devices and warheads, purportedly to ensure peace. Soon, there will be about ten thousand. I suppose peace will be even more "secure" then. Such perverse numbers, together with the revived propaganda about the "Danger from the East," prepare the people for the possibility of a new war; at the same time, domestic contradictions are covered up by an imagined exterior enemy.

West Germany is the deployment zone for the German army and the foreign NATO troops stationed here against the COMECON states. In the case of a war, it would be destroyed completely; military officers and government officials are cynical enough to not even deny that. Given such a gloomy outlook, it is only logical—and important—that a new, broad antiwar movement will emerge, fighting both the possibilities of a nuclear holocaust and further NATO armament and the resurgence of German militarism.

What happened in Bremen on May 6, and later in Bonn, Hanover, and other places, was an expression of this struggle.[14] Among the reasons the left joins forces with old antifascists, pacifists, and other opponents of war are opposition against turning human beings into robotic fighting machines and the rejection of slavish obedience. Struggling under the motto "War Against War" means to attack those who develop and prepare for war in your own country: the NATO strategists, the arms manufacturers, the revanchists, and all of their henchmen. In the end, this is about class war. The named groups and their military mindset are responsible for armament against foreign enemies going hand in hand with armament against domestic enemies. Armament inevitably increases repression in the country where it takes place.

Apart from the possibility of absolute destruction through war, there also looms the danger of gradually eliminating life on earth due to large-scale technological projects that are impossible to control, contaminated ghost towns, poisoned regions like Seveso,[15] cities drowned in concrete, people dying of unknown viruses because some geneticist let bacteria escape from the lab, and a total, computerized control machinery in the spirit of Orwell's *1984*, able to detect rebellions before they even start and capable of destroying them with heavily armed police and military units.

These are not happy perspectives, but they might define the future—a future hardly worth living. Whether reality will indeed look like this depends on each one of us. It depends on whether each one of us will fight or do nothing but try to live their last days in relative peace. But: anyone who surrenders their hope and their will to resist will inevitably lose their freedom and future.

We know that the environmental clock is ticking. There is not much time to stop the gradual destruction of the earth. If you weren't aware of it before, the accidents of Harrisburg and Seveso should have served as a wake-up call.[16] The antinuclear movement with its numerous groups and participants forms a cross-class alliance, a broad front against the projected nuclear state.

But there's another clock ticking, and it is hardly noticed: we need to stop the computerization of repression, which is leading to total control. If we don't, the intelligence gap between the state and us will become so big that each rebellion will be able to be predicted and smashed before it has even started. Even though the radical left suffers more than everyone else from computerized strategies, it leaves the discussion to reformists who talk about little else than data privacy laws.

Nuclear power plants are hard to miss in any landscape, and their consequences are measurable. Computers are for the most part stored away, in climatized bunkers. The danger they pose is concentrated in tiny electronic circuits. It is precisely this subtle threat, so hard to grasp, that makes the danger so big. The mass accumulation of data and its digital analysis form the technological basis for bourgeois domination and social control. Without computers, there is no "German Model."[17]

Knowledge is power—that's a platitude, but it becomes very real when considering preemptive catalogs of fingerprints, writing samples, blood and hair samples, voice recordings, and digitally analyzed photographs. In computerized regional dragnets, forms filled out by hand at state agencies are analyzed, while international telephone wires are monitored for particular voices and cue words. For example, if anyone phoning London is using the word "IRA," they can be sure that some secret service will be listening in. As part of their overall rationalization, the federal mail service is acquiring machines able to identify handwritten addresses; these machines are connected to the computers of the Federal Criminal Agency.

The collection of data is one side of this dirty coin, and the access to it is the other. Small, transportable terminals shall soon link each patrol car and each cop to a big database. Pushing a button will be enough to know everything about a person, from their shoe size to their criminal record to current legal proceedings. Thanks to the so-called household files of social services, they'll even know about the contents of people's garbage bins. A state security informant could probably compile a list of all acquaintances an activist has had since elementary school, based on secret intelligence.

If practically all information about us as individuals is centrally accessible, then it is possible to determine if and when we might begin to resist. Informants, social workers, or whoever else can then be deployed against us preemptively. This wouldn't be possible if it wasn't for the extensive sharing of data between state agencies, from the health services to the secret services. And we must not forget the suppliers: community centers, welfare agencies, and unemployment offices.

The ones with access to the data will always have more power than the ones whose data is collected, no matter the social and political context. We're not advocating Luddism, nor do we demonize the personal computer on the office desk, but we should seriously consider attacking centralized computer systems and servers. In France, Action Directe has already done so several times; they managed to destroy military programs to steer nuclear missiles. In West Germany, it is time to massively disrupt further computerization, both by obstructing the collection of data and by hacking into the computer systems of IBM, Honeywell, or Siemens.

I opened my closing statement stressing that the radical left has to join forces with the social mass movements of the 1980s. Neighborhood struggles, especially squatting, already provide an example. The left is ready to rumble, and there is a necessity for social change that the state cannot tolerate without losing power. The same will happen in other areas of life in the coming years. The growing contradiction between social necessity and state interest is a chance for us.

Traditionally, factories, schools, and families installed discipline among the population. Today, they play a lesser role. There is the most friction, and the most resistance, in the neighborhoods. The state therefore tries to bring them under control. It deploys more cops, including plainclothes ones, small precincts are replaced by fortress-like stations, and social workers flood youth and recreation centers. Even the undercover units have switched from hippie to punk camouflage, frequenting events where they provoke brawls and have people arrested. Apart from gathering data, the state's presence in the neighborhoods shall sow fear and distrust and undermine solidarity among the neighborhood rebels.

There are plenty of examples where the police turn a blind eye to big heroin dealers while junkies are arrested without mercy. Almost ten years ago, the Black Panthers proved in Harlem that heroin was used as a particularly perfidious means to pacify the revolting youth, to individualize their problems, and to undermine solidarity and organized resistance. What the FBI has tolerated for a long time can hardly be beyond German cops. By now, everyone knows that Turkish fascists are the biggest players in the heroin trade in Germany. Their role is akin to that of the Mafia in Harlem. However, they are rarely caught. We also hear from Zurich that heroin has been flooding the market since the political protests have taken off. Leftists cannot sit idle or focus solely on reformist therapy programs when big dealers undermine resistance in the neighborhoods.

Little is done about the fascist Grey Wolves,[18] while the immigration police and the employment agency join forces in targeting left-wing immigrant workers, prompting their deportation or, at the very least, obstructing their political work. The immigrant comrades, too, try to work in the neighborhoods, and it would be an example of practical internationalism to join forces with them. Furthermore, it would allow German leftists to benefit from experiences of leftists in other countries.

It is part of the state's counterinsurgency methods to tear down old neighborhoods and move the population to new suburbs, planned with the involvement of the Federal Police Agency. All of the new high-rise housing estates are built so that they can be monitored easily. The way they are structured makes it difficult for bigger groups of residents to come together. Most of them drown their frustration in alcohol and sit in front of the TV. Together with the construction companies' thirst for profit (only satisfied in the case of wholesale redevelopment), this paradigm of control, and the efforts to undermine solidarity, are responsible for why many cities today look just like they did after World War II: concrete everywhere.

There are further reasons that prompt people to fight for worthy living conditions, among them higher rents, less rent protection, and the destruction of bigger apartments. Housing subsidies will soon be hard to come by, and city councils are too corrupt to do anything more than saving public housing associations from bankruptcy by granting them deductions. The alternative is an endless series of construction scandals. Well, in West Berlin that's no longer even an alternative: both bankruptcies and scandals have become daily occurrences.

There are also those who reject on principle that houses are treated as commodities by their owners, and who increasingly help themselves to what they need. This is both a model for those on the brink of eviction and an expression of self-management and counterpower, piercing through the administrative demands and the control of the state as well as defying the state monopoly on violence. This is what bothers the fat cats much more than people living in empty buildings. The latter they can tolerate as long as their profits from redevelopment projects aren't threatened and as long as they have an eye on the squatters and what they are up to. But as soon as the houses turn into liberated zones, the boundaries of what the state can handle are crossed.

Until a couple of weeks ago, the broad and militant support of the left for the squatters kept the Berlin senate from evicting them. The senate didn't even dare to send search troops. Now, this has changed, unfortunately. The movement is no longer as united as it was earlier, and not even in the heart of Kreuzberg do mass arrests or evictions give rise to days of street fighting and millions of Deutschmark worth of property damage. The so-called Berlin line, a tactical application of the carrot and the stick, is abandoning the carrot. The last one on offer was possible legalization, an attempt by the senate to reestablish control and pacify the situation by integrating some of the movement's currents.

A couple of hundred people have been arrested and registered in recent months, and some have been imprisoned as a deterrent. The reason for me speaking at length about computerization and data collection was that I am not sure whether everyone on the outside is aware of the long-term plans attached to it. In 1968, most of the people who later went underground were hard to identify and surveil. The data that the state had about the earliest members of the armed groups was very thin. In order not to find themselves in a similar situation, the authorities are now registering as many leftists as possible preemptively, which makes them easier to monitor and, if need be, to eliminate. After 1968, state security tried to infiltrate the movement with the help of informants, and they are doing the same today. It has become mandatory to carry out militant action in ways not allowing digital systems to identify you.

The most recent nightly "cleanups" have resulted in relatively high losses and arrests.[19] We need to consider other means of struggle to defend ourselves against evictions, attacks on the movement, and the cops' new arsenal. We need to change tactics and not bury our heads in the sand or in the muesli bowl. To rely on negotiations is an apparent solution only for those unable to look past their own backyard and risk more politically. All those who see the housing struggle as a terrain among many in a broader struggle for autonomy have to ask themselves the age-old question: "What is to be done?"

Karl Marx once wrote that history repeats itself, the first time as a tragedy, the second time as a farce. I don't believe that everything after 1968 was a tragedy, but we must ensure that the new militant movement won't be a farce. In order to do so, we need to learn from the history of the urban guerrilla. The endurance tests of organization and reliability must be added to spontaneity and the readiness to fight, or our struggles will be fleeting.

As the identification of the ordinary people with the state withers away and the state monopoly on violence is weakened, counterpower can and has to develop. Otherwise, the relative weakness of the rulers will never translate into a strong left. The struggles of the coming years, which will involve big sections of the population, can only be led with commitment and intensity if we make these struggles our own. Autonomist groups have to be present in all social movements, whether it's the women's movement, the squatters' movement, or the antinuclear movement. Autonomist self-organization around single issues is one thing. What we need are alliances beyond that, based on the realization that they are necessary, not because anyone forces them on us. The coming together of different left-wing currents and groups defines the movement's strength. The internal contradictions will reflect the contradictions in society as a whole. They'll prevent one-sidedness and stagnancy. Strength doesn't come from a sterile and pure political line, but from unity in diversity. Uniformity is only appealing when you know little about dialectics. Without debate and critique, including self-critique, there is no development and no progress.

What is true for the individual groups and their self-determination within the movement is also true for our means. They have to be self-determined as well. We need to figure out whether they are justifiable, whether they are beneficial to the movement, and whether they weaken the enemy. To be autonomous means to choose one's form of struggle and not to let others tell you what to do and not to do. We must not allow the law to limit our choices. Nor must we think in capitalist terms of competition, presuming that there are more and less valuable forms of struggle. The form of an action says nothing about its political quality. The contents and the goals are at the center; the form derives from there. We cannot repeat it often enough: the way an action is carried out is determined by politics and the objective conditions at any given time. Politics command the gun, not the other way around!

Under certain circumstances, a printing machine can be more important than a gun. The Gestapo put more efforts into finding printing presses than arms depots. There are, of course, enough situations where legal or nonviolent methods hit a dead end. Then you need to resort to other means. You can remove the pylons from a nuclear power station whose construction couldn't be prevented by legal means. You can militantly defend a squat that's of importance to the movement. Or perhaps you need to do something as banal as acquiring money to continue the struggle—after all, leftists don't come by generous loans as easily as capitalists who have driven their companies into bankruptcy. Even bank robbers have to work harder for a few thousand Deutschmark than Garski for his 125 million. It's easy to say who the bigger criminal between a bank robber and a Garski is.[20] Social crimes of gigantic dimensions have always enjoyed impunity in capitalism.

No matter which means are used, none can be successful alone. Only a diversity of methods and flexible strategies render a political movement strong and resilient. It can only help if leftists learn different methods in the struggle, thereby adding subversive means to legal ones.

We need to form armed autonomous groups within our movements— groups able to militantly intervene in conflicts and to help dismantle the current power structure. Organized militancy helps overcome the individual's fear and sense of powerlessness vis-à-vis the state. It shatters one of the foundations of the state's domination. There has been a blend of mass militancy and subversive actions in recent struggles to a degree that we have never seen before in the history of West Berlin and West Germany. It is up to us to strengthen these struggles and to take advantage of the possibilities they are offering to the left in the coming years.

I began my closing statement with a few questions—questions about where we stand, what we want to achieve, against whom we struggle, with whom we struggle, and with whom we *have* to struggle. We are no know-it-alls. We believe that the answer to these questions lies in practice. We don't know whether we'll be victorious one day, but we know that we certainly won't be if we don't dare to fight.

We don't want to be accused of not having tried to do something for a better future—a future that will see us all in the streets together, sweeping away the remains of the current system and building something new. See you then!

Postscript, October 1981

The text printed in *Radikal*, which I had written as a closing statement for my trial in January, has a few shortcomings, as it didn't address the most recent events and, therefore, wasn't able to draw conclusions from them. Especially the peace movement with its strength in numbers and its radical, reformist, and neonationalist currents received too little attention. It helps to illustrate the connections between mass action, militancy, and the urban guerrilla, connections that will help us to advance our struggle. The peace movement demonstrates how spectacular individual actions with limited political meaning in and of themselves can become a mobilizing factor in connection with a mass movement. (We are speaking about the actions here—the communiqués are a different story.)

The background to the new US foreign policy and military strategy has become clearer during the past year. US hegemony over NATO partners and economic competitors with medium-power ambitions, such as Europe and Japan, shall be reinforced. The open economic war that Reagan has declared both on the Third World and his own people shall be secured by new imperialist weapons systems. Meanwhile, the "German model" is crumbling. Apart from a solid pillar of ideologically integrated and economically halfway-satisfied white-collar and blue-collar workers, there is an increasing number of marginalized groups who get less state subsidies but are confronted with more cops. A certain level of resistance by these groups is expected by the state, but the state tries to keep the resistance at a manageable everyday level. The state knows how to contain that sort of resistance, at least as long as it isn't organized and doesn't morph into actual counterpower.

In recent discussions about autonomy (also in *Radikal*), the term sometimes rings rather hollow. It can mean everything and nothing. If we don't want this vagueness to erode the foundations of the movement (see the current case of Zurich), then we need at least some theory derived from our practice. We've had lots of practice in recent years! Often, autonomy is merely understood in personal terms, as an existential concept and not as a strategy for advancing the struggle. We fight autonomously (self-determined, with our methods arising from the base) in order to include more groups and in order to work on more issues, with the goal to one day elevate individual autonomy to organized counterpower. ("To elevate" here means both to preserve and to reach a higher level.) Counterpower without the strength and the will to eventually elevate doesn't have much power.[21]

Those who rail against any form of power under the label "autonomous politics" render themselves irrelevant, and the powerful won't even thank them for it.

It will take years to form broad counterpower. Political autonomy is a strategy for today, tomorrow, and the day after tomorrow, not just for late afternoon. The cops are looking for quick solutions in the struggle against us. We must not look for quick solutions in the struggle against them. We must focus on the long run and keep the struggle alive. This also means to go beyond pure spontaneity, which has become ever more urgent since the latest offensive of the Berlin senate. Given its logistical and theoretical weakness, spontaneity will remain reduced to attacking the most obvious and most superficial targets. It will reach neither the roots nor the corridors of bourgeois power.

Of course, there need to be protests to "clean up" every once in a while, if for nothing else than because these protests serve for many as an entry point into political politics.[22] But it is about time to turn to other methods and goals as well, even if they are not self-evident and don't follow the "throw, smash, and run" model. (As an aside, it is obvious that the cops want to battle things out on the streets of our neighborhoods, where neither debris and rubble nor frightened residents bother them, but why should we go along with this and let the cops pick the terrain of confrontation?)

The squats are important for autonomous organization and struggle, but if we stick to a monoculture of organization and struggle, the squats can become an Achilles' heel. We need to expand our activities into other areas and diversify our methods; otherwise, there'll be more losses and setbacks. We must also prepare for a time when there'll be less squats. This has nothing to do with defeatism, only with caution. We'll need to make some practical adjustments. How, everyone needs to figure out for themselves.

I have consciously avoided presenting a list of guidelines here. They would only disappear with all the other "hot pamphlets" on a leftist bookshelf, and that would be just about the last thing I wanted.

PRISON

US IN HERE, YOU OUT THERE: A LETTER FROM KNOFO FROM HEARTBREAK HOTEL

(ca. 1977)

Norbert "Knofo" Kröcher

Included in volume 1 of the text collection *Der Blues* (1982) as "Wir hier drinnen—ihr da draußen. Ein Brief vom Knofo aus dem Heartbreak Hotel."

———

"Good morning, my dears, it is 5:30 a.m., please get up!" Nice words are floating from the stereo in my apartment. With a song in my heart and a smile on my lips, I throw back the cushy covers, leap up, take off my silk pajamas, and scurry into the pleasantly hot shower. I've barely turned the water off when, with a gentle scraping, a key slides into the hole from outside and is turned once, twice, three times. The lock clicks cheerfully, once, twice, three times. The extra chain rattles happily. All for my protection. The door opens, and there they are, eagerly awaiting me, my four personal pages in their perky green uniforms. One is carrying my breakfast, one an enormous key ring, one a portable telephone, and one is waiting discreetly in the background.

What treat do we have this morning? Mmm, two cans of delicious lukewarm water and—of course—four slices of excellent bread, half-baked and soggy, the way I love it. Along with it, wonderful gold-yellow margarine with a strong sour smell. "No, thank you, my dears, that will be it." I am—as is almost always the case—perfectly content.

After presenting me with my typewriter—it always rests in front of my cell overnight—my four friends withdraw with submissive smiles. The door closes, and the locks, bolts, and chains sing, "Scrape, scrape."

After enjoying several cups of lukewarm coffee (that was what the water was for, because the prison coffee is too strong for me), I puff on a few cigars and turn to my daily tasks. Many pages calling for armed struggle must be written, orders for the foot soldiers of the revolution must be formulated, and a mountain of fan mail awaits response. The neon light buzzes quietly, the screen hums gently on the window of my attic, the typewriter clatters pleasantly, and the hours fly by. Hey, it's such joy to be in prison!

Then comes yard time. It's at a different hour every day to nurture my sense of time. You can call it part of guerrilla training. Under the benevolent gaze of my four friends, I don a fresh suit in the combined changing/visiting room of my two-room residence—that's among my privileges—before I happily scuffle to the yard. When I get to the yard, it is always devoid of humans, no matter whether I'm in my own private yard or the one the common criminals are also allowed to use. Should any of the regular hoodlums dare to disturb my time in the sun—perhaps by pushing a fist through the bars separating me from them, or by making an obscene gesture—my four bodyguards leap into action: they call for additional green uniforms to descend onto the yard, and then, with the help of large white numbers on the wall, the cheeky fellow's cell is located and he receives a warning. Should he dare try this again, he will be tossed in the hole. Rightly so! Nobody asked him to disturb my creative solitude with a stupid grin or a silly hand gesture.

After the yard, it's time to change my suit again, and then—back to work. Oh, it's already noon, and lunch is served. I sharpen the plastic utensils, and, aaahh, Peking duck, truffles (flown in fresh by the feds), and with that a 1966 Châteauneuf-du-Pape. "Thank you, my dears, only half a bottle today, I'm still expecting a visit from one of my terrorist lawyers." After ice cream, mocha, and a Brazilian cigar, I relax for an hour until one of the pages appears to announce the lawyer's arrival.

A speedy change of suits, the listening device switched on, and, boom, I'm face to face with the legal counselor.

What nice things does he have with him today? Thick and heavy are the files he has put on the table, smelling of bookbinder's glue. No, no bazookas or hand grenades this time, rather something for the soul: a handful of light green leaf tips from a killer marijuana plant, fresh from Lebanon, a small courtesy of Dr. Habbash.[1] After enjoying a few joints, we discuss the coming week: nothing special, the usual bombings, arsons, kidnappings, and killings. Quickly we exchange a few coded messages from the Moscow wirepullers, and the visiting period is over. "My regards to Carlos!"[2]

Another quick change of suit, a light in my bum, x-rays, and a full body search later, I remove the drugs from the lawyer's files and hide them behind the baseboard of my cell. My steaming hot dinner and the twenty-seven terrorist magazines I subscribe to are waiting for me there. I watch a little color TV, crochet a cloth ladder for an hour or so, and then it's already 10 p.m. and time to turn off the lights—well, for almost everyone, but not for us privileged few. So I read a little bit in the *Anarchist Cookbook* before I fall dead tired into bed and drift peacefully off to sleep, not without some friendly thoughts about those responsible for my prison conditions.

Okay, Let's Be More Concrete...

Numerous months of uninterrupted solitary confinement (in my case, it's "only" been a year); screens or metal partitions with small holes covering the windows (absorbing about a third of the light); extra locks and chains on the door; constant surveillance; double the guards; no common activities, solitary yard time, solitary showers, etc.; chow delivered by a guard; daily cell searches, weekly mine-seeking festivities with a complete redo of the interior, toilet and sink included, leaving the cell as if it were Dresden 1945;[3] every screw in the cell coated with red varnish; frequent cell transfers; suit changes from two to eight (!) a day; every couple of months, "suicide watch" with constant lighting, observation every five minutes, plastic cutlery (oddly, razor blades and belts are permitted), and sleep deprivation by waking me up at short intervals.

A specialty is the refrigerator cell: bare cement floor, the linoleum ripped apart, likewise the tiles above the sink. The temperature is between 13 and 15 degrees Celsius,[4] and an icy draft comes through the broken window. After an hour of sitting at the table, your legs are frozen stiff and your kidneys hurt.

Then there's the contact ban: numerous weeks alone with yourself and your thoughts. No newspapers, no radio, no visits, no lawyer, no nothing. Raging headaches for three to four days at a time. Pissing every five minutes. Complete loss of sense of time. Panic and anxiety, constant sweating, trembling limbs.

"Little things" can accumulate until you lose it. For example, a typewriter being "examined" by the Federal Criminal Police Office for ten weeks. When the machine is returned, all that remains is a pile of junk. A replacement machine is "examined" for three months (!). Letters disappear in the mail or take four weeks to arrive. Newspaper clippings, glue, or more than four felt pens in a cell are considered a "security risk"—of course, why wouldn't they be? Seeking permission to make handicrafts is—of course—suspect from the outset. In addition, unacceptable political censorship of letters, newspapers, and books. Rarely does a publication arrive without mutilation—even the *Stern* is censored if it contains anything about prisons. Visits are denied constantly, while the federal prosecutors, often successfully, try to ban the lawyers of our choice.

If a prisoner is close to losing it, or if public pressure keeps piling up, there's the occasional treat: church twice a month, and maybe even the monthly cultural highlight, a movie or something of that kind. (Is this what they call "easing solitary confinement"?) The movies and church services follow the usual formula: a change of suit before and after, a seat in the last row (about three kilometers away from the other felons), extra guards. It's all for the show! What makes it worse is that by seeing your imprisoned brothers from afar, the desire to talk to them and to touch them becomes stronger and makes your isolation even more painful. Of course, you still join the church service or the movie, because at least you can see for a few meters without a screen getting in the way. It makes you tolerate the priest's shenanigans, and even the likes of Heinz Rühmann and Adele Sandrock,[5] or whoever the stars of the films are that they show.

Survival Training—November 1977

Some weeks ago, I was taken by helicopter to Ossendorf, once again. And, once again, bad news: Ingrid is now also in the happy hunting ground, and I feel shittier and shittier.[6] I just survived the contact ban, after complete isolation for six weeks. There's been a lot of fear since Stammheim, and the horror continues and becomes even worse.[7] I'm increasingly losing hope. Whenever you think, "It can't get any worse than this," reality proves you better.

For the first four days, they wouldn't let me sleep at all. Every five minutes, the spyhole was opened, every two minutes, keys banged against the door until I moved, day and night. The neon light was buzzing twenty-four hours a day, I only got plastic cutlery, and so on. The last two nights, I managed to sleep two to three hours each, divided up into short intervals. My eyes hurt.

Now it's afternoon. From the morning until noon (so, for four to five hours), the guards hammered on the door like madmen every few minutes. The noise in my cage was unbearable. My left hand has been trembling frantically for a couple of hours now, and there is nothing I can do to make it stop. My right hand is still numb from the chains during the flight. Occasionally, I have uncontrollable twitches in my face, and every noise makes me jump. I drop things. The situation and the shape I'm in are difficult to describe. I cannot concentrate, and my memory is failing me. I no longer remember what yesterday's dinner was (the "evening meal" that's served way ahead of the evening). They ransack my cell several times a day, and every couple of days they replace the furniture and fixtures, so there's always a mess. A photo of you was taken off the wall and torn apart. All my letters are scattered around for the guards to see. Almost everything has been taken away. Today, they took all the felt pens, I don't know why. My body is always wet from cold sweat, and I'm freezing. I don't know when I'll stop being human. There's gotta be a limit somewhere. What is human dignity?

I take slight comfort in the fact that many other rebels have had it worse. But what does this change about my situation? I'm afraid I'm going crazy. Yesterday, I punched my fists bloody against the wall, and it felt like it wasn't my blood. It was like the pain only reached me through a filter, it didn't feel real. When I screamed, my voice sounded alien to me, as if someone else was screaming. The buzzing light affects your brain, and when they bang on the door, it feels as if they are banging on your head.

You hear them commenting on Ingrid's death in front of the window ("The easiest way out," "If necessary, you give them a helping hand"), and there's almost always someone peeking into the cell. Here in prison, under these conditions, tomorrow's super-terrorist is being cultivated, compared to whom Ravachol, Gershuni, Henry, or Nechayev were choirboys.[8] And that's very bad. Even, or especially, for us.

I don't know whether you can imagine what it's like when your personality disintegrates and disappears. How your personality, all the small pieces of the puzzle that make up the aggregate *you*, vanishes, bit by bit. All nuances, all individual characteristics, everything is gone. First, you can no longer see problems from different angles, and you can't look at their specific characteristics in order to understand them in their complexity. You only see black and white. Your feelings and desires, your wishes, your dreams, your needs lose complexity too. Your personality shrinks and you can't do anything about it. Eventually, only basic instincts remain, animalistic hunger, thirst, and fatigue. Sex? Lost, sublimated into eating, reading, whatever. You start to react like an animal. The unity of body and soul—gone. Only remnants are left. Your soul hovers two meters above you, unreachable. No sensual perception, or almost none. No gray zones. Only hunger, thirst, heat, cold—and hatred! The latter frighteningly and overwhelmingly powerful.

I don't yet grasp everything, things are blurry. I'm wondering: What was it like to have sex? I no longer know. Tenderness, what was that? Caresses? I can no longer imagine, don't even have an idea. Skin to skin? Feelings? What it is that you feel? There's not even raw, instinctive sexual desire, probably because of the grub they are serving . . . It's hard to process it all, there's only black and white, no variations, no range of anything, no spectrum.

I'm fading. I sit next to myself, I observe myself. Cold, almost scientifically, dissecting my soul with plastic cutlery. I'm a spectator, interested, but not understanding, just monitoring. I don't know how far this can go before it's irreversible, before you know that now it's too late. Or maybe you don't know when it's too late. When is it too late? I want to climb down the ladder, I don't want to get all the way to the top. What awaits you there? The super-terrorist, cold, inhumane, a machine? Or a customized, manipulated being, the Pavlovian man, sweating on signal, drooling, under remote control, apathetic, following orders, only speaking when asked to.[9] *Shut up!* Feelings, senses, emotions, all on demand, as determined by the feds. Happiness as determined by the warden. You turn into a zombie.

Right now, I can still observe, I'm not completely dead—but when will I be? Lots of despair, close to the bottom.

THE YEARS IN PRISON

(1990)

Ralf Reinders

This is an abridged version of a conversation between Reinders and old comrades on September 14, 1990, during a furlough. It was originally published under the title "Die Jahre im Knast" in the 1995 Edition ID-Archiv book *Die Bewegung 2. Juni. Gespräche über Haschrebellen, Lorenzentführung, Knast*.

...and then I heard the voice: "It's Bär."[1] I say, "Who?" "Bär." I said, "Forget it. Bär on the telephone? That's impossible." It took a while to realize that you were actually calling me. That was in 1986.
From 1986 on, we were allowed to use telephones. We had been in House 3 in Moabit for two years.

What was it like to be able to call the outside for the first time?
Very strange. I don't like phones anyway. And from prison—when you don't see anybody and only hear a voice, no facial expression, no smiles, no nothing. Plus, there is always someone sitting next to you, listening in. It's terrible. But the phone calls were necessary to regain a touch of normality.

Were you allowed to call whoever you wanted?
We were allowed one call a week for five minutes. Every day, four prisoners per unit in House 3 were allowed to call. Every Monday, you had to put your name on the list. There were forty to forty-four prisoners in a unit,

but only twenty-eight fit on the list. You had to stand in line to put down your name. If you were last, you were out of luck. The calls were made between 6 and 8 p.m.

How else did you maintain contact with the outside?
Through letters and visits. There were no other options.

Were the letters monitored?
Yes, until the very end.

The visits as well?
Yes, until March 1985. Around the same time, we were allowed to join the family unit meetings, held once a month. They let twelve to fourteen prisoners sit down with their relatives over coffee and cake with no recordings.

What was it like when you called me after all those years in prison? Did you have an image, a sense of me sitting in the kitchen of a collective house, together with others, the walls plastered with posters?
It was similar to receiving visits. Mainly, it was about having someone to talk to. Feelings for how the people lived on the outside were buried. That came much later.

You lose the feeling for life on the outside?
Of course. You remember how it was before you got in, how you used to live. That's deep within you, and that's your sense of life on the outside. That doesn't change because you hear some stories about new developments while you're locked up. Intellectually, you understand that things are changing, but the emotions can't follow. You are isolated. The gap is huge. You only realize that after your release.

What is it like to go to Skalitzer Straße in Berlin after fifteen years in prison and watch the cars go by?[2]
The smells are important. The exhaust fumes got on my nerves quickly. Once you enter Kreuzberg, it's the Oriental smells, each eatery has a different one. I felt that very intensely. It's incredible to leave Berlin, like we did last week. To leave the city by car, to just keep on driving—it was the

first time I regained a sense for distance, for space. The horizon was so incredibly wide, the fields had been harvested. Clear water for a change! I had forgotten about that in prison.

But let us start at the beginning: how was it to enter prison?
In the beginning, we were totally isolated. They tried to interrogate us. Once they realized that they wouldn't be successful, they lifted total isolation. That meant that we had a half hour of yard time every day with the other prisoners. The other twenty-three and a half hours you remained isolated. But at the time, those were normal conditions for prisoners in remand.

It's still the same, right?
More or less. Today, it's an hour of yard time, and on occasion you'll be allowed to meet with other prisoners inside. But very little, maybe two hours each weekend. It's not enough.

We had a strict regime until summer 1976, and then Entebbe came.[3] That led to a week of total isolation. It was the first time we weren't allowed any contact to the outside at all. And just when the ban was lifted, the women escaped from Lehrter Straße on July 7, 1976.[4] After that, we were isolated for three and a half months. The order came from the oh-so-liberal justice senator Baumann, hailed for his "prison reform," when, in reality, he made remand in Berlin much tougher.[5]

What was he like?
A liar through and through. He even came to prison, into our cells, to ask what we wanted. We said we wanted normal prison routines, to be treated like anyone else, no special conditions. And the next day we read what he said at the press conference after the visit: "I will not give in to the entirely inappropriate wishes of these elitist people who want to remain among themselves."

When he came to my cell, I was completely unprepared. I had not expected him to show up. When he did, I thought, "Hmm, don't I know this fellow?" I was just washing my hands, and he came with a whole entourage—state security agents? When he started to introduce himself ("I am your justice . . ."), I realized who he was and took a swing at him. I missed. He jumped out of the cell with the tap still running, and I managed to spray some water in his direction. At least he got a little wet.

Did the cops use political arguments during the interrogations?
They tried to get you to talk. They used everything they knew about us
to start a conversation, our personal circumstances and, of course, our
political convictions. It is quite funny when you sit there for four hours
without saying a word and they are already blue in the face but are still
trying to get you to open your mouth. And when you ask for a coffee, they
are super happy, because you've finally said something. But they only
try this a few times, and then they stop. Still, at that point you know a lot
about their private lives and their problems with the wife or the children,
who might be doing poorly at school or whatever.

All of this is to get you to talk. I remembered some of them from
1970, when I was arrested for the first time. I didn't sign any statements
then either, but we did talk to the cops a little, since we had nothing to
do with the things they had arrested us for. We were a little naive, kinda
like, "We have nothing to hide!" That's why they brought in the same
fellows again, because they thought, "Well, they had a chat with them at
the time. They'll find something to chat about now."

They really tune in on each individual. At first, they want to see how
you react. This can become rather absurd and very cliché, for example,
when they try to act tough. The first time I was interrogated, there were
six cops in the room. One of them essentially mirrored me. He mimicked
every gesture I made. I thought he had serious issues. He acted like a
fool. Another fellow was super tough, saying things like, "He should get
a good hiding," or, "Unfortunately, we can't do it Chile style." Yet another
wanted to discuss Marxism, quoting from books I didn't even know. Their
problem was: if you don't respond to anything, they can do whatever they
want without getting anywhere.

They brought me to the interrogation room six days in a row, for
about six hours each. For four days, I said nothing, not even whether I
wanted to eat or drink. Then they tried something new. I got lunch from
the state security folks. Otherwise, they would have had to return me to
prison. One day, I heard them shaking the bucket of food. Finally, an agent
brought it in and said, "No, you can't offer this to anyone, that's inhumane."
Another had a look and said, "Ugh!" before turning to me: "Shall I get you
something from the canteen?" I said, "Yes." It was the only thing I said all
day. The next day, the guy who had offered to get me food from the canteen
started to talk, and he talked and talked, and suddenly he looked at me,
saying, "I don't understand. Yesterday, we had such a great conversation,

and today, you return to saying nothing at all." That was a highlight. One word seemed like a great conversation to him!

You understand how it's going for the others when a cop suddenly blurts out stuff like, "They are all making fools out of us: one says he would never talk to us, only shoot us (must have been Meyer), one sucks his thumb (Teufel, of course), and another only drinks coffee (must have been Ronny)." I should add that they weren't too tough here in Berlin. But, unlike in West Germany, no cops were ever shot in Berlin either. And the Lorenz kidnapping had been really popular with the population. Even Lorenz himself had good things to say about us during the press conference after his release, emphasizing how well he had been treated. The cops didn't want to come across as the total opposite. So, in general, they treated us correctly, except for the torture weekend of 1977—but that was the federal prosecutors' fault.

When exactly was that, and what was it about?
It was about a lineup. Already the third. It was in May 1977. Some of us had been in remand for more than two years. Then they organized yet another lineup with all the witnesses from the trial. Based on the witness statements, they cut our hair, trimmed our beards, and tried to make us fit the descriptions. It didn't matter that we had never looked that way, but it made it more probable that we would be identified.

How many of you were there?
The six from our trial, and they had flown in Knofo and Manne Adomeit as well. Eb Dreher was also there.[6] And the about two hundred witnesses they led by us behind a one-way mirror.

Can you describe the scene?
The first confrontations were because of the haircuts and shaves. This caused a few bruises. Needless to say, we didn't want them to "fix our hair." They told us to look friendly. Ronny closed his eyes, opened his mouth, and stuck out his tongue. It caused them to tighten his handcuffs really good, and they pierced his tongue with a ballpoint pen. My handcuffs were so tight that my nails started to bleed. Ronny had his thumb dislocated. We were covered in bandages for weeks. Even the prison doctor, usually not very sensitive to our needs, complained. That had never happened before.

Did you file a report?
Yes, but the investigation was dropped. Amnesty International also filed a complaint, but the court concluded that it wasn't torture because the lineup had been legal.

What was the situation like for you in autumn 1977: Schleyer, Mogadishu, Stammheim?
We were in total isolation at the time and depended on the help of other prisoners for information. Some dangled their radios out the window on broomsticks so that we could hear the news. The reports about the hijacking shocked us, particularly the shooting of the pilot. We had not thought it possible that folks claiming to be revolutionaries would target innocent people, not least because of the fierce debates after Entebbe.

But you had confrontations with prison guards even before that, right?
During the first years, there were a number of conflicts, but they weren't planned from our side. They were the outcome of a logical development. For the prison authorities, we were troublemakers. That's why they wanted to keep us isolated. They ignored court orders and pressured the guards to enforce nonsensical rules against us. They would ban sugar from our cells and take our radios. This created a powder keg of tensions ready to explode. At some point in 1977, we played with a homemade soccer ball, and the guards told us not to. They were prepared. Everything was under lockdown, and they were waiting in line, ready to go. They wanted a rumble.

Why?
The prison administration wanted to totally isolate us again. After that day, they had an excuse. That's what they had been looking for. What happened that day? The guards stormed the yard and pounced on us. They pulled us around, and we tried to hit back. But we were in poor shape by then, and our resistance wasn't very effective. It was a pretty quick rout for them.

Was that an isolated incident?
No, there was another battle in the yard in 1979 as well as some more confrontations. But when the trial began, the situation changed. Since

we had been in remand for so long, we were promised two hours of yard time, one in the morning and one in the afternoon. But on trial days, we couldn't do the morning hour, and according to the prison administration we couldn't get two hours after 4 p.m. because the number of guards on site wasn't sufficient. That was just absurd. On some trial days, we only got half an hour of yard time. When we complained in court, the presiding judge said, "Yes, I did order two hours, but I don't have a police unit that I can send inside to enforce it." So we thought, "Okay, then we'll enforce it ourselves." The next day, we refused to leave the yard after an hour. They came to get us. They prepared for it. We waited for an hour. Then they sent out six guards per prisoner and a few extra ones. But, somehow, they got their orders mixed up and weren't the bravest. They knew that Fritz was the weakest of us and that his glasses made it more difficult for him to fight back, and so even the guards assigned to Klöpper and me went for Fritz. That caused chaos. For the first time, they suffered some painful losses: a broken nose, a broken vertebra, a knocked-out tooth. But we didn't look pretty either.

Did they have batons?
No, but some of them used their key rings. They knew, though, that we had the public watching the trial. This made them a little more cautious. With regard to other prisoners, they didn't care at all. We saw them smash other inmates against railings until their bones were crushed. The guard whose nose got broken that day had once hit a prisoner transferred to Moabit from Tegel in the face with his key ring, while the prisoner was constrained by his colleagues. When the prisoner fell to the ground, the guard kicked him. The guard with the broken vertebra had not long before smashed the face of a Russian prisoner into a railing. Everything was broken: cheekbone, jaw, nose. So we got the right ones. It was the first time there was a sense of retribution, a little joy. We had prepared for that day for a year.

Later, when we were moved into the special unit, there were almost weekly fights for three months. This was mainly about the prison administration wanting to reintroduce the partitions during private visits. At first, the partitions had been removed after us moving into the special unit, because the whole point was that security there was so high that it wouldn't make any such measures necessary. There were also two guards and two state security agents present during every visit. What did they think could happen?

The guards were writing reports about incidents that had never occurred, and they constantly provoked confrontations. When the partitions came up again, we were mad, of course, and we cursed them, with the result that the visits were broken off altogether.

The visits were always sensitive. If they were broken off, a fight would inevitably follow. That was already the case before we were transferred to the special unit. For us, there could be no compromises regarding the visits. With all else, you could back down on occasion; you can't fight for years on end. But the visits were the limit. Human contact was necessary, touching people was necessary, and to speak in relative freedom was necessary, at least as far as possible. So, when it came to that, we could get pretty aggressive.

The routine was the following: we had a visitor, and a guard would get us from the cell. On the way to the visiting room, he would give us the rundown: "No touching, no physical contact!" Or: "Well, I'm the generous type, a handshake is okay." Usually, we didn't talk to them. So they would ask: "You know that, right? I assume you have understood everything. No physical contact!" It's easy for aggression to build up under such circumstances. With some of the guards, our fuses blew. With others, it was easier. When we hugged our visitors, they looked the other way.

Doesn't there come a point when you think it'd be easiest to simply give in ...
Once you think that, you have lost. There are moments when you question everything, when you have all sorts of thoughts, but if you give in, you'll lose your identity.

Many on the outside forget that much of what happens in prison is like life outside, only much more concentrated. Everything is piled on you at once. It's hard to imagine. Everything is more extreme. You reflect on when it makes sense to resist and when it's only going to be futile. It's always a balancing act. You disobey them, but a big fight every day is not sustainable; eventually, you'll no longer have the strength. But if you give in, you will lose a part of yourself. You need to think much more carefully about every move you make than on the outside. On the outside, it's much easier to avoid conflict.

Did you ever consider pretending to give in to be moved into general population?

That's an excuse for giving in. I don't think it's possible. You can't live a life pretending, not even temporarily. As soon as you pretend to make a compromise, you're making the compromise. In prison, everything you do or say is registered. Each one of the guards writes a report about you. These are things prisoners often forget. If you decide to greet one of the guards one day, it will appear in his report: "The prisoner has become much friendlier, he appears approachable now." The lines are too strictly drawn to say, "All right, I will fool them." I don't know of a single prisoner who made a bogus offer of collaboration and got away with it. Your options are limited. For me, any such attempt would have been impossible.

And there is yet another thing. Every once in a while, you wonder: Are they getting to you? Are you going soft? How can I defend my integrity in this space? Like, you refuse to leave the cell during the three minutes they're opening it for you. Otherwise, if that's what they'll do one hundred, two hundred, or three hundred days in a row, you'll become a cog in their machine and function under their orders. To be aware of this danger, to observe processes of adaptation, is the requirement not to be absorbed by the machine.

Is resistance the only way to keep you alive as a person?
Yes, that's absolutely true, at least if you're in there for many years. Of course, you can say, "If I get two years in prison, I keep a low profile, I won't make a fuss," and so on. But I don't know if anyone can do that and remain healthy. You can't just swallow the years that way.

Did reflections of that sort play a role when you rejected calls for an amnesty for prisoners from the militant left in the 1980s? You wrote: "No amnesty for class justice!"[7]
No, that was purely a political dispute, in which our personal situation played a secondary role.

On the one hand, you want to survive and leave prison intact. On the other hand, your behavior in prison has political significance, both for yourself and for those on the outside.
You don't go to prison thinking, "What am I gonna do for the next fifteen years?" You have thought about that before. You were aware of what you were doing, what you were doing politically, what your response to the

system was, and what the consequences might be. Then you sit in your cell and need to figure out where to go from there, how to continue what you had started, but now under different circumstances. You try to gather as much information as possible. At some point, though, you'll reach a limit, because—and this is something where we might differ from intellectuals—you, or at least I, have great difficulty in dealing with something over a long period of time on a purely abstract level. It has to be something that can be put into practice. But in prison it's hard to do that. It was only possible for things that directly related to the prison experience.

Were you prisoners like any other for the prison staff?
No, we never were. Look at all the special security measures we were dealing with. We were watched much more closely, and that alone created a special situation.

Many of the guards hated us. Some were right-wing extremists. Others might have had some respect for us. Because—and they still say this today—we weren't some fellows who snatched some granny's purse. That made a difference. Besides, when other prisoners had fights with prison staff, they were usually alone. Between 1976 and 1980, twenty-two or twenty-three of us were at the Moabit prison. If the guards messed with one of us, they never knew where the response would come from. That made them more cautious. It was probably the first time they experienced collective resistance; that experience was new to them. It was easier for them to divide the other prisoners and to wear them down individually. There are some prisoners who resist with violence, who don't put up with shit. But in those cases, the warden sends in fifty guards who bash them up and put them in the hole. Over time, that wears everyone down. It's practically impossible to take that year after year.

What was your relationship like with the other inmates, the so-called social prisoners?
During the early years, and whenever isolation was extreme, we received much solidarity. We also organized common actions such as the hunger strike of 1979 for better prison conditions in the general population.

A guard once told me: "You don't even have to do much." What he meant was that other prisoners are encouraged by politically conscious inmates who know how things work, who have a plan and experience. Their resistance inspires everyone. Suddenly, prisoners who have always kept quiet start to speak up. They start filing complaints, get lippy with the guards, and so on. As a result, the guards lose a bit of control over them.

Were you harassed a lot by the guards?
Yes, some would spill jam over our clothes during searches, or soap powder, or they tore down pictures or scattered our things around. But that was a minority.

Another form of harassment were special regulations. There were plenty when the trial started: trial in the morning, trial in the afternoon, and then yard time. In the morning, before you went to court, you were strip-searched. When you returned from court, you were strip-searched. When you returned to court, you were strip-searched. When you returned from court, you were strip-searched. At some point we said: "That's enough, we will no longer go along with that." Tensions were high.

Then they started to dismantle the cells every day. Sometimes, when I returned, my cell looked as if a bomb had gone off. All my things were lying there in one big pile. In such moments, it's easy to lose it. Permanent stress that can easily throw you off balance. It's massive. While you try to improve your conditions, they mess with you again and again. It creates extreme anger, and you don't know what to do with it. And if you try to work on something, no matter what, you need a minimum level of concentration.

They could give you yard time at seven in the morning or at six in the evening or at any hour in between. For "security reasons," the hour was always different, and you were never told beforehand. That means that you never knew when they were coming to get you, when you were taken outside. In the beginning, they coordinated searching your cell with the yard time. At some point, they started to do the search at a different time, locking us into an empty cell while they were at it. When you returned, you needed an hour to put everything in order again.

They keep you busy all day for nothing. In reality, nothing is happening, you are totally isolated, but you're kept on your toes by the prison staff. In the special unit, there was a period of heavy confrontations with the guards. After some fights, they wanted to divide us into smaller groups. (We were seven in a group at the time.) The warden asked the court to create groups of two or three. This was discussed publicly during the main trial.

One incident helped us: there had been a fight among the guards. We said, "Well, even the guards fight among themselves. They come to prison voluntarily and can leave every day, but even they don't know what to do with their aggression. So what are you expecting from us?" From that day, the issue was off the table, and the guards left us alone. From then on, they came in, a dozen of them, with helmets and batons, brought our food, locked the door, and then we could do in the unit whatever we wanted. It was the end of the fights.

When was that?

It started on April 13, 1980. That day, a guard got his nose smashed in and his eye bashed up. The cause was, once again, a visit that had been broken off. That was the main reason why they wanted to divide us into smaller groups.

Once we left the special unit, there were no more fights. The guards avoided all confrontations. When directives came from above, and they knew that we'd resist, they found ways to defy those directives.

Did you ever have normal conversations with them?

Yes, with some of them. There were different ones. Some were pigs, and some we never had any problems with. I mean, even the latter were guards, they stood on the other side, but they didn't go out of their way to harass us. They followed the rules and always tried to, I'm tempted to say, "act humanely." They simply believed their job was necessary. Not all are the same. Some left the cell more orderly after a search than it had been before. Most were very conservative and strict, but they stuck to the rules. They organized my closet better than I was capable of.

Do you ever get a sense of "home" in prison?

Never. Some inmates, who are in there for a long time, they might develop a sense of home. They polish the floor and have tablecloths and curtains and such things. But their heads are already done in. I never felt at home in my cell. But it all depends on how you approach it. There's a difference between being in prison and knowing why you're there and being there only because you tried to improve your standard of living. Let's say you've committed a robbery and end up in prison, and you can't even justify it and are dealing with a guilty conscience. It's common, at least when you're there for the first time. By the third time, the guilty conscience might be gone, but then it's already too late. What do these people have to hold on to? This can lead to some form of super-adaptation.

Everyone needs their own space, and you notice it by the way you get agitated. If it was just water rolling off your skin, you wouldn't get agitated. You wouldn't get agitated when returning from the yard and finding your cell looking like a battlefield. You wouldn't care. You wouldn't take it personally. But it is personal. It's about your life and the conditions you can do things under. And it is a constant struggle for your own space.

Were you ever scared?

Yes, I was scared of fights. Well, what does being scared mean? It's a feeling—yes, I was scared, but that feeling wasn't dominant. It didn't lead me to say, "Okay, I won't do it." Much rather, I got angry for not doing something. Any missed opportunity caused a lot of anger.

We had discussions about how to deal with the guards. We always said that the "little guy" didn't really interest us. So we decided to deal with the guards according to the motto "You reap what you sow." Eventually, they understood that. They realized that if they behaved correctly and reasonably, nothing would happen. During the last years, our relationship with them was defined by that. I think that it had to do with us not randomly attacking guards only because we were frustrated. We picked our targets.

Did the public eye provide protection?

I think a little, yes, even if it wasn't any protection in a legal sense. But because of the media attention we received, we had eyes on us, especially during the trial. When one of us appeared bashed up in the courtroom, it didn't look so good for them. It caused a bad impression. You can report a beating, but seeing someone beaten black and blue lifts it to another level. Yes, that had an impact.

We talked a lot about fights. Maybe because a violent situation makes violence the main means of conflict resolution. This affects your entire thinking.

AMNESTIES ARE NO GIFTS

(ca. 1985)

Ralf Reinders and Ronald Fritzsch

During the years in which numerous urban guerrilla militants were incarcerated in Germany, there were repeated discussions about amnesty, with members of different groups and factions disagreeing about the direction and focus of relevant campaigns. This is a contribution to the debate by Ralf Reinders and Ronnie Fritzsch from the mid-1980s. The text circulated among comrades and has not been published before.

—

Dear lovers of sports, the national championship fight between Günther State and Norbert Guerrilla is over. The event has gathered international attention due to its many highlights and an impressively high level of performance. But the audience still wonders about the weak final rounds. The fighters were tired. Now they want to go home. And we want to go home too! With pleasure! Now!! It's a no-brainer. Twenty-four hours a day in the soft and warm arms of our beloved with the delicious scent. But back to our topic . . .

Amnesties are no gifts. They are part of a political compromise negotiated between those who rule and those who resist. They happen in the context of social change or shifts in the balance of power. Which political groups in West Germany have both the interest *and* the strength to push through an amnesty for prisoners? The armed groups don't frighten the state at the moment. Neither them nor the legal left have the political strength to extort any concessions. In 1971, this might have still been possible. The power struggle of the ruling parties and the unstable political situation that followed caused the minister of the interior at the time, Genscher, to contact Ulrike Meinhof in secret and offer the end of the persecution of RAF members if the RAF would no longer be active and its most prominent members would go into exile. Today, the price for an amnesty would be much higher. Without an ace up your sleeve, without any political strength, you can only submissively beg for it, but you cannot gain it in a fight.

The proponents of an amnesty have so far not used an inch of their lengthy written statements to explain the reasons for an amnesty politically. Their arguments are moral and idealistic and raise more questions than they claim to answer. The resignation bemoaned by the comrades Wackernagel and Schneider is the consequence of thinking purely in military categories.[1] These two comrades are not alone in seeing themselves as participants of a military confrontation but not as instigators of political and social confrontation, that is, of class struggle. Armed groups in crisis easily make the mistake of raising the military stakes in order to get out of the crisis. They prioritize the military aspect—armed confrontation—over the political one. But militancy and armed struggle are in and of themselves no political statements. They need to be part of a political strategy. What they can contribute depends on the politics. Some discussions in and around the peace movement remind us that this needs to be stressed time and again.

The belief that one must raise the military stakes in order to compensate for earlier military (and political) defeats led directly to the biggest political catastrophe of the guerrilla and the entire militant left in West Germany: Mogadishu. The hijacking of the *Landshut* was political suicide. That was the defeat, not the plane being raided. It doesn't help to come up with excuses, for example, that it was the Palestinians who carried out the action.

Those who still reference Mogadishu when looking for proof for how terrible the imperialist state is have learned nothing—in fact, they have no interest in learning anything. They have no interest in rectifying mistakes and developing a new perspective.

The arguments used by Wackernagel and Schneider confuse a means to pursue political goals with the political goals themselves. They ignore the complexity and the dynamics of social life. This produces statements like the following: "The left has not won, there is no victory in sight, and there is no sign of strength that would make victory possible."

In what political and historical dimensions do comrades think when it comes to the struggle of the RAF, which they supported? Did they really believe that they could beat the world's second-biggest and most advanced military apparatus, NATO, with a few guns? The tiniest of police stations stores more guns! Did they really believe that the social conditions in the most stable country of the capitalist world could be overthrown in five, ten, or fifteen years?

> What succumbed in these defeats was not the revolution. It was the prerevolutionary traditional accessories, results of social relationships that had not yet reached the point of sharp class antagonisms—persons, illusions, conceptions, projects from which the revolutionary party before the February Revolution was not free, from which it could be freed not by the victory of February, but only by a series of defeats.[2]

If it is true that defeat is the mother of all success, then there must be political and personal experiences that cannot disappear without a trace. When fourteen years ago, the armed struggle began, none of the people involved had the slightest experience that would have qualified them for it. Each action served as a lesson to gain experience. Theory can only be tested in practice, and errors made in practice reveal the theoretical shortcomings. There is no point in feeling ashamed of errors. The experiences of both the small victories and, especially, the defeats are needed to learn how to do things right.

What are fourteen years? Once upon a time, we could hear people say with revolutionary fervor: we can be killed or imprisoned, but our ideas will live on! What kind of ideas are ideas that don't last fourteen years before they are thrown in the dustbin of history due to a few defeats? The principles of the Paris Commune of 1871 have lost nothing of their truth despite the commune's defeat. The German November Revolution of 1918 failed, but its goals are still valid. The Chinese Cultural Revolution was killed, but its ideas remain alive.

Even in times of the worst defeat, it remains our duty to search for the right ways forward and the rights means to follow them. The goal of our politics, of our struggle for freedom, equality, and humanity, remains untouchable. There is a whole number of examples for drawing consequences from defeats. But neither this nor the general political development are mentioned by our comrades. They recognize neither the political and social struggles nor the resistance against imperialist politics and the class struggle from above.

Pohrt uses the position paper of the Revolutionary Cells as a starting point for demanding amnesty in one of his articles, but there's no discussion of the Revolutionary Cells in the piece, and not in similar contributions to the debate either.[3] That is rather strange. The Revolutionary Cells have consistently reflected on their defeats, and they are the only radical group that has developed political strategies on a solid foundation. For years, this has been ignored by pretty much everyone.

The politics and the practice of the Revolutionary Cells is hardly considered in the amnesty debate, especially not by its proponents. Is the reason that only a few members of the Revolutionary Cells are in prison? We don't think so. People don't want to discuss the goals of the struggle. They insist on focusing on the defeats. The reason for this seems clear. What might appear as concern for the prisoners is really a way of abusing them. Prisoners begging for freedom shall make the pointlessness of militant action and the lack of perspective for radical politics obvious. Conveniently, this covers up the defeat of the peace movement. As bourgeois pacifism has reached its end with this defeat, people instead talk about failed armed and militant politics. Pohrt does indeed manage to turn the enormous defeat of pacifism into "the loss of any political operational basis for militancy." In light of mass unemployment, increasing social misery, and imperialist armament, he also reduces a social-revolutionary orientation to a "legal discussion circle," dismissing it entirely. Flick sends his regards![4]

The original goal of the peace movement—fighting imperialist armament—has long been revised due to the doctrines of bourgeois pacifism. Today, the peace movement serves as a transmission belt for domestic stability.

> The analysis of the world from a class perspective is overshadowed by a fake moralist dualism that doesn't distinguish between the top and the bottom but between good and evil. The new ideal is not new at all. It is, in fact, ancient, namely, the peace-loving man who understands class contradictions as a consequence of human errors, which can be resolved by a moral "renewal." Resistance and

grassroots struggles reveal to him the same aggressive desires as imperialism's inhumanity. This is dangerous thinking because it ignores the material conditions of our existence. Peace becomes the result of "personal mass disarmament," not the result of struggling against structures of oppression and exploitation.[5]

Bourgeois pacifism is the bourgeoisie's weapon against class struggle. It distracts from the root causes of imperialist armament, that is, capitalism's need of expansion. SS 20 and the Jena Peace Circle make anticommunism palpable.[6] Meanwhile, the imperialist warmongers can go about their bloody business. All of this reveals the true role of bourgeois pacifism: to take the moral high ground and prevent class struggle.

Demanding an amnesty for only a few dozen prisoners, while ignoring more than seventy thousand people behind the walls of prisons and psychiatric wards, doesn't exactly make a huge contribution to class consciousness and solidarity. It pays no attention to social relationships and the role of oppressive institutions in the capitalist state.

The bourgeois legal system is the violent manifestation of social inequality in capitalism. Several facts indicate clearly for whom, and against whom, the current legal system works. Ninety-nine percent of the prisoners in West Germany come from the lower social strata, the Nazi mass murderers get away, and the professionals target the left. There are probably more raped women in prisons than rapists. The Lambsdorffs and Flicks are not bothered by any of this, while seventy-year-old retired ladies land in prison because they've stolen a bar of soap.[7]

The purpose of class justice is to subdue collective resistance, to break those who refuse to conform, to isolate and intimidate those who try to find their own escape routes, ending up as "criminals" in the process.

The demand for an amnesty for "political" prisoners is an acknowledgment of class justice. It writes off all those who land in prison because they've been chewed up in the turning wheels of pursuing profits by exploitation. Amnesty, yes. But for everyone!! That's only possible (if it is possible at all) through a new justice campaign that raises people's consciousness about class justice, explaining its function and its crimes. The demand for amnesty must be the basis for a new way of thinking, striving for the abolition of all prisons and psychiatric wards. But this seems of little interest to the proponents of a limited amnesty.

No amnesty for class justice!! Freedom for all!!!

PRISON ROUND TRIP
(2003)

Klaus Viehmann

This text was originally published under the title "Einmal Knast und zurück" in the left-wing magazine *Arranca!*, no. 26, January 2003. The English translation appeared first as a pamphlet titled *Prison Round Trip*, published by PM Press and Kersplebedeb in 2009. It has been slightly edited for this volume.

Bang. The door to your cell is shut. You have survived the arrest, you are mad that you weren't more careful, you worry that *they* will get others too, you wonder what will happen to your group and whether a lawyer has been called yet—of course you show none of this. The weapon, the fake papers, your own clothes, all gone. The prison garb and the shoes they've thrown at you are too big—maybe because they want to play silly games with you, maybe because they really blow "terrorists" out of proportion in their minds—and the control over your own appearance taken out of your hands. You look around, trying to get an understanding of where you'll spend the next few years of your life.

What is the point of talking about survival strategies today—years later? Is it worth trying to organize and sum up your experiences? It is, at any rate, difficult to bring them into words and sentences. Yet for those who will spend time behind bars in the future, they might be useful. Besides, since the experiences of (political) prisoners are neither extra-societal nor ahistorical, their survival strategies might also help those comrades who experience their everyday life as little more than a somewhat coordinated form of "getting by." To focus on what's essential, to plan your everyday life consciously, to use your energies in meaningful ways—these are all qualities that are useful. Everywhere. Survival strategies are personal (which is why this text is, also rhetorically, directed at *you*, no abstract third person), but not egotistical. Emancipation and liberation do not happen within the individual—they are socio-historical processes. In the words of Peter Brückner,[1] "It was only the late bourgeois who has turned freedom and independence into a question of 'inwardness.'" This shows the limits of all individual survival strategies. Surviving can only turn into living through social liberation. But this is another story, one in which prisons will hardly play a role . . .

In prison, the necessity of survival strategies is immediate; without them you are at the mercy of the enemy. Prison is a hostile environment, and it has been designed as such by people who see you as their foe. Have no illusions about that. In regular prisons—especially old-fashioned ones—conditions are often atrocious and sometimes violent, but there are at least social structures. In isolation or maximum-security units, social relations are controlled, regulated, abolished. Isolation means the absence of social life and the presence of yourself. You have nothing but yourself, and you have to find ways to deal with it. This is possible, but it is not possible to know beforehand who will get through prison okay and who won't. For someone with little life experience, limited political self-motivation, and uncertain (possibly egotistical) future plans, it will be difficult. A colorful biography in which prison does not mark the first rough period, optimism even in the face of a dire situation, and the ability not to take yourself too seriously all help.

Ernst Bloch might have said that "those who acquire their knowledge only from books should be put onto shelves," but it is not necessarily a tragedy if the knowledge about certain things only comes that way.[2] I have not experienced physical torture, death threats, or confinement in dark cells. Personal or literary descriptions of such experiences, however, can help you to understand your own experiences better and to get through them.

The empirical basis (if you will) of this text are fifteen years' imprisonment. Seven years—after 1978—were spent in isolation or with small groups of inmates, five out of these in maximum-security units (in Moabit and Bielefeld). From 1986 until my release in 1993, I was in a special "security cell" in Werl, an old German prison. I had one hour in the yard every day with other inmates. My visits and my mail were monitored, I was separated from my lawyers by a bulletproof glass window, I was hardly ever allowed to buy extra supplies, had no visits of other prisoners in my cell, showered alone, was allowed a maximum of thirty books, no radio, and five or six subscriptions to newspapers and magazines. Mail restrictions were eased during my last years there, and from 1991 to 1993 I was permitted to jog in the yard twice a week. What I am writing here is the quintessence of my experiences. During the first five or six years of my imprisonment, I learned the survival strategies that got me through the last ten. These are the experiences I'm summarizing here.

Back to the first day in prison. You have no conception of the day you will be released. Five thousand, five hundred days are beyond what is imaginable, even when I look back at it. What you see at the time is what you need to know to survive right there and then: Where do I get reading and writing material? Where do I hide secret messages? When should I expect a cell search? Where are the cells of my comrades? There is a lot to do. Boredom is the least of your concerns. Besides, you know why you are in there—an enormous advantage compared to those who have no idea. It was a radical political challenge that got you there; one that you could see as "just another step" in a life that you had chosen by engaging in militant left-wing politics. Sure, *they* were one up on you at that point, but prison was a new terrain and they still had to prove that they could break you. This is exactly what you must not allow them to do—and this, in turn, defines your struggle from the first day to the last.

To have a clear objective and clear front lines enables you to fight well. You must never allow them to persuade you that there are no clear front lines and that "big brother" is your friend. Ulrike Meinhof's declaration that "the fight of the people against power is the fight of remembering against forgetting" sums this up perfectly. The ability to remember requires political and/or moral conviction. Those who lose this conviction refuse to remember and get lost in self-reflection, self-pity, and lack of orientation. This is the steep decline where desperation can turn into suicide and political denial into betrayal. Solitary confinement and the control of social contact (letters, visits, news), you can also call it brainwashing, aim at causing you to forget and to become egotistical. Resistance, solidarity, responsibility, collectivism, and a corresponding personality shall vanish.

Maximum-security prisons also follow the bourgeois-capitalist principle of "everyone is his/her own best friend." Those who adopt this principle do not survive—they turn into someone else. Not because they grew and achieved emancipation, but because they regressed and desocialized. The consequences are depoliticization and the disintegration of the personality. True survival means to experience yourself as a human being who is socially, politically, mentally, and emotionally autonomous and self-responsible. This requires breaking your isolation and finding reference points outside your cell. Those who cannot transcend their own imprisonment and who cannot understand it in a wider context will be unable to find meaning in their arduous situation. The narrower your horizon, the more paralyzing and desperate your personal fears. Jean Améry[3] once described these "reference points" in connection with the most extreme of all experiences, that of Auschwitz:

> "You must realize," a believing Jew once told me, "that your intelligence and education is worthless here. Me, however, I know that God will take revenge." A German leftist comrade, in the camp since 1933, expressed this more bluntly: "There you are, you bourgeois know-it-alls, and you shiver when the SS appears. We do not shiver, and even if we will perish in here miserably, we know that the comrades who follow us will line them all up." Both these men transcended themselves and projected themselves into the future. . . . Their belief or their ideology gave them a stable point in the world that allowed them to see the downfall of the SS-State.

Günter Anders has called this the "paradox of hopelessness creating hope."[4]

In the much less dangerous world of West German high security prisons, it is rare that your physical survival is threatened. There is enough food, clothing, warmth, and hygiene—an enormous difference from the conditions in, for example, military prisons in Latin America. Despite such differences, however, you have to figure out how to survive with your personality intact. How do you protect yourself? How do you organize your defense? And when do you have to attack? The first impulse of course says: *Always!* But to act politically means to assess power balances and the consequences of your actions—also in prison. For example, there is no point in destroying your cell if no one on the outside will ever know about it. It might be fun, sure, but it will almost certainly cause time in the hole and repercussions. However, when in 1980 the first prisoners were meant to be transferred to the newly constructed maximum-security unit in Moabit, it made sense to barricade yourself behind the dismantled furniture of your cell. This was a sign that you refused to go to this unit voluntarily, that you refused to accept a worsening of your conditions without resistance. If you do not show such resistance, it will make *them* overconfident and you will feel powerless in your new surroundings. In the case of Moabit, comrades protested on the outside, there were militant actions, and the media coverage was huge. For surviving the maximum-security conditions, this was all extremely helpful.

The hunger strikes of the 1970s and 1980s were—despite the critique of their exact circumstances and certain demands—"survival strategies" for prisoners in isolation and maximum-security units. The solidarity campaigns that followed the deaths of Holger Meins and Sigurd Debus— killed by medical negligence and force-feeding—definitely helped the survival of their imprisoned comrades. Here is an example for an imme- diate survival strategy from my own experience: In 1983, the authorities intended to implement a new model of isolating small groups of prisoners in the maximum-security unit in Bielefeld. It was planned to supplement the maximum-security architecture with an extremely rigid regime: for a dirty sink, you would lose three days in the yard, turning off the common room's idiotic, prison-selected TV program meant confinement to your cell for two weeks, etc. Forced labor programs were added to this: assem- bling three thousand clothespins in an eight-hour workday, five days a week, under CCTV surveillance, with disciplinary measures for poor output. The enforcement of repetitive and mind-numbing activities is essential in all psychological conditioning, a classical means of brain- washing directed at the body. To assemble clothespins for years equals a slow mental death. Punishment for work refusal was the hole. Since a hunger strike (possibly of several weeks) is difficult under such circum- stances, and since everything seemed at stake anyway, the only available means was a thirst strike. Thirst strikes do not last long—one way or another. Public pressure has to be mounted fast, and this pressure has to become stronger than, in this case, *their* interest in implementing the new maximum-security forced-labor model. The survival strategy in this case was to challenge them to explain why three thousand clothespins a day were worth a human being's death. Besides, there was an unspoken, yet clear, understanding that if they did implement forced labor within the maximum-security units, attacks on the prison labor system would become so strong that it would be impossible to maintain prison labor even in the regular units, which would have caused substantial loss of income. *They* gave in after five days, having suffered significant property damage: the Revolutionary Cells (Revolutionäre Zellen, RZ) had bombed the prison bureau and the offices of two companies profiting from prison labor. Added to this were demonstrations, a riot in the maximum-security unit in Köln-Ossendorf, and bad press. Since then, no further attempt has ever been made to implement forced labor in maximum-security facilities.

Most times, however, the life of a prisoner is less heroic. After all, the natural enemy of the hero is daily routine. Here is an example, though, of a tiny survival strategy: If your request to see the prison dentist remains "overlooked" for two days, you can tape it to the toilet which can then be demounted and, at the next opportunity, placed in front of your cell—just so it won't be "overlooked" any longer. This will lead to some money being taken from the solidarity account and will result in a disciplinary measure, but you will see the dentist. Such an action works because the denial of dental services becomes official with the property damage, which needs to be registered. This means you will have the option of filing a legal complaint—something that the prison administration usually does not want to deal with in such petty cases.

Of course, you cannot rattle your bars or kick against your door all day. You won't be able to keep that up for very long. However, not being able to tear down the bars or to kick in the door does not mean that you have to accept the prison's regime and be forced into norms that are a lot narrower than those on the outside. You can keep your individuality only by resisting these norms. Live or be lived. An acceptance of the norms means an end to your own development. You lose interest in social contact and refuse to accept that circumstances and situations change. To adapt to the prison regime means to forget individual strength and success. The adaptation reproduces itself endlessly, both because you fear the actual regime and the personal consequences of resistance. You lose hope. Eventually, accepting the wrongs turns into embracing the rules. Not only optimism is dependent on activity, resistance is too. Being lethargic makes you dumb. Merely thinking about resistance (what the Nazi pawns called "inner emigration") is no survival strategy; it is cynicism: you think one thing, but you do another, or you refuse to draw the consequences of your thoughts.

The praxis of imagined resistance has a name: expected behavior. When you are passive, you internalize fear and hopelessness. This creates—and reproduces—the obedient, neurotic prisoner. This prisoner's daydreams about spectacular escapes or unexpected pardons fall under the authority-sanctioned category of "Give-us-our-daily-illusion." Within the "false life" of prison, there can be no absolutely correct ways of acting. However, fundamental decisions about your actions can still be made—decisions that are an important part of your survival strategies. They are not dogmatic. They have to be revised again and again. Is it wrong to give in? Are the old principles still valid? You always have to know this; you always have to convince yourself anew. Your responses must not just be habits. You ought to be curious and open when it comes to the experiences and perspectives of others, and you ought to appreciate friendly advice.

To make clear decisions on the basis of your memories and your knowledge, while accepting contradictions and acknowledging the change of social and political realities, in other words, to think dialectically, is a solid basis for your own conviction. Rigid and inflexible thinking can only make an exterior frame that does not even allow for the tiniest of cracks. If one detail seems off, everything seems off . . . This is why it is such tiny cracks that can sometimes cause those who once professed a "150 percent" conviction to crumble. The next thing they do is to look for a new frame. Not one that necessarily makes much sense, but one that might lead to an earlier release. Look at the example of Horst Mahler: after a lot of ideological meandering, he finally settled on the far right when, after studying the relevant literature extensively, he came to the brash conclusion in the late 1970s that Marx had misunderstood Hegel and that we all ought to reconsider our understanding of the state. In a *Spiegel* interview, he managed to outdo even the minister of the interior in his praise for the state institution. He was released early.

Of course, you will develop politically, reflect on the political praxis you were engaged in before you went to prison, etc. Yet dialectical thinking will only foster your conviction that exploitation, oppression, poverty, and war will not disappear without the overthrow of the prevailing order. This is what will always separate you from a minister of the interior.

The question of whether it is "false to give in" can be put into simple terms: Do you want to talk to someone who locks you up during the day and who is ready to shoot you if you attempt to escape during the night? Do you want to talk to the head of a prison who prohibits any commemoration of those who, in 1943, were sent to die in Mauthausen from the very yard you walk in every day? Or do you want to talk with the one who attends military training as a "reserve captain"? Do you want to strike a deal with the Federal Criminal Bureau (Bundeskriminalamt, BKA), an organization maintaining a department called "TE" for "terrorism" (formerly "Sicherheitsgruppe Bonn" and established by former officials of the Nazis' Reich Security Head Office [Reichssicherheitshauptamt]) that spies on your visitors and was involved in the death of Wolfgang Grams?[5] Do you want to bow in front of them in exchange for nothing more than a few perks? The "reason" that they demand of you rocks the cradle of both madness and betrayal, and the "common sense" they evoke "is the little man in the grey suit who never makes a mistake in addition—but it's always someone else's money he's adding up" (Raymond Chandler).

> It is sweet but dangerous to wait for letters . . .
> to lay awake till the morning and stare at the ceiling . . .
> Forget your age, beware of the spring evenings . . .
> It is bad to dream of roses and gardens, but good to think of mountains and oceans.
> My advice to you would be: read and write as much as possible—
> and ignore the mirror
> —Nâzım Hikmet, letter to a fellow prisoner[6]

Nâzım Hikmet's lines express pure survival strategies. Letters are important fractures in the prison walls, but to focus on receiving them makes you dependent. Be happy when they arrive—look for something else to be happy about when they don't. To lie awake until morning and stare at the ceiling does not change anything. To read and write until morning, however, might, as it means that you are active. To forget one's age and the mirror eradicates the worries about missing out on life. Beautiful spring evenings can cause terrible yearning for the world outside. To dream of roses and gardens appeases you in a place where you shouldn't be appeased. To think of untamed mountains and seas puts your own problems into perspective. To read and write as much as possible is the most crucial advice; in the long term, this is the most important require-ment of each and every survival strategy in prison.

Books can transfer you into a different world when the one you are facing is intolerable. They allow you to travel even though you are trapped. This is of inestimable value in solitary confinement. Besides, it helps your survival strategies in the long run to engage with thoughts and people through reading and writing. It might be difficult against the backdrop of the exhausting monotony of prison, but it is the precondition for you to be engaged. Being engaged means new social relationships and new thoughts that keep you alive. Nobody wants to hear the same stories from you year after year, about shoot-outs or eternal truths or your problems inside. The Salvation Army might want to listen to your laments, but nobody who sees you as a political subject will.

Once you have managed to resist repression during your first months and years of prison, time becomes your main enemy. Physically you can stay fit—you can exercise even in a prison cell, and cigarettes, coffee, and sweets are too expensive anyway. The sheer length of the years, however, affects the possibilities of creating a life trajectory, of experiencing life as a whole—something that forms an identity. It is difficult to understand your own patterns of behavior as coherent and meaningful. On the outside, you can be relatively certain in your knowledge that you are a person who—despite developing, of course—is always the same person, with his or her interests, ideas, reasoning, and self-confidence. Now you always have to check your personality, your consciousness, and your ability to think and see if all this hasn't somehow changed without you noticing. Without a rigorous self-reflection about your thoughts, emotions, and actions, you cannot be certain that you still think and act rationally—something you could take for granted before.

"You can understand things by changing them," Bertolt Brecht said dialectically, and it is this praxis of realization that Nâzım Hikmet describes above. To read Marx and Gramsci, Rosa Luxemburg and Assata Shakur, Malcolm X and Primo Levi, Vera Figner and Peter Weiss,[7] or to read about the history of the Peasants' War or the Black Panthers, or about internationalism, natural sciences, art history, or chess games—all this does not cut through the bars of your cell, but it helps you to preserve your ability to think and discuss. In the worst case, you can use the Bible as the only book allowed in the hole: "To open eyes that are blind, to free captives from prison and to release from the dungeon those who sit in darkness" (Isaiah 42:7).

To read is an active exchange of thoughts with others. Language is practical consciousness. Writing is production. Intellectual activity that does not result in communicable thoughts, i.e., in speaking or writing (for others), turns, in the long run—not only in prison—into a Sisyphean task. You do not live and think and write on a mythical mountain, though, but in a specific social situation. In this case: in prison. You ought to be aware of the impact that the contradictions of your situation have on your thoughts. Certain essential political realizations might in fact come more easily with some distance from the hustle and bustle of everyday life, but you ought to be very careful with all evaluations that require sensual experience. . . . In any case, it is the connection of your theoretical reflections to the current problems of the left, i.e., the problems of your comrades and friends on the outside, that gives your learning and writing a practical meaning—something that can get you through many years.

Bang. The door is shut again. This time, however, you are on the outside. This does not come as surprisingly as the arrest and is significantly more pleasant. It is similarly confusing, though. You spin around like a Matchbox car. It takes a while—and hitting a few corners—before you stop and are able to really take a good look around. Your prison survival strategies helped you deal with an environment that is not really suitable for human life. Now all the strategies that you internalized get in your way. The prison experience teaches you to keep what is important to yourself, not to reveal anything, not to make yourself vulnerable. On the outside this appears—to put it mildly—as being insensitive. Friends cannot understand your (lack of) reactions. Others—certainly not your friends—raise "ex-prisoners" onto pedestals that are, in fact, closets. It is neither uplifting nor a political program to have spent time in prison. The inevitably acquired ability to make decisions for yourself often leads to avoiding challenging collective discussions. Not wanting to be dependent on anything complicates possible bonds. The ability to be alone turns into a desire to be so. Your resistance to norms and your struggle to stay afloat as an individual now makes you skeptical toward groups. After the seriousness of the prison experience, disputes within the left often appear irrelevant or even ridiculous—yet when you show this, you appear arrogant. It is difficult to switch off the control over your emotions that you have worked so hard to attain, just so that *they* wouldn't be able to use your emotions against you. Love, hate, passion—everything is secured in an intellectual bag, and you look over your shoulder carefully before you untie anything. Sure, you keep misery away from you that way. But happiness too. With time, this becomes less severe. Things become easier. Still, what a former Tupamaro described with the following words will stay with you: "You realize that one . . . cannot live a lie comfortably without being disgusted by oneself, because you believe that those who understand but live inactively in comfort will break."[8] In any case, there is life after survival, and it is worth living. Sean McGuffin's comment that "age and trickery will always beat youth and strength" is as much a comfort to you as the useful degrees of persistence, patience, and endurance that you could only acquire as a prisoner.[9] You are still here, and you are still curious.

DISSOLUTION
(OR NOT)

STATEMENT DISSOLVING THE 2ND OF JUNE MOVEMENT

(1980)

The following document was presumably written by RAF members in France. It was read out in court during a trial against 2nd of June Movement members in June 1980 by Gabriele Rollnik, who supported it together with her codefendants Angelika Goder and Gudrun Stürmer. Codefendant Klaus Viehmann immediately distanced himself from the document. Days later, he read out a critical response in court, authored by him together with Ronald Fritzsch and Ralf Reinders. The controversy split the 2nd of June Movement into two factions and effectively marked the end of the group. The faction supporting the dissolution statement joined the RAF. The faction opposing it felt much closer to the autonomist movement and the social-revolutionary strategy of the Revolutionary Cells.

—

After ten years of armed struggle, we want to reflect critically on our history and clarify why we have decided to dissolve the 2nd of June Movement in order to continue the anti-imperialist struggle within the RAF, as the RAF.

The 2nd of June Movement was founded in contradiction to the RAF with the vague purpose of carrying out "spontaneous proletarian politics." We considered revolutionary theory and analysis—which is mandatory to develop strategy, tactics, continuity, and perspective—to be unimportant. We "jumped into the struggle" with the goal of "turning on" young people. Our practice was determined by what we thought would "excite" people, rather than by identifying imperialism's real contradictions and frictions, which we needed to attack.

The 2nd of June Movement was conceived as an alternative to the RAF, appealing to comrades for whom the uncompromising struggle went too far. For ten years, this has caused splits, competition, and disorientation within the left and the guerrilla. It has prevented our own revolutionary development. We followed a populist line, not offering any political direction or mobilization against the strategy of the pigs.

It is never the responsibility of the guerrilla to please the people and to win their praise, but rather—in a country where Nazi fascism and a social democracy tied to US imperialism have deprived the working class of any proletarian organization—to be at the forefront of the struggle, to escalate the main political contradictions through armed attacks in order to push the state into a political crisis. The guerrilla can only be one thing in the metropole: the political explosive in the imperialist structure, the attack that forces open the breach between society and the state. In this breach, revolutionary politics can emerge by enabling proletarian, anti-imperialist organization and by shifting the balance of power. The political attack, materialized by the gun, is always victorious because it anticipates and introduces this process, even when there is military defeat. The continuity of the guerrilla is to be found in its strategy, despite the defeats.

That is also the difference between Schleyer and Lorenz. Today, we are in a position to critique our most important action. In the Lorenz kidnapping, we find all the errors that we've made over the past ten years, but we have learned from them. The 1975 kidnapping unfolded in a politically charged situation in Berlin. The struggle of the comrades in Stammheim had given rise to national and international mobilization, which peaked in the widespread hunger strike that pushed Schmidt against the ropes. We not only completely ignored this context, but we gave the momentum to the enemy by our choice of prisoners. This, as well as choosing Lorenz (a fellow from a party who is no longer of importance for imperialist strategy), meant that tactical considerations were more important for us than strategic ones. In our propagandistic efforts during and after the kidnapping, the short-sighted victory, that is, the consumable ritual, took precedence over the political and military level needed in order to break the imperialist strategy. These are the roots of the perverted "fun guerrilla" of Reinders, Teufel, and others. The RAF's

1977 offensive and the reaction by the state raised the question of political strategy anew for us.

The year 1977 caused a watershed in the development of imperialist strategy as well as in the direction of the guerrilla in the metropole. After the massacres of Mogadishu and Stammheim, Schmidt defined the political agenda of Western Europe under the leadership of West Germany: Western Europe should defend an imperialism in crisis against the liberation struggles both in the Third World and in the metropole.

The unconditional integration of Western Europe into US military strategy, and the militarization of the metropole through an increasingly hegemonic apparatus, are imperialist responses to the simultaneous rise of revolutionary struggles worldwide. Revolutionary strategy becomes increasingly international by anti-imperialist groups recognizing both the US as the main enemy and the intentions of Western Europe. The US and its allies know that another strategic defeat anywhere in the world will put them on the track to ultimate defeat.

The "post-Vietnam era"—that is, the attempt to recover from US imperialism's politico-military defeat in Vietnam through a new politico-economic strategy—collapsed due to the events in Iran. These events had been announced by a chain of uprisings from Angola to Kampuchea. Imperialist politics now seek a military solution that cannot be achieved. Its preparation for total annihilation reveals the naked expression of its content. The imperialists try to prevent a new, and probably final, strategic military defeat in the Third World by launching a war in Europe, conceived right from the start as a nuclear war. The notion of a "limited war" receives a new meaning in this perverse context.[1]

This war shall not divide the world among imperialist rivals. At stake are revolution and counterrevolution. This is the decisive phase of the struggle. The outcome of the war will be decided in the metropole, since the Third World liberation movements that have come to power will be forced to position themselves within the East-West contradiction as long as the imperialist center blackmails them militarily as well as economically ("dependence on the world market").

All that's at the center of world revolution—the destruction of the state, self-determination, identity—has matured and taken on a special dimension in the most recent struggles for communism in the metropole. It will materialize now or not at all.

The question facing the entire Western European left is whether it will live up to its historical responsibility during this escalation that will settle things one way or another. Or will it betray this responsibility?

Unity in the Anti-imperialist Armed Struggle!

For the last time: 2nd of June Movement
June 2, 1980

REGARDING THE ALLEGED DISSOLUTION OF THE 2ND OF JUNE MOVEMENT

(1980)

Ralf Reinders, Klaus Viehmann, and Ronald Fritzsch

Response to the "dissolution statement" (see above, "Statement Dissolving the 2nd of June Movement") by Ralf Reinders, Klaus Viehmann, and Ronald Fritzsch. Read out in court by Klaus Viehmann in June 1980 and published in the autonomist journal *Radikal*, no. 80, July 1980.

━━

Brilliant, the faction that has been pushing hard for the 2nd of June Movement to adopt the RAF line for three years has now joined the RAF. In the heat of the moment, the comrades have drowned the entire 2nd of June Movement in an ocean of words.

Some comrades have asked us who the authors of this unpolitical baloney are. But the question isn't phrased right. If this was all "baloney," we wouldn't have to fear that it will lead to idiotic actions, such as hijackings. We take the warning of comrade Mao Zedong seriously: one cannot leave unaddressed the subjective bullshit that comes from some comrades when trying to assess the political situation. After all, there are always inexperienced comrades who embrace such theories and, as a consequence, not only hurt themselves but us, the entire left. The "dissolution statement" entails no materialist analysis, only phraseology.

One more thing before we start: since the "roots of the perverted 'fun guerrilla' of Reinders, Teufel, and others" have now been exposed, we declare that the fun guerrilla was dissolved in its dissolution a long time ago. We have taken the critique of uncompromising "fighters" for "leadership" and "strategy" seriously. "Reinders, Teufel, and others" did confirm it with their thumbprints: the fun guerrilla has been dissolved! Yes! For years we made our own perversion the cornerstone of resistance. No more! Fun is perverse! And fun in struggle is perverse fun. We've been flagellating ourselves for weeks now, with delight. "Smack . . . aaahh . . . smack . . . aaahh!"

However, not everything in this "dissolution statement" is so funny. For instance, the assertion that the 2nd of June Movement "was founded in contradiction to the RAF." The 2nd of June Movement resulted from the fusion of three West Berlin groups that wanted to develop and organize the armed struggle. The largest group was the Tupamaros West Berlin, which started to carry out actions in Berlin in 1968. They attacked imperialist and Zionist institutions and symbols, factories that sacked workers, and, especially in the context of the APO's 1969 Justice Campaign, courthouses, judges, and state prosecutors. The 2nd of June Movement's orientation was based on this practice. Its long-term goals, and the means and methods it chose, derived from the experiences of the youth rebellion at the time.

It is certainly correct that the 2nd of June Movement did not present a theoretical "urban guerrilla concept" like the RAF. However, it was impossible to conceive of any such concept in a credible manner. Germany was a country in which, after twelve years of Nazi terror and twenty years of anticommunist hysteria, a youth movement was finally returning to socialist ideas. A group of proletarian youth, with no unbroken tradition to lean on, took up the struggle against oppression and exploitation, against apathy in the face of genocide and imperialism, and against the absurd capitalist machinery of consumption, which abuses human needs for the ugly face of profit. Their resistance developed out of their own distress, and their strategic and tactical understanding was based on their experiences and reflections on social reality. This dialectical development of theory and practice is what Marx had recognized as the precondition for revolutionary politics to succeed.

There wasn't enough practical experience in Germany at the time to present a "concept" as definitive as the RAF did. The fact that the RAF wasn't able to put their concept into practice proves this.

The contradictions between the RAF and the 2nd of June Movement were the results of the different ways in which the groups formed. The 2nd of June Movement came out of a shared cultural context, while the

RAF was based on a theoretical revolutionary model. The RAF had a centralized organizational structure; the 2nd of June Movement preferred autonomous, decentralized structures. Another point of conflict was the question of cadre going underground, which the RAF insisted on by principle. The forerunners of the 2nd of June Movement provided practical proletarian alternatives. There was no competition, but there were different ideas of revolutionary struggle. In the beginning, there was strong mutual support between both groups, even joint actions, for example expropriations at three banks in West Berlin in September 1970. At the time, the groups still agreed that the future would determine the long-term potential of their respective political lines.

In the obscure "dissolution statement," Lorenz's kidnapping by the 2nd of June Movement and the subsequent liberation of a number of prisoners is heavily attacked. It is argued that "all the errors that we've made over the past ten years" are to be found in it. Of course, we made mistakes prior to 1975, and even during the Lorenz kidnapping. The setback of September 1975 proved that all too clearly.[1] But what is passed off here as political "self-criticism" is incredibly ignorant and, indeed, preposterous. Apparently, the Stammheim comrades' struggle "had given rise to national and international mobilization, which peaked in the widespread hunger strike that pushed Schmidt against the ropes." Is that why, in 1975, he always hunched his shoulders?

Seriously: Lorenz was kidnapped four weeks after a hunger strike had been broken off because the prisoners had all been moved to Stammheim and it was clear that nothing more could be achieved. And what was the "politically charged situation" the authors of the "dissolution statement" hint at? The hunger strike? The elections in Berlin? What about the struggle in Wyhl?[2] Was that not part of the "political context"? Mass unemployment? Inflation? And so on and so forth. And Schmidt? He was able to cope with a lot more. (Unfortunately.)

The "dissolution statement" reads as if the hunger strike nearly led to the downfall of West Germany, prevented only by the 2nd of June Movement—those bastards of history—because we "ignored this context" by our "choice of prisoners." Apparently, that was how Schmidt could escape an otherwise hopeless situation. The 2nd of June Movement, Schmidt's aide and savior of the nation! (Helmut, where are our Federal Crosses of Merit?![3]) Meanwhile, the RAF was only moments away from tipping the balance of power in their favor. Would you believe it?

To be blunt: whoever dares to throw this much shit at the Lorenz action, the only big victory in twelve years of armed struggle, must have completely lost their mind. But the statement itself explains how these comrades can arrive at such a mad conclusion. It tries to sell us revolutionary politics as an "attack" that "forces open the breach between society and the state." Go figure! That's what we are supposed to do? Open the breach between capitalist society and its expression, the bourgeois state? That sounds like: free the ladders from their rungs, then we'll finally have free ladders. (And true, at least that would be ladders no one can fall off of.)

The "dissolution statement" is full off bloated prose, flippancy, hubris, arrogance, contempt for the masses, and resignation. Underneath all of its contradictory assertions lies a mirror image of bourgeois society: while capitalist interests dictate social conditions, armed struggle degenerates into an end in itself. The human being disappears. Everyone reunites in alienation.

Régis Debray described this process correctly in *A Critique of Arms*:

> Thus we cannot consider the problem of what forms of organization the revolutionary struggle demands without first asking: what are the class interests which the guerrilla force exists to serve? To consider technical problems of method independently of the aims and aspirations of the masses that method is to serve; to consider the organizational problems of the vanguard independently of the class, or alliance of classes, whose instrument that vanguard is; this is to take the means for the end, to set foot on the empty air. The theoretical steps which lead to such a lamentably real fall can be analysed as follows: first, you begin by separating the military instrument from the social class, the armed method from the economic and social conditions in which it is being used; then, logically, the instrument takes precedence over the class, the method over the concrete conditions, and instrument and method become the predominant and determining factors ("the principal aspect in the dialectically united pair of opposites"); finally, the instrument—the army or Party—replaces the class whose instrument it is, and the method—the armed struggle—replaces its political and social objectives. In other words, the instrument now determines its own actions, and the revolutionary armed struggle becomes "left-wing terrorism."[4]

What kind of guerrilla rejects "to please the people and win their praise"? For what and, more importantly, with whom can such a guerrilla hope to struggle? To construct a dichotomy such as "populist line versus political line" makes no sense. There is no false "populist line," unless the guerrilla lags behind the interests of the people and their willingness to struggle. Yes, the 2nd of June's actions were meant to be populist, but by "populist" we mean "popular." The actions meant to win people over to our side, instead of finding them rally around the state.

There's nothing particularly revolutionary about disregarding the sympathies of the people. Being "praised" in the sense of gaining approval for an action, or for the politics of the guerrilla, means to cut through mainstream consciousness and to make popular support for revolutionary politics possible. "Praise" creates the sea, which the guerrilla relies on for growth, mobility, logistics, and operations. Ten years ago, we all claimed to "serve the people." But in Mogadishu, we abused the people. We've been trying hard to counter the cops' propaganda that even "the flower girl on the corner" could fall victim to one of our actions. With Mogadishu, our credibility was washed away.

The difference between terrorism, which can hit anyone indiscriminately, and revolutionary struggle is that revolutionary action, both in its means and in its ends (targeting class enemies and their henchmen), does not provide the cops with cheap arguments. Otherwise, the actions easily rebound against those who carry them out. This is not a question of tactics, but a question of principle!

Revolutionary politics can only develop from within the potentially revolutionary class, and not against it. Those who constantly complain about comrades "showing no solidarity" should take a moment to consider why that is, and how their own errors have contributed to it. One of the main errors is to fetishize the armed struggle, turning it into a struggle fought for the sake of struggling: "The political attack, materialized by the gun, is always victorious because it anticipates and introduces this process, even when there is military defeat." This sentence is a masterpiece of dialectical thinking! Or, let's say: of mental acrobatics. The punch always lands, even if it hits nothing but air, because it anticipates and introduces this process . . . But we decide on a political attack on the basis of whether it serves a purpose, whether it is advantageous to us, whether it weakens the enemy. We choose the means—armed/legal/

illegal—based on the same criteria. It is the political content that determines the form of the struggle, not vice versa!

A guerrilla that distinguishes between political and military aspects in the way the "dissolution statement" does is an affront to all "classics," from von Clausewitz to Mao and Che.[5] Continuous military defeat is always the result of political errors. Not paying attention to one's base, losing the connection to the everyday struggle of the people, incorrectly analyzing the political and concrete national/regional conditions of the struggle—these are the cardinal errors! Any sober assessment also reveals that there is little "continuity of the guerrilla . . . to be found in its strategy." Yet this is nothing to be ashamed of. It wouldn't speak for your politics if you stuck to one and the same strategy for ten years, ignoring all developments and changes.

To address the geopolitical assumptions made in the "dissolution statement" is almost impossible. For example, "Schmidt defined the political agenda of Western Europe under the leadership of West Germany: Western Europe should defend an imperialism in crisis against the liberation both in the Third World and in the metropole." Trying to fill this sentence with political meaning is a task as difficult as emptying the North Sea with a sieve. The "unconditional integration of Western Europe into US military strategy" is simply a fabrication, something that should be obvious to everyone since France's factual withdrawal from NATO.

NATO is an expression of its members states' common interest to maintain and extend the "Free West" against the Soviet Union. Within this common strategic interest, there is competition between the different centers of the metropole, from the EC-US steel war to the Japan-USA-EC automobile war, and from the EC's boycott of Iran (which really isn't a boycott) to Japan's economic advances in China against US-EC interests. The imperialist states were once appropriately described as "hostile brothers" united by a common enemy, the Soviet Union.

That the countries of the metropole undergo militarization is characteristic of any capitalist state; they must do so in order to suppress their own citizens in times of crisis, not because there is a "simultaneous rise of revolutionary struggles worldwide." Only someone with the mentality of a hoarder can believe the latter, someone who sees an "objective" connection between an uprising in Southeast Asia with the latest collective agreement at ÖTV, disregarding all specific conditions of particular struggles, their reasons, the classes that drive them, and so forth.[6] But the masses who make history make it only where they are. If you live in Europe but set your watch by the time of Tehran or Hanoi, you subscribe to illusions that lead nowhere and have nothing do with proletarian internationalism.

Those who try to convince themselves again and again, in an almost Teutonic display of catastrophism, that imperialism's defeat in the Third World is around the corner and that imperialism is about to depart from the world stage with sound and fury, is throwing sand into their own eyes and those of others. The "chain of uprisings from Angola to Kampuchea" is only impressive if you ignore imperialism's victories: in Egypt, Somalia, and China, most probably in Iraq, and with certainty soon in South Korea. The everyday realities of imperialism and the way imperialism develops are mistaken for its final stages.

The death of imperialism will come in the metropole. It is here where the wealth is produced that provides the imperialist system with the power to rule over other nations. It is wealth produced by working people. The national liberation of a country in the Third World does not pose unsolvable problems for imperialism. "Imperialist politics now seek a military solution that cannot be achieved. Its preparation for total annihilation reveals the naked expression of its content." Sentences for the funhouse mirror. "Seeks, doesn't find, annihilates the naked expression." Of the content? Or are we talking about the expression of nakedness? Does anyone know what this means?!

The authors of the "dissolution statement" assume that a nuclear war is being prepared in Europe in order to prevent "a final, strategic military defeat in the Third World." The imperialists would be out of their fucking minds if they attempted to secure their assets in the Third World by destroying Europe, where they have invested much more. If a "limited nuclear war" were to become possible in Europe, it would be because of the US interest in containing the Soviet Union. If there really was a "limited nuclear war" in Europe (which is unlikely), it would be because US imperialism calculated that a cunning competitor—the European Community—and a strategic opponent—the Soviet Union—could both be decisively weakened without the US being directly attacked.

Since the "dissolvers" occupy themselves with monumental problems like "limited nuclear war," one would think that they'd offer some handy solutions. Alas, there are none. And that despite the fact that the paper correctly notes that the "outcome of the war will be decided in the metropole." Those who want to struggle in the "belly of the beast," as Che called it, must be familiar with the problems of the struggle here, and must engage in it.

The "dissolution statement" is the printed expression of what has caused the guerrilla's political crisis. While reams of paper have been churned out about the international situation, NATO committees, and the like, most of the actions of recent years had nothing to do with the struggle of the left and even less with people's everyday resistance. Even the exceptions—actions by autonomists and the Revolutionary Cells— have been unable to prevent the guerrilla's isolation.

Some comrades have recognized this. They understand that only a politics tied to the people's everyday struggles can prevent total defeat at the hands of the counterrevolution. To escape isolation means to gain approval not only among those who already subscribe to our politics, but also among those who are not on our side yet. In the current phase of the struggle, it means that we have a lot to learn and a lot to forget. Old drawers, which we've used far too long to carelessly place comrades and groups in ("they don't want a guerrilla movement," "they're nonviolent," "they're revisionists," "they're like the Green Party," and so on) need to be cleared out. We need to look at both, the things that separate us and the things that connect us.

Considering the state of the West German left, no one can deny the need for a "politics of alliance" (*Bündnispolitik*). A politics of alliance doesn't mean to betray one's own position but to identify the common- alities among different groups during a specific phase of the struggle. It is a requirement for closing in on our goal of winning the majority of the people for social revolution. We want to develop social-revolutionary politics, a socialist alternative to social democratic crisis management.

In the 1980s, unemployment and inflation will reach dimensions in Western Europe that were not thought possible. Through new technol- ogies such as microprocessors, rationalization will increase rapidly and speed up labor for everyone who hasn't lost their job yet. The intense competition in a relatively crowded world market will expedite currency devaluation in the imperialist states and lead to a decline in real wages. Since, in pursuing capitalist interests, the state must use more and more social wealth for subsidies and arms expenditures, the "social safety net" (which is paid for by those who require it) will become ever more porous.

Broad sections of the population will be declassed/proletarianized and slip below the poverty line.

Since the powerful know very well that this will increase the tensions between themselves and the population, they prepare for social conflict. First, in the time-honored tradition of refining and upgrading their repressive apparatus. Second, by social democratic leaders and technocrats trying to deceive the people with reformist slogans, the kind of "dialogue" offered by Baum.[7] They want to prevent the discontented, aggrieved, and oppressed from joining forces with the left opposition, which would prompt mutual radicalization. For the same reason, they want to neutralize and buy off the left to prevent any movement that might question the legitimacy of the state. How successful they will be depends not least on whether we succeed in intervening in current conflicts in ways that the state cannot resolve or defuse with reforms. It will then have no choice but to respond with violence. This is true with regard to any particular issue, be it the antinuclear movement, the squatting movement, the women's movement, antimilitarism, the struggles of the unemployed, or industrial action in the factories. The fundamental problems behind the facade of the "social welfare state" can, in the end, only be resolved by violence. A capitalist factory will always remain a site of exploitation and inhumane working conditions, despite comanagement, collective agreements, and factory councils. In this country, profit remains, after all, the measure of all things.

To protect the state, a few thousand cops will be deployed if opportune. Gorleben was violently cleared because if construction at the site had been obstructed further, the entire nuclear energy program would have been delayed. The West German monopolies cannot afford this if they want to remain competitive and profitable on the world market based on the know-how they've acquired.

Wherever the economic or political interests of the powerful have met massive resistance, the state has responded with violence: from Grohnde to Brokdorf, from the Westend to the Dreisameck,[8] from the swearing-in ceremony in Bremen to the occupation of the America House in West Berlin,[9] from the legal rubber-stamping of the lockouts to the clubbing of striking printers.[10] In all these struggles, the state attempts to defend its monopoly of violence, a precondition for the smooth functioning of capitalist exploitation. That's why the state tries to silence any discussion about the legitimacy of the monopoly of violence. If we want to break through the monopoly of violence—both practically as well as in popular consciousness—we must intervene in the people's struggles with militant action. We must carry out exemplary actions that can be understood and copied by many people, and we must clarify that illegal action is necessary.

A nuclear power plant that couldn't be prevented despite occupations of the construction site and demonstrations can still be neutralized if the power poles are knocked over. A crane is only a useful tool for a real estate speculator until it is torched. A slumlord destroying living quarters gets a sense of what it's like when his own place is "renovated." A municipal planning office will find it difficult to administer deforestation when its offices are burned down. A prison warden learns less about daily life in prison from petitions and protest letters than from a couple of bullets in his leg.

All the small and big enemies of the people can no longer bask in their glory if they need to fear being held accountable for their scummy behavior!

The interventions in everyday struggles must, of course, not lose sight of the long-term goal: the bringing together of all sources of resistance. Only then can a broad militant and revolutionary movement develop, dismantle all oppressive structures, and carry out the social revolution in the metropole.

We must never lose sight of this goal—the social revolution—even if it seems utopian; otherwise, we will lose ourselves in sects, transcendental theories, and political irrelevance.

A final comment on the "dissolution statement": social-revolutionary politics, as they are practiced by the 2nd of June Movement and others, cannot be "dissolved" like some petit bourgeois gardening club.

Berlin-Moabit, June 1980
Reinders, Viehmann, Fritzsch

EVALUATION

HOW IT ALL BEGAN
(ca. 1992)

Norbert "Knofo" Kröcher

Written under the title "Wie alles anfing" (a reference to the Michael "Bommi" Baumann book of the same title) in the early 1990s. The circulation history is unclear. The version translated has been uploaded to www.haschrebellen.de/wie-alles-anfing.

———

June 2, 1878: Accompanied by a horde of cavalry guards from the security unit "Potsdam," a luxurious carriage dashes through Berlin's Tiergarten. The passenger is none other than Kaiser Wilhelm I. His Majesty is on the way to the opera, where he—this is no joke—intends to enjoy a little culture with the Shah of Persia.[1] But that never happens. Behind some bushes, the Berlin doctor and antimonarchist Nobiling is lurking, republicanism in his heart and a double-barreled shotgun in his hand. When the carriage slows down for a pedestrian crossing, Nobiling starts firing. Diving for cover, the Kaiser catches a load of buckshot in his most Serene Highness. Nobiling escapes. However, he has been recognized and shoots himself, sustaining severe injuries, as police officers try to arrest him.

According to contemporary reports, the coachman of the prisoner transport ordered to Nobiling's house smashed his head on a low gateway, falling from the coach unconscious. Ninety-nine years later, when the useless chronicler and author of these lines was arrested in a foreign country, the secret car delivering him to the airport for the purpose of deportation to the former Kaiserreich ran out of gas. Not much has changed.

But let's return to the Kaiser. Lying on his belly, he orders his guards to take him back home immediately. The removal of the foreign lead in his behind is so painful that Wilhelm—in fury, this was already the second assassination attempt that year—lets loose on the chancellor who has rushed to his bed. In turn, this chancellor, none other than Bismarck, immediately steamrollers through the notorious socialist laws.[2] Wilhelm's behind was so damaged that—after gleefully watching a number of social democrats, anarchists, and other scum disappear behind the walls of the Spandau fortress—he took a step back from governmental affairs.

When, about a good lifetime later, a descendant of the Shah of Persia was invited to the Berlin Opera again (no joke: as in 1878, *The Magic Flute* was to be shown), a mob of democracy-conscious youth rocked the gates to the cultural temple, while, on a side street, a plainclothes cop shot a fleeing student in the back of his head. The student, Benno Ohnesorg, did not survive, and, a few years later, the event prompted the Central Council of the Roaming Hash Rebels (the Blues, for short) to name the daring organization they founded together with other groups after that sad day.

As we all know, things didn't go too well for the Shah either. For another few years, he listlessly let his stooges torture and murder some more, until cancer did him in in exile. At that point, Nobiling and the Kaiser's punctured bum were forgotten.

It went better for the daring organization. It developed well, with joy and laughter, and it was popular with the people of Berlin, even legendary. Quite a few of Berlin's bigger and smaller children recall with pleasure the occasional chocolate kiss received from it while wanting to pay the rent or open a bank account.

You might say that it was a clandestine organization whose popularity stemmed from only accepting proletarian informants in its ranks, being open to the tender green of indica cannabis ("Don't legalize it—smoke it!"), and respecting no other flag than the one German speakers refer to when a good night out leaves the traces of alcohol on your breath.[3]

What were the highlights in the organization's history? It did plenty for Berlin's culture and transport system and the pockets of the proletarian population (for example, by printing tons of counterfeit tickets for rock concerts, subway rides, and factory canteens, while burning the Berlin transport system's files on fare-dodgers); it arranged Berlin's biggest "smoke-in" to date, at the Olivaer Platz along Kurfürstendamm; and it repaired the pants of the former Berlin CDU chairman, Peter Lorenz, who, for this purpose, was even housed free of charge in one of the organization's lodgings. The Berlin government was so moved that it released five comrades from prison, flying them to Yemen. They were accompanied by Heinrich Albertz—voluntarily—who, in 1967, when Benno Ohnesorg was killed, acted as Berlin's mayor and host to the Shah of Persia.

These are, of course, only a few examples of the diverse and varied activities of the organization. If we started to list all of the big and small actions securing jobs at Berlin's fire department, we'd have to fill volumes. There is not much data. But after threatening the boss of the Federal Gang Ministry to be raped by five hundred Yorkshire pigs, the ministry provided the following information: approximate membership in Berlin 379,000, worldwide about two hundred million. There are no age restrictions. The youngest member is apparently eleven months old, the oldest 108 years old. It is noteworthy that most members don't seem to know anything about their membership, probably because admission is automatic after regular fare-dodging, repeated shoplifting, arson at the centers of big capital, squatting, and occupying the factory you work in. Records? No.

As proof of the extraordinary cleverness of the daring organization—whose name will still remind people of the murder of Benno Ohnesorg a hundred years from now, and who will probably still be around when it officially no longer exists—let us reference the creation of its former mascot Bommi, akin to the English soccer team's billy goat. A book written under his name is still seen as a legitimate historical account by naive fellow citizens. Even the feds fell for it, using wanted posters to look for Bommi. But he doesn't exist, and—after reading his book—it is doubtful that he ever existed.

Since the early 1980s, there circulates a rumor in more or less dubious circles that the movement has dissolved, or, worse, joined the ranks of the Rough Army Faction. All nonsense. You can't just dissolve the FC St. Pauli either, can you?[4] It is true that the RAF has been dissolved by the Treuhand, just like all East German operations.[5] The 2nd of June Movement, however, has achieved its goal: complete failure.

Let us close the account here. It should be noted, however, that if the decision on the capital city won't be reversed (Bitterfeld is located much better[6]), the 2nd of June Movement will claim the other 364 days of the year as well. Then, my friends, you'd better get prepared! After all, Fritz Nietzsche already recognized with crystal clarity that "it would be foolish trying to stop an earthquake."[7]

Good Morning,
Knofo

WHAT'S NOT WRITTEN
(June 1997)

Klaus Viehmann

Originally published as "Was nicht geschrieben steht" in *Arranca!*, no. 12, June 1997.

———

1997: The Year of the Pigs?

The year 1997 risks proving the nasty joke that history is nothing more than the sum of lies that people have agreed upon twenty years later. Whenever there is a twentieth or thirtieth anniversary, there are television films, talk shows, book releases, and newspaper features filled with terror and guerrilla stories, presented—"Important, important!"—by a crude blend of federal prosecutors, *Spiegel* reporters, Federal Crime Agency journalists, and, especially, former urban guerrillas. To challenge this cartel of schmaltz and nonsense on the media market is impossible. All the bourgeois media is interested in are people distancing themselves from their past. Those who don't play the game are ignored or denied, such as the people still in prison. A book like the one by Rossana Rossanda and Mario Moretti about the history of the Red Brigades, fulfilling the need for a left-wing historiography based on political reflection and not dependent on renunciation, is read by one or two thousand people in Germany.[1] A revisionist film made for television about the Schleyer kidnapping (paid ghost writers: the crown witnesses Peter-Jürgen Boock and Silke Maier-Witt) will be watched by millions.[2]

The situation would be different if there currently was a stronger (militant) left, and perhaps an armed practice, but now, toward the end of the 1990s, when the armed struggle of the 1970s no longer exists, when few of the old folks stick to their revolutionary goals, and when hardly any of the younger ones discover any, a critique of the 1997 remembrance shenanigans will remain reduced to a few circles within the left and not find a mass audience. Astonishingly, some of the new publications find their way even into other circles within the left, especially the memoirs of dropouts who still claim a leftist identity.[3] But why do left-wing projects invite dropouts to their events, giving them a platform to tell their skewed stories?

Bang! Bang! Babbling Until the Very End

What's the appeal of dropout memoirs? Why do political stories and discussions find much less interest than a personalized cabinet of curiosities about the armed struggle? In theory, everyone knows that people lie in memoirs, that they distort things and sweep others under the rug. So what is it that leads even left activists to appreciate terrible books and to believe in obvious caricatures of the truth?

Memoirs offer a glimpse into an intimate, hidden world—often a strange but seemingly interesting one. (Or one made interesting by sensationalist stories.) Who would not want to know how it really was? Who would not want to know who has said what or done what or thought what?

Sure, it is more entertaining to read in flashy magazines like *Goldenes Blatt* about queens and princes than to dive into a historical and critical study of feudalism and its remains. Everyone knows that there's a difference when it comes to the truth, but the flashy magazines can be read without using your brain, while the studies require an intellectual effort. That's why the latest gossip from the scene is so popular: you get information without having to think . . . The same is true for the "insider reports" from the urban guerrilla: illustrious figures, villains, and heroes instead of political backgrounds and reflections; lines full of love and resentment instead of fairness and nuances; good versus evil instead of real people. The writing is often terrible, but the readers get a peek at machine gun fire, dark dungeons, and sex in the underground.

There are some good personal accounts. The testimonies by former Tupamaros, for example, combine personal experience (and all its contradictions) with political consciousness and resistance against the ruling system. They are characterized by self-criticism and fairness toward former companions.

However, this is not what the capitalist market wants. The capitalist market is looking for a kick, relationship gossip, cool dudes, possibly even strong women. It wants people to renounce their past, to find closure in the realization that it was all for nothing, that the armed struggle was a mistake, and that no one should ever make the same mistake again. Resistance against the system and dull honesty don't pay.

Vanity at the Ministry of Truth

In historical accounts of communist parties, some people and political positions are glossed over, while the significance of others is exaggerated. It all depends on the political situation. In a history about the Brandenburg prison, published in several editions in East Germany, the role of the later dissident Robert Havemann became less important with each one of them, until his name eventually disappeared completely.[4] Meanwhile, Erich Honecker developed, edition by edition, from a simple medical assistant to a central figure in the resistance movement. The difference to the dropout memoirs is that they don't mention some people and political positions even in the first edition. Important is only one person: the author. Have mistakes been made? Sure. By others.

There's a human trait that enjoys seeing one's own personal account in a high print run: vanity. You are the hero and the center of the story, while the old collective remains silent in the background, a prop to your self-portrayal. Left-wing histories are written by many; a memoir is written by one person only. That person has no desire to debate their version of the story or to be corrected. If the story was written collectively, they wouldn't be able to invent things. Rarely do they present facts. They evoke old friendships and settle old scores, all depending on what they get out of it today, what their personal interests are, and what they feel like saying. Accounts from the (former) underground allow them to use the smoke-without-fire trick: to hint at something without spelling it out, so that it becomes impossible to be refuted. The only thing that counts is leaving an impression. By using a blend of code names, real names, and fake names, a gray zone is created, where insinuations, omissions, and defamations float freely. If anyone asks, you have both options: "Yes, this is the one I mean," or, "I can't tell who this is about, sorry." That's terribly convenient to avoid any criticism. You can even use different names for one and the same person, allowing you to distribute praise and admonition at the same time.

What the writers of memoirs don't distribute are the profits. While the anticapitalist story was created collectively, the profits from the books, talk shows, and lectures are collected individually. You don't even bother asking the old comrades if the money should be donated. The movement is not important. The money comes from a bourgeois audience, guaranteeing high sales and ratings. Having excerpts printed in *Der Spiegel* or appearing on TV satisfies the ego more than a program on an alternative radio station or a discussion with a left-wing panel where you can't use the stage to tell an idolizing audience whatever you want.

To be successful on the market, a dropout story has to find the right balance of renunciation. You can't go as far as you did when securing a shorter prison sentence by talking to the cops and prosecutors. You need to find the right balance between declaring that you have now "come to your senses," which is mandatory for securing a broad audience, and keeping the veil of authenticity that allows you to sell your story as that of an "insider."

Consumer satisfaction and vanity go together nicely. Neither is interested in errors the author might have committed, but both are interested in presenting their "weaknesses" as caused by circumstance ("tragic hero") and inner turmoil ("romance or guerrilla"). The audience can revel in this kitsch for the soul, and since it is printed ten thousand times, the author can feel flattered.

In prison, vanity doesn't get you very far. It's not a place for loudmouths and wannabe celebrities. You gotta survive on your own for ten, fifteen years. For the dropouts, their personal fate is more important than their former political conviction. In prison, they are looking for a way out—anything!—and if escape is impossible, they find tactics to get out (earlier) in some other way. To remain in prison for a long time and watch yourself grow old is unbearable for vain people.

What's Not Written…

Why even bother to address books like Inge Viett's *Nie war ich furchtloser*? Some of the former group members no longer want to hear about it, others are annoyed (to varying degrees), and the dead can't defend themselves. I myself pondered for a long time whether it's worth commenting on. If it was just any book, it wouldn't be, but in 1997 it represents the attempt to once and for all close the urban guerrilla chapter. And it stands for a very sloppy way of writing history. Since, considering the lack of collective historiography, such books are often read as a substitute for real history, they need to be disputed.

There are also personal reasons. Mainly, being flabbergasted by the way people and events are presented that you remember all too well yourself. Inge Viett is writing about a time when I was living underground for almost two years. Some things are unrecognizable, while others read like an attempted theft of one's own history to the point of defamation.

You can't evaluate the book without considering how it came about and who the author is. Anyone who has read the newspaper articles, or Inge Viett's verdict, has known for years that Inge Viett talked to the feds and got a crown witness deal, even if she wants you to believe the opposite. At least she's talked less than the others who escaped to East Germany.[5] Had she kept quiet after that, there wouldn't be any particular need to let the public know about this. But with writing a book the way she did, criticism and reactions are inevitable.

In the book itself, the crown witness deal and her early release aren't mentioned with a single word, and to this day there hasn't been any (self-)criticism. When organizers of a book presentation asked her to say something about it, she canceled on short notice. What got her the crown witness deal were statements about the cooperation between the RAF and the Stasi in the early 1980s, especially training sessions that, according to her, happened before the RAF action against US general Kroesen.[6] Because of these statements, federal prosecutors brought charges against four or five former Stasi agents in the early 1990s. They were imprisoned in remand but only for a few weeks or months, since a judgment by the federal constitutional court on the criminal liability of deeds committed on East German territory was still pending. Later, Viett's statements didn't suffice for a conviction. Some RAF prisoners also made contradictory statements.

In Viett's verdict, the crown witness deal is justified by the warrants against the Stasi people and the "destabilization of the RAF," whose members might have been "deterred from committing further criminal acts." (You can find the exact wording in the August 26, 1992, Koblenz Higher Regional Court verdict.) Why Inge Viett would incriminate all of the Stasi representatives who had helped her come to East Germany, although she speaks so highly of the country, I don't know. She does not give an explanation.

Charges against her with regard to the Lorenz and Palmers kidnappings were dropped, even though in other trials they led to sentences of fifteen years in prison. The time that Viett spent in remand in the 1970s was deducted from the thirteen-year sentence she received, a very generous move by the federal prosecutors. To do six years for the (attempted) "murder of a police officer" is highly unusual considering the sentences usually handed down under such circumstances. Anyone who knows the prison system also knows what you have to do for benefits like furlough, day passes, and being housed in an open institution. You have to diligently do mind-numbing work for ten Deutschmark a day, keep your mouth shut, and develop a good relationship with the shrinks and social workers.

Inge Viett wrote her book during that time, behaving in exactly that manner. The manuscript was checked by the prison authorities before it went to the publisher. No surprise that it was written in a way that wouldn't jeopardize her release after six years. To say anything positive about the RAF was impossible, since her strategy of defense was based on the claim that she had already turned away from the RAF when she shot that police officer in France. This is of relevance, since active RAF members were always charged for "intent to kill" with subsequent life sentences, translating into an effective prison time of sixteen to twenty years. So, no matter what Inge Viett's real view on the RAF and the armed struggle was, she couldn't have written anything other than what she wrote. She doesn't explain with a single sentence how she was able to circumnavigate a life sentence. No word about the crown witness deal, about furlough, or about her early release.

If Inge Viett does have a critique of the RAF or the armed struggle, she should have explained it politically. But that doesn't happen; it's all personal. It gets nasty when, in her book, she criticizes her former comrades on a very personal level—comrades who have done much more time in prison than her, with some still doing time because they did not, contrary to her, make statements, and because they cannot or do not want to use the (bourgeois) public to defend themselves against the history presented in her book. She herself says that prison isn't the best place to write a book as there is no one who can help you remember things. So why did she do it then? She could have waited and talked to former comrades after her release. There was no pressing reason for writing the book in prison.

In the book, Inge Viett writes about her time in prison both in the 1970s and in the 1990s. If you compare the accounts, you understand what separates the Inge Viett of the 1970s from the Inge Viett of the 1990s. In the 1970s, she rebelled against the prison system. In the 1990s, she sees prison as the power controlling her life. During both periods, the most important thing is to get out. But she uses different methods: in the 1970s, a duplicate key; in the 1990s, the federal prosecutors. In the 1970s, she saw other political prisoners as "family"; in the 1990s, she writes about her "survival instincts." Politics are replaced by self-centeredness.

Excerpts from her book were sold for prepublication, together with the exclusive rights to an interview, to *Der Spiegel* and Spiegel TV for about 50,000 Deutschmark. (*Der Spiegel* threatened *junge Welt* and *taz* with six-digit fines should they ignore the contract and print their own interviews.) To use a medium like *Der Spiegel* for promotion, which essentially passes as the feds' own publishing organ, and to accept paid appearances throughout the country clearly contradict the principles of any left-wing approach to writing and debating history. Sell, sell—that's the capitalism that the urban guerrilla fought against, and that the German Democratic Republic, praised by Viett, wanted to overcome.

Hanni and Nanni Go Underground[7]
What follows is not a complete book review. The purpose is to illustrate how the general mechanisms of dropout memoirs manifest in Inge Viett's book.

First Example
Inge Viett mentions the RAF and the 2nd of June Movement innumerable times in her book, but the Revolutionary Cells or the Rote Zora not once. All of the legal supporters are absent from her account too. When she writes about things that would make the omissions obvious, she covers them up with lies and distortions.

We had good contact to the Revolutionary Cells and the Rote Zora at the time. With them disappearing, their positions disappear as well. They had a very different understanding of the guerrilla struggle than the RAF. In fact, they were very close to the old 2nd of June Movement. As such, they didn't fit into Inge Viett's narrative, since Viett joined the RAF. For her, alternatives only seem bothersome. And there's something else that might have played into it, namely the fact that the Revolutionary Cells, the

Rote Zora, and legal supporters were quickly dismissed by comrades who felt superior. Statements like "You can't take them seriously" or "They don't *really* dare to fight" were often heard. In any case, the omissions are so blatant that there must be a reason for them. They are no coincidence.

Second Example

Inge Viett uses disparaging comments about people whenever she tries to justify her actions without really being able to do it, considering the way she has chosen to tell the story today. While Viett criticizes the RAF for pathologizing people, recalling herself as a target, she shamelessly does the same with respect to former comrades. There's jealousy, competition, and censorship, right out of Hanni and Nanni.

The example Nada: When describing the November 1977 Palmers kidnapping in Vienna, which gave the 2nd of June Movement almost 5 million Deutschmark, the comrade "Nada" is mentioned. (She was one of the prisoners liberated during the Lorenz kidnapping and passed away two years ago from cancer.) The Palmers kidnapping had a few political shortcomings. For example, young Austrian anti-imperialists had been recruited for an action they weren't prepared for, in the end making statements and disappearing in prison for years despite them. It was bitter. Viett, however, seems to know exactly who was to blame. She writes: "Nada fell in love with a Vienna comrade, and he was included in our action way too fast." The truth is that the Austrians had been approached by Viett, because she had heard them arguing for a "new anti-imperialist line" in tune with Viett's views. The people preparing for the Palmers kidnapping in Berlin only got to know the Austrians when they already were fully included. Inge Viett uses a "Nada in love" to dodge her own responsibility.

The example Biene: A pretty brutal example for resentment and late retaliation is the description of "Biene," easily identifiable as Juliane Plambeck, who died in a car accident in 1980. Viett writes about her: "Biene was always indecisive, whether it concerned political or practical questions. She could only make decisions under pressure, even when it came to the most trivial things. . . . Her closet was full of clothes, because her indecisiveness led to her buying everything in various sizes and colors. . . . She had always been deeply opposed to the RAF . . . but when she was more lost than ever, she quickly joined the RAF, since it appeared strong and steadfast. . . . She had fallen in love with Christian."

In other words, "Biene" was a nonpolitical, opportunistic twat. A few pages later, Viett doubles down. About the RAF's suspicion that there "was competition, with Biene as the second in command being oppressed by me," Viett writes: "Biene was much too indecisive and phlegmatic for taking on the responsibility for the group's direction. . . . Quietly, I began to despise her." Yes, quietly. We must assume that Viett never said this to Biene when she was still alive. But twenty years later, all readers finally get to know the truth about Juliane Plambeck. She was too weak, no competition for Inge Viett. It's appalling.

The example Kowalski: When the name first appeared in the book, I didn't think it could refer to myself. After all, I didn't meet Viett, as she claims, for the first time in Vienna in late 1977, but in July 1976 after her escape from the women's prison at Lehrter Straße. For weeks, we shared a cramped living space. During that time, the decision was made for me to transfer from legal supporter to the underground. We had a lot of contact until early 1978. State prosecutors saw us not only involved in the Palmers kidnapping together but also in a number of bank robberies.

I joined the 2nd of June Movement as a supporter in 1975–76, at a time when the group had suffered harsh setbacks. But it still stood for a social-revolutionary practice. The "new anti-imperialist line" that would later lead to the RAF didn't exist yet.

I was also very friendly with the Revolutionary Cells. Around the time of the Lehrter Straße escape, my apartment was searched, as I was accused of distributing *Revolutionärer Zorn* (Revolutionary fury), the Revolutionary Cells' newspaper. Later, when I met a Revolutionary Cells member as a 2nd of June representative under very conspiratorial circumstances, we had a good laugh when we realized that we knew each other from the legal scene and had, in fact, run into each other just the day before.

At times, the collaboration between the 2nd of June Movement and the Revolutionary Cells was close. In fall 1976, when the women who had escaped from Lehrter Straße had moved to the Middle East, we even prepared a common action, namely, the liberation of Till Meyer from the prison in Berlin-Tegel. Four people, of whom three are no longer with us, waited anxiously and well-armed at the outside wall, while a jammer neutralized the police radio. Yet an inmate heard the saw screeching, and it fucked everything up. We had put much work into the action and taken significant risks. It was supposed to be a follow-up to the Lehrter Straße escape. It wasn't so much about Till, but in Tegel, there was a chance to get someone out, while in Moabit, where the others were, there wasn't. At some point, someone—there aren't many options—volunteered to give details, including the names of the participants, to the Stasi. I saw the files years later.

As stated above, Inge Viett ignores the Revolutionary Cells and the Rote Zora completely in her book, although, in 1976–77, there was much discussion about whether we should join forces with them or the RAF. Inge Viett's stance was clear: no collaboration with the Revolutionary Cells. She didn't take them seriously, and she didn't like their texts.

Every time collaboration with other groups was discussed (RAF, Revolutionary Cells/Rote Zora, PFLP), the contradictions between the different "lines" in the underground came to the fore. (We weren't many, so often a "line" was represented by two or three people.) The same happened every time we planned an action. To carry out good actions was a strength of the 2nd of June Movement, but its weakness was not to have its own political direction. The RAF, the Revolutionary Cells, and the Rote Zora covered all the possible urban guerrilla concepts. The 2nd of June Movement had to search for its place and found itself adrift. Today, it is clear to see that, already in 1976, the 2nd of June Movement no longer had the strength to develop its own position and concept. Unity was makeshift, produced through carrying out actions that everyone—or at least most members—felt okay with; we agreed on the lowest common denominator. Of course, there were love affairs as well as personal animosities alongside the political mash-up, but this was always secondary to the politics. To use the personal relationships as an explanatory tool and present them to a broader public without the consent of the people involved can be left to the likes of Inge Viett.

We, the members of the 2nd of June Movement, made different experiences in our everyday lives, and the discussions we had caused tensions despite the common planning and carrying out of actions. Those who maintained contact with legal comrades in Berlin had, for example, a different view of airline hijackings than people like Inge Viett, who had spent much time in the Middle East with the PFLP and had lived in some foreign country without contact with the legal left in Germany. As she writes herself, she lived a very different life in those places.

There were important discussions at the time about a particular question that Inge Viett writes nothing about. Others remember it very well: the planning of an airline hijacking together with a Palestinian group. It could have become the 2nd of June Movement's Entebbe. Luckily, it never came to that action, even though a small circle, including Viett, wanted to go ahead with it despite explicit objection by a person she now calls Kowalski. (In the original manuscript, something about this must have been included, which a note at the end of the book reveals. It is clear that the note ought to have been removed, as it doesn't refer to anything in the main text.) This was the time when the 2nd of June Movement should have split. In hindsight, it was a mistake that it didn't.

In fall 1977, the *Landshut* hijacking to Mogadishu led to new discussions about airline hijackings and whether they could be justified, but we never discussed these things properly. We probably felt that such a discussion would bring unbridgeable differences to the surface, and no one wanted to face the consequences. The members living underground only had meetings every other month or so. Most of the discussions happened in smaller groups that had little contact with one another. After Stammheim, there was also the question of whether the RAF hadn't suffered too many setbacks to make future collaboration feasible.[8] Some disagreed. In late 1977, legal comrades in Berlin heavily criticized airline hijackings, calling for the abandonment of the 2nd of June's anti-imperialist line. They were right. Our infrastructure was weakened. To save it, a new strategy was needed.

Instead of having the discussions that we should have had, and instead of developing a new strategy, an action was supposed to patch up the political differences once again. (Money was no longer an issue after the Palmers kidnapping.) For quite some time, we had been considering liberating all of the six 2nd of June members imprisoned in Moabit during yard time. The action would have required the involvement of pretty much everyone in the underground, and it would have probably led to a firefight with the guards on the watchtower and the cops descending on the scene. The risk stood in no proportion to the likelihood of success, and the action was called off. Meyer's liberation later was the small-scale version of this, since according to the intelligence we had, the cells where the prisoners met with the lawyers were a weak spot.

There were differences in our group with regard to whether the Meyer action was doable or not. There were also differences in assessing our infrastructure's strength in light of the large-scale manhunt that we had to expect after it. Finally, there were discussions about doing something other than liberating prisoners, to counter the prevailing image of the "liberate-the-guerrilla guerrilla." That the commando that claimed Meyer's liberation called itself "Nabil Harb Commando," after a Palestinian shot dead in Mogadishu, was a clear nod to the *Landshut* hijacking. Viett says nothing about it in her book.

During the discussions about whether it was worth risking the remaining presence in Berlin for Meyer's liberation, it was clear that the views of the group members living abroad differed from those who still wanted to work with the legal left in Berlin and the Revolutionary Cells. After some 2nd of June members who Viett doesn't bother to mention had been imprisoned, it was the underground member who she calls Kowalski who, together with some legal comrades not mentioned by Viett either, stood for the "Berlin line." But too half-heartedly, too late, and too inconsistently. A split was, as already stated, long overdue, and the rift became crystal-clear during discussions about the odds of success and the meaning of the Meyer liberation. When Viett offers her readers a relationship drama that caused political differences and a split, she is lying. The accusation of "cowardice," constructed after the fact in a vulgar psychological manner to satisfy the audience, serves only to dismiss criticism, using the time-tested accusation that the critics "simply didn't want to fight."

People who have held their ground in prison for many years don't have to feel ashamed when they admit to fear in certain situations. But no one opted out of the Meyer action because of fear. We were all pretty fearless back then. You learn to control fear when you've been through a number of actions and had close calls with the cops, which, after two years underground, you inevitably had. Feelings of fear were also repressed by the silly illusion that you might be giving your life in a more or less meaningful way to the revolution. We also repressed the possibilities of many years in prison or serious injury.

The one who Viett calls Kowalski left the 2nd of June Movement, that is true. But he didn't leave alone; he left together with some of the few remaining legal comrades, none of whom was a dropout but all of whom wanted to engage in a different kind of politics. (State security and police later alleged that I and some unknown others were involved in actions in spring 1978 such as the kneecapping of a court-imposed lawyer in the Lorenz trial, an action later claimed by the Revolutionary Cells. Five years later, the Revolutionary Cells and the Rote Zora did a few actions in support of a hunger strike in the Bielefeld high-security unit, calling me a "friend and comrade.")

I was captured a week after the Meyer liberation, as I was trying to get into a car that the Nabil Harb Commando had left me. The authorities were on it, and a special task force was waiting for me. Two mistakes at once: I wasn't told the car was hot, and I should have double-checked. For the first mistake, I never received an explanation, and there is none in Inge Viett's book either. Because of this car, I later received thirteen years for the liberation of Meyer. I never said anything about it, because I wasn't up for an "It wasn't me!" defense. Plus, the Palmers kidnapping and a few bank robberies were enough for the fifteen years I got anyway.

In Viett's book, the one she calls Kowalski is suspected of having stolen a million Deutschmark from the Palmers money. On the next page, she reveals that the group hadn't been searching properly, eventually finding the money buried in the woods a second time. I've heard the story about me stealing the money more than once. It went around in 1978. The denunciation even made its way into prison via a kite—RAF prisoners received vague warnings about me. Such a "There's no smoke without fire" denunciation can drive you nuts in prison. You're enraged, as you're not confronted with the accusation directly, it's just rumors and no facts. And you can never catch it; it's sly like a stray dog that years later still pisses in your boots. I still don't know how many people were told at the time ("clandestinely") that I had stolen money from comrades, and there might be some who still believe I did. When the money had been found, no one, according to my knowledge, deemed it necessary to do anything about the rumor that had been set loose. Now, Inge Viett has done it—twenty years later. Should I be grateful for that?

I have spent more than fifteen years in prison, a time done until the very last day in my own cell without any privileges. Furlough? Forget it! I rejected each single offer from the police and the courts. Anyone who cares can try to imagine what it feels like to now be ridiculed in a book by someone like Inge Viett, who, during that time, enjoyed eight good years in freedom in East Germany and never did more than a few years behind bars due to a crown witness deal. If you call someone a "deserter" in 1978 for no other reason than the person choosing a different political approach, and if you yourself leave the armed struggle entirely four years later, you should be more concerned about your own personal and political integrity than that of others.

Till and the Detectives

One shouldn't really say anything about crime novels like Till Meyer's *Staatsfeind* (Enemy of the state), where you find phrases like "the wedding night took place on a prison toilet" or "suddenly the machine gun let loose." One thing, however, is typical of dropout memoirs: in renouncing your past, you can either gloss over things, like Inge Viett, or you can cheat, like Till Meyer. When he addresses my being transferred from the Moabit high-security unit, he shifts years and incidents. He writes that I had "asked to be transferred to West Germany" and that he "shed no tears" about it (tough fellow). He adds that he himself, Ralf, and Ronnie remained in the unit. Allegedly, we had called him a "pig" and a "traitor." All nonsense. The truth is that, in mid-1982, Berlin's justice senator sent people to our unit announcing that Till, Ralf, Ronnie, and I would soon be transferred to West Germany if we remained unwilling to discuss a "different prison regime." I didn't go to the meeting. Ralf and Ronnie did, but refused to say anything political. Till, on the other hand, denounced the armed struggle behind our back and distanced himself from his small prison team. He wanted under no circumstances to be transferred to West Germany. True, we were already annoyed by the Stalin images in his cell and the constant watching of East German television, and we found his argument that the East German nuclear power plants were safe because they were serving the people to be tragicomic, but we hadn't thought of him as a traitor. When, after his "conversations" with the justice senator stooges, I told him bluntly that we had already parted ways long ago and that he should stop lying to us, he threw a fit before disappearing into his cell never to be seen again. A few days later, he distanced himself from us publicly in the *taz* and the *Tagesspiegel* (August 4, 1982), as demanded by the justice senator. Till's reward was to be moved into general population on August 27, 1982. Later, he got an early release. Ralf, Ronnie, and I remained another year in the special unit. Through a hunger strike and negotiations, Ralf and Ronnie were, after much back and forth, allowed to leave the unit during the day to work in general population. I did not want to do that, and since I now would have been in the unit by myself all day, I refrained from taking legal action against a transfer that the justice senate decided on. So, in late June 1983 (see *taz*, June 29, 1983), I was transferred to West Germany, where I landed in the new Bielefeld high-security unit, with instant trouble awaiting. Ralf and Ronnie left the Moabit unit for good in August 1983.

That Till Meyer has not many things, and certainly no good things, to say about me in his book is a result of the circumstances: the risk taken for him in the failed Tegel action of 1976; the rejection of the action to get him out in 1978; and the fact that, in 1980, when we met in the same unit, he hardly talked to me as a member of the "other faction."[9] Later, he was released after two-thirds of his sentence, while I remained behind bars—ironically, sentenced, among other things, for his liberation. Yes, it's hard to be chummy under these circumstances.

2002: Forward to Not Forgetting!

Dropout memoirs only find a place within the left because there are no better accounts of our history. It's up to the ones who haven't distanced themselves from their past to present a comprehensive account. The two old *Der Blues* volumes or the small book by Ralf Reinders and Ronnie Fritzsch is not enough.[10] One is too old, one is too short, and they both lack commentary. Sure, there are more important things to do, and nobody pursuing leftist politics wants to make digging through dusty files their main pursuit. Yet it would probably be better to dedicate a year of one's life to this than having to forever tolerate the crap presented by Viett and Meyer. We should manage before the thirty-fifth anniversary of June 2, 1967, or the twenty-fifth anniversary of the "German Autumn," shouldn't we?[11]

SERVANT OF MANY RULERS

(ca. 1997)

Norbert "Knofo" Kröcher

Circulated under the title "Diener vieler Herren" by various radical outlets in Berlin.

History is written, onward! Thirty years ago, on June 2, 1967, the cop Karl-Heinz Kurras shot dead Benno Ohnesorg. Today, Inge Viett allows Spiegel TV and Küppersbusch to look into her nostrils.[1] No weekend without seminars, meetings, and veterans' roundtables on *the topic*: APO, the radical left, and a republic that would never be the same after the whirlwind of the 1960s and 1970s (paraphrasing Rudi Dutschke). Those were the days!

Even the regular Joes chime in, people who were there, and people who would have wanted to be there. Ancient injuries and vanities reemerge from the depths and are thrown at the audience by a half dozen through open letters published in *Die Zeit* and other forums.[2] *Der Spiegel*, of all publications, exploits the events with particular zeal. Well, they changed the country more profoundly than any other after the war.

Needless to say, it's always the same dubious figures who appear when the attention turns to the (otherwise completely ignored) 2nd of June Movement: Bommi Baumann and Till Meyer. The first one a junkie, who made a run for Asia with money from the movement in the early 1970s ("before everything began"[3]), as well as a loudmouth and a scaredy-cat whose statements about 2nd of June Movement members fill dozens of pages in Stasi files (and not only there); the other, Till Meyer, no less dodgy, spying for the Stasi on the *taz*, where he worked as a volunteer, for years, and also on the few friends he still had after his release from prison.

History is written. You cannot leave the task to those who distort, falsify, and author memoirs full of lies. The coming generations have a right to proper information! This (re-)review of Till Meyer's book *Staatsfeind* (Enemy of the state) is meant to be a small step in the right direction. It will include a few remarks that reach beyond the book itself.

Meyer, go ahead and make a characteristic movement with your hand:[4] "Clicking away, I emptied the entire magazine of the pump action one last time—all of the cartridges passed through cleanly and flew out smoothly." All right!

Just a couple of pages later it's all clear: here, a true proletarian put pen to paper. He does not tire in assuring us of that. His proletarian family lived in a 150-square-meter apartment with four bedrooms in the nice Berlin suburb of Friedenau, and the proletarian dad works for the Nazi broadcasting company. (Cut. Air Force and Red Army make a quick appearance and those with the mercy of being born after the war can now be proletarians in school again for no other reason than being too dumb to be anything else.) To summarize: there are people who'd rather be someone else. They are prone to creating a legend about themselves based on wishful thinking. And there are also people who simply alter history to be the one they always wanted to be.

Let's move to the year 1972. Till Meyer founds the 2nd of June movement, and "Hedwig" invents the name.[5] Fascinating. Because, incidentally, that very year, the 2nd of June Movement is founded a second time, in the basement of a former Kreuzberg bakery. Present are the author of these lines, Ralf Reinders, Ina Siepmann, Gabriele Kröcher-Tiedemann, and some others—but there's no Meyer. Odd! Some time earlier, the author of these lines did indeed meet a Till Meyer. But it could not have been the Meyer from the book *Staatsfeind*—because that Meyer had already founded half of Berlin's radical movements by then, launching one antiauthoritarian initiative after the other, working hard at the grass roots, suffering, fighting, and even puffing on a joint on occasion. He had sat with Ulrike Meinhof on a panel, patted the knee of Rudi Dutschke, and engaged in deep conversation with Andreas Baader. So who was the Till Meyer I met at the outermost periphery of the antiauthoritarian youth revolt? (Which, today, in university seminars is often, and falsely, presented as a "student revolt.") A shady figure, more interested in quick

deals with equally shady figures than in what we understood as the "politics in the first person"?[6] Together with his companion P., he committed
cowardly robberies. They would gang up on elderly doorkeepers until
the poor fellows, sometimes badly bruised, surrendered a few bills that
Meyer would take to the brothel.

In 1975, a 2nd of June commando arrested the West Berlin CDU chairman Lorenz. After a few days, Lorenz was released in exchange for five
prisoners, who were flown to South Yemen. Meyer claims that he had
carried detailed plans of the Lorenz kidnapping in his pocket for years
before he finally met the characters who would pull the thing off under
his guidance. That these characters remember things very differently
can only be a result of their jealousy toward the mastermind Meyer—see,
for example, the interviews by Ralf Reinders and Ronald Fritzsch in the
Edition ID-Archiv book *Bewegung 2. Juni*.[7]

The truth is that Meyer is a genius of tactics and prophecy. We need
to introduce a few women who came into the 2nd of June Movement
fairly late. They had never been too impressed by the Hash Rebels, whom
they considered nonpolitical, and would have found a better home in
the Stalinist RAF. When the RAF was on the brink of demise in the late
1970s, they declared the 2nd of June Movement dissolved in true putschist,
Bolshevist tradition—or, to be precise, they said it was now a part of the
RAF.[8] At this moment, we saw Meyer at his best: he secretly agreed with
the statement but denied everything in front of his comrades. His genius
also showed in how he removed himself from the special unit in Moabit:
secret negotiations with the authorities, behind the backs of fellow prisoners. Well, of course it was their problem if they were too stupid for an
ingenious move of that sort.

The true Meyer does not understand the world, but he is best at
interpreting it: 1. Politics are shit. 2. Morality is shit. 3. Money doesn't
stink. 4. Power is hot. And if you don't have any power yourself, you gotta
get in bed with those who do, as their power might rub off on you. Then
you're no longer excluded from playing with the big guys! The logic? Rebel
against those at the top until you belong to them yourself.

Ladies and gentlemen, the true Meyer has now reached his cruis-
ing altitude: "One summer afternoon, there was a knock on the door of
my Kreuzberg apartment." Finally, *the firm* has come to see you![9] (There
are indications that there was contact between Meyer and the firm
long before.) Meyer's new friend complains: "Even the weather report

is anticommunist here." Meyer wastes no time: "Everyone knows that I have always defended the German Democratic Republic and the division of Germany." Such an opinion deserves special respect when held by a well-to-do man from the West, suffering under the weight of consumerism and free travel.

A side note by the author of these lines: When I came out of the can in 1984, the Stasi had a big file on me, but I never had problems traveling to and through East Germany (if we look past the thorough searches that the East German border police were known for). When Meyer was released from prison, everything changed, after I had told him what I thought of the pseudo-socialist joke of history called the German Democratic Republic. I was refused entry again and again, the last time on the very day that Schabowski brought down the wall by mistake.[10] Honi, soit qui mal y pense.[11]

"Enemy of the state number one"—nothing less will do for Meyer. The feds may be amused by the significance that this cheap criminal seemingly had for the Stasi, but it seems confirmed by the fact that his entire file was destroyed.[12] Apparently, the federal prosecutors dropped their preliminary proceedings against Meyer because of that. But how trustworthy does that make the Stasi turncoat, who, in 1992, convinced Meyer to out himself? And how trustworthy is his own detailed self-incrimination? Questions over questions . . .

Then everything happens really fast. Meyer is not in Berlin when the beloved wall comes down. He is on important secret business in Chile. "La caida del Muro en Berlin . . ." Meyer cries and wants to turn the tanks loose: "There will be a civil war! They won't hand over the state to the counterrevolution, will they? Where is the party?! Where is the youth organization?! They ought be on the streets and resist!" No wonder he ends up being depressed. "I lay in bed for weeks, very ill. I refused to listen to the news."

Meyer wouldn't be Meyer had he not eventually got over his depression and put on a new coat. With his old handler now in jail, the question was: Where would he find a new one? By that time, Meyer knows all about business. He benefits from a change in the editorial office of a well-known German news magazine.[13] Integrity is a fine thing, but the audience is demanding, and the competition by the tabloids strong. Dear reader, you can already guess the outcome: Meyer once again finds a place to be and makes a few bucks! His new handler pays all right. Meyer now lives near

Kurfürstendamm, wears the finest garments, and mixes with people of importance and influence. Our spies in Meyer's proletarian circles whisper under their breath: there are plenty of architects and lawyers! Back on deck is also the old handler, released from the imperialist dungeon: "Let's go West, Meyer, a real estate firm in Trier is waiting for us. There are tons of stupid farmers just waiting to be ripped off." Then, however, the old handler gets to know who had ratted on him and put him behind bars. To be continued . . .

JUNGE WELT INTERVIEW
(2003)

Andreas Thomas Vogel

The following interview was conducted by Thomas Seibert for the socialist daily *junge Welt*, published on June 27, 2003.

If you want to tell a story, you need a beginning. Once you choose a beginning, you place yourself within a web of stories and a mix of voices that sometimes contradict each other. You will speak here about the history of the urban guerrilla in Germany. Where do you begin and who will you contradict?

I have chosen not one but two beginnings. The first one takes us back to the years after 1968 when the urban guerrilla emerged. The second one goes back way further, which doesn't make it less important. Let us start with the second one: the origins of our armed struggle date back to the confrontation with fascism and the defeat of the KPD. We concluded that this must never happen in Germany again. The KPD was the biggest communist party outside of the Soviet Union, and it was basically wiped out overnight. Tens of thousands of cadres were arrested. Any immediate resistance, which would have been necessary, was prevented. Three million members waited for the signal from Berlin or Moscow to join an armed uprising. The signal never came. For us, forming an armed organization meant to build counterpower. It gave us the opportunity to act independently. Contrary to what's currently been said about us, and the New Left in general, we determined the form and the means of our struggle based on our reflections about fascism. This separated us from the DKP, its youth organization, and the K-groups, which focused on the political legacy of the KPD alone, apart from the historical circumstances of its dissolution.

On the other hand, the reflections about fascism among parts of today's Antifa and, especially, among the Antideutschen, leads to a completely ahistorical adaptation of the historical circumstances.[1] We always stressed the difference between the situation today and the situation of the 1930s—which brings me to our second starting point, which was determined by the international dimension of the uprisings that connected ours with the struggles of the South, but also with those in the so-called socialist camp, for example in Poland in 1970.[2] This was a very new situation. We drew conclusions from the workers' movement's history and connected them to the unprecedented possibilities of the current moment. It was very important for our development. It happened in the late 1960s and early 1970s, that means after 1968. We fought against the post-fascist remodeling of West Germany, against the bosses in the factories, authoritarianism in schools and universities. Had 1968 only been a students' movement, there wouldn't have been uprisings in every factory, every school, and every town.

Solidarity with anti-imperialist struggles was already important before you came. What was new, for example compared to the 1960s solidarity movement with Algeria?

Our politics were no longer reduced to solidarity. It was about a common struggle. People today see the anticolonial liberation movements as anachronistic, as attempts at national liberation carried by bourgeois forces. But that didn't concern us much. We had few illusions about those struggles. What was important was that the anti-imperialist struggles were part of an international movement that included struggles in the metropole—where, perhaps, some of the most crucial confrontations were to take place. That was the meaning of the famous Lin Biao quote about the villages encircling the towns on a global scale.[3] It summed up the political stakes of the left-wing forces worldwide. We related to one another, both spontaneously and in organized manners. We fought here in Germany, others fought in Vietnam or Latin America, and together we were fighting the same enemy. Us coming together was meant to show what was possible. If you assess these movements today, your opinion will depend on whether you look at what has been achieved or whether you take the historical effort of the people involved into perspective. In the former case, you write the history of the victors, denying that those who lost had any chance of winning at all. But it's only the defeat that makes the goals of the time illusionary. I still believe that the encircling of the towns by the villages was a possibility. My critique of the struggles at the time is based on that. History remains open.

You have spoken of two beginnings: one was the defeat of the communist movement by fascism, and the other the worldwide anti-imperialist struggle. How did you combine the two?

In our understanding of class struggle. The communist movement took the industrial working class to be the revolutionary subject. Class struggle was assumed to intensify continuously, even if it could be obstructed, disrupted, or temporarily halted. Fascism proved this belief to be untrue. And in the context of the worldwide revolutionary movements later on, the role of the industrial working class in the metropole was that of a "labor aristocracy." This led us to two convictions: one, the class is not given, it is formed in struggle; two, this struggle does not progress continuously, it needs to be rekindled again and again. And since we started from a position of weakness, both due to the history of fascism and our position in the international context, we wanted to first liberate the class struggle itself as a precondition for a fighting class being able to emerge. The arena for this was neither the factory nor the neighborhood but the struggle itself, which had to be led everywhere. Its subject was not the workers but everyone who was fighting, no matter where they came from. From the position of a radical minority, this meant to challenge the omnipotence of the state by demonstrating with exemplary actions that resistance was possible and that you had the chance of fighting and winning. We also wanted to make it clear that we were serious, both to the enemy and to the people we meant to bring to our side. The struggle demanded to bring our own subjectivity to the table, precisely because there was no "revolutionary subject," because you first had to create this subject. We thought that world revolution was possible. And, objectively, the transition to communism would have been possible in the metropole. We wanted to help create the subjective requirements for this.

Let us look at the critique levied against the guerrilla, and the undogmatic anti-imperialist left in general. You were criticized for espousing a strategy of escalation that intended to bring the state's

"fascist" characteristics to the fore. You were also criticized for anti-revisionist and antireformist rhetoric, which included comparing the US with the Third Reich and portraying West Germany as a "US colony."

Well, those critiques are all very German and very academic, because you judge a situation not from what is happening, but from what is written in certain texts, and in texts you'll always find things to criticize. Words are taken as the absolute, but you overlook that people were trying to think in new ways, that they wanted to transcend the conditions they lived in. When, in 1972, the RAF attacked US military facilities in Germany, facilities that were directly connected to the military engagement of the US in Vietnam, we were also dealing with the division of Germany, the rivalries between the East and the West, the relationship between the US and West Germany, and the limited sovereignty of West Germany. In the context of the imperialist power structure, we saw ourselves to be part of the anti-imperialist resistance, connected and organized with Latin American and Palestinian comrades. We exchanged experiences that were radically different, and we had to find terms for them. Of course, there was plenty that was wrong, slogans such as "USA-SA-SS," and the definition of West Germany as a "US colony." And, of course, we trivialized fascism when we spoke of things like "reform fascism." But a precise evaluation of the Third Reich was not our priority. We wanted to understand the current moment, for example the connection between capitalism and repressive modernization. It had started with fascism and defined our experience. I would no longer call high-security units "concentration camps," and I would no longer use "SS" as an abbreviation for state security. After a hundred leaflets, it became old.

What concerns antirevisionism and antireformism—characteristic for both the spontis and the K-groups—there is an important element besides the historical role of social democracy and party communism, namely, that the majority of the left openly supported capitalist modernization during the Brandt-Schmidt era, be it in the DKP or the SPD and the trade unions, and therefore in the state apparatus. This happened very fast; we couldn't keep up. You mentioned the escalation of conflict: we felt we needed to stop a fatal development, we weren't interested in correct academic language. But, true, you cannot separate one from the other, the terms form the practice that they are supposed to set into motion or defend.

Okay, let's talk about terms and practice, specifically, terms and violence.

Violence was and is foremost the violence of those in power. You find it unmediated in the apparatuses of repression, and mediated in the structures of exploitation. Our violence was violence against their violence; it was violence against imperialism and modernization. These tensions defined the 1970s, fueled by the state and the New Left. 1977 was the year of extreme escalation: from our side in the struggle for the prisoners, which led to defeat and many prisoners' deaths; from the state's side (and this is something ignored today, even by many on the left) in the systematic attack not only against the guerrilla but against the entire post-1968 emancipatory movement, which affected all levels of society.

When we started out, we were aware of our minority position and the weakness that this position entailed. That was a difference to most of the K-groups and the spontis, who thought they represented an imaginary workers' mass movement. With the escalation of 1977, it became clear that our position was more grounded in reality, that it had to be the foundation for formulating and developing radical politics. Over the next few years, the left split into two camps: on the one hand, tens of thousands supported the Green Party (some passively, some actively) and narrowed their political horizon to gradually participate in state power; on the other hand, there was a chance for the guerrilla groups, radical currents within the left, and militant social movements to unite.

In the 1980s, quite a few people saw this as a possibility, people who defended their political projects militantly, for example in the squatting movement. It was also clear that the strength of the antinuclear movement, the movement against the Startbahn West,[4] and the movement against armament came at least partly, or perhaps mainly, from their militancy. Here, we saw the fighting class whose emergence we had intended to instigate, people who rejected the ruling order. Violence played an important part in establishing counterpower and rejecting cooptation.

My historical perception differs. Of course, it is true that large parts of the left were rapidly co-opted after 1977 and that a radical rejection of the ruling order was increasingly reduced to the militant left. But I also felt there was self-isolation on the part of the radical left at the time, a denial of social reality, a process of "hardening" within the

guerrilla, and even within the autonomist movement. Hand in hand with this came a moralization of one's own behavior, which led to unattainable ambitions as well as judgmental bigotry. This went against my political intuitions. Oscillating between the two poles, violence seemed to be more of a catalyst, a reflex of defeat.

All of that was there, and terrible mistakes were made. There was also indifference, to the point of cruelty. But a common accusation is not true, namely, that the persecuted and oppressed become persecutors and oppressors themselves by using violence. This just doesn't apply to organized counterviolence, save perhaps individual incidents. But even if there are many of them, and even if they can't be excused as individual errors, it doesn't change the overall tendency. Our violence always came from a minority position, and in that sense it was different from the violence of the state, both in terms of quantity and, more important, in terms of quality. We weren't soldiers. This was proven in prison, where I found myself together with many other comrades. In prison, you have your back against the wall and the violence of the state apparatus is coming right at you. We saw prison as an arena of struggle, first and foremost together with the social prisoners, but also by struggling against the special conditions we were held in, and finally in connection with the struggles that were led against the prison system on the outside. These struggles were an important part of the social movements, where the guerrilla and militant politics could—at least potentially—win a mass base. It was mandatory for us to deny the state the possibility to rob our actions of their political content. This marked a historical rupture and continued into the second half of the 1980s. Before us, the communist left saw prison as a place detached from class struggle. We questioned the prison system and brought struggles on the inside and the outside together, with increasing support by thousands of people. This broadened the theoretical and practical rejection of the status quo.

Appearing "self-centered" and "hard" were consequences of our inability to adapt our violence to certain social developments. To return once more to the first half of the 1980s: at the time, the militant left was growing in connection with social movements turning more radical; at the same time, the ruling status quo was massively modernized, and there was a global imperialist offensive, foreseeing the defeat of the struggles in the South and the collapse of the Soviet bloc. I believe what would have been needed in that situation was a reconstitution of the radical left, recognizing these three moments. We, as well as the autonomists, but also the socialist, communist, and even the reformist left, would have had to reorientate ourselves. Yet there was no such new beginning. That resulted, on the one hand, in the hardening of those who stuck to the militant path, and, on the other hand, in the corruption—or at least resignation—of innumerable other leftists. We are talking about the majority of the 1968 generation, and also the 1977 generation.

What could a new beginning have looked like?
We reflected on the possibilities of connecting the guerrilla, the broad left, and radicalized social movements. We knew that this couldn't be done by the guerrilla alone, or by a party, or by the autonomist movement. Each of these limited approaches had to be overcome. When we found no proper way to do it, we tried to persevere, to carry on in some manner, hoping for a new possibility to present itself. But that never happened, and the perseverance became a goal in itself, which led to defeat. The longer you persevered, the hollower your positions and your analysis became.

It was all over when, during the triumph of capitalist modernization and imperialism in 1989 (at a time when social movements were basically nonexistent), people were made to believe that the state was opening up, that violence should be abandoned, and that we should enter into negotiations with the state in order to get out the prisoners that we hadn't been able to free by militant means. The militant left no longer had any prospects, and self-isolation and hardness became their characteristics. Just look at the "Germany, Never Again!" (*Nie wieder Deutschland!*) demonstration in Frankfurt in 1991. What was sold there as a new beginning was a declaration of bankruptcy. The left had nothing to offer and tried to turn that into a virtue. That was a decisive moment for us and the entire left. Not only were we no longer able to challenge the status quo, but we could no longer escape our defeat. The consequence was the building of barricades around our own marginalization. The Antideutschen turned the defeat into proof of their own superiority, which, in reality, meant to make peace with the status quo.

That brings us right to the present day. You mentioned the imperialist breakthrough of the late 1980s. Today, the US Army is in Baghdad, and tomorrow it might be in Damascus. Confronting this military machine with arms is, obviously, doomed to fail. Al-Qaeda has shown

that the US can be attacked. But there is nothing emancipatory about the violence of September 11.

Already during the Second Gulf War, so, in 1991, it became clear that the "protracted people's war" and the possibility of "villages encircling the towns" belonged to the past. The Iraqi assault on Kuwait was as reactionary as the Iraqi regime itself. It was not anti-imperialist. And the Soviet invasion of Afghanistan years earlier wasn't either. The killing of thousands of Iraqi soldiers by the US military was the cruel proof of a fundamental shift in international power relations and the use of violence in cementing the new order. Since then, the countries of the South and the East have become places of never-ending carnage and massacres. We can think of Rwanda, Angola, and the Congo, but also of Yugoslavia and Grozny. That's all part of the history of September 11, which marked a rupture. It is true that, on that day, the "South" had once again attacked the "North," and Al-Qaeda did disclose imperialism's vulnerability. But it was a scenario that had nothing to do with "villages" and "towns." Lin Biao's metaphor captured a historical moment in global class contradictions, but it had nothing to do with Al-Qaeda. September 11 proved this. The attack was reactionary, not least because it was indiscriminate, targeting an artificially homogenized "enemy." And that at a time when, finally, there was a new internationalist movement emerging in the metropole.

Global class contradictions aren't obsolete. They still form the departure point for emancipatory politics, but the fronts of the struggle have become much more complex today than they were during the end of the last century, because today we find the South in the North and the North in the South. This is why we still need to liberate the class struggle itself, but under entirely different conditions.

THE URBAN GUERRILLA AND CLASS STRUGGLE—REVISED
(2006)

Klaus Viehmann

Originally published as "Stadtguerilla und Klassenkampf—revised" in the 2006 book *Klassen und Kämpfe*, edited by the jour fixe initiative berlin.

———

The world in which the proletarian élite grows up is not academies but struggles in factories and unions. . . . The revolutionary career is not a series of banquets and a string of honorific titles, nor does it hold the promise of interesting research or professors' salaries. It is a passage toward the unknown, with misery, disgrace, ungratefulness and prison as its way stations. Only an almost superhuman belief illumines it, and merely talented people therefore choose it only rarely.

—Max Horkheimer[1]

Stop lounging around . . . counting up petty details. Build an effective distribution system. Forget about the cowardly shits, the bootlickers, the social workers, those who only attempt to curry favor, they are a lumpen mob. Figure out where the asylums are and the large families and the subproletariat and the women workers, those who are only waiting to give a kick in the teeth to those who deserve it. They will take the lead. . . . Develop the class struggle—Organize the proletariat—Start the armed struggle—Build the red army!

—RAF, "Build the Red Army [2]"[2]

I will start with some biographical remarks because the jour fixe initiative berlin considered this helpful to understand my analysis and to outline a biography that was anything but exotic during the 1970s.

My first "political action" was distributing leaflets against the NPD in 1969, when the party came close to entering parliament.[3] Nazi history has strongly shaped my generation's perception of Germany. I knew what kind of crime West Germany was built on, and I knew that many of those who were responsible were still around. In general, knowledge about fascism and the Holocaust was much, much more limited than it is today. In terms of antifascist literature, there was 1 percent of what exists today.

In 1972, I, like many other conscientious objectors, came to West Berlin, where you were exempt from military service because of the four-power agreement. During the following years, I got to know people from different factions of the left while working in collectively run bookstores. Private life—which was political, or at least it was supposed to be—focused on collective houses and communes. Universities I only got to know as places for political events, not as sites of learning. For me—and not only for me—much changed between the military coup in Chile in September 1973 and the death of RAF prisoner Holger Meins in November 1974. (Holger Meins died during a hunger strike against solitary confinement.)

In the early 1970s, our view of the urban guerrilla was based on "critical solidarity." Now, their writings and practice seemed to make much more sense. The overthrow of Allende had destroyed the last illusions about a "peaceful transition to socialism." On September 11, 1973, we had to watch how a reactionary army subjugated much larger, but unarmed, forces of the left. It was harsh.

The most important aspect of the Chilean example for me concerned self-defense, the "arming of the revolution." The reactions by some West German companies and politicians, who welcomed the coup, as well as my personal experiences with police repression at demonstrations and raids at the bookstores I worked at (the police were looking for illegal publications), also contributed to my radicalization.

In 1975, I made contact with the 2nd of June Movement. I belonged to the current that sympathized with the social-revolutionary wing of the Revolutionary Cells. We were opposed to the "anti-imperialist" attempts at collaboration with Palestinian groups and the RAF. Internal conflicts, brought to a head by the airline hijackings to Entebbe and Mogadishu, led to a split from the faction that joined the RAF in 1980.

After a sentence that came about somewhat randomly, I was imprisoned from 1978 to 1993. I certainly wasn't blessed with any "almost superhuman belief," referenced by Horkheimer in the quote above, but I was unwilling to engage with cops, the prison system, and the legal system. (Left-wing radicals on the outside do not engage with them either.) Instead, I dedicated much time to reading and writing. Pondering theory in prison is intellectual training. You do it to stay in touch with the real world, not to gather credit. That's one aspect. The other is that you're doing theory in prison under circumstances in which repression is a daily reality. This helps avoid fancy hairdos on a bald head of abstractions and mega-theories.

We were not allowed to have more than twenty books in our cell (which was searched daily), and we had highly educational contact with proletarians and migrants (at least once solitary confinement had been lifted). Theory in the sense of reflection both of yourself and the reality beyond the prison walls is necessary for survival. Otherwise, it's all too easy to drown in the prison routine. Theory prompts thorough and critical thinking. If your thinking remains to the left, it won't help you get an early release or better conditions on the inside. Opposition is costly, which is another reason for careful consideration. I had much time to think, but I could not find good reasons to abandon leftist convictions. This, however, doesn't mean that I wouldn't criticize certain things that I have said, thought, or done in the past.

When, after thirteen years, I was allowed to have a TV in my cell, the first images I saw were those of the racist pogrom of Rostock-Lichtenhagen.[4] Welcome to the new Germany!

The introductory quote by Max Horkheimer on revolutionary biographies recalls personal decisions that weren't in tune with bourgeois careers. At times, in places, and under circumstances different from ours today, you might be forced to make such decisions. They can also be demanded from people on the left—this is what the RAF did thirty-five years after the end of the Third Reich.

Urban guerrilla and class struggle are always bigger than academic discussions. One reason is that they raise the question of violence.

Revolutionary activists will sooner or later clash with a system that claims a monopoly on violence to secure its domination and defend the existing structures of property and exploitation.

Why should we reflect today on a practice of class struggle by an urban guerrilla that no longer exists, especially when the left has changed as much as it has? Perhaps because today's "antiglobalization movement" could learn from the experiences of the internationalism of the 1960s, '70s, and '80s, at least to avoid old mistakes. Or perhaps because the social cutbacks of recent years are a consequence of the class struggle from above, which makes the necessity of a radical class struggle from below obvious. Social movements must develop into social-revolutionary movements, an ambition of APO, or at least some of its currents.

If the only legacies of '68 are Joschka Fischer and RAF memorabilia, the history of an entire generation is wiped out.[5] It is no coincidence that people like to speak of '68 but not of APO. The most urgent issues for the so-called New Left were the remilitarization of West Germany, the persecution of communists, the Vietnam War, the colonial wars of France and Portugal (supported by West Germany), the exploitation of the Three Continents, the emergency laws passed by the "big coalition" of CDU/CSU and SPD, the professional bans, and not least the repressive sexual morals and culture. Within APO, a women's movement emerged that challenged blind spots and oppressive structures within the left, both in theory and practice. Not everyone in APO was happy with that.

None of this appears in the hegemonic way in which this history is written today. There are various examples: the Hamburg Institute for Social Research favors decontextualized, personalized, and often defamatory accounts about radical left networks and debates.[6] The "RAF exhibition" in the Berliner Kunstwerke painstakingly avoided any features that could have possibly been interpreted as sympathetic. During the planning phase, politicians objected to a question such as, "What ideas and ideals of the RAF stand the test of time and can't be dismissed as naive?" They were concerned the exhibition might glorify things and rekindle activities they believed to be dead. In the end, the only part of the exhibition that didn't consist of artwork consisted of magnified *Bild*, *Spiegel*, and *Stern* articles with dubious contents, and RAF texts crammed into dark display cabinets without commentary. Any analysis or evaluation of the era that could benefit left-wing politics has to be avoided.

The APO's Lines

There were certain strains, or "lines," in APO that influenced the different urban guerrilla groups. One was the internationalist line (which we'll soon talk about more), strongly influenced by the Vietnam War and the decolonization struggles in the "Third World." The APO current that focused on the traditional workforce in the factories, where they thought the revolutionary subject was based, found their way into the DKP, sometimes into the trade unions, and into a few Marxist-Leninist micro-parties that recycled class struggle concepts of the 1920s, usually a recipe for failure.

The new mass worker of the factories worked on assembly lines and often came from abroad. Italian and Spanish workers brought with them experiences of workplace struggles in their countries of origin. They became reference points for operaist factory groups, which I will return to.[7] Largely, class struggle had been abandoned in the factories, especially by skilled workers, after the persecution of communists and the layoffs (sometimes arrests) of entire strike committees during the 1950s, in the midst of the German economic miracle wonderland. Throughout the 1960s, there were wildcat strikes in which workers saw their demands met despite the lack of union support. But these strikes were limited to single factories and mainly directed against production quotas and the living conditions of the "guest workers" (*Gastarbeiter*), who were often housed in barracks. When, in 1967, employers cut bonuses, there were wildcat strikes in the mining, metal, and electronic industries, involving around two hundred thousand workers. But the relationship between APO and the working class was difficult, and compared to the 1960s in Italy or France (May '68 in Paris), there were much less experiences of common struggle. The cultural barriers and the political differences were huge.

Yet APO was not simply a student movement. Its antiauthoritarian and cultural aspects appealed to proletarian youth, to young workers and apprentices as well. In light of the relatively complacent and (apparently) pacified "social partner society" of West Germany,[8] one line in APO embraced the so-called marginal group strategy, which focused on the sub-proletarian and migrant milieus—milieus where the adherents of this line saw a stronger revolutionary potential. The sub-proletariat and the migrants had concrete interests to defend themselves against bosses, managers, and teachers. An apprentice's monthly wage was around eighty Deutschmark in 1970.

There was a movement of independent youth centers, with the Rauch House in West Berlin as its unofficial headquarters. This movement resonated with youth in the smallest and most isolated of towns. In the neighborhoods of the big cities, there were left-wing base groups trying to organize tenants. There was unrest in the disciplining institutions of post-fascist society: in schools, apprentice hostels, and prisons. The frequent prison revolts could only be contained by the 1972 prison reform.[9] From these circles there emerged in the following years quite a few urban guerrilla members. Proletarian youth had participated in APO demonstrations and—in contrast to the students less used to physical confrontation—successfully attacked and fought the police. For some, this confirmed the marginal group strategy.

Agit 883, at the time the most important radical left journal in West Berlin (of ninety issues, sixty were confiscated), had good contacts in the proletarian and sub-proletarian milieus of Kreuzberg and Neukölln, while the student left was concentrated near the technical university in Charlottenburg. On the front page of the May 20, 1969, edition of *Agit 883*, it said: "Some workers say, 'If the students didn't throw rocks, we could join them.' Some students say, 'If the workers joined us, we wouldn't have to throw rocks.'"

Certain SDS circles repeatedly discussed guerrilla strategies as a possibility after the killing of Benno Ohnesorg by a West Berlin police officer on June 2, 1967. Ohnesorg was shot dead during a protest against the visit of the Shah of Persia. The protesters had been dispersed under the command of a former SS officer. There were also discussions about organized violence on the left during the famous Vietnam Congress of February 1968, which served as a platform for the internationalist line.[10] This was half a year after Che Guevara's death in Bolivia. Peter Weiss, today known as the author of *The Aesthetics of Resistance*, stressed in his speech the importance of "organizing the resistance in the metropole."[11] He added: "Ideas have to become practical, and action must have consequences. Action must mean sabotage whenever possible. This requires personal commitment, and it will change our private political life. The resistance needs to become as broad as possible.... We must be willing to make sacrifices to build new international proletarian solidarity." Hans-Jürgen Krahl, one of the theoretical SDS figureheads,[12] propagated a "Destroy NATO" campaign: "Capitalism's internal contradictions must be turned into a qualitative broadening of the mass base, into a second front against imperialism in the metropole! . . . The struggle in the metropole cannot be based on an uncritical adaptation of the guerrilla strategy, yet the guerrilla strategy provides a model for uncompromising struggle."

Krahl demanded that "the organizational conditions be built to launch a struggle against the NATO bases in all of Western Europe, to take measures against the transport of American war materials to Vietnam, and to take action against facilities of the American armament industry in Western Europe." Rudi Dutschke said in his keynote speech: "We dare to attack American imperialism politically, but we do not yet dare to break with the apparatus of domination at home, to carry out militant actions against the centers of manipulation, for example the inhumane machinery of the Springer corporation. We do not yet dare to destroy the inhumane war machinery. Comrades! We don't have much time left. . . . We're on the right course, but we must act faster. Vietnam is coming closer, and in Greece the first units of the revolutionary liberation front are taking action."[13]

The Twists and Turns of the RAF . . .

After the liberation of Andreas Baader from prison, the RAF released a statement in June 1970 that became known as its founding document. It includes the quote used at the beginning of this article. One would think that the RAF statement would have been widely distributed. In truth, it was published on page 6 of an *Agit 883* issue (the RAF had sent the statement to the editors)—effectively, under "Miscellaneous," but at least together with two letters that welcomed the action, one from a "Berlin worker."

The first pages of that *Agit 883* issue focused on a militant protest outside the America House in Berlin, the repression against the Gauche prolétarienne in France,[14] and the "proletarian struggle against the bourgeoisie." The RAF statement criticizes nonchalantly "slimy leftists" and references social conflicts and proletarian problems to justify the armed struggle: "Without forming the Red Army, any conflict, any political work in the factory or in Wedding, in the Märkische Viertel, or in the Plötze [two working-class neighborhoods and a youth prison], as well as in the courtrooms, will turn into reformism, meaning: You are only enforcing better means of discipline, better means of intimidation, better means of exploitation. . . . Without building the Red Army, the pigs can do whatever they want, can continue to imprison, fire, impound, steal kids, intimidate, shoot, dominate."[15] (It becomes clear from these lines that quite a few of the RAF founding generation had worked in homes with foster children. Some of these children would later join the RAF.)

The same social-revolutionary line can be found in two subsequent RAF texts, "The Urban Guerrilla Concept" (April 1971) and "Serve the People: The Urban Guerrilla and Class Struggle" (1972).[16] Both texts address the social conditions in West Germany, in particular the situation of workers, youths, and marginal groups. The texts were released at a time when the first shootouts with the cops occurred, and when some RAF members were already in prison or dead. In other words, the confrontation with the security apparatus had taken on a new dimension. These experiences clearly impacted the development of the RAF, as we shall see soon. We will also see that the RAF increasingly veered toward an anti-imperialist line, no doubt related to some members visiting a Fatah camp in Jordan and having political experiences outside of the West German context. From this perspective, West Germany appeared not only as part of the metropole but, specifically, as an imperialist US subcenter, an ally in the exploitation of the Three Continents. To view West Germany as a class society with different political actors and interests was no longer the focus.

In "The Urban Guerrilla Concept" from April 1971, written roughly a year after the first RAF text was published in *Agit 883* and with a few months of illegal practice behind them, we find a remarkably apolitical explanation for abandoning the social-revolutionary practice heralded by the RAF only shortly before:

> Our original organizational concept implied a connection between the urban guerrilla and the work at the base. We wanted everyone to work in the neighborhoods, the factories, and the existing socialist groups, to influence the discussions taking place, to have some experience, to learn. It has become clear that that doesn't work. The degree to which the political police can monitor these groups, their meetings, their appointments, and the contents of their discussions is already so extensive that one has to stay away if one wants to escape this surveillance. It is impossible to combine the legal work with the illegal work.[17]

With such a technical-organizational explanation, where the enemy controls the situation, it is not surprising that it is no longer "the sub-proletariat and the women workers who are waiting to take the lead."[18]

Now there were two forms of practice: the urban guerrilla and the overall political struggle. "We are not saying that the organization of armed resistance groups can replace the legal proletarian organizations, that isolated actions can replace the class struggle, or that armed struggle can replace political work in the factories or neighborhoods. We are arguing that armed struggle is a necessary precondition for the latter to succeed and progress."[19]

The marginal group strategy was more or less abandoned as well: "[The students'] identity was not based on class struggle here, but rather on the knowledge that they were part of an international movement, that they were dealing with the same class enemy as the Viet Cong, the same paper tigers, the same pigs."[20] Contrary to the letter sent to *Agit 883* in June 1970, the RAF now presented an anti-imperialist line:

> If it is true that American imperialism is a paper tiger and can be defeated, and if struggles against it have erupted all over the world . . . then there is no reason to exclude or leave out any country or any region from the anti-imperialist struggle. . . . By supporting the US wars of aggression through development aid and military support, the Federal Republic of Germany profits from the exploitation of the Third World. . . . It is no less aggressive than US imperialism.[21]

In light of the RAF emerging as an illegal and armed group, "The Urban Guerrilla Concept" evokes for the first time a certain revolutionary romanticism: "'Victory means to accept the principle that life is not the most precious thing for a revolutionary' (Debray). . . . Cleaver said, 'Either you're part of the problem or you're part of the solution. There is nothing in between.'"[22]

A dualism of personal decision-making replaced the positioning of oneself in a historical setting, in the dialectics of class struggles. People who make that transition see themselves as different, and, quite likely, as more important, than people doing political work without risking their lives.

In the April 1972 text "Serve the People: The Urban Guerrilla and Class Struggle," the RAF, at first, describes capitalist normalcy in West Germany: "5,000 people die every year at their workplace. . . . 12,000 commit suicide. . . . 1,000 children are murdered."[23] Then they tie these numbers to the following observation: "The fact that the working class in West Germany and West Berlin can only think and act in the national context, while capital thinks and acts in a multinational context, is first and foremost an example of the splitting of the working class, as well as of . . . weakness."[24]

An extensive analysis of the 1971 strike in the chemical industry also ends in an internationalist vein: "The workers suffered a setback, because of the use of slave labor in Africa, Asia, and Latin America to put pressure on wages, because investments are used to get the labor force off their backs, and because concentration is used to secure economic and political mobility and flexibility."[25] The RAF does say in its text that "this terror [they mean the "search for terrorists" in the 1970s] is not directed against the RAF, but rather against the working class . . . the development of the coming class struggle."[26] However, in contrast to the statement sent to *Agit 883*, they see the subproletariat off: "The poor are not spontaneously and of their own accord revolutionary. They generally direct their aggression against themselves rather than against their oppressors. The objects of their aggression are usually people even poorer than them."[27]

When the proletarian struggles and the solidarity the RAF hoped for in 1970 didn't materialize, the RAF veered away from a class-struggle perspective in West Germany and turned to an anti-imperialist practice characterized by confrontation with the state apparatus. On May 14, 1972, it bombed the US Army headquarters in Frankfurt to protest the "US imperialist mine blockade of North Vietnam."[28] On May 16, 1972, three bombs were set off at the police headquarters in Augsburg and the State Office of Criminal Investigation in Munich to show "that they can't liquidate any of us without having to anticipate that we will strike back."[29] On May 20, 1972, a bombing targeting the federal high court judge Buddenberg in Karlsruhe failed. The attack was directed against "isolation [which is] institutionalized fascism in the justice system. It is the beginning of torture. . . . Freedom for the political prisoners!"[30] Only the communiqué in connection with the action against the Springer building in Hamburg on May 20, 1972, still includes references to class struggle in West Germany: "Our demands of Springer: that his newspapers stop the . . . hysteria . . . against working class solidarity actions such as strikes, and . . . that the Springer Press stop spreading lies about foreign workers here."[31] However, this particular action went haywire. Since the building wasn't cleared despite several warnings, the explosions of several bombs injured seventeen employees.

The anti-imperialist action against the European headquarters of the US Army in Heidelberg on May 25, 1972, was meant to delay further bombings of Vietnam. It probably did, because the central computer of the US Air Force was damaged. But the communiqué included a risky comparison: "In the last seven weeks, the American Air Force has dropped more bombs on Vietnam than were dropped on Germany and Japan during World War II. Apparently, millions of tons of explosives will still be dropped. . . . This is genocide, the slaughter of a people; this is 'the final solution'; this is Auschwitz. The people [note: "the people," not "the workers" or the class-struggle subjects of earlier RAF texts] of the Federal Republic of Germany don't support the security service in its search for those who attacked the US military facilities, because they want nothing to do with the crimes of American imperialism and the support it receives from the ruling class here; because they haven't forgotten Auschwitz, Dresden, and Hamburg; because they know that the bomb attacks against those who commit mass murder in Vietnam are just."[32] To arouse solidarity with the people of Vietnam by referencing "Auschwitz, Dresden, and Hamburg," and to equate the US bombings with the "final solution," was anything but proletarian internationalism. At least, such arguments, which are reminiscent of a 1965 *Konkret* column by Ulrike Meinhof, were no longer used thereafter.[33]

In November 1972, when almost the entire first generation of RAF members was in prison, the RAF released their last longer text for quite some time, "The Black September Action in Munich: Regarding the Strategy for Anti-imperialist Struggle."[34] The text strongly supported the anti-imperialist line, focusing on the Black September action against the Israeli Olympic team and making the government of West Germany responsible for the Fürstenfeldbruck massacre.[35] The text also includes a reckoning with the legal left in West Germany. The earlier references to the "marginal groups" as revolutionary subjects are basically gone.

. . . And Four Reasons for It

In my opinion, the RAF abandoned the social-revolutionary, class-struggle approach and turned to the anti-imperialism of a small, forceful, and vanguardist guerrilla organization because it wasn't able to combine illegal activities with a participation in the legal left. It was a decision tied to the reality of illegal activism, but it had far-reaching consequences for the RAF's theory and practice. It violated the rule that politics command the gun and not vice versa.

That was one reason for the RAF's turn. A second was that the state arresting and killing RAF members made the confrontation with the repressive apparatus a priority. In such a confrontation, class struggle and legal left-wing movements are of little significance.[36] A third reason was that the RAF understandably resorted to anti-imperialism when the revolutionary hopes for Germany didn't materialize. It was tempting to think that higher personal risk (struggle until death), more effective means (better logistics, better weapons), and an alliance with liberation movements in the Three Continents might encircle and weaken, perhaps even revolutionize, the imperialist metropole. Under these premises, internationally active, small, armed organizations that were often (and inevitably) tied to intelligence agencies (in the 1970s, the main example was the group around Wadie Haddad that had split from the Marxist PFLP[37]) were more eager to work with an urban guerrilla group from West Germany than a factory group or neighborhood committee, or even the Red Brigades of Italy, who stuck to a class-struggle perspective. They were much more responsive to an anti-imperialist line and relevant strategies, group structures, and enemies. Finally (a fourth reason for the RAF turn), it is true that class struggle without internationalism leads to nationalist narrow-mindedness. But internationalism without a social-revolutionary practice based in the class society of the country where you operate leads to the kind of anti-imperialism that uses a "friend versus foe" logic. As a consequence, it is easy to neglect the power structures and social contradictions in the metropole, which ought to be crucial reference points for left-wing theory and practice. Such an anti-imperialist world view, separating a "revolutionary Third World" from a "criminal First World," fits in with an indiscriminate struggle against the populations of the metropole, down to airline hijackings. The social-revolutionary line of the early RAF got buried under these consequences and developments.

Factory Guerrilla

Throughout the year of 1973, there were spontaneous wildcat strikes in at least three hundred workplaces across West Germany. About 275,000 workers were involved. They were mainly unskilled and migrant workers as well as women (both German and non-German). This marked a difference to the strikes of 1969. Apart from demands for higher wages and better working conditions, the striking workers also demanded longer holidays, a slower pace at the assembly lines, and the elimination of low-wage groups. Union leaderships often portrayed the strikers as "detrimental to union interests," calling on them to return to work.

During the strikes, there were factory occupations and, especially, sabotage at the assembly lines. Workplace security, together with police and right-wing unionists, sometimes interfered violently. It shouldn't be surprising even today that in such a context—proletarians ready to fight on the one hand, and a repressive reaction by capital on the other—militants entertained the idea of a social-revolutionary factory guerrilla, which would support one side and fight the other. Left-wing groups with an operaist orientation had entered the factories in the early 1970s, among them Revolutionärer Kampf (Revolutionary Struggle) in Frankfurt, the Proletarische Front (Proletarian Front) in Hamburg, and Arbeitersache (The Workers' Cause) in Munich. Together, they published the newspaper *Wir wollen alles* (We want everything), which reported on factory and housing struggles, neighborhood actions by migrants, and the armed struggle. It appeared for two or three years.[38]

How concrete the plans for a factory guerrilla became will not be addressed in this article. The approach was special in the context of guerrilla strategies. The idea was to sign up in a factory under a false name, to enter the personal milieu of the workers, and to develop an illegal social-revolutionary practice. The people discussing this saw revolutionary potential by looking beyond the skilled German worker, who was fighting for a bigger share of the capitalist cake rather than against wage labor. Studying the militant workplace struggles of the Italian operaists and the old American Wobblies (IWW) naturally tied in with discussing the urban guerrilla and class struggle. People also studied the early practice of the Red Brigades, since the Red Brigades had emerged in the factories, where they had also carried out their first actions.

During these discussions, a new understanding of class emerged, based on the "moral economy" of migrant workers rather than on the disciplined West German worker. The militants involved in the discussions thought that attacking the factory regime and the logic of profit and exploitation would pose a bigger challenge to capitalist normalcy than demands for a higher wage that didn't question the extortion of surplus value as such. The goal was a struggle against work. The assembly line was to be abolished, not "humanized." The struggle was to give birth to a new revolutionary subjectivity, hostile to work. The hope was that work refusal would drive capitalism into a crisis, with the polarization between increasingly repressive requirements for work and the refusal to go to work spawning revolutionary struggles in the factories—struggles of an entirely different quality than APO actions that had barely touched on capitalist production and ownership of the means of production. Outside of the factory, there were also actions, for example in Hamburg, where people demanded better living conditions for migrant workers, who were housed in barracks. Fences were dismantled and workplace security guards trying to interfere were beaten.

In the factory, a guerrilla practice would have focused on sabotage. It could have focused on the just-in-time production that was very new then. Just-in-time production is dependent on a precisely scheduled flow of deliveries of finished parts. Spreading out production sites over the entire country and even Europe required highly complicated logistics, and each interruption caused losses. (It is no wonder that the downing of pylons, which can lead to factory standstills, later became a crime under section 129a.)[39]

A factory guerrilla could have been the armed wing of the migrant and underprivileged workers. It could have centered on self-organization, not vanguardist ambitions. The militants would have been required to be present in the factories and work there (of course, as little as absolutely necessary). Why didn't much come of it? The attempt to form a factory guerrilla met the fate of the Red Brigades in Italy. Capital reacted quickly. Many of the most militant workers were laid off, often with the support of factory councils. The organization of labor changed too. Unruly factory departments were shut down or relocated, often abroad. Certain duties on the assembly line were automated under supervision of a few loyal skilled workers. The recruitment of migrant workers slowed down significantly. They were replaced by politically cautious Germans returning from abroad, so-called late repatriates (*Spätaussiedler*).[40]

After having been chased from the factories, the Red Brigades attacked the "heart of the state," that is, the political class and the organs of repression. The fledgling factory guerrilla in West Germany didn't take that step. It retreated in the mid-1970s, just like legal left-wing radicals in the factories. The newspaper *Wir wollen alles* stopped publication. Many leftists were laid off. Others preferred to take temporary jobs and secure their survival with student subsidies, unemployment money, welfare checks, or green-alternative cooperatives. The hopes that had been tied to entering the factories had not been fulfilled.

Backs Against the Wall?[41]

Workers have retreated following the struggles of recent years. The bosses' attack, which, at first, was primarily directed against migrant and young, unskilled German workers is now targeting the entire working class. . . . The summer of 1973 was a short summer of fresh air, of courage, and of hope for more humanity in the factories. For the bosses, it was a summer of panic, insecurity, and fear. That's why their response to the demands for slower assembly lines, less working hours, no wage grades, longer breaks, and longer vacation came swiftly and violently. . . .

German skilled workers don't experience the same pressure as their Turkish, Greek, Yugoslav, and Spanish colleagues, both men and women. The pressure the workers feel has many reasons: mass layoffs, raids, deportations, reduced child allowance, termination of apprenticeships, pressure in vocational schools, evictions of youth centers. Strongly affected are also those who are supposed to mediate between the exploited and the state: social workers have to deal with fewer rights, shorter contracts, transfers, and sackings, and there are professional bans for teachers and other public servants. Leftist groups working with minorities among the working class can also feel the heat. The "Winter Journey" (a nationwide wave of raids following the von Drenkmann assassination in 1974) was the largest police assault in West German history. The police raided one hundred homes and collectives. It was much more than just a demonstration of power. The raids meant to spread fear at the heart of the social resistance movements: in the factories, the immigrant ghettos, the youth centers, the prisons. . . .

It is clear that the first response, the apparent humanization of labor, provides a cover for the second, the enslavement of workers as industrial androids. The requirement to produce surplus value doesn't lead to the abolition of mass work but rather to its reconstruction. It may be that much mind-numbing assembly line piecework will disappear, but only to chain automated supervisors and workers, both responsible for several semiautomated machines, more strongly to the production line than ever before. . . . Should the assembly lines in West Germany cease to run smoothly, the bosses will either restructure them or relocate them to the European periphery and, in particular, to the most stable economic regions outside of Europe. . . .

The increasing pressure in the factories has an immediate impact on working-class neighborhoods. . . . Illegal immigrants are controlled, hunted—on their way to work, on public transport, or randomly on the street—and deported. Restricted immigration shall allow the state to regain control over the immigrant ghettos. . . . But not only immigrants are threatened. The bosses have made it clear to young German workers that they, too, can be sacked at any time given the ongoing restructuring of production. . . . Women workers, already at the bottom of the pile, are heavily affected by the restructuring of labor. In many factories, low-wage categories are reintroduced. (In some, they never disappeared, despite the struggles of recent years.) Progressive abortion laws are revoked by the legal mafia. The women's rebellion is being crushed, and everything is done to prevent an uprising by women workers. The overexploited sections of the working class are under siege, with the situation of the working class worsening overall. . . . The Schmidt-Genscher government dropped all ambitions for stronger government control of investments. The massive reduction in social policy has drastically expanded capitalism's room to maneuver . . . with the consequence of one and a half million people being unemployed. . . . West German employers are still the most powerful in Europe, able to control their employees better than anyone else. . . . With Schmidt, the axis Washington-Bonn has become a reality. For the US, Bonn has become the main ally in the extraction of Third World raw materials. By all means and for all purposes, West Germany acts today as an imperialist superpower. . . .

Where do we still find pockets of counterpower? Are new ones emerging? While the workers are put on the defensive, the left has fragmented into a thousand pieces. There are no more common evaluations of the class enemy. In light of petty factional quibbling, fear of armed actions, and discouraging experiences, many have retreated. The situation is depressing—as it almost always is when the class enemy has seized the initiative. . . . The antireformist left was splintered, weak, and only able to provide limited agitation during the workers' struggles of 1973. It could not take any major initiative, even though the undogmatic groups, neighborhood initiatives, Red and Black Aid organizations, and migrant groups—for example, the Spanish Center in Essen—made a bigger effort than the K-groups to connect with the migrants, workers, and proletarian youth. The problem wasn't so much a lack of contact between the social resistance movements and the antireformist tendencies, but rather the inability to create autonomous approaches to organizing that could have served as a basis for proletarian counterpower, enabling open and subversive resistance. To overcome this inability seems crucial for our attempts to develop the possibilities of real counterpower....

The RAF disregards the struggles of the most exploited: women, foreigners, and young German unskilled workers. Any practical attempt to involve militant proletarians in the armed struggle has been rejected by the RAF. Instead, the RAF comrades act as a revolutionary "secret service," looking only at the liberation movements of the Three Continents.... But in the summer of 1973, they should have engaged with a workers' resistance that was strong enough for anyone to notice....

During the student movement, another militant and eventually armed group emerged besides the RAF in a much less spectacular manner: the 2nd of June Movement. Contrary to the actions of the RAF, the actions of this group, based in West Berlin, are carried out by proletarian comrades. The support for them doesn't come from left-wing celebrities and the left bourgeoisie, but from their own social circles.... The 2nd of June Movement has learned that revolutionary force does not consist of a left "scene," but rather of the mass worker, the apprentice, the imprisoned prole, the rebellious woman in the factory and the neighborhood.... The current retreat of the left will only stop when an armed proletarian movement will make the social liberation of the exploited masses possible, regardless of the economic doctrines of the employers and the state.

There is a history of the armed mass line in the German working class. In 1920, the Red Ruhr Army, the partisan movement in central Germany, and armed farmers in Mecklenburg brought large areas under their control. The 1921 uprising in central Germany, as well as the 1923 uprising in Hamburg by an urban guerrilla group, are not simply "heroic battle stories." They are the living memory of old workers.... In 1943–44, not even public executions could prevent the armed resistance by forced laborers from different countries and young German proletarians. The violent rebellion spread widely. In Berlin, there were illegal groups of the KPD; in Hamburg, there was the Swing Youth (Swing-Jugend); in Cologne, there were the Edelweiss Pirates (Edelweißpiraten). They all chased Nazis out of bombed areas and working-class neighborhoods, and sometimes,

THE URBAN GUERRILLA AND CLASS STRUGGLE—REVISED

when they could get their hands on a machine gun, they killed them. They liberated city blocks and were engaged in bitter battles with SS and Gestapo units. . . . There is a historical tradition behind the activities of today's armed groups engaged in struggles for revolutionary workers' power and the destruction of the capitalist system. We are facing two options: either the armed mass line will become resilient enough to survive and continue its attacks, or West Germany will once again become a center of repression, this time enforcing the social massacre against the international workers' movement and the Third World liberation movements together with the USA.

The Revolutionary Cells and the Rote Zora as Social Revolutionaries

That the RAF's "anti-imperialist turn" wasn't inevitable is indicated by the history of the Revolutionary Cells and the Rote Zora, which unfolded differently. During their existence, they repeatedly carried out actions to support and radicalize social struggles. Contrary to the RAF, the Revolutionary Cells and the Rote Zora took a turn from an anti-imperialist to a social-revolutionary perspective in the 1980s. It helped that their members were living legally in West Germany and were not subjected to the same constraints as the members of the RAF. This means that they could move from anti-imperialism and an illegal infrastructure to social-revolutionary actions based on a kind of semi-legality. They were also fortunate in being a lesser target of state repression and media slander than the RAF, and in not being forced to make the question of prisoners and prison conditions a priority.

What follows are a few examples to illustrate the Revolutionary Cells' and Rote Zora's urban guerrilla and class struggle practice: In January 1980, a "Revolutionary Cell of the Unemployed" bombed the federal employment office in Nuremberg. The reasons given were the "daily experiences of the unemployed," the long time of processing applications for unemployment money, and the "reasonability provision" (*Zumutbarkeitsklausel*) introduced at the time, which allowed employment agents to assign jobs to people despite long commutes and overqualification. For the Revolutionary Cells, the acceptance of "federally appointed jobs at low wages without holiday and Christmas benefits" and the "prioritizing of laying off women, foreigners, and the elderly" proved that the federal employment office supported the "rationalization of capital." They called the office "a bastion of the modern slave trade" and demanded "production with less labor and more free time for everyone" as well as "self-determined decisions of what to produce and where and how." This still sounds relevant, doesn't it?

In 1985, there were no less than three internationalist Revolutionary Cells actions in connection with the miners' strike in the UK, where the National Union of Mineworkers had been on strike for over a year to protest the mass layoffs and the neoliberal policies of Margaret Thatcher's government. In the Revolutionary Cells' communiqué, it said: "The courage and the commitment of the people on the picket lines and the tenacity and the strength of the women in the solidarity committees have demonstrated what class consciousness and solidarity are capable of when they are more than hot air." The actions targeted the employers' association Ruhrbergbau (literally, Mining in the Ruhr Valley) because it had increased coal exports to England during the time of the strike by 1,000 percent; a shipping agency that had transported the coal; and the headquarters of the miners' union IG Bergbau und Energie, because it had done its best to sabotage the UK strike in order to ruin the National Union of Mineworkers, which saw itself as a class organization.

There were many notable Rote Zora actions related to the topic of "the urban guerrilla and the class struggle," for example an attack on the data center of Creditreform in Neuss, which contained Europe's largest database of credit and rental information. The database stored information about any individual that had ever been in contact with banks or landlords, facilitating debt collection when people were unable to make payments. Credit reform served as a henchman in the capitalist war against the poor. In June 1987, nine attacks on shops of the clothing chain Adler were carried out almost simultaneously. The cause was an April 1987 strike of women workers in the South Korean textile factory Flair Fashion, owned by Adler. The 1,600 employees (about 90 percent women) fought for higher wages and better working conditions. The Adler management, all Germans, called on the military police and goon squads to suppress the uprising. The women at Flair Fashion worked up to twelve hours a day, six days a week, for less than fifty cents an hour, with no pay for overtime. The company's boss, whose name was indeed Fürchtegott Adler,[42] once said: "Without the black-haired Koreans with their almond-shaped eyes, the fast rise of the Adler company would not have been possible."

The attacks were also directed against the relocation of production to South Korea, which had made thousands of women workers in West Germany unemployed. Furthermore, the women workers in Adler's stores only received temporary contracts, often below the 430 Deutschmark poverty line. The Rote Zora wrote: "The class compromise in the metropole has become fragile but is maintained by cheap consumer products at the cost of the people in the Three Continents. In West Germany, too, women are subjected to double exploitation in the form of housework and wage labor." In the spirit of the internationalist class struggle, they added: "Capitalist accumulation turns all human activities, expressions, and material conditions for survival into commodities. Those responsible are here among us! The gender division of labor, and the exploitation and violence women are subjected to, are part of the patriarchal system of domination, without which imperialism both in the Three Continents and in the metropole cannot be understood. Women's collective experience of struggle transcends national borders!"

And Now?

So much for the history of the urban guerrilla and the class struggle. Relevant as ever is the call to resist work! Yet strategies of class struggle against the global post-Fordist offensive and the Agenda 2010 need to be more complex than thirty years ago.[43] A new class analysis must merge with analyses of racism and gender relations as well as their intersections.[44] The old Marxist concept of labor needs to be reexamined. We also require a new left analysis of the role of the nation-state and international relations and the function and strategies of the bourgeoisie. The bourgeoisie is an enemy in the social-revolutionary struggle that remains oddly obscure behind the protest images from Seattle or Genoa.[45]

Who, and what, can be a strong force of resistance today? What kind of subjectivity is possible under, and against, commercialization? Who, and what, is able to lead today's resistance movements? How can militants on the left account for the social realities of those who engage in struggle? This is a crucial question for the sustainability of left-wing organizing. In recent years, "the left" has been increasingly proletarianized. But issues such as consumption and education remain more important for many left-wing activists than their position in the production process, which was once at the center of class analysis. Misery today is more material and tangible (not "only" psychological); it is a concrete form of social exclusion and of "not being valued."

The struggle against work will probably redefine the old rascal of the workers' movement, sabotage. The highly complex networks of production and communication, and the possibilities of resistance they offer for relatively small groups, can interrupt current strategies of commercialization more effectively than strikes could thirty years ago.

All considered, the odds of left-wing resistance have increased. In the resistance against the class struggle from above, conditions that have been deemed unchangeable are changing. Things in motion are always better than fossils. We will see whether concepts once declared dead will gain new significance.

NOTES

Introduction: The Blues

1   From a 2005 letter by Karl Heinz Roth to the organizers of a teach-in on the thir-tieth anniversary of the Peter Lorenz kidnapping. Roth declined to participate due to disagreements about the focus of the meeting. Quoted from https://www. bewegung.nostate.net/absagen.html.

2   Ilija Trojanow, *Macht und Widerstand* (Frankfurt/Main: Fischer, 2013), 43–44.

3   The term *Rhine capitalism* (*Rheinischer Kapitalismus*) refers both to the West German capital Bonn, situated along the Rhine River, and the SPD party plat-form of 1959, which was passed in the Bonn suburb of Bad Godesberg. The term signifies the "social market economy" characteristic for West Germany in the 1960s.

4   The "Springer press" refers to the publications of the conservative Springer publishing empire, whose most notorious newspaper is the tabloid *Bild*.

5   Panel discussion in the Auditorium Maximum, Technical University Berlin, May 3, 1996. Quoted from https://haschrebellen.de/optimismus-von-damals.

6   J. Smith and André Moncourt, eds. and trans., *The Red Army Faction: A Documentary History*, vol. 1, *Projectiles for the People* (PM Press: Oakland, 2009), 82.

7   The Tupamaros were founded as a liberation movement in Uruguay in the 1960s and soon developed into an underground guerrilla. Over the years, it split into various factions, with one of the most influential being part of the left-wing party platform Broad Front today. José Mujica (born 1935), president of Uruguay from 2010 to 2015, was a prominent Tupamaros member and longtime prisoner during the 1973–85 military regime.

8   Horst Rieck (born 1941) wrote for several German newspapers and magazines. Baumann, von Rauch, and Weisbecker had falsely suspected him to be the author of a *Quick* magazine piece criticizing the Tupamaros West Berlin. Rieck later gained fame as the journalist behind the bestseller *Christiane F.: Wir Kinder vom Bahnhof Zoo* (Christiane F.: We children from the zoo railway station, 1978), a biographical account of a teenage heroin addict.

9   Angelika Goder (born 1950) was arrested as a 2nd of June Movement member in

1978 and sentenced to fifteen years in prison. In 1980, she joined the 2nd of June faction that united with the RAF (see the chapter "Dissolution (or Not)" in this volume). The quoted statement is from a 2001 interview in *Flensburger Hefte*.

10   Danyluk quotes from a text titled "Widerstand gegen die Staatsgewalt. Erfahrungen aus der Bewegung 2. Juni" (Resistance against state violence: Experiences from the 2nd of June Movement), included in Michael Sontheimer and Otto Kallscheuer (eds.), *Einschüsse* (Berlin: Rotbuch, 1987).

11   Smith and Moncourt, *Red Army Faction*, vol. 1, 490.

12   Smith and Moncourt, *Red Army Faction*, vol. 1, 494.

13   J. Smith and André Moncourt, eds. and trans., *The Red Army Faction: A Documentary History*, vol. 2, *Dancing with Imperialism* (Oakland: PM Press, 2013), 232.

14   Inge Viett, *Nie war ich furchtloser* (Hamburg: Nautilus, 1997). See the preface in this volume and Klaus Viehmann's text "What Was Not Written."

15   "Autonomist movement" and "autonomists" are translations for the *autonome Bewegung*/the *Autonomen*, a militant, radical-left, extraparliamentary counterculture blending anarchist, left communist, and social-revolutionary ideas. Autonomists were very influential in the German left throughout the 1980s. See the book *Fire and Flames: A History of the German Autonomist Movement* (Oakland: PM Press, 2012).

16   Quoted from *Die Früchte des Zorns. Texte und Materialien zur Geschichte der Revolutionären Zellen und der Roten Zora*, vol. 1 (Berlin/Amsterdam: Edition ID-Archiv, 1993), 35.

From the Hash Rebels to the 2nd of June Movement

1   Residents of West Berlin were exempted from military service.

2   Rotaprint was a well-known offset printing press manufacturer in West Berlin.

3   *Gammler* means "bum." The subculture emerging around the term was based on a conscious rejection of wage labor.

4   The Kaiser Wilhelm Memorial Church (in German usually shortened to *Gedächtniskirche*) in Berlin-Charlottenburg was severely damaged during World War II. It has never been fully restored and serves as a memorial for the atrocities brought by the war. It is popular both as a tourist site and a gathering place.

5   Alfred "Shorty" Mährländer (1942–2023) and Hans-Peter "Knolle" Knoll (born 1949) were Tupamaros West Berlin members.

6   The Sozialistische Einheitspartei Westberlins (SEW) was a West Berlin sister party to the SED, which ruled in East Germany.

7   *Roter Punkt* (red spot) actions targeted increases in public transit fares. A red spot on private vehicles indicated that the drivers were willing to provide lifts to passengers during public transit boycotts.

8   The Rote Garde (Red Guard) was the youth organization of the pro-Albanian Kommunistische Partei Deutschlands/Marxisten-Leninisten (KPD/ML), one of the era's notorious "K-groups" (*K* for *Kommunismus*; see also "Backs Against the Wall," note 7).

9   Bernhard "Bernie" Braun (1946–2009) later joined the RAF; he was arrested in 1972 and sentenced to twelve years in prison.

10   The Young Pioneers (Jungen Pioniere) was the SED's children's organization.

11   In the communist bloc, including East Germany, International Children's Day was celebrated with numerous events on June 1.

12 At the Battle of Tegeler Weg, a mixed crowd of SDS members, APO activists, proletarian youth, and rockers engaged in violent confrontations with the police on November 4, 1968. The reason was a trial against the left-wing lawyer and later RAF member Horst Mahler. The "battle" is regarded as a pivotal moment for the radicalization of the German left. For Horst Mahler, see "Protagonists" in this volume.

13 Bolle was a West Berlin supermarket chain.

14 Friedrich Geus (n.d.) was a Berlin judge. He presided over the "Lorenz-Drenkmann trial," which is featured later in this volume.

15 RIAS (Rundfunk im amerikanischen Sektor, or Radio in the American Sector) was a West Berlin radio station founded by US military forces in 1946.

16 Estrongo Nachama (1918–2000) was the chief cantor of West Berlin's Jewish community; he also performed in West Germany.

17 The Harnack House is a prominent research center in Berlin. At the time, it was controlled by the US military.

18 For Alfred "Shorty" Mährländer, see "From the Hash Rebels to the 2nd of June Movement" note 5. Hella Maher (n.d.) was a short-lived member of the Tupamaros West Berlin who, at nineteen years of age and addicted to heroin, made extensive statements about the group's activities.

19 Klaus Schütz (1926–2012) was an SPD politician and mayor of West Berlin from 1967 to 1977.

20 Dirk Schneider (1939–2002) was a prominent leftist activist who later became a Green Party member; for years, he served as a Stasi informant.

21 The Tricontinental Conference took place in Cuba from January 3 to 16, 1966. It brought together revolutionary movements from Africa, Asia, and Latin America.

22 It is unclear which statement this refers to. The only known interview from prison with Reinders involved is "The Unrelenting of the Spree" (included in this volume), and the statement is not included there.

23 Linhof is a Munich-based company producing film cameras. They had a branch in West Berlin.

24 The *Bayernkurier* was a CSU newspaper that appeared from 1950 to 2019. Its first editor-in-chief was Franz Josef Strauß.

25 Rainer Hochstein (1946–2011) was rejected as a 2nd of June Movement member because he appeared unreliable; during the Lorenz-Drenkmann trial he appeared as a crown witness of the prosecution.

26 Karl-Heinz Ruhland (born 1938) moved in RAF circles. After his arrest in late 1970, he served as a crown witness of the prosecution in trials against RAF members.

27 The German term used at the time was *Negerküsse*, literally "Negro kisses." It is no longer commonly used.

28 Reference to the occupation of the West German embassy in Stockholm, Sweden. See the timeline in this volume.

29 The leaflet is quoted in its entirety in Klaus Viehmann's text "A Nest Egg for the Revolution," included in this volume.

30 Michael Grünhagen (n.d.) was a state security agent who infiltrated radical left circles under various code names.

31 Wolfgang Möllenbrock (1940–2016) was a West Berlin prosecutor who participated in 2nd of June Movement investigations.

32   Hans-Jürgen Przytarski (n.d.) was a West Berlin prosecutor who participated in 2nd of June Movement investigations.

2nd of June Movement Program
1   NATO's Prometheus plan was designed to prevent a communist takeover in Greece in the 1960s and facilitated the military coup in 1967.
2   Movimento de Libertação Popular, a short-lived (1970–71) guerrilla group in Brazil.
3   The Gauche prolétarienne was a French Maoist organization that existed from 1968 to 1973.

A Nest Egg for the Revolution: The Banks of the 2nd of June Movement
1   During a bank robbery in Munich in August 1971, one of two robbers and a hostage were killed; it was the first time that a hostage was killed during a bank robbery in West Germany. See the references to Hans Georg Rammelmayr on page 63 and "The Lorenz Kidnapping" note 16.

2nd of June Movement Leaflet
1   Putte, Fuchsbau, Belzigerstraße, and Weisbecker House were squatted buildings and youth centers. The Steglitzer Kreisel and the Zehlendorfer Tunnel were development projects. Ford saw the biggest of the wildcat strikes of the 1970s. There were also big strikes at Hella, an automotive parts supplier based in Lippstadt, North Rhine-Westphalia.

Those Who Sow Violence...
1   Ian McLeod was a Scottish businessman shot dead through his bedroom door when police raided an alleged RAF safe house on June 25, 1972. Günther Jendrian, a Munich taxi driver and alleged RAF sympathizer, was shot dead by police during a raid on his home on May 21, 1974. Günter Routhier, a member of the pro-Albanian Kommunistische Partei Deutschlands/Marxisten-Leninisten (KPD/ML), died after police brutally cleared a courtroom in Duisburg during a trial on June 5, 1974. Seventeen-year-old Richard Epple, driving without a license, was shot dead by police in Tübingen on March 1, 1972, when he ran a roadblock during a manhunt for RAF members.
2   This refers to incidents of particular prisoner abuse in different prisons in West Germany and West Berlin. Klingelpütz was a prison in Cologne.

Regarding the Assassination of Berlin's Highest Judge: Terror or Resistance?!
1   The KaDeWe, short for Kaufhaus des Westens, is one of Europe's largest department stores; it opened in 1907.
2   *Tagesspiegel* is a liberal daily, founded in Berlin in 1945.
3   For short background information on most of the people listed here, see the chapter "Protagonists" in this volume. For Schelm, see page 21 of the introduction. For Epple, Jendrian, Routhier, and McLeod, see "Those Who Sow Violence . . ." note 1.
4   Reference to an upcoming memorial service for Günter von Drenkmann; public servants and the employees of many of Berlin's biggest private workplaces got the day off and were expected to attend.

Friends, Throw Away the Gun
1   Siemensstadt is a neighborhood in the west of Berlin that was originally built
    as a company town for the industrial manufacturer Siemens.

Bommi Baumann: How It All Ends
1   Johannes Mario Simmel (1924–2009) was a best-selling Austrian author.
    Christian Semler (1938–2013) was one of the founders of the Maoist KPD/AO.

Backs Against the Wall?
1   In April 1974, high-ranking SPD member Günter Guillaume (1927–95) was
    exposed as a longtime Stasi informant. SPD chancellor Willy Brandt stepped
    down one month later.
2   Helmut Schmidt succeeded Willy Brandt as chancellor on May 16, 1974; FDP
    politician Hans-Dietrich Genscher became vice chancellor and minister for
    foreign affairs.
3   The European Economic Community was founded in 1957 as a predecessor to
    the European Union.
4   On December 12, 1969, a bomb planted by the far-right paramilitary organization
    Ordine Nuovo at the headquarters of the National Agrarian Bank in Milan killed
    seventeen people and injured eighty-eight.
5   IG Metall organizes metalworkers and is Germany's largest and most powerful
    trade union. The strike at Ford was the biggest and most covered of the 1973
    wildcat strikes in West Germany.
6   *Wir wollen alles* was published from 1973 to 1975 by groups from Germany's
    operaist milieu.
7   "K-groups" (*K-Gruppen*) refers to a large variety of small communist organi-
    zations that were active in Germany in the 1970s. ("Communist" is spelled
    kommunistisch in German.)
8   On May 11, 1972, the RAF bombed the headquarters of the US Army V Corps in
    Frankfurt, killing one person and injuring thirteen; on May 25, the RAF bombed
    the European headquarters of the US Army in Heidelberg, killing three soldiers
    and severely injuring five more people. The attacks were part of the RAF's "May
    Offensive," responding the US carpet bombing in Vietnam.
9   The "Committees Against Torture" (Komiteen Gegen die Folter) were groups
    across Germany protesting the conditions that prisoners from the urban guer-
    rilla were held under; they were often seen as important gathering places for
    RAF sympathizers.
10 2nd of June Movement member Heinz Brockmann (born 1948), arrested in May
    1973, made extensive statements, incriminating his former comrades.
11 In March 1921, there were unsuccessful communist insurrections in several
    German towns; in October 1923, a communist uprising in Hamburg failed.

Regarding the Death of Our Comrade Werner Sauber
1   A reference to the RAF's April 24, 1975, occupation of the West German embassy
    in Stockholm. See the timeline in this volume.

The Lorenz Kidnapping
1   Reference to a demonstration after the November 9, 1974, death of RAF member

Holger Meins as a result of a weeks-long hunger strike and declined medical care.

2   Karl Heinz Pepper (1910–2003), merchant and real estate baron. The Europa-Center in Berlin-Charlottenburg is a high-rise office building that includes a shopping mall; it was opened in 1965 and is a Berlin landmark.

3   Herbert Wehner (1906–90) was chairman of the SPD's parliamentary club from 1969 to 1983.

4   Sigurd Debus (1942–81) was a communist militant arrested in February 1974; he died in April 1981 while being force-fed during a weeks-long hunger strike.

5   Heinrich Lummer (1932–2019) was the chairman of the CDU club in the Berlin parliament.

6   *Juso* stands for Junge Sozialisten (Young Socialists), the youth organization of the SPD. NPD stands for Nationaldemokratische Partei Deutschlands (National Democratic Party of Germany), a far-right party founded in 1964. Having had modest electoral success, it changed its name to Heimat (Home) in 2023.

7   Verlag Roter Stern in Frankfurt/Main, closely associated with the early 1970s militant left in West Germany, published a selection of Tupamaros texts in German translation in 1974 under the title *Wir die Tupamaros* (We, the Tupamaros).

8   *Avus* stands for Automobil-Verkehrs- und Übungsstraße (Automobile Traffic and Training Track), a public road in Berlin that doubled as a race track between 1921 and 1998.

9   The Funkturm (Radio Tower) in the Westend neighborhood of Berlin, erected in the 1920s, is one of the city's best-known historical landmarks.

10   The Bund Freies Deutschland (Alliance Free Germany) was a short-lived conservative party in West Berlin in the early 1970s, supported by the likes of CSU chairman Franz-Josef Strauß and Axel Springer, head of the Springer publishing empire (see "Introduction" note 4).

11   The Ohnsorg Theater of Hamburg has been staging theater plays, mainly comedies, both in high German and in the low German dialect (*Plattdeutsch*) since 1910. The plays started to be broadcast on German television in the 1950s.

12   Section 218 of the German penal code prohibits abortion. In 1976, the section was amended so that abortions are no longer punishable as long as a number of conditions (consultation, terminations no later than twelve weeks after conception, and others) are met.

13   Karsten Klingbeil (1925–2016) was a Berlin-based sculptor and building contractor.

14   For Rainer Hochstein, see "From the Hash Rebels to the 2nd of June Movement" note 25.

15   Sender Freies Berlin (SFB, Radio Free Berlin) was West Berlin's German radio and television service; RIAS (Radio in the American Sector) was West Berlin's US radio station.

16   On the evening of September 5, 1972, fifteen people, including nine hostages of the Israeli Olympic team, died at the airport of Fürstenfeldbruck, near Munich, when attempts by German police to free them failed. The Israelis had been taken hostage earlier that day by a commando of Palestinian militants during the Munich Olympic Summer Games; five of the Palestinian militants were killed during the shootout. Hans Georg Rammelmayr was killed during a bank

robbery, alongside a hostage he had taken, in Munich in August 1971 (see also "A Nest Egg for the Revolution" note 1).

17   Reference to the FDP minister of the interior Gerhart Baum (born 1932), who promised early release for imprisoned members of urban guerrilla groups if they renounced the armed struggle.

18   For a few years during the 1980s, Mahler supported the FDP and the party's liberal economic program.

19   Kurt Biedenkopf (1930–2021) was a highly influential figure in the CDU, often regarded as the intellectual strategist behind longtime chancellor Helmut Kohl.

20   This information appears to be incorrect. According to reliable accounts, it was Ina Siepmann who instructed the pilot.

21   Hans-Jürgen Wischnewski (1922–2005) was an SPD diplomat who earned the nickname "Ben Wisch" due to his many contacts in the Arab world.

22   The entire text is included later in this volume.

23   A reference to the Steglitzer Kreisel, a huge office complex being constructed at the time in the Steglitz neighborhood of Berlin. There were widespread accusations of corruption, incriminating high-ranking Berlin officials.

24   Sigrid Kressmann-Zschach (1929–90) was an architect responsible for numerous development projects in Berlin, including the Steglitzer Kreisel.

25   The small town of Wyhl in Baden-Württemberg, southern Germany, gained significance for Germany's antinuclear movement when mass protests in 1975 prevented a planned nuclear power plant near the town from being built. "Community group" is a translation for the term *Bürgerinitiative*, which, more literally, could also be translated as "citizens' group." *Bürgerinitiativen* played an important role for the green-alternative movement of the 1970s and '80s in West Germany, often formed around ecological, and to a lesser degree social, (single) issues.

26   The leaflet is included in the chapter "Drenkmann" in this volume.

27   Putte was an occupied youth center in Berlin-Wedding that existed in 1973–74.

28   DeTeWe is a telecommunications company founded in Berlin in 1887. Loewe, founded in Berlin in 1923, manufactures consumer electronics.

29   Berthold Rubin (1911–90) was a far-right historian who faked his own kidnapping by the RAF in 1971 with the intention of increasing repression against the left in Germany. He was active in circles around the CSU.

30   Elisabeth von Dyck (1950–79) and Willi Peter Stoll (1950–78) were RAF members. Von Dyck was shot dead by police in a Nuremberg safe house on May 4, 1979; Stoll was shot dead by police in a Dusseldorf restaurant on September 6, 1978.

31   Rolf Heißler was released from prison in 2001; he died in 2023.

32   Rolf Pohle died of cancer in 2004; he was still living in Athens.

33   RAF member Günter Sonnenberg (born 1954) was seriously injured during the incident; he spent fourteen years in prison.

34   2nd of June Movement member Christian Möller (born 1949) spent eleven years in prison in Switzerland.

35   See the timeline in this volume.

The Kidnapping as We See It

1   A reference to the Steglitzer Kreisel; see "2nd of June Movement Leaflet" note 1.

2   For Sigrid Kressmann-Zschach, see "The Lorenz Kidnapping" note 24.

3   For Wyhl, see "The Lorenz Kidnapping" note 25.
4   For Karsten Klingbeil, see "The Lorenz Kidnapping" note 13.
5   For RIAS, see "From the Hash Rebels to the 2nd of June Movement" note 15.
6   The United Arab States was a 1958–1961 confederation of North Yemen and the
     United Arab Republic consisting of Egypt and Syria.

Tunix

1   The phrase "march through the institutions" was coined by the prominent SDS
     agitator Rudi Dutschke in 1967. It references the "long march" of the Red Army
     in China.
2   In September 1976, the Revolutionary Cells bombed the Cologne home of the
     real estate speculator Günter Kaußen. In August 1977, they bombed a plant of the
     engineering company MAN, which supplied the South African nuclear program.
     The Berlin transport authority BVG (Berliner Verkehrsbetriebe) was the target
     of frequent attacks during transit fare hikes. Section 218 regulated Germany's
     antiabortion legislation (see also "The Lorenz Kidnapping" note 12).
3   Daniel Cohn-Bendit (born 1945) is a French-German green-alternative politician
     who was a prominent member of both the French and German extraparliamen-
     tary left in the late 1960s and early 1970s. Sozialistisches Büro (Socialist Bureau)
     and Langer Marsch (Long March) were left-wing collectives in Germany opposed
     to the urban guerrilla strategy.
4   In 1974–75, bombs exploded in a number of main West German railway stations,
     causing property damage and injuries. They were alleged to have been planted
     by the urban guerrilla, but all urban guerrilla groups denied involvement.
5   A reference to the hijacking of the *Landshut*—see the timeline and several texts
     in this volume.
6   See "Backs Against the Wall?" in this volume.
7   The Feuerwache (Fire Station) was a squat in Berlin-Kreuzberg used as a social
     center for six weeks in May–June 1977.
8   For the arrest of "our printers," see note 11 below; for the Springer publishing
     empire, see "Introduction" note 4.
9   *Kontaktbeamte* (literally "contact agents") are police officers who attempt to
     become friendly with community members and build trust for the police; in
     left-wing circles, they are often seen as infiltrators.
10   *Info BUG* was a radical left-wing magazine published in Berlin from 1974 to 1977.
     It printed many relevant pieces, including communiqués, by and on the urban
     guerrilla groups. *BUG* stood for "Berliner undogmatische Gruppen" (Undogmatic
     Groups of Berlin).
11   In 1977, the *Info BUG* printers were arrested and accused of "supporting a terrorist
     organization"; they were sentenced to prison sentences from nine to thirteen
     months without parole.
12   Reference to the sponti magazine *Pflasterstrand*, a German wordplay on a popular
     slogan during the May 1968 uprising in France, "Sous le pavé, la plage" (Beneath
     the pavement, the beach). *Pflasterstrand* literally means "pavement beach."

Indians Don't Cry, They Struggle

1   A wordplay: *Ernst der Lage* means "The situation is serious."
2   Eduard Bernstein (1850–1932) was the most prominent early-twentieth-century

theorist of the SPD's revisionist wing, while Rosa Luxemburg (1871–1919) stood for the SPD line that led to the founding of the KPD in 1919. Luxemburg was murdered alongside her longtime comrade Karl Liebknecht (1871–1919) after the failed Spartacus Uprising of January 1919.

3   A reference to the lawyer and former RAF member Horst Mahler, who, by the time this text was released, was moving in liberal circles; later, he turned to the far right (see "Protagonists" in this volume). *Hotte* is a German nickname for Horst.

4   The reference to Ayatollah Khomeini might seem puzzling, but the Iranian Revolution was hailed by many on the left as a victory for anti-imperialism. The Marxist factions in the revolution were overstressed, and the Islamic ones underestimated. See also relevant comments in Ralf Reinders's "The Lorenz Trial Closing Statement Marathon" in this volume.

5   Probably a reference to Horst Mahler's public explanation for refusing to be liberated during the Peter Lorenz kidnapping in 1975.

6   See the timeline in this volume.

7   In the course of the trial, it became clear that Teufel could not have taken part in the Lorenz kidnapping.

8   See the timeline in this volume.

9   Patrice Lumumba (1925–61), a pan-Africanist who served as the first prime minister of the independent Republic of the Congo, was overthrown and executed by political rivals with support of the old colonial power Belgium and the US.

10   Idi Amin (1925–2003) served as the president of Uganda from 1971 to 1979.

11   Reference to a six-year court case in Düsseldorf (stretching from November 1975 to June 1981) in which sixteen people who had served at the Majdanek concentration camp in Poland during World War II were accused of mass killings. CDU politician Hans Filbinger (1913–2007) served as the minister-president of Baden-Württemberg from 1966 to 1978; he had been a Nazi party member during the Third Reich and sentenced at least four people to death as a military judge.

12   The GSG 9 is a special antiterrorist unit of the German police established in 1972 in response to the Black September attack during the Olympic Games in Munich (see "The Lorenz Kidnapping" note 16).

13   In 1919, following the turmoil of World War I, short-lived council republics were established in Hungary and Germany.

14   Friedrich Ebert (1871–1925), Gustav Noske (1868–1946), and Philipp Scheidemann (1865–1939) were decidedly antirevolutionary SPD leaders, facilitating the post–World War I transition from the German Kaiserreich to the Weimar Republic.

15   In the 1970s, the towns of Wyhl, Germany, and Malville, France, were sites of mass mobilizations against the planned construction of nuclear power plants. During the same time, serious accidents occurred at a chemical manufacturing plant in Seveso, Italy, and a nuclear power plant in Harrisburg, Pennsylvania, US. Contergan is a brand name for the drug thalidomide, which, in the 1960s, caused thousands of deaths and birth defects among infants after the drug had been prescribed to their mothers during pregnancy.

16   Teufel was one of the few political prisoners who only partially participated in hunger strikes. In his 1978 text "Hungerstreik und Solidarität" (Hunger strike and solidarity), he lists both political reasons ("I am fed up with the hunger strikes of the imprisoned guerrilla, particularly the way in which they are conducted,

prepared, and evaluated—or, let's say, not evaluated") and personal ones ("I was no longer able to do it—the efforts seemed to outweigh the benefits").

17   See "The Lorenz Kidnapping" note 25.

Our Contribution to the Teach-In on January 27

1   EB stands for Eberhard Dreher—see "The Unrelenting of the Spree" note 13.

2   In December 1976, the students Peter W. and Christoph D. were arrested at the Berlin subway station Thielplatz after an altercation with plainclothes cops, accused of various crimes, and held in remand. After a broad movement demanded their release, they were freed after three weeks and sentenced to moderate fines.

May 9 Declaration in Court

1   Krupp and Siemens are powerful German companies named after their founders. Hermann Josef Abs (1910–94) was a German banker responsible for the confiscation of Jewish property during the Third Reich.

2   Hans-Joachim Rehse (1902–69) was a judge at the Berlin "People's Court" (*Volksgerichtshof*) during the Nazi regime, signing at least 231 death sentences. Hanns Martin Schleyer (1915–77) was a German industrialist and former SS officer who was kidnapped and killed by the Red Army Faction in 1977 (see several texts in this volume). CDU politician Kurt Georg Kiesinger (1904–88) was chancellor in West Germany from 1966 to 1969; during the Third Reich, he had been a Nazi party member. For Filbinger, see "Indians Don't Cry, They Struggle" note 11.

The 1977 Torture Weekend

1   Egon Bahr (1922–2015) was a highly influential SPD member during the Schmidt years. "Deutsche Jusos" (*Jusos* refers to the SPD youth association) was a polemic against far-left tendencies published in 1978.

2   Wolfgang Paetzelt (n.d.) acted as judge in trials against alleged urban guerrilla members in Berlin.

3   The small town of Gorleben in Lower Saxony has been the site of antinuclear mass mobilizations since a nuclear waste storage facility was erected there in 1983.

The Unrelenting of the Spree

1   "Occupying forces" (*Besatzungsmächte* or, as in this case, *Besatzer*) refers to the Allies of World War II (France, the UK, and the US) and the Soviet Union, who were administering postwar Germany. Today, the expression is controversial, as some believe it denies the contribution that the Allies and the Soviet Union have made to the liberation of Germany from fascism; these people rather speak of "liberating forces" (*Befreiungsmächte*).

2   Reference to the 1971 antifeminist book of the same name by Esther Vilar (German original: *Der dressierte Mann*).

3   Brokdorf in Schleswig-Holstein and Grohnde in Lower Saxony were sites of mass mobilizations against the construction of nuclear power plants in the 1970s. In Frankfurt, women's groups were active in opposing section 218, the law limiting access to abortion.

4   A reference to Horst Mahler's 1971 text *Über den bewaffneten Kampf in Westeuropa* (Regarding the armed struggle in Western Europe).

5   For Grohnde and Brokdorf, see "The Unrelenting of the Spree" note 3. The prison of Stammheim, near Stuttgart, contained the most notorious high-security wing for urban guerrilla prisoners. BEFA stands for Beobachtende Fahndung, literally, "observant manhunt," a network of police surveillance strategies. DISPOL stands for Digitales Integriertes Sondernetz der Polizei, literally, "digital integrated special web of the police," a computerized data surveillance program.

6   Baumann had suggested in interviews that "terrorist organizations" had access to nuclear weapons.

7   Astrid Proll (born 1947) was a founding member of the Red Army Faction.

8   For Filbinger, see "Indians Don't Cry, They Struggle" note 11.

9   For "community groups," see "The Lorenz Kidnapping" note 25.

10   Karl Marx, "The Eighteenth Brumaire of Louis Napoleon" (Marxists Internet Archive, 1999), https://www.marxists.org/archive/marx/works/1852/18th-brumaire.

11   The "*Spiegel* affair" refers to a controversy around articles published in the weekly news magazine about the state of the German defense forces in 1962; CDU and CSU politicians prompted security forces to arrest several *Spiegel* journalists on treason charges, but the case never made it to court.

12   See "Tunix" notes 10 and 11.

13   In 1978, Eberhard Dreher (born 1946) was sentenced to four years in prison for allegedly having supported the 2nd of June Movement.

14   Jürgen Baumann (1922–2003) was a prominent FDP legal expert and justice senator of Berlin from 1976 to 1978. He was forced to resign due to the liberation of Till Meyer from Moabit prison in May 1978.

The Lorenz Trial Closing Statement Marathon

1   Ernst Bloch (1885–1977), a German Marxist philosopher, was well respected by the 1960s student movement and the New Left. He is best known for his three-volume work *Das Prinzip Hoffnung* (The principle of hope), published in the 1950s.

2   In the Potsdam Agreement of 1945, the Allies (France, the UK, and the US) and the Soviet Union divided postwar Europe into different spheres of influence.

3   This 1947 CDU program on economics and social policy claimed to go "beyond capitalism and Marxism."

4   During the elections for the Hesse parliament in 1946, a referendum was conducted on the possibility of nationalizing banks and industries; 62 percent of the casted votes were in favor.

5   General Lucius Clay (1898–1978) was the military governor of the US Occupation Zone in Germany from 1947 to 1949. He is known as one of the administrators of the Berlin airlift from June 1948 to September 1949, when Soviet troops cut off all land access to West Berlin.

6   Joseph Goebbels (1897–1945) was the Nazi party's propaganda minister.

7   A reference to Judge Geus.

8   KPD members who received prison sentences after the party was outlawed in 1956.

9   At the concentration camp in Buchenwald, the inmates took control over the camp in 1945 before the US Army arrived.

10   On July 20, 1944, a group of government and military officials attempted to assassinate Hitler with a suitcase bomb.

11   Hans Josef Maria Globke (1898–1973) and Theodor Oberländer (1905–98) were examples of Nazi officials who held important posts in postwar CDU governments. CDU member Karl Heinrich Lübke (1894–1972) was the president of Germany from 1959 to 1969; toward the end of his term, it was revealed that he had collaborated with the Nazis during the Third Reich. For Filbinger, see "Indians Don't Cry, They Struggle" note 11; for Kiesinger, see "May 9 Declaration in Court" note 2. Abs, Schneidewind, Krupp, and Thyssen are powerful German industrialists that did business with the Nazis during the Third Reich. For Schleyer, see "May 9 Declaration in Court" note 2. Adolf Heusinger (1897–1982) was in the Wehrmacht's high command during the Third Reich, and from 1961 to 1964 was chairman of the NATO Military Committee.

12   SPD member Walter Sickert (1919–2013) was the chairman of the Berlin chapter of the German Trade Union Confederation (Deutscher Gewerkschaftsbund, DGB) from 1960 to 1982.

13   Ernst Thälmann (1886–1944) was the chairman of the KPD from 1925 to 1933, before the party was outlawed by the Nazis; Thälmann was arrested in 1933, held in solitary confinement, and executed in 1944.

14   See "The Lorenz Trial Closing Statement Marathon" note 9.

15   Das Braunbuch (Brown Book), authored by Albert Norden, was published in 1965. It identified 1,800 former Nazis and war criminals in prominent positions in West German society. The third edition was seized by security agents at the Frankfurt Book Fair in 1967.

16   Freie Deutsche Jugend (Free German Youth) was the official communist youth organization in East Germany; its West German affiliate was banned in 1951. It regularly organized Jugendkarawanen (youth caravans), usually to rally for peace.

17   Since 1960, the peace movement in Germany has been mobilizing for mass peace marches on Easter weekend.

18   Ernest Mandel, An Introduction to Marxist Economic Theory (London: Resistance Books, 2002), 47. First published 1967. Ernest Mandel (1923–95) was a German-Belgian Marxist economist popular with the left-wing movements of the 1960s.

19   The America House in Berlin was a regular target of political actions. Here, Reinders is referring to an occupation by activists demanding to close the recently built high-security wing in Moabit. Four of the involved activists were sentenced to three to four years in prison.

20   Regarding the protests against the nuclear waste storage facility in Gorleben, see "The 1977 Torture Weekend" note 3. Wendländer (literally, "those from the Wendland") refers to the activists who regularly travel to the Wendland region around Gorleben to protest, some even settling down there.

21   Reference to the coup d'état in Chile in September 1973, toppling the democratically elected socialist government under president Salvador Allende (1908–73).

22   Source unknown, translation by G.K. The "Luxembourg Convention" of 1953 is officially known as the "European Convention on Social and Medical Assistance."

23   In 1948, far-right Israeli paramilitaries bombed the Semiramis Hotel in the Katamon neighborhood of Jerusalem, killing at least twenty-four people; they massacred more than one hundred people in the village of Deir Yassin close by.

24 Menachem Begin (1913–92), conservative prime minister of Israel from 1977 to 1983.

25 Matzpen was a revolutionary anti-Zionist organization founded in Israel in 1962; it split into different factions in the early 1970s.

26 Quoted from Matzpen: The Socialist Organization in Israel, "General Declaration by the ISO, 22 March 1968," https://matzpen.org/english/1968-03-22/general-declaration-by-the-iso.

27 Yasser Arafat (1929–2004), leader of the Palestine Liberation Organization (PLO) from 1969 to 2004 and president of the Palestinian National Authority from 1994 to 2004.

28 Bruno Heck (1917–89) belonged to the right wing of the CDU ("The 1968 rebellion has destroyed more values than the Third Reich") and was chairman of the CDU-affiliated Konrad Adenauer Foundation from 1968 to 1989.

29 Regarding section 218, see "The Lorenz Kidnapping" note 12.

30 After the reform of the abortion law in Germany, women who wanted to get an abortion still had to undergo mandatory psychological screenings and medical tests.

31 For Klaus Schütz, see "From the Hash Rebels to the 2nd of June Movement" note 19; Hermann Oxfort (1928–2003) was chairman of the FDP club in the Berlin parliament from 1963 to 1975.

32 The leaflet is included in this volume.

33 The five prisoners flown to South Yemen as well as the two prisoners released after the Holger Meins demonstration.

34 Schering (pharmaceuticals), Rollei (optical instruments), and Siemens (manufacturing conglomerate) are German companies; Schering was bought by Bayer in 2006.

35 For the squats named after Tommy Weisbecker and Georg von Rauch, see "Protagonists" in this volume. They were regular targets of police raids.

36 Carl von Clausewitz (1780–1831) was a Prussian general and influential military theorist.

37 The Trilateral Commission was founded in 1973 by David Rockefeller to improve relations between North America, Western Europe, and Japan. IMF stands for the International Monetary Fund, founded in 1944.

38 The COMECON (Council for Mutual Economic Assistance) was the Eastern European pro-Soviet bloc's answer to the Western European OEEC (Organization of European Economic Cooperation).

39 From the leaflet "The Main Enemy Is at Home!" (1915).

40 From a leaflet of the same name (1915).

41 On May 6, 1980, militant activists disrupted the swearing-in ceremonies at the NATO twenty-fifth anniversary celebration in Bremen.

Pigs to Outer Space

1 A far-right bomb attack at the Munich Oktoberfest on September 26, 1980, killed thirteen people and injured more than two hundred.

2 The socialist El Salvadorian Farabundo Martí National Liberation Front (Frente Farabundo Martí para la Liberación Nacional, or FMLN), which led a guerrilla war from 1980 to 1992, had much support among the West German left. Today, the FMLN is a legalized political party.

3   Translating as "chaotics," the term *Chaoten* is often used in German media for
     militant activists engaging in property destruction and street fights with the
     police.
4   Julen Agirre, *Operation Ogro: The Execution of Admiral Luis Carrero Blanco* (New
     York: Quadrangle/New York Times, 1975), 193. ETA stands for the militant Basque
     liberation movement Euskadi Ta Askatasuna (Basque Country and Liberty),
     which existed from 1959 to 2018. Luis Carrero Blanco (1904–73) was killed by an
     ETA bomb in his car on December 20, 1973; the detonation was so heavy that
     Blanco's car flew over a Jesuit monastery and landed on the second-floor balcony
     of a building behind it ("the halfway ascension to heaven").
5   See "Tunix" note 11.
6   For Horst Mahler and his unconventional political biography, see "Protagonists"
     in this volume.
7   Ernst Albrecht (1930–2014), CDU politician and minister-president of Lower
     Saxony from 1976 to 1990. For Grohnde, see "The Unrelenting of the Spree" note
     3.
8   Reference to a weeks-long hunger strike involving dozens of political prisoners
     in early 1981.
9   For Sigurd Debus, see "The Lorenz Kidnapping" note 4.
10   Judge Giovani D'Urso (1933–2011), who had assigned numerous prisoners to
     high-security units, was kidnapped by the Red Brigades in December 1980. The
     Red Brigades wanted the notorious Asinara Island prison to close and demanded
     that statements written by their imprisoned comrades would be read on tele-
     vision. D'Urso was released when the demands were met on January 15, 1981.
11   The Camp David Accords, signed by Egyptian president Anwar Sadat (1918–
     81) and Israeli prime minister Menachem Begin (1913–92) in September 1978,
     normalized relations between the two countries.
12   KWU stands for Kraftwerk Union, a German company that built nuclear power
     plants (and some others) from 1969 to 2000.
13   "Friede den Hütten und Krieg den Palästen" (Peace to the shacks! War on the
     palaces!) is the title of a revolutionary tract authored by playwright George
     Büchner (1813–37); it was first circulated in 1834.
14   A reference to militant disruptions of military swearing-in ceremonies.
15   See "Indians Don't Cry, They Struggle" note 15.
16   For Harrisburg and Seveso, see "Indians Don't Cry, They Struggle" note 15.
17   *Modell Deutschland* was the name given to the capitalist powers' economic
     restructuring program for Germany during the postwar period; it was hailed
     as a model for rapid economic growth.
18   The Grey Wolves are a Turkish nationalist paramilitary organization known for
     attacks on left-wing activists.
19   A reference to the so-called Putzgruppe, or "cleanup squad," a street-fighting
     unit associated with the Frankfurt sponti group Revolutionärer Kampf
     (Revolutionary Struggle) of the 1970s. The later German Green Party politician
     and vice chancellor Joschka Fischer was a member (see "The Urban Guerrilla
     and Class Struggle—Revised" note 5).
20   Dietrich Garski (born 1931) is an architect and real estate agent who embezzled
     millions of Deutschmark after the Berlin government had pledged a loan in
     connection with a construction contract of Garski's company in Saudi Arabia.

21   In the original, Viehmann uses the term *aufheben* (for "elevate") in the sense of
     Hegelian-Marxian dialectics; the term is notoriously difficult to translate.
22   See note 19 above.

Us in Here, You out There: A Letter from Knofo from Heartbreak Hotel

1   George Habbash (1926–2008) was a founder and key member of the Popular
    Front for the Liberation of Palestine (PFLP).
2   A reference to Ilich Ramírez Sánchez (born 1949), better known as "Carlos,"
    a Venezuelan militant who worked closely with the Popular Front for the
    Liberation of Palestine (External Operations), a splinter group from the PFLP.
    German militants cooperated with him on a number of occasions. Since 1994,
    Carlos has been serving a life sentence without parole in France for the 1975
    murder of two police officers.
3   A reference to the heavy bombing of Dresden by UK and US forces in February
    1945.
4   Roughly, 55 to 60 degrees Fahrenheit.
5   Heinz Rühmann (1902–1994) and Adele Sandrock (1863–1937) were German
    movie stars.
6   RAF prisoner Ingrid Schubert (1944–1977) was found hanged in her cell in the
    Munich prison of Stadelheim on November 13, 1977.
7   A reference to the morning of October 18, when RAF members Andreas Baader,
    Gudrun Ensslin, and Jan Raspe were found dead in their cells in Stammheim
    prison.
8   The French anarchists Ravachol (François Claudius Koenigstein, 1859–92)
    and Émile Henry (1872–94) were protagonists of the "propaganda by the
    deed," committing random acts of violence. The social-revolutionary Grigory
    Gershuni (1870–1908) was involved in a number of assassination attempts
    against Russian government officials. His Russian compatriot Sergey Nechayev
    (1847–82), an anarchist, is best known as the author of the merciless *Catechism
    of a Revolutionary* (1869).
9   Ivan Pavlov (1849–1936) was a Russian neurologist most famous for documenting
    the "conditioned reflex" in dogs.

The Years in Prison

1   "Bär" (Bear) is Ralf Reinders's nickname.
2   Skalitzer Straße is a main road in the activist neighborhood of Berlin-Kreuzberg.
3   Reference to the hijacking of an Air France airliner that ended in Entebbe; see
    the timeline and several texts in this volume.
4   See the timeline in this volume.
5   For Jürgen Baumann, see "The Unrelenting of the Spree" note 14.
6   For Eberhard Dreher, see "The Unrelenting of the Spree" note 13.
7   See the text "Amnesties Are No Gifts" in this volume.

Amnesties Are No Gifts

1   Christof Wackernagel (born 1951) and Gert Schneider (born 1948) were arrested
    as alleged RAF members after a shootout with police in Amsterdam in 1977.
    Both spent ten years in prison. In January 1984, the daily *taz* published letters by
    them that responded positively to a suggestion for political amnesty by left-wing

journalist Wolfgang Pohrt (1945–2018); Pohrt later became a prominent figure among the Antideutschen (see "*junge Welt* Interview" note 1). In their letters, Wackernagel and Schneider suggested that the militant struggle had ended in irreversible defeat.

2   Karl Marx, *The Class Struggles in France, 1848 to 1850* (Marxists Internet Archive, 2010), https://www.marxists.org/archive/marx/works/1850/class-struggles-france.

3   Regarding Wolfgang Pohrt, see note 1 above.

4   Friedrich Flick (1883–1972) was a German industrialist profiting from the expropriation of Jewish-owned businesses. Sentenced to seven years in prison after the war for the exploitation of forced prison labor, he returned as one of Germany's most powerful industrialists in the 1950s. In the early 1980s, it was revealed that the Flick industrial empire had ensured business deals through donations to all of the leading West German parties.

5   Revolutionary Cells, "Krieg—Krise—Friedensbewegung. In Gefahr und höchster Not bringt der Mittelweg den Tod" (War—crisis—peace movement: At the moment of the highest danger compromise means death), *Die Früchte des Zorns*, vol. 2, December 1983, 492.

6   The SS 20 was an intermediate-range ballistic missile with a nuclear warhead, deployed by the Soviet Union from 1976 to 1988. The Jena Peace Circle (Jenaer Friedenskreis) was a pacifist opposition group in East Germany.

7   Otto Graf Lambsdorff (1926–2009) was an FDP minister for economic affairs who had to resign in the wake of the Flick bribery scandal (see note 4 above).

Prison Round Trip

1   Peter Brückner (1922–82) was a psychologist popular with the 1960s protest movement.

2   For Ernst Bloch, see "The Lorenz Trial Closing Statement Marathon" note 1.

3   Jean Améry (1912–78) was an Austrian author, resistance fighter, and Auschwitz survivor.

4   Günther Anders (1902–92) was a German philosopher.

5   RAF member Wolfgang Grams (1953–93) died during a shootout with police at the railway station of Bad Kleinen, a small town in Mecklenburg-Vorpommern.

6   Nâzım Hikmet (1902–63) was a Turkish poet and communist.

7   Primo Levi (1919–87) was an Italian author, partisan, and Auschwitz survivor. Vera Figner (1852–1942) was a Russian social-revolutionary who spent twenty years in prison due to her involvement in the assassination of Tsar Alexander II. Peter Weiss (1916–82) was a communist German author best known for the three-volume novel *Die Ästhetik des Widerstands* (1975–81; in English as *The Aesthetics of Resistance*, 2005).

8   The quote is attributed to David Cámpora in Ernesto González Bermejo, *Los manos en el fuego* (Montevideo: Banda Oriental, 1985). Here it was translated from the German edition: *Hände im Feuer* (Giessen: Focus, 1986), 79.

9   Sean McGuffin (1942–2002) was an Irish novelist imprisoned in the 1970s for alleged IRA membership.

Statement Dissolving the 2nd of June Movement

1   In conflict studies, a "limited war" (as opposed to a "total war") is one where

the involved parties do not use all military means at their disposal, for example nuclear weapons.

Regarding the Alleged Dissolution of the 2nd of June Movement

1   In September 1975, a number of 2nd of June Movement members were arrested in short succession.
2   For Wyhl, see "The Lorenz Kidnapping" note 25.
3   The German term is *Bundesverdienstkreuze.*
4   Régis Debray, *A Critique of Arms* (London: Penguin, 1977), 185–86.
5   For von Clausewitz, see "The Lorenz Trial Closing Statement Marathon" note 36.
6   ÖTV is the acronym for the Öffentliche Dienste, Transport und Verkehr (public service, transport, and transit) union. In 2001, it became part of the labor union ver.di.
7   For Gerhart Baum, see "The Lorenz Kidnapping" note 17.
8   For Grohnde and Brokdorf, see "The Unrelenting of the Spree" note 3. The neighborhoods of the Westend in Frankfurt and the Dreisameck in Freiburg were hot spots of the squatters' movement.
9   In Bremen, militant activists disrupted the swearing-in ceremonies at the NATO twenty-fifth anniversary celebration in 1980. The America House in West Berlin, a cultural center funded by the US government, was a regular target of militant protests from the 1960s to the 1980s. The same was true for America Houses in other German cities.
10   Reference to a printers' strike at Druckhaus Tempelhof in 1980.

How It All Began

1   A reference to the fact that Benno Ohnesorg was killed on June 2, 1967, during protests against a visit to Berlin by yet another Shah of Persia. However, the dates are not correct. The Shah of Persia visited Berlin in 1873. He was not with Kaiser Wilhelm I on the day indicated here.
2   The "socialist laws" (*Sozialistengesetze*) prohibited any form of socialist organizing in Germany from 1879 to 1890.
3   *Eine Fahne haben* (literally, "to have a flag") is a German saying indicating that you can smell alcohol on someone's breath.
4   The FC St. Pauli is a sports club from the St. Pauli neighborhood in Hamburg popular with left-wing fans worldwide.
5   The Treuhandanstalt (Trust Agency) was established by the East German government to administer the privatization of state companies prior to the reunification of Germany in 1990.
6   There was much debate about the temporary West German capital during the division of Berlin. The reference to Bitterfeld, which is located in Saxony-Anhalt, East Germany, is a joke. Bitterfeld was significant for GDR history, both as a center of the 1953 protest movement and because of a 1959 conference trying to strengthen the ties between GDR cultural and manual workers (the *Bitterfelder Weg,* or "Bitterfeld Way").
7   This might be a variation on a Nietzsche quote (if so, probably with reference to *Thus Spoke Zarathustra*), or something made up by Kröcher. The literal quote doesn't exist.

What's Not Written

1   Viehmann is referring to the German translation of Mario Moretti and Rossana
    Rossanda's book *Brigate Rosse. Una storia italiana* (1998). The book has not been
    translated into English.
2   Both Peter-Jürgen Boock (born 1951) and Silke Maier-Witt (born 1950) are former
    RAF members who turned into outspoken critics of urban guerrilla politics;
    Boock provided ample evidence to authorities and the media, much of it fabri-
    cated. The film that Viehmann is referring to is called *Die RAF* (The RAF); it was
    released in 2007 and codirected by Stefan Aust, author of the 1985 bestseller *Der
    Baader-Meinhof Komplex* (The Baader-Meinhof complex).
3   The most important of these memoirs are listed in the preface in this volume.
4   Robert Havemann (1910–82), a chemist, resistance fighter during the Third Reich,
    and prominent East German dissident in the 1960s, criticizing dogmatism in
    the sciences. The book that Viehmann refers to is Max Frenzel, Wilhelm Thiele,
    and Artur Mannbar, *Gesprengte Fesseln* (Berlin: Militärverlag, 1978).
5   A number of Red Army Faction members had found sanctuary in East Germany
    in the 1980s—see the timeline in this volume.
6   In 1981, General Frederick Kroesen (1923–2020) was injured in a Red Army Faction
    attack on his armored vehicle near the US Army garrison in Heidelberg.
7   *Hanni und Nanni* is the German title for the *St. Clare's* series (1941–45) by popu-
    lar English children's writer Enid Blyton; the series revolves around a pair of
    mischievous twin girls.
8   The reference to Stammheim concerns the deaths of the Red Army Faction
    members Andreas Baader, Gudrun Ensslin, and Jan-Carl Raspe in their
    Stammheim prison cells on October 18, 1977. See also the timeline in this volume.
9   See the chapter "Dissolution (or Not)" for the two main factions within the 2nd
    of June Movement.
10 The "small book" by Reinders and Fritzsch is the 1995 Edition ID-Archiv release
    Die Bewegung 2. Juni. Gespräche über Haschrebellen, Lorenzentführung (The 2nd
    of June Movement: Conversations on Hash Rebels, the Lorenz kidnapping, and
    prison). The main texts of the book—the interviews "From the Hash Rebels to
    the 2nd of June Movement," "The Lorenz Kidnapping," and "The Unrelenting of
    the Spree," as well as Ralf Reinders's piece "The Years in Prison"—are all included
    in this volume.
11 The "German Autumn" refers to the events of late 1977, with the RAF kidnapping
    and killing of industrialist Hanns Martin Schleyer, the *Landshut* hijacking, the
    deaths of RAF members Andreas Baader, Gudrun Ensslin, and Jan-Carl Raspe
    in Stammheim, and the hard-handed reaction by the West German state. See
    the timeline in this volume.

Servant of Many Rulers

1   Spiegel TV is a video news production company launched by the news magazine
    Der Spiegel in 1990. Friedrich Küppersbusch (born 1961) is a popular German talk
    show host specializing in political programs.
2   *Die Zeit* is a prominent liberal weekly newspaper.
3   A reference to the Bommi Baumann book *How It All Began*—see the preface in
    this volume.
4   This is a reference to a popular former German TV show, *Was bin ich? Das heitere*

Beruferaten (What am I? The humorous guessing of trades), in which prominent jury members were to guess the profession of invited guests. Each program started with the guest making a hand movement characteristic for their trade. The show ran from 1955 to 1989.

5   Pseudonym used in Meyer's book; unclear which (if any) real-life person it refers to.

6   *Politik der ersten Person* was an important concept for the antiauthoritarian wing of Germany's radical left in the 1970s and 80s. It rejected representative politics and hierarchical structures.

7   The interviews are all included in this volume. See "What's Not Written" note 10.

8   See the chapter "Dissolution (or Not)" in this volume.

9   A reference to the Stasi.

10 Günter Schabowski (1929–2015) was a high-ranking SED official who declared the inner-German border open "immediately" during a rushed press conference on November 9, 1989.

11 Anglo-Norman maxim, most commonly translated as "Shame on anyone who thinks evil of it."

12 In the chaos following the surprisingly sudden reunification of Germany, the Stasi only managed to destroy the most delicate of files.

13 In 1994, Stefan Aust (born 1946) became editor-in-chief of *Der Spiegel*. His 1985 book *Der Baader-Meinhof Komplex* is the most widely read account of the history of the Red Army Faction.

Junge Welt Interview

1   The Antideutschen (literally, Anti-Germans) emerged as a faction within the German left in the early 1990s. Under the impression of an aggressive German nationalism following reunification, the Antideutschen rejected nationalism in all forms, including anticolonial national liberation movements. They became most notorious for their uncompromising defense of the state of Israel as a necessary safe haven for the Jewish people. Their view of the German left of the 1960s and 70s is marked by this perspective.

2   In December 1970, there were widespread uprisings in Polish cities triggered by price increases for staple foods and consumer goods.

3   Lin Biao (1907–71) was a military leader during the Chinese Revolution and a high-ranking official in the Chinese Communist Party.

4   The Startbahn West (Runway West) is an extension of the Frankfurt airport, whose construction in the early 1980s drew militant mass protests.

The Urban Guerrilla and Class Struggle—Revised

1   Max Horkheimer, *Dawn & Decline* (New York: Seabury, 1978), 41, quoted from https://platypus1917.org/wp-content/uploads/readings/horkheimer_dawnex.pdf. *Dawn & Decline* is the English edition of *Dämmerung. Notizen in Deutschland* (1934), published under the pseudonym Heinrich Regius.

2   J. Smith and André Moncourt, eds. and trans., *The Red Army Faction: A Documentary History*, vol. 1, *Projectiles for the People* (PM Press: Oakland, 2009), 82.

3   For the NPD, see "The Lorenz Kidnapping" note 6.

4   For four nights in August 1992, nationalist mobs attacked a reception center

for asylum seekers and the adjacent apartments of Vietnamese workers in the Lichtenhagen neighborhood of Rostock.

5   Joseph "Joschka" Fischer (born 1948) is a sponti turned Green Party politician who became vice chancellor and foreign minister during an SPD-Greens coalition government in Germany from 1998 to 2005.

6   The Hamburg Institute for Social Research is a research center founded in 1984 by industrial heir Jan Philipp Reemtsma (born 1952).

7   Operaism is a left tendency focusing on workers' power and self-organization popularized in Italy in the 1960s and '70s.

8   "Social partner society" refers to the concept of *Sozialpartnerschaft*, a class compromise between industrialist and trade union organizations characteristic for Germany and other Western European countries.

9   In 1972, German authorities introduced leaner conditions but also more thorough surveillance in German prisons.

10   The February 1968 *Vietnamkongress* in Berlin was a pivotal event for the radicalization of the 1960s protest movement in Germany.

11   For Peter Weiss, see "Prison Round Trip" note 7.

12   Hans-Jürgen Krahl (1943–70) was, alongside Rudi Dutschke, the main student leader of the German protest movement of the late 1960s. He died in a car accident.

13   Translations of the Krahl and Dutschke quotes by G.K.

14   For the Gauche prolétarienne, see "2nd of June Movement Program" note 3.

15   Smith and Moncourt, *Red Army Faction*, vol. 1, 81 (slightly edited).

16   Both texts are included in Smith and Moncourt, *Red Army Faction*, vol. 1.

17   Smith and Moncourt, *Red Army Faction*, vol. 1, 98 (slightly edited).

18   Smith and Moncourt, *Red Army Faction*, vol. 1, 82.

19   Smith and Moncourt, *Red Army Faction*, vol. 1, 86–87.

20   Smith and Moncourt, *Red Army Faction*, vol. 1, 90.

21   Smith and Moncourt, *Red Army Faction*, vol. 1, 88–89, 96 (slightly edited).

22   Smith and Moncourt, *Red Army Faction*, vol. 1, 95, 105.

23   Smith and Moncourt, *Red Army Faction*, vol. 1, 123.

24   Smith and Moncourt, *Red Army Faction*, vol. 1, 126.

25   Smith and Moncourt, *Red Army Faction*, vol. 1, 132–33 (slightly edited).

26   Smith and Moncourt, *Red Army Faction*, vol. 1, 142.

27   Smith and Moncourt, *Red Army Faction*, vol. 1, 145 (slightly edited).

28   Smith and Moncourt, *Red Army Faction*, vol. 1, 174.

29   Smith and Moncourt, *Red Army Faction*, vol. 1, 175.

30   Smith and Moncourt, *Red Army Faction*, vol. 1, 176.

31   Smith and Moncourt, *Red Army Faction*, vol. 1, 177.

32   Smith and Moncourt, *Red Army Faction*, vol. 1, 178 (slightly edited).

33   *Konkret* is a left-wing German news magazine. At the time Ulrike Meinhof wrote for it, it was highly influential in the German left. The editor was Ulrike Meinhof's then husband Klaus Rainer Röhl (1928–2021).

34   Smith and Moncourt, *Red Army Faction*, vol. 1, 187–203.

35   See "The Lorenz Kidnapping" note 16.

36   Note by Klaus Viehmann included in the German original: "My argument is not directed against the personal decision to accept the consequences of one's political, and politico-military, engagement. But I know from personal experience

that it changes you when comrades are killed or when you understand how they are treated in prison. Yet this change must not lead to an elitist self-perception, in which political criticism of the militant struggle can only be interpreted as an unwillingness to take the struggle to its ultimate conclusion."

37 Wadie Haddad (1927–78) was the leader of the PFLP-EO—see "Acronyms and Abbreviations."

38 From March 1973 to June 1975, twenty-seven issues of *Wir wollen alles* were released.

39 Section 129a of the German penal code criminalizes the formation and support of a "terrorist organization." It has been frequently used in the persecution of left-wing militants since it was added to the code in 1976.

40 The name *Spätaussiedler* is used for people of German descent who migrated to Germany from Eastern Europe (mainly from Poland, Romania, and former Soviet republics) after January 1, 1993, when new regulations in Germany's migration law were implemented. People of German descent who migrated from those regions to Germany before January 1, 1993, are simply known as *Aussiedler* (repatriates).

41 This is an abbreviated version of the 1975 text by "Werner Sauber and comrades," included in this volume in its entirety. Notes added to the full-length text have not been added to this excerpt.

42 *Fürchtegott* literally means "Fear God!"

43 Agenda 2010 was a package of social and economic reform plans introduced by the German SPD-Greens coalition government of the early 2000s. It was meant to stimulate economic growth by curtailing labor rights and unemployment benefits.

44 In 1990, Klaus Viehmann was the main author of a booklet titled *Drei zu Eins: Klassenwiderspruch, Rassismus und Sexismus* (Three to one: Class contradiction, racism, and sexism), which introduced the concept of "triple oppression" to the German-speaking world. The publication was both influential and controversial.

45 A reference to the mass protests against the 1999 WTO summit in Seattle and the 2001 G8 summit in Genoa.

INDEX

ABOUT THE CONTRIBUTORS

Roman Danyluk is a worker, grassroots labor unionist, and writer from Munich. He is the author of *Blues der Städte: Die Bewegung 2. Juni—eine sozialrevolutionäre Geschichte*.

Gabriel Kuhn is an Austrian-born writer, translator, and union organizer living in Sweden. Among his book publications are *All Power to the Councils! A Documentary History of the German Revolution of 1918–1919* and *Turning Money into Rebellion: The Unlikely Story of Denmark's Revolutionary Bank Robbers*.

ABOUT PM PRESS

PM Press is an independent, radical publisher of critically necessary books for our tumultuous times. Our aim is to deliver bold political ideas and vital stories to all walks of life and arm the dreamers to demand the impossible. Founded in 2007 by a small group of people with decades of publishing, media, and organizing experience, we have sold millions of copies of our books, most often one at a time, face to face. We're old enough to know what we're doing and young enough to know what's at stake. Join us to create a better world.

PM Press
PO Box 23912
Oakland, CA 94623
www.pmpress.org

PM Press in Europe
europe@pmpress.org
www.pmpress.org.uk

FRIENDS OF PM PRESS

These are indisputably momentous times—the financial system is melting down globally and the Empire is stumbling. Now more than ever there is a vital need for radical ideas.

In the many years since its founding—and on a mere shoestring—PM Press has risen to the formidable challenge of publishing and distributing knowledge and entertainment for the struggles ahead. With hundreds of releases to date, we have published an impressive and stimulating array of literature, art, music, politics, and culture. Using every available medium, we've succeeded in connecting those hungry for ideas and information to those putting them into practice.

Friends of PM allows you to directly help impact, amplify, and revitalize the discourse and actions of radical writers, filmmakers, and artists. It provides us with a stable foundation from which we can build upon our early successes and provides a much-needed subsidy for the materials that can't necessarily pay their own way. You can help make that happen—and receive every new title automatically delivered to your door once a month—by joining as a Friend of PM Press. And, we'll throw in a free T-shirt when you sign up.

Here are your options:

- **$30 a month** Get all books and pamphlets plus a 50% discount on all webstore purchases

- **$40 a month** Get all PM Press releases (including CDs and DVDs) plus a 50% discount on all webstore purchases

- **$100 a month** Superstar—Everything plus PM merchandise, free downloads, and a 50% discount on all webstore purchases

For those who can't afford $30 or more a month, we have **Sustainer Rates** at $15, $10, and $5. Sustainers get a free PM Press T-shirt and a 50% discount on all purchases from our website.

Your Visa or Mastercard will be billed once a month, until you tell us to stop. Or until our efforts succeed in bringing the revolution around. Or the financial meltdown of Capital makes plastic redundant. Whichever comes first.

Since 1998 Kersplebedeb has been an important source of radical literature and agit prop materials.

The project has a non-exclusive focus on anti-patriarchal and anti-imperialist politics, framed within an anticapitalist perspective. A special priority is given to writings regarding armed struggle in the metropole, the continuing struggles of political prisoners and prisoners of war, and the political economy of imperialism.

The Kersplebedeb website presents historical and contemporary writings by revolutionary thinkers from the anarchist and communist traditions.

Kersplebedeb can be contacted at:

Kersplebedeb
CP 63560
CCCP Van Horne
Montreal, Quebec
Canada
H3W 3H8

email: info@kersplebedeb.com
web: www.kersplebedeb.com
        www.leftwingbooks.net

Kersplebedeb

The Red Army Faction, A Documentary History— Volume 1: Projectiles for the People

Edited by J. Smith and André Moncourt
with Forewords by Russell "Maroon"
Shoats and Bill Dunne

ISBN: 978-1-60486-029-0
$34.95   736 pages

The first in a two-volume series, this is by far the most in-depth political history of the Red Army Faction ever made available in English.

Projectiles for the People starts its story in the days following World War II, showing how American imperialism worked hand in glove with the old pro-Nazi ruling class, shaping West Germany into an authoritarian anti-communist bulwark and launching pad for its aggression against Third World nations. The volume also recounts the opposition that emerged from intellectuals, communists, independent leftists, and then—explosively—the radical student movement and countercultural revolt of the 1960s.

It was from this revolt that the Red Army Faction emerged, an underground organization devoted to carrying out armed attacks within the Federal Republic of Germany, in the view of establishing a tradition of illegal, guerilla resistance to imperialism and state repression. Through its bombs and manifestos the RAF confronted the state with opposition at a level many activists today might find difficult to imagine.

For the first time ever in English, this volume presents all of the manifestos and communiqués issued by the RAF between 1970 and 1977, from Andreas Baader's prison break, through the 1972 May Offensive and the 1975 hostage-taking in Stockholm, to the desperate, and tragic, events of the "German Autumn" of 1977. The RAF's three main manifestos—*The Urban Guerilla Concept*, *Serve the People*, and *Black September*—are included, as are important interviews with *Spiegel* and *le Monde Diplomatique*, and a number of communiqués and court statements explaining their actions.

Providing the background information that readers will require to understand the context in which these events occurred, separate thematic sections deal with the 1976 murder of Ulrike Meinhof in prison, the 1977 Stammheim murders, the extensive use of psychological operations and false-flag attacks to discredit the guerilla, the state's use of sensory deprivation torture and isolation wings, and the prisoners' resistance to this, through which they inspired their own supporters and others on the left to take the plunge into revolutionary action.

The Red Army Faction, A Documentary History— Volume 2: Dancing with Imperialism

Edited J. Smith and André Moncourt
with an Introduction by Ward Churchill

ISBN: 978-1-60486-030-6
$26.95   480 pages

The long-awaited *Volume 2* of the first-ever English-language study of the Red Army Faction—West Germany's most notorious urban guerillas—covers the period immediately following the organization's near-total decimation in 1977. This work includes the details of the guerilla's operations, and its communiqués and texts, from 1978 up until the 1984 offensive.

This was a period of regrouping and reorientation for the RAF, with its previous focus on freeing its prisoners replaced by an anti-NATO orientation. This was in response to the emergence of a new radical youth movement in the Federal Republic, the Autonomen, and an attempt to renew its ties to the radical left. The possibilities and perils of an armed underground organization relating to the broader movement are examined, and the RAF's approach is contrasted to the more fluid and flexible practice of the Revolutionary Cells. At the same time, the history of the 2nd of June Movement (2JM), an eclectic guerilla group with its roots in West Berlin, is also evaluated, especially in light of the split that led to some 2JM members officially disbanding the organization and rallying to the RAF. Finally, the RAF's relationship to the East German Stasi is examined, as is the abortive attempt by West Germany's liberal intelligentsia to defuse the armed struggle during Gerhart Baum's tenure as Minister of the Interior.

Dancing with Imperialism will be required reading for students of the First World guerilla, those with interest in the history of European protest movements, and all who wish to understand the challenges of revolutionary struggle.

"This collection is not simply a documentary of the West German revolutionary Left at a particular point in the Cold War 1970s. It is more important for the insights it provides into the challenges, obstacles, and opportunities of waging armed struggle within the context of a wealthy, well-resourced, Western capitalist state. In this, the experiences and activities of the RAF are unique in the lessons they might teach organizers in Western capitalist milieus. In our own context, it is likely that future conditions of radical social change, and certainly revolutionary struggles, will more closely approximate those engaged by the RAF in 1970s West Germany than the much more influential examples of Russia in 1917 or Spain in 1936."
—Jeff Shantz, *Upping the Anti*

Fire and Flames: A History of the German Autonomist Movement

Geronimo
with an Introduction by George
Katsiaficas and Afterword by Gabriel
Kuhn

ISBN: 978-1-60486-097-9
$19.95   256 pages

Fire and Flames was the first comprehensive study of the German autonomous movement ever published. Released in 1990, it reached its fifth edition by 1997, with the legendary German *Konkret* journal concluding that "the movement had produced its own classic." The author, writing under the pseudonym of Geronimo, has been an autonomous activist since the movement burst onto the scene in 1980–81. In this book, he traces its origins in the Italian *Autonomia* project and the German social movements of the 1970s, before describing the battles for squats, "free spaces," and alternative forms of living that defined the first decade of the autonomous movement. Tactics of the "Autonome" were militant, including the construction of barricades or throwing molotov cocktails at the police. Because of their outfit (heavy black clothing, ski masks, helmets), the Autonome were dubbed the "Black Bloc" by the German media, and their tactics have been successfully adopted and employed at anti-capitalist protests worldwide.

Fire and Flames is no detached academic study, but a passionate, hands-on, and engaging account of the beginnings of one of Europe's most intriguing protest movements of the last thirty years. An introduction by George Katsiaficas, author of *The Subversion of Politics*, and an afterword by Gabriel Kuhn, a long-time autonomous activist and author, add historical context and an update on the current state of the Autonomen.

"The target audience is not the academic middle-class with passive sympathies for rioting, nor the all-knowing critical critics, but the activists of a young generation."
— *Edition I.D. Archiv*

"Some years ago, an experienced autonomous activist from Berlin sat down, talked to friends and comrades about the development of the scene, and, with Fire and Flames, *wrote the best book about the movement that we have."*
— *Düsseldorfer Stadtzeitung für Politik und Kultur*

Turning Money into Rebellion: The Unlikely Story of Denmark's Revolutionary Bank Robbers

Edited by Gabriel Kuhn

ISBN: 978-1-60486-316-1

$19.95   240 pages

Blekingegade is a quiet Copenhagen street. It is also where, in May 1989, the police discovered an apartment that had served Denmark's most notorious twentieth-century bank robbers as a hideaway for years. The Blekingegade Group members belonged to a communist organization and lived modest lives in the Danish capital. Over a period of almost two decades, they sent millions of dollars acquired in spectacular heists to Third World liberation movements, in particular the Popular Front for the Liberation of Palestine (PFLP). In May 1991, seven of them were convicted and went to prison.

The story of the Blekingegade Group is one of the most puzzling and captivating chapters from the European anti-imperialist milieu of the 1970s and '80s. *Turning Money into Rebellion: The Unlikely Story of Denmark's Revolutionary Bank Robbers* is the first-ever account of the story in English, covering a fascinating journey from anti-war demonstrations in the late 1960s via travels to Middle Eastern capitals and African refugee camps to the group's fateful last robbery that earned them a record haul and left a police officer dead.

The book includes historical documents, illustrations, and an exclusive interview with Torkil Lauesen and Jan Weimann, two of the group's longest-standing members. It is a compelling tale of turning radical theory into action and concerns analysis and strategy as much as morality and political practice. Perhaps most importantly, it revolves around the cardinal question of revolutionary politics: What to do, and how to do it?

"This book is a fascinating and bracing account of how a group of communists in Denmark sought to aid the peoples of the Third World in their struggles against imperialism and the dire poverty that comes with it. The book contains many valuable lessons as to the practicalities of effective international solidarity, but just as importantly, it is a testament to the intellectual courage of the Blekingegade Group."
—Zak Cope, author of *Dimensions of Prejudice: Towards a Political Economy of Bigotry*

"The story of how some pro-Palestinian activists become Denmark's most successful bank robbers is more exciting than any thriller."
—Åsa Linderborg, *Aftonbladet*

The Global Imagination of 1968: Revolution and Counterrevolution

George Katsiaficas with a Preface by Kathleen Cleaver and a Foreword by Carlos Muñoz

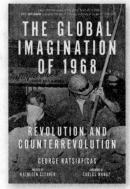

ISBN: 978-1-62963-439-5
$24.95   360 pages

This book brings to life social movements of the 1960s, a period of world-historical struggles. With discussions of more than fifty countries, Katsiaficas articulates an understanding that is neither bounded by national and continental divides nor focused on "Great Men and Women." Millions of people went into the streets, and their aspirations were remarkably similar. From the Prague revolt against Soviet communism to the French May uprising, the Vietnam Tet offensive, African anticolonial insurgencies, the civil rights movement, and campus eruptions in Latin America, Yugoslavia, the United States, and beyond, this book portrays the movements of the 1960s as intuitively tied together.

Student movements challenged authorities in almost every country, giving the insurgency a global character, and contemporary feminist, Latino, and gay liberation movements all came to life. A focus on the French general strike of May 1968 and the U.S. movement's high point in 1970—from the May campus strike to the revolt in the military, workers' wildcat strikes, the national women's strike, the Chicano Moratorium, and the Black Panther Party's Revolutionary Peoples' Constitutional Convention in September—reveals the revolutionary aspirations of the insurgencies in the core of the world system. Despite the apparent failure of the movements of 1968, their profound influence on politics, culture, and social movements continues to be felt today. As globally synchronized uprisings occur with increasing frequency in the twenty-first century, the lessons of 1968 provide useful insights for future struggles.

"A well-informed survey of the global 'New Left' of 1968."
—Eric Hobsbawm, author of *The Age of Extremes: A History of the World, 1914-1991*

The Mohawk Warrior Society: A Handbook on Sovereignty and Survival

Louis Karoniaktajeh Hall
Edited by Kahentinetha Rotiskarewake,
Philippe Blouin, Matt Peterson, and
Malek Rasamny

ISBN: 978-1-62963-941-3
$27.95   320 pages

The first collection of its kind, this anthology by members of the Mohawk Warrior Society uncovers a hidden history and paints a bold portrait of the spectacular experience of Kanien'kehá:ka survival and self-defense. Providing extensive documentation, context, and analysis, the book features foundational writings by prolific visual artist and polemicist Louis Karoniaktajeh Hall (1918–1993)—such as his landmark 1979 pamphlet *The Warrior's Handbook*, as well as selections of his pioneering artwork. This book contains new oral history by key figures of the Rotisken'rhakéhte's revival in the 1970s and tells the story of the Warriors' famous flag, their armed occupation of Ganienkeh in 1974, and the role of their constitution, the Great Peace, in guiding their commitment to freedom and independence. We hear directly the story of how the Kanien'kehá:ka Longhouse became one the most militant resistance groups in North America, gaining international attention with the Oka Crisis of 1990. This autohistory of the Rotisken'rhakéhte is complemented by a Mohawk history timeline from colonization to the present, a glossary of Mohawk political philosophy, and a new map of Iroquoia in Mohawk language. At last, the Mohawk Warriors can tell their own story with their own voices, and to serve as an example and inspiration for future generations struggling against the environmental, cultural, and social devastation cast upon the modern world.

"While many have heard of AIM & the Red Power movement of the '60s and '70s, most probably do not know the story of the Mohawk warriors and their influence on Indigenous struggles for land and self-determination, then and now. These include the 1974 Ganienkeh land reclamation (which still exists today as sovereign Mohawk territory), the 1990 Oka Crisis (an armed standoff that revived the fighting spirit & warrior culture of Indigenous peoples across North America), and the Warrior/ Warrior Unity flag, a powerful symbol of Indigenous resistance today commonly seen at blockades & rallies. The Mohawk Warrior Society tells this history in the words of the Mohawks themselves. Comprised of interviews with some of the key participants, as well as The Warrior's Handbook *and* Rebuilding the Iroquois Confederacy *(both written by Louis Karoniaktajeh Hall, who also designed the Warrior/Unity flag), this book documents the important contributions Mohawk warriors have made to modern Indigenous resistance in North America."*
—Gord Hill, Kwakwaka'wakw, author of *500 Years of Indigenous Resistance* and *The Antifa Comic Book*

Remembering the Armed Struggle: My Time with the Red Army Faction

Margrit Schiller with a Foreword: Ann Hansen, Afterword by Osvaldo Bayer, and Appendix by J. Smith & André Moncourt

ISBN: 978-1-62963-873-7
$19.95   256 pages

Margrit Schiller was an early member of the Red Army Faction, the West German urban guerrilla group. In 1971 she was captured and charged with a murder she did not commit, and upon her release she returned to the underground, being captured again in early 1974. She would spend most of the 1970s in prison, enduring isolation conditions meant to break the human spirit, and participating hunger strikes and other acts of resistance along with other political prisoners from the RAF.

In *Remembering the Armed Struggle*, Schiller recounts the process through which she joined her generation's revolt in the 1960s, going from work with drug users to joining the antipsychiatry political organization the Socialist Patients' Collective and then the RAF. She tells of how she met and worked alongside the group's founding members, Ulrike Meinhof, Andreas Baader, Jan-Carl Raspe, Irmgard Möller, and Holger Meins; how she learned the details of the May Offensive and other actions while in her prison cell; about the struggles to defend human dignity in the most degraded of environments, and the relationships she forged with other women in prison.

Also included are a foreword by Ann Hansen, who situates the draconian prison conditions inflicted on the RAF within the context of a global counterinsurgency program that would help spawn the plague of mass incarceration we still face today, an afterword by the late Osvaldo Bayer, and an appendix by J. Smith and André Moncourt summarizing the politics and history of the RAF in the 1970s.

"Margrit Schiller's life story Remembering the Armed Struggle, *is not meant to mark a hard break with the Red Army Faction, but is more of a critical reflection in the spirit of solidarity. Even those who do not share Schiller's perspective well find it interesting to join her as she looks back on her years underground and in prison."*
—*diesseits*

"Schiller's recollections are profoundly honest and to the point. She neither glorifies the Red Army Faction nor does she repent or distance herself from her past."
—*taz*

Creating a Movement with Teeth: A Documentary History of the George Jackson Brigade

Edited by Daniel Burton-Rose
with a preface by Ward Churchill

ISBN: 978-1-60486-223-2
$24.95   320 pages

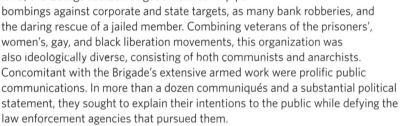

Bursting into existence in the Pacific Northwest in 1975, the George Jackson Brigade claimed 14 pipe bombings against corporate and state targets, as many bank robberies, and the daring rescue of a jailed member. Combining veterans of the prisoners', women's, gay, and black liberation movements, this organization was also ideologically diverse, consisting of both communists and anarchists. Concomitant with the Brigade's extensive armed work were prolific public communications. In more than a dozen communiqués and a substantial political statement, they sought to explain their intentions to the public while defying the law enforcement agencies that pursued them.

Collected in one volume for the first time, *Creating a Movement with Teeth* makes available this body of propaganda and mediations on praxis. In addition, the collection assembles corporate media profiles of the organization's members and alternative press articles in which partisans thrash out the heated debates sparked in the progressive community by the eruption of an armed group in their midst. *Creating a Movement with Teeth* illuminates a forgotten chapter of the radical social movements of the 1970s in which diverse interests combined forces in a potent rejection of business as usual in the United States.

"Creating a Movement with Teeth *is an important contribution to the growing body of literature on armed struggle in the 1970s. It gets us closer to knowing not only how pervasive militant challenges to the system were, but also the issues and contexts that shaped such strategies. Through documents by and about the George Jackson Brigade, as well as the introduction by Daniel Burton-Rose, this book sheds light on events that have until now been far too obscured.*"
—Dan Berger, author of *Outlaws of America: The Weather Underground and the Politics of Solidarity*; editor of *The Hidden 1970s: Histories of Radicalism*.

Ingrid Schubert: Letters from Prison 1970-1977

Ingrid Schubert
Edited and translated by Gerti Wilford
and Jo Tunnard

ISBN: 979-8-88744-108-5
$24.95   256 pages

Ingrid's letters reveal the daily struggle of a political
prisoner resisting repression.

Ingrid was one of the first members of the RAF, and among the first to be
imprisoned. This volume contains original letters from prison to her sister,
showing her efforts to maintain her integrity, political identity, and at the same
time a meaningful exchange with her family.

A collection of photos and mementos complement the letters.